LOST MELBOURNE

Acknowledgements

We gratefully acknowledge the assistance of the following: The State Library of Victoria, the National Library of Australia, Natasha Kamanev (Bayside Library Service), Fiona Campbell (East Melbourne Library Service), Simone Sharpe (Stonnington History Centre), Liz Gay (Brighton Historical Society), Carol Stals (Glen Eira Historical Society), Dorothy Lobert (St Kilda Historical Society), Dianne Temby (Master of Museum Studies), Peter Maltezos, Diana Gold, Melissa Gilmour (Richmond Library Service).

Thanks also to: Anthony Tonna (Collingwood Library Service), Lisa Burns.

Picture credits

All images are courtesy of State Library Victoria, except for the following:

Dianne Temby: 10 (left).
Caroline Simpson Collection: 10 (right).
Stonnington History Centre: 22.
Museum Victoria: 62.
National Gallery of Victoria: 63.
National Library of Australia: 81, 141.
Courtesy of Collingwood Local History photograph collection: 82, 83 (right).
© Mark Strizic (1928–2012), Courtesy the Estate of the Artist: 105.
The cooperation of Carlton & United Breweries in the sourcing of its historical photos is gratefully acknowledged: 107 (top).
Graeme Butler: 128 (middle top), 139 (bottom).
Corbis: 130.
Getty Images: 136, 137.

First published in the United Kingdom in 2015 by
PAVILION BOOKS,
An imprint of Pavilion Books Company Ltd.,
1 Gower Street, London WC1E 6HD, UK

ISBN: 978-1-91049-674-9

A CIP catalogue record for this book is available from the British Library.

10 9 8 7 6 5 4 3 2 1

Repro by Colourdepth
Printed by 1010 Printing International Ltd, China

LOST MELBOURNE

Heather Chapman and Judith Stillman

PAVILION

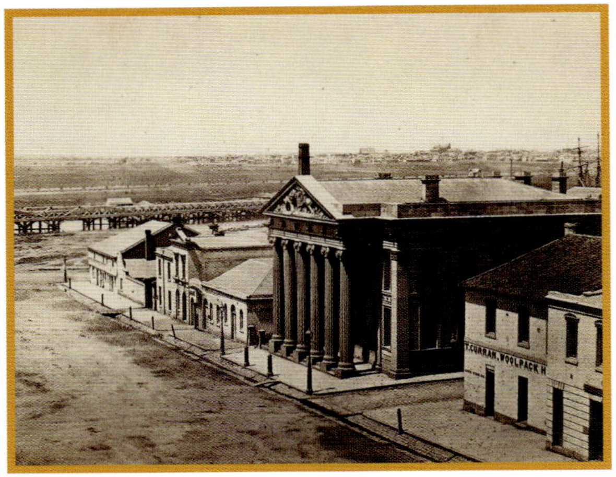

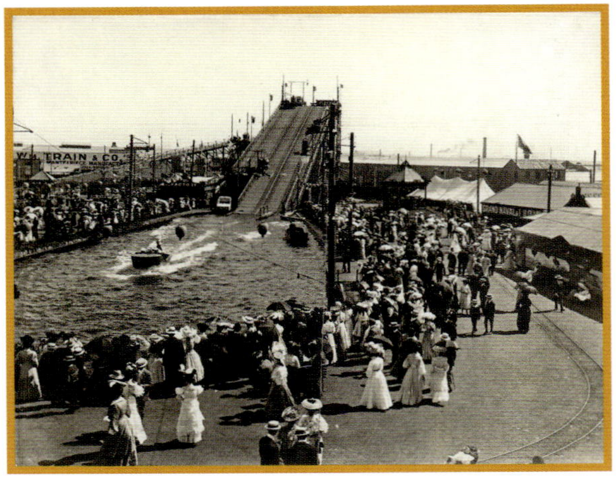
W. TRAIN & CO.

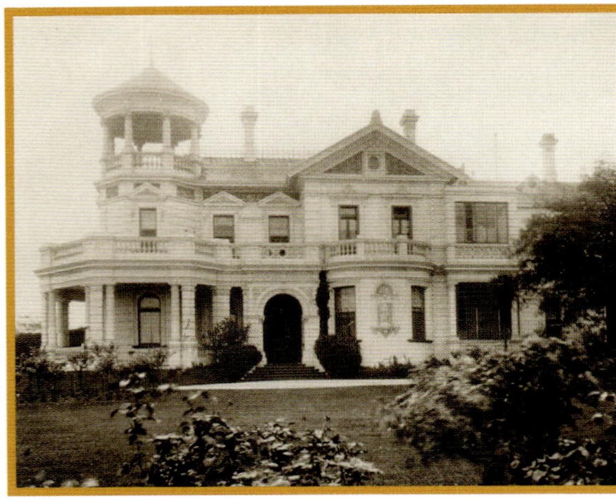

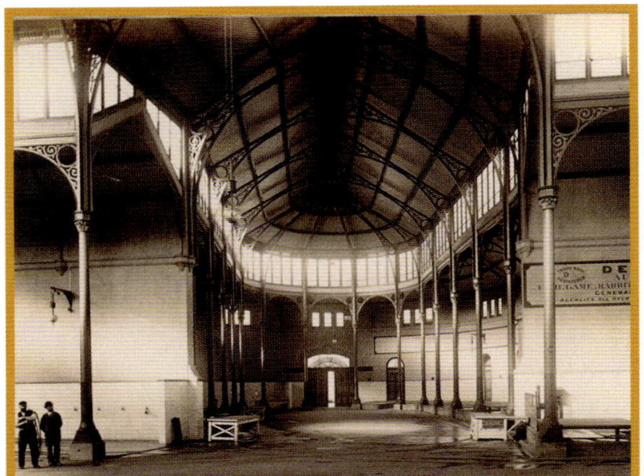

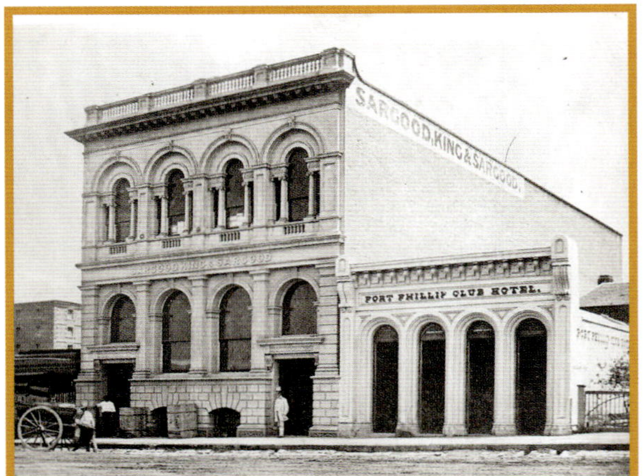
SARGOOD, KING & SARGOOD.
PORT PHILLIP CLUB HOTEL.

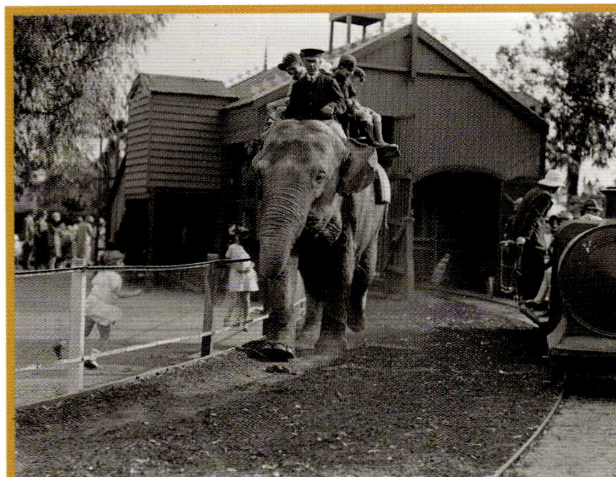

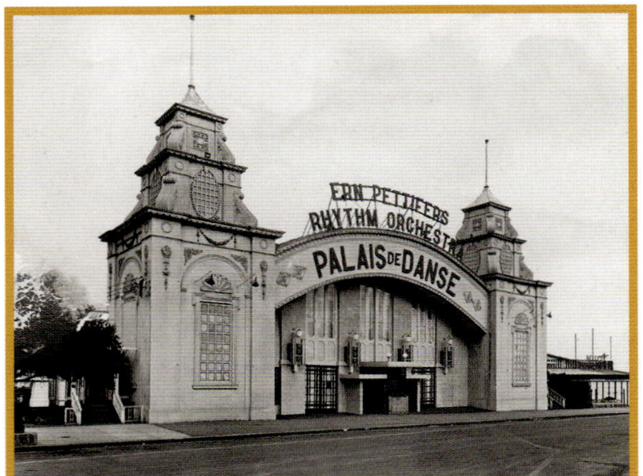
ERN PETTIFERS
RHYTHM ORCHESTRA
PALAIS DE DANSE

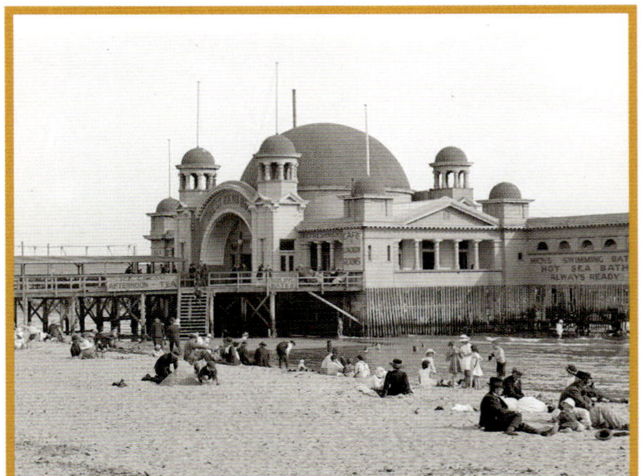

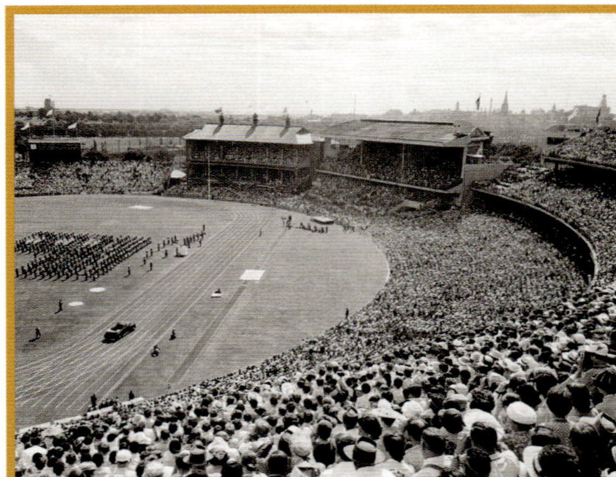

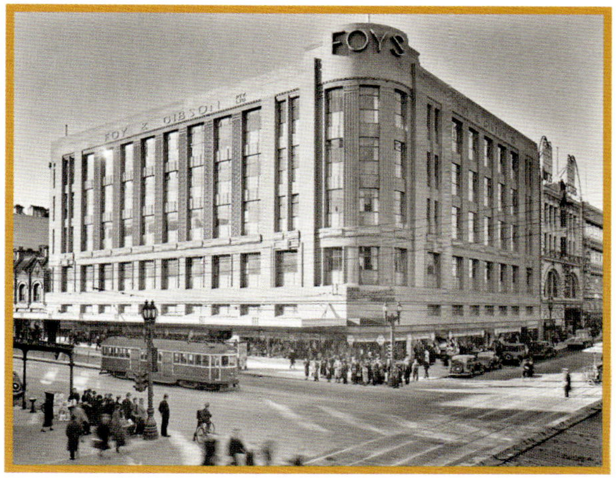

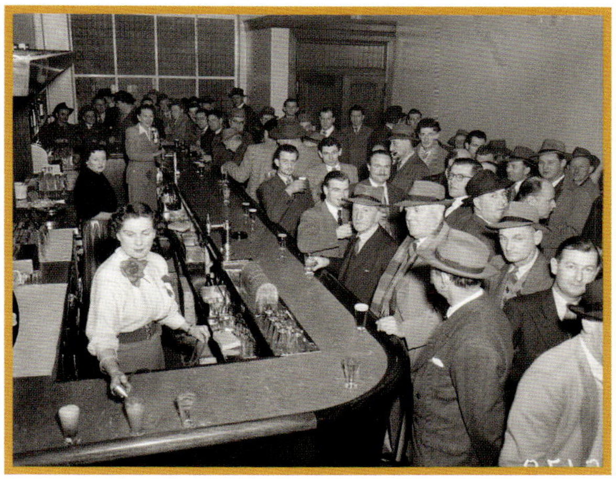

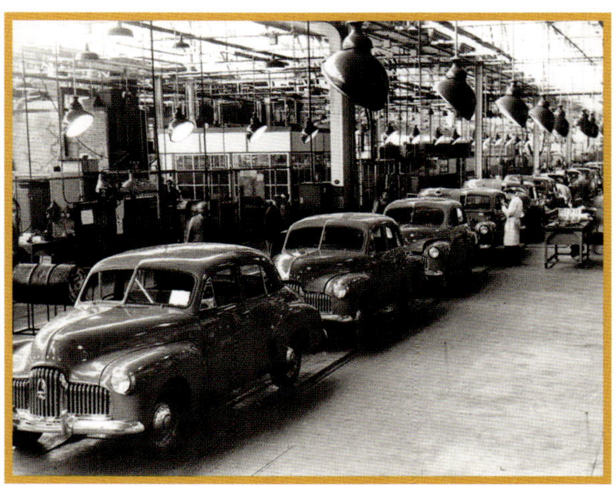

LOST IN THE...

1880s	page 8
1890s	page 10
1900s	page 12
1910s	page 14
1920s	page 16
1930s	page 18
1940s	page 24
1950s	page 28
1960s	page 42
1970s	page 76
1980s	page 96
1990s	page 114
2000s	page 128
2010s	page 138

Index page 144

INTRODUCTION

Melbourne was first settled in 1835, where fresh water was available in the Yarra River. The land to the north of the river was relatively flat and low hills lay to the west, east and north, bisected by small streams running down to the Yarra. Because the southern banks of the river were lower lying and swampy, Melbourne settled on this northern bank. Surveyor Hoddle's grid of streets, almost 30 metres wide, followed the course of the river. In 1837 Hoddle had no high mountains, deep gorges and fast-flowing rivers to contend with. Even the land to the west was able to be flattened, when it became necessary to do so, for the railway development at Spencer Street.

Until the 1850s, settlement grew steadily. And then gold was discovered. Tens of thousands made their way to the goldfields, with Melbourne the port of call for most. Melbourne's population grew from 4,000 in 1837 to 300,000 in 1854. They came from as far as California, Britain, Europe and China, all with a desire to make their fortune. A total of more than £100 million worth of gold was won from the earth in the 1850s. Even if they didn't find gold, many of them became successful in other ways by catering to the miners. Many were skilled and ambitious men, determined to succeed. Entrepreneurs such as E. W. Coles, Pearson Tewkesbury and Mark Moss used their drive and energy to develop businesses and grand buildings during these years. As a result of this wealth, Melbourne's major public buildings such as the State Library, Parliament House, the Town Hall and the GPO were built on land allocated by Hoddle for public use. While these public buildings remain, so many others built in this period have been lost. The wealth first generated in Melbourne from the gold rushes was to make Melbourne a world city in the next 30 years. This is when it became known as "Marvellous Melbourne".

In the 1880s, Melbourne was the largest and wealthiest city in Australia, with a population of 500,000. London banks were willing to lend money to men of wealth and vision, and there were many of these men in Melbourne who wanted to speculate in land and build grand edifices. The Craig, Williamson, and Thomas store, the Prell's Buildings, the Menzies Hotel and the Equitable Building were constructed during this period, and it is all of these that have been lost. Many stately mansions, now gone, were also built at this time.

The vagaries of nature played a part in the loss of some buildings in the early years, but it was not the major factor. Fire was responsible for destroying some city buildings, particularly during the huge 1897 conflagration. Later, Princes Court was burnt, although it wasn't really suitable for an all-year-round outdoor fun park given Melbourne's weather. The Brighton and St. Kilda Sea Baths were twice destroyed by storm and high seas.

Public attitudes to development and building styles change over time. Melburnians came to see multi-storey, glass-fronted rectangular structures as being modern and more attractive than the 19th-century ornamental architecture. Many of the 19th-century buildings, such as the Federal Coffee Palace and the State Bank of Victoria, so familiar from childhood money boxes, were demolished to be replaced by often unremarkable substitutes. In Melbourne, historically important buildings have not always been retained; maximising profits has sometimes taken precedence over conservation and heritage values. Occasionally, there was the realisation that the new building was out of tune with the area in which it had been built. The Gas and Fuel Buildings are a good example. They interfered with the familiar vista of St. Paul's Cathedral from Princes Bridge, and to the south over the Botanic Gardens and St. Kilda Road. They have now been demolished.

As our ideas of what is a pleasing building have waxed and waned, so too has our choice of entertainment. Music halls and vaudeville and other live theatre, so popular in the 19th century, were replaced by cinemas, whose audiences were then influenced by the introduction of TV in 1956. The Tivoli became a cinema, then a flea market and finally a shopping arcade.

Technological advances and economic changes have been most important factors in the loss of many of our buildings. Even the introduction of lifts enabled developers to successfully find tenants for upper floors in higher buildings. Government regulation, which substituted the building limits imposed in 1916 with the plot–ratio formula in the 1960s, permitted buildings to go higher as long as they allowed open space at ground level. This meant much greater financial return for the developer from the same size plot of land. It was cheaper to pull down and start again than it was to build on what already existed, otherwise we might still have the Australian Building and the APA Tower.

In Melbourne's history there have been times when the city has lost population and popularity. Better transport and the magnetic pull of often large, one-stop shopping malls outside of the central business district have drawn people away. The loss of trade has been a factor in the demise of some city businesses and the consequent demolition of their buildings. Sometimes, business did not move with the times. Craig, Williamson, and Thomas's large drapery store did not adopt the innovations that were to make department stores like Myer so successful. Thus they eventually went out of business, and their premises were sold and demolished. Some activities became redundant. The wharves on the Yarra could not accommodate the changes in shipping needs and the building of bridges across the Yarra effectively meant their demise. Port activity moved elsewhere.

The 1950s to 1970s were a time of rapid change in Melbourne. These were the decades where demolition reigned supreme and are often referred to as the years of the wreckers: the decades of demolition. Many of the 19th-century buildings, with their towers and turrets and ornamentation, were seen as passé and have been lost to us.

Today, Melbourne has once more become a dynamic city: a 24-hour city. People have moved back, and inner city factories like the Denton Hat Factory have become prized residential properties, while the Queen Victoria Hospital site is now a CBD village.

Melbourne hasn't lost all its built heritage. Many of the old buildings, or at least their facades, are now protected. Much of old Melbourne is hidden and some of it has migrated to other buildings and locations. The question for all of us is how can we preserve our cultural and historical identity and yet allow for progress and innovation? It is a balancing act. This book touches on some of what has been lost to Melbourne. Although we are fortunate that examples of our built heritage remain, many of the pressures that brought about the losses of the past still exist.

RIGHT *Flinders Street, circa 1910. The turreted Fish Market was demolished in 1959* *(see page 40).*

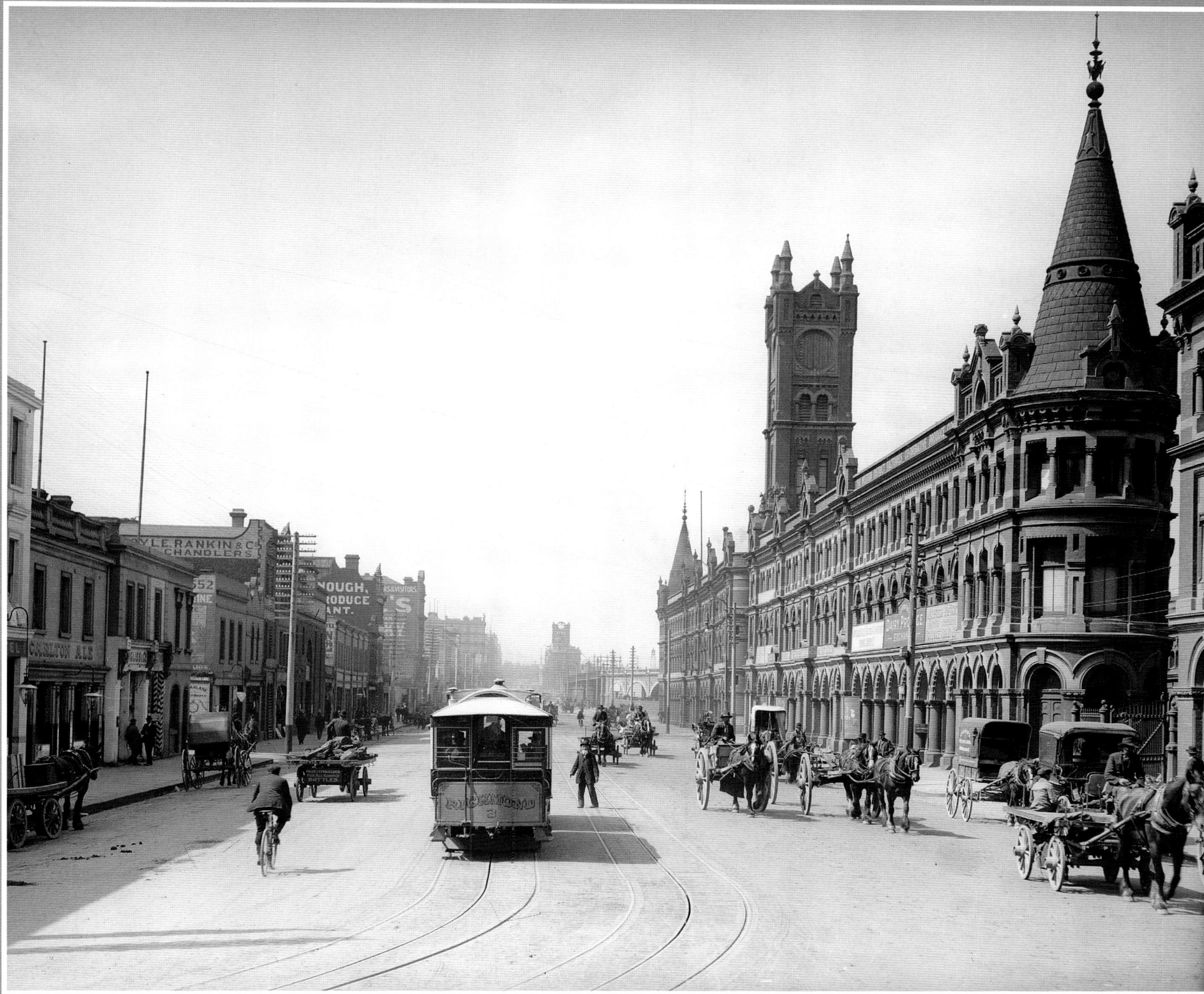
CHANDLERS
CARLTON ALE

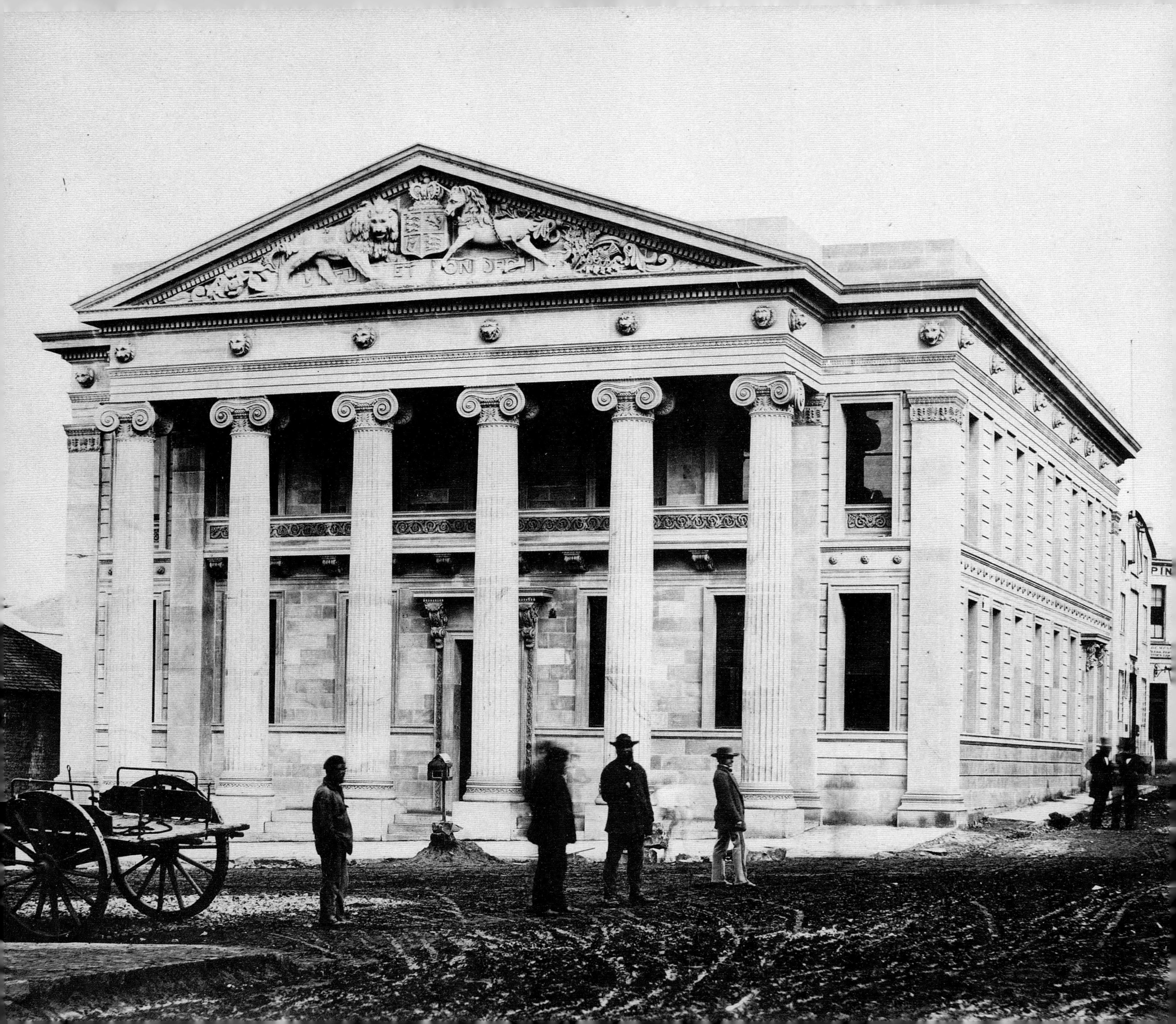

Oriental Bank DEMOLISHED MID-1880s

The 1850s were boom years in the fledgling city of Melbourne, with money from the gold fields and enthusiasm for the future. Melbourne was growing quickly from a muddy town into a city with streets, businesses, grand buildings up to four storeys in height and elegant mansions. Banks, offices and clubs were reinterpretations of the buildings seen overseas. Such an economy needed credit and a place for savings. Banks and financial institutions came into prominence and new banks were attracted by the opportunity to do business.

Most of these banks were branches of existing ones but the Oriental Bank Corporation was an English bank. It was established in Bombay in 1842 under the name of the Bank of Western India. It moved its headquarters to London in 1845 and changed its name to the Oriental Bank Corporation. It was chartered in 1851 to allow competition with the unpopular East India Company's opium billing monopoly. The Oriental Bank Corporation became a large organisation with branches in many countries. The bank wanted to capitalise on the growing Chinese population who were indentured to work in Australia in the industries surrounding Melbourne and Sydney. The name of the bank was purposely chosen by the original investors to appeal to the demographic market. The Oriental Bank Corporation's first Australian branches opened in Melbourne and Sydney in 1852 and it was able to issue its own banknotes. These banknotes would be accepted as currency by other banks until 1884.

The Oriental Bank in Melbourne was located at the corner of Flinders Lane and Queen Street. It was built in 1856 as the result of a competition held by the bank. The architects were Robertson and Hale who used a Greek temple-themed design for their plan. The building's classical facade and grand scale dominated Queen Street and the surrounding area. The portico of the double-storey bank featured a colonnade supporting a pediment with coat of arms in tympanum.

In 1867 the bank was robbed but as the result of an anonymous communication most of the bills were recovered. In the *Bendigo Advertiser* of 5 February, 1867, it was stated that "the fact of the bills having being discovered intact seems to raise an impression that temporary annoyance to the superior bank officials was intended rather than to deprive the bank of its property."

Poor management of the bank in London led to a suspension of payments in 1884. A cablegram was received from London indicating the difficulties the Oriental Bank was experiencing. A notification was placed on the front door explaining that the Queen Street bank would not be open for the transaction of business until further instructions from London. The bank was in trouble on a number of fronts. There were heavy losses encountered by sugar plantations held by the bank in Mauritius, there was the coffee disease in the plantations in Ceylon and there were losses in London and other parts of the world. The Oriental was reconstituted as the New Oriental Bank Corporation, but it was never successful and closed its doors in 1892. The Oriental Bank building in Queen Street was demolished shortly after the bank went out of business in 1884. Today the site is occupied by a modern office building.

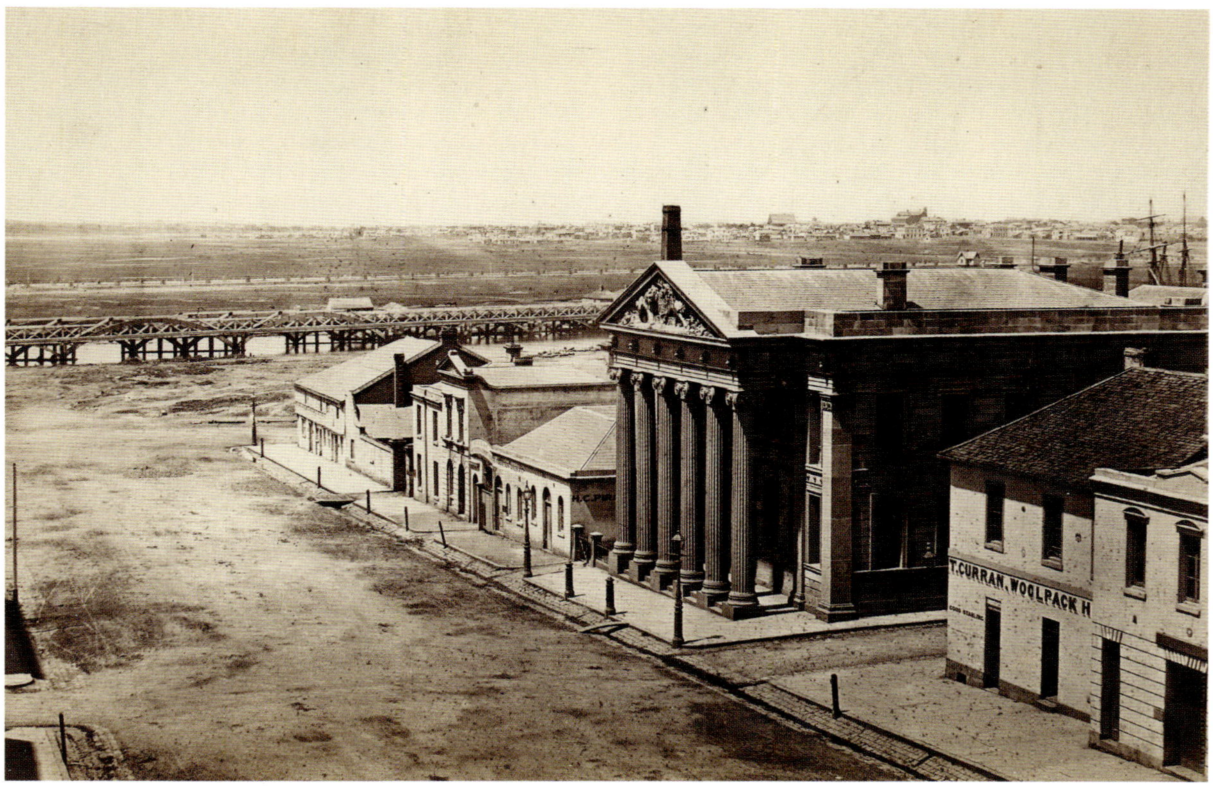

LEFT *This is part of Queen Street showing the Oriental Bank and the suburb of Emerald Hill (now South Melbourne).*

OPPOSITE *The bank's Greek temple-themed design was the product of a competition amongst Melbourne's architects.*

Iron Houses IMPORTATION CEASED 1890s

Many prefabricated homes, made of timber, zinc and slate, were brought to Melbourne by the new migrants in the early days of the settlement. Charles Joseph La Trobe, the first Lieutenant-Governor of Victoria, brought two timber houses with him and one of these is still in existence, located in Kings Domain.

Corrugated iron had been patented in England in 1829 and in 1830 it was already being used in Sydney. The corrugated sheets of steel were very strong and flexible. They were exported to all the colonies but particularly to Australia, because they were a cheap building material, didn't require a skilled tradesman to erect, were easily transported, and resistant to termite infestation. Many of the buildings used for schools, shops, churches, chapels and stables were made of corrugated iron. Dr. Adam Cairns brought two portable buildings with him when he came to Victoria, complaining that the cost of transport was almost as much as the cost of the buildings.

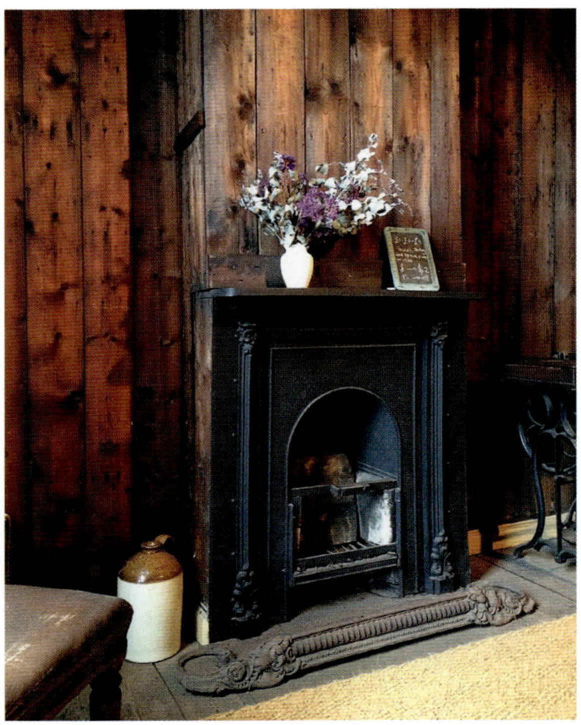

The discovery of gold in Victoria in 1851 brought thousands of emigrants from overseas, seeking their fortunes on the Victorian goldfields. Between 1850 and 1860 Melbourne's population quadrupled to 120,000. Housing such numbers seemed an impossible task and Emerald Hill, now South Melbourne, was a settlement of tents. People living in this "Canvas Town" had to pay five shillings a week for them. The first land grants in the South Melbourne area took place in 1852 and the 68 blocks were quickly sold at £300 per acre. In response to the critical shortage of housing, Governor La Trobe also commissioned the importation of one hundred portable houses.

Colonists who wanted to import their own houses could choose them from a catalogue. The dismantled unit would arrive from Britain, sometimes complete with floors, ceilings, walls, carpet and even a water closet. Most of the 22,000-plus portable houses that came into Victoria in 1853 were timber, but 6,369 of these were made of iron. The cost of a small cottage was about £10. In the South Melbourne area local speculator Robert Patterson erected 21 iron houses in "Tin Pan Alley". Kitchens and bathrooms were separate from the main cottage. They had no running water, which was only enjoyed by the wealthy. When temperatures soared in summer, children often slept in the downstairs passage, with front and back doors open so that a cool breeze could blow through. The people who lived in these were merchants and stonemasons, builders, clerks and public servants. Families of up to 10 would live in these tiny dwellings until they could afford something larger. There were almost one hundred portable houses in this area in 1854 and 1855.

Some portable houses came from other parts of Australia but most were imported from England and Wales. Others were brought in from New Zealand, Germany, Singapore, India and the United States. The main suppliers of portable houses were C. D. Young and W. and P. McLellan from Glasgow, Samuel Hemmings from Bristol, E. T. Bellhouse from Manchester and other suppliers from Liverpool and Birmingham. E. T. Bellhouse had patented cast iron stanchions to fit the corrugations in the iron. His work so impressed Prince Albert that he had a portable ballroom constructed at Balmoral Castle. Almost all Melbourne's iron portable houses have gone and only one Bellhouse cottage remains in its original position, while another has been relocated nearby, and a third, manufactured by Moorewood and Rogers of London, is now in South Melbourne under the watchful eye of the National Trust.

Portable iron houses were very important in the early days of Melbourne and provided much-needed accommodation for poorer families. The 1890s Depression meant that importation of them almost ceased and construction slowed. Although there were people living in iron houses in the 1930s and some even in the 1960s, the era of the portable iron house had passed and their place was taken by houses of brick and weatherboard.

LEFT *Timber shipping crate boards, sometimes covered with hessian, canvas, newspaper or wallpaper, lined the walls of this remaining Bellhouse-manufactured South Melbourne iron cottage.*

RIGHT *"A Portable Town for Australia", showing the church and parsonage ordered to be sent to the Bishop of Melbourne about 1853.*

OPPOSITE *A 1943 street scene showing the first portable iron houses to be imported to North Melbourne.*

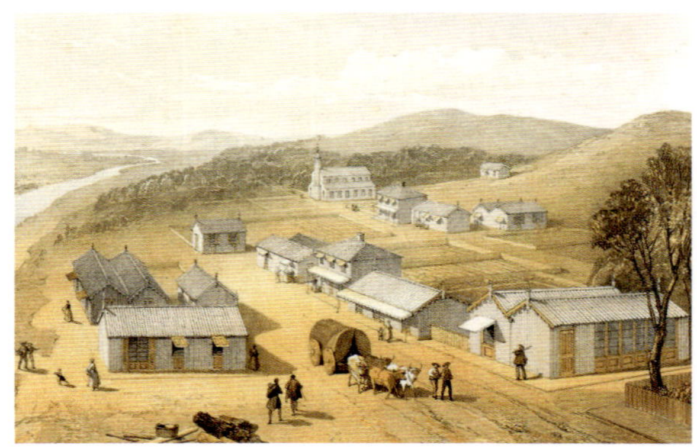

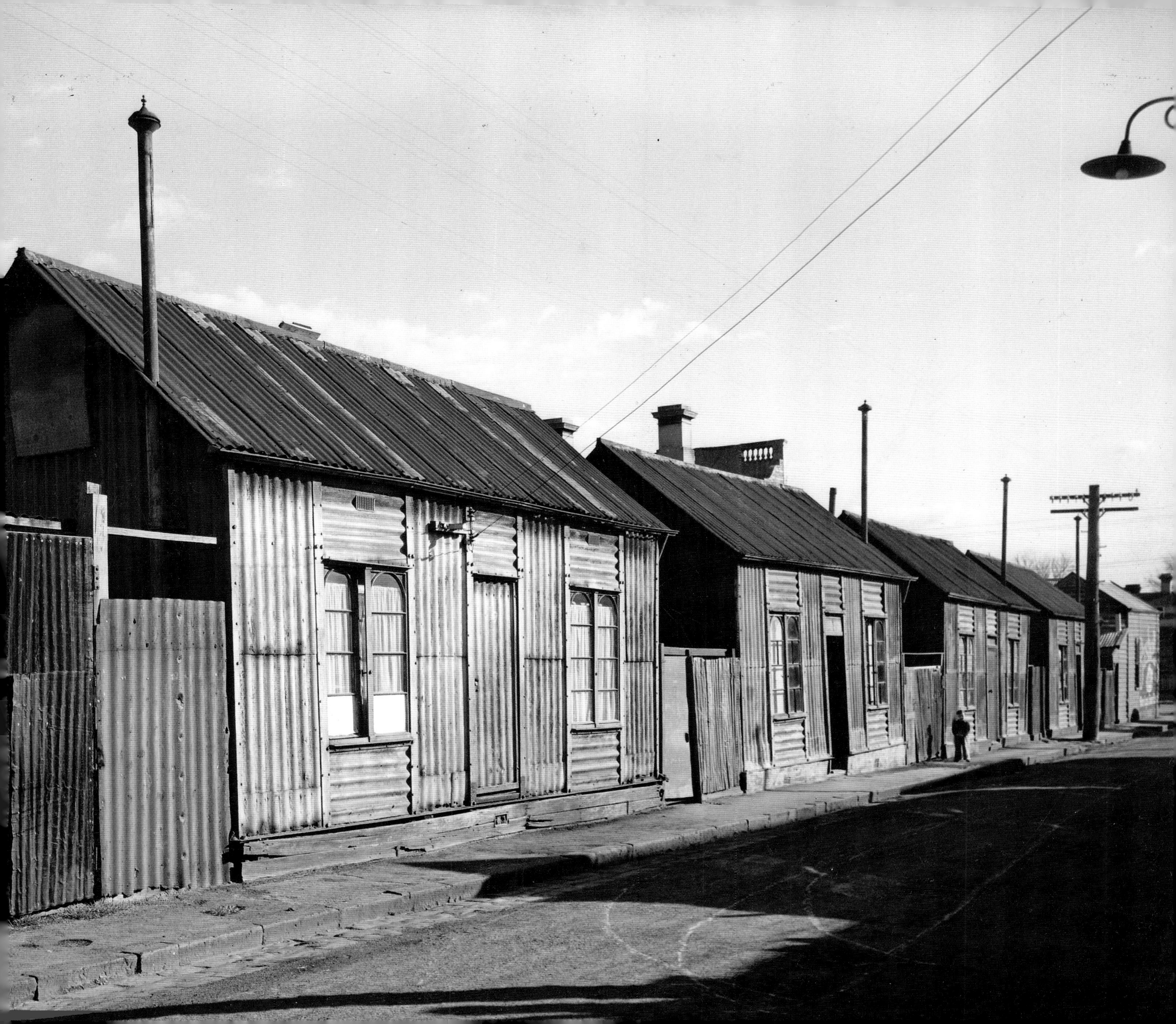

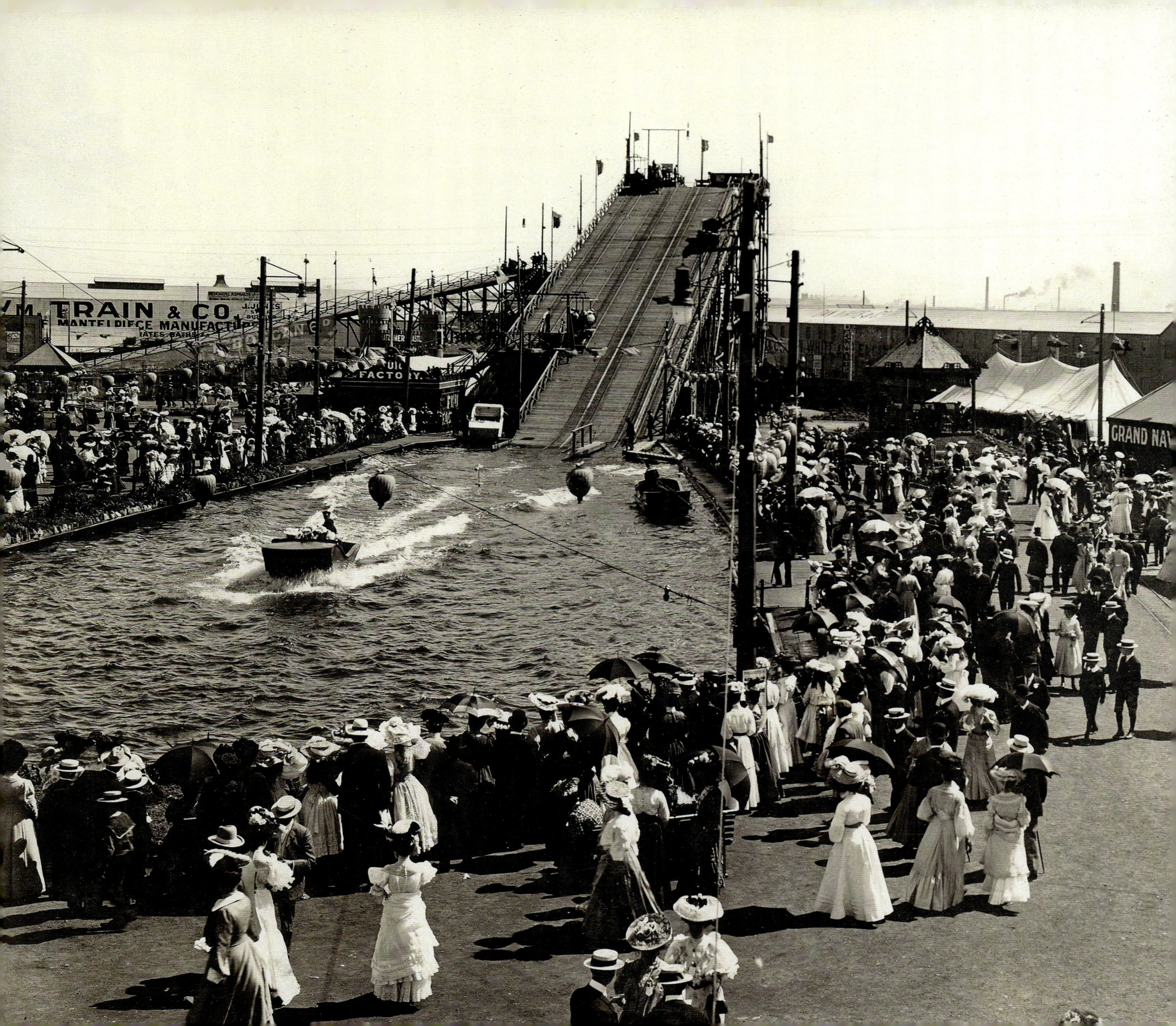
TRAIN & CO
FACTORY

Princes Court CLOSED 1909

The Camel Back toboggan and the Canadian Water Chute were two of the major attractions at Princes Court. Both were elevated structures and the participants, with many squeals, plunged from a great height and at a fast rate into the water below. Princes Court was the name given to the entertainment precinct in St. Kilda Road beside Princes Bridge and was established adjacent to FitzGerald Brothers' Circus buildings in 1904.

This piece of land had been a popular spot for Melburnians since the late 1800s. It was regarded as public space and any attempt to commercialise it was resisted. Given its position as an entrance to the city proper there were many attempts to make use of this area of land for private gain. The big top, or circus, first came to the vicinity in 1877 and for the next 80 years there was always a circus of some sort. In 1901 the FitzGerald Brothers moved there and set up a regular venue for boxing tournaments. With so many people flocking to the Snowden Gardens (built on what was once the city's rubbish tip) adjacent to the Princes Bridge and the water's edge, the FitzGeralds decided to create an amusement park there. They called it Princes Court.

Melburnians sought amusements and distractions and during its short-lived life, Princes Court satisfied these desires. It was built in 1904 and some of the other attractions were a rifle range, the Café Chantant with a Pierrot variety show, a tug of war and the open-air theatre that resembled a Chinese temple. Roller skating and bicycle races were also popular, as were diving displays. Those who found the activities a little strenuous or daring could always enjoy watching the more adventurous, or relax in the Japanese tea house or watch the Biograph films that opened in 1908. The *Prahran Telegraph* reported in 1905 that "if Princes Court patrons are not delighted beyond measure with the good things provided… at this wonderland of fun and frolic, then they must indeed be hard to please."

Two of the more notable performers at the Princes Court were Annette Kellermann (1886–1975), who by 1905 held all the world records for ladies' swimming. She performed a mermaid act at Princes Court entertainment centre. Kellermann was called the Australian Mermaid and Diving Venus, and with her skimpy, for the time, costume, went on to do much to emancipate women from the neck-to-knee bathing suit. The other was Beatrice Kerr (1887–1971) who was a competitive swimmer and a strong rival of Annette Kellerman. In a 20-week season in 1905, she completed 366 swimming and diving performances at Princes Court.

During its short-lived life, Princes Court raised money for the Women's Hospital by hosting such events as a jumble carnival, which included a spectacular Chinese procession and a grand continental bazaar that entertained thousands. In 1906, the FitzGerald brothers died. Without their support, the amusement park went into decline. The unpredictability of Melbourne's weather, combined with the fact that many of the activities were outdoors, plus the non-payment of rent, meant that the Princes Court Company was removed from the site. The Princes Court closed in 1909. Part of the site today is occupied by the Arts Centre.

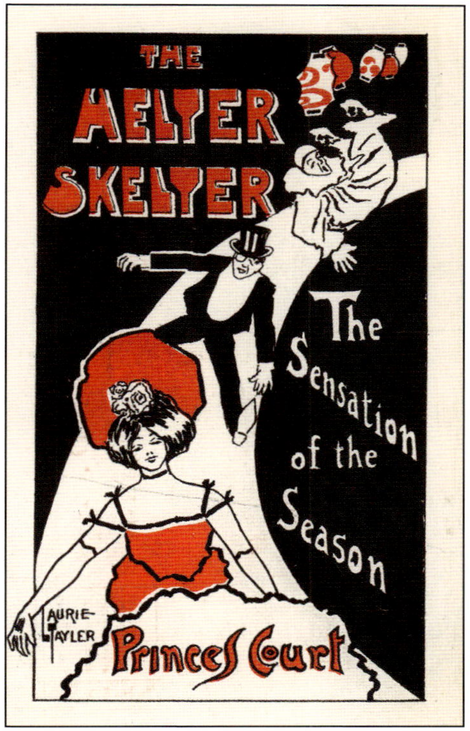

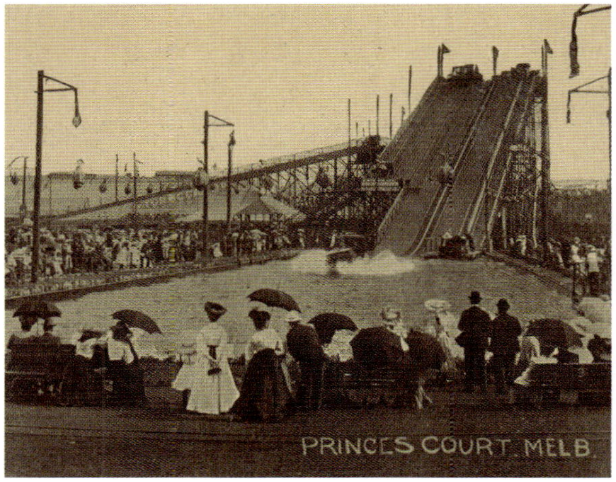

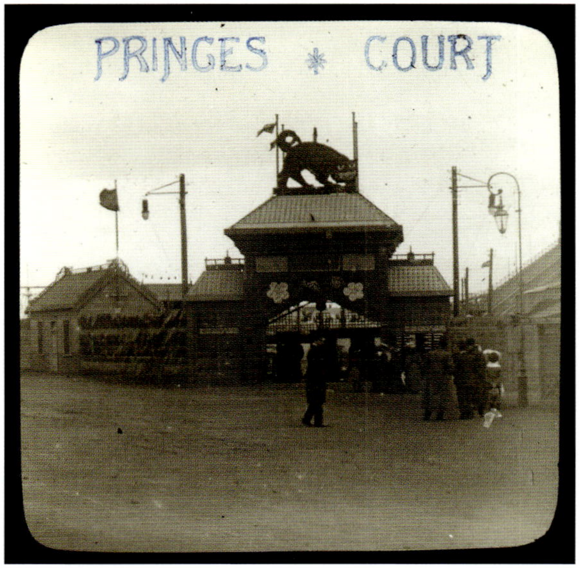

LEFT AND RIGHT *The Canadian Water Chute, one of the park's major attractions.*

FAR RIGHT *The entrance to the Chinese-themed, open-air theatre.*

FAR RIGHT, TOP *A Toulouse Lautrec style poster for the Helter Skelter, "The Sensation of the Season", circa 1905.*

Benevolent Asylum, North Melbourne

DEMOLISHED 1911

There were always poor and sick people in the early days of settlement at Port Phillip, but, with the discovery of gold in 1850, people flooded into the colony from all over the world. The alluvial gold quickly ran out and fossickers who could not afford to buy more expensive mining equipment returned to Melbourne in search of work, many destitute and starving. The Victorian Benevolent Society, a group of philanthropic citizens, was concerned about the welfare of the poor, and encouraged the City of Melbourne Councillors to request that the government of the colony put land aside so a building could be constructed that would house and look after the sick, poor and infirm.

In 1850 Governor Fitzroy granted the Benevolent Society 1,000 acres at North Melbourne where a few years before there was only a scattered collection of buildings. The gold-rush immigrant Albert Mattingley had described the area as being "richly carpeted with grass and studded with noble redgum trees", where Aboriginal tribes still occasionally camped. They were also granted £1,000 so that a facility could be built. This money was to be matched by an equal amount raised by public subscription. At the time, *The Argus* described the site as being beautiful, with a view to the bay, but others thought that it was too far out in the bush and there was no road access to it. It was two kilometres from the centre of the Melbourne Township.

Charles Laing, the Chief Surveyor of Melbourne, built the huge Benevolent Asylum building and by the time it was finished and opened in 1851 it had cost £3,272. Initially it was to house immigrants but then it looked after the blind, orphans, lunatics and the aged poor. The building was extended four times until it had 685 beds. An article in *The Argus* in 1862 begs the public to give more support to the Benevolent Society, saying that it "is the only form in which public relief is given to the helpless and decrepit people who are every week thrown upon our hands." At the time there were 350 inmates and no more could be admitted. It cost £24 a year to keep each one and new buildings hadn't yet been paid for. A sum of £10,000 had been voted by Parliament for the asylum but only on the condition that one third more be raised by public subscription.

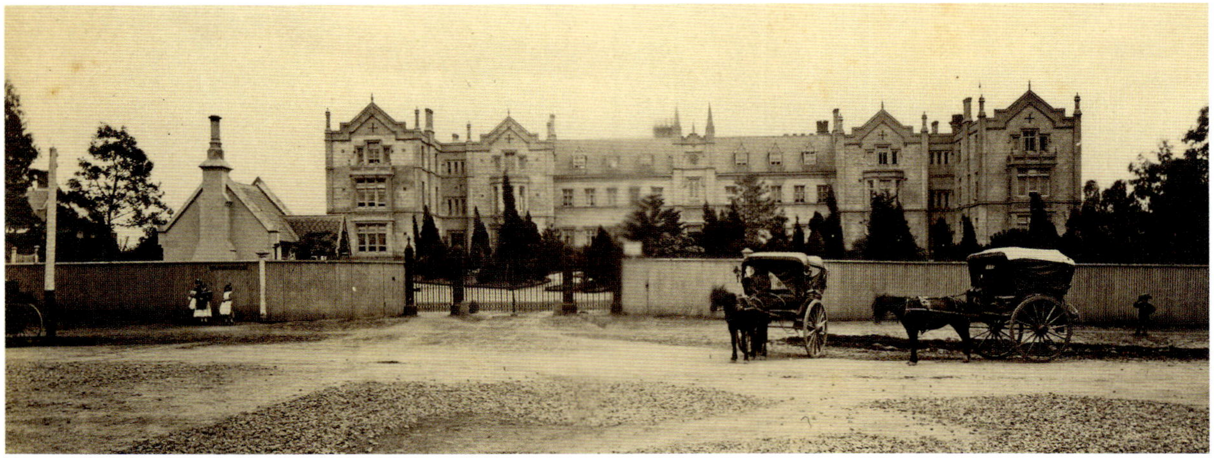

ABOVE *Buggies and horses wait for passengers on the unmade road outside the Benevolent Asylum in 1890.*

RIGHT *The gardens and building of the Benevolent Asylum and Hospital for the Aged and Infirm in 1868.*

RIGHT *Christmas Day at the Benevolent Asylum in 1895, showing the ladies' dining room and men being given gifts of tobacco.*

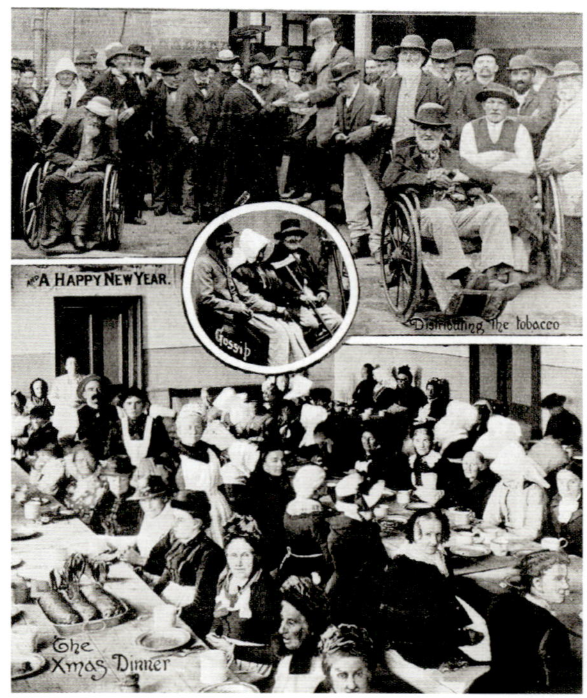

In a report from 1880, the asylum was described as being "filled to repletion with aged and infirm persons, whilst every week numbers of gaunt hungry and distressed persons ... vainly implored admission." The Depression of the 1890s created an even greater number of desperately poor people and the Benevolent Asylum could not possibly accommodate them. Another site needed to be found. A site at Cheltenham had been set aside in 1887, and a foundation stone had been laid in 1909 by the Governor of Victoria, Sir Thomas Carmichael but the first patients at this new Cheltenham Asylum were not admitted until 1911. In the end, 515 patients were transferred to what would later be called the Kingston Centre for the Care of the Aged and the massive neo-Gothic Benevolent Asylum at North Melbourne finally closed and was demolished in 1911.

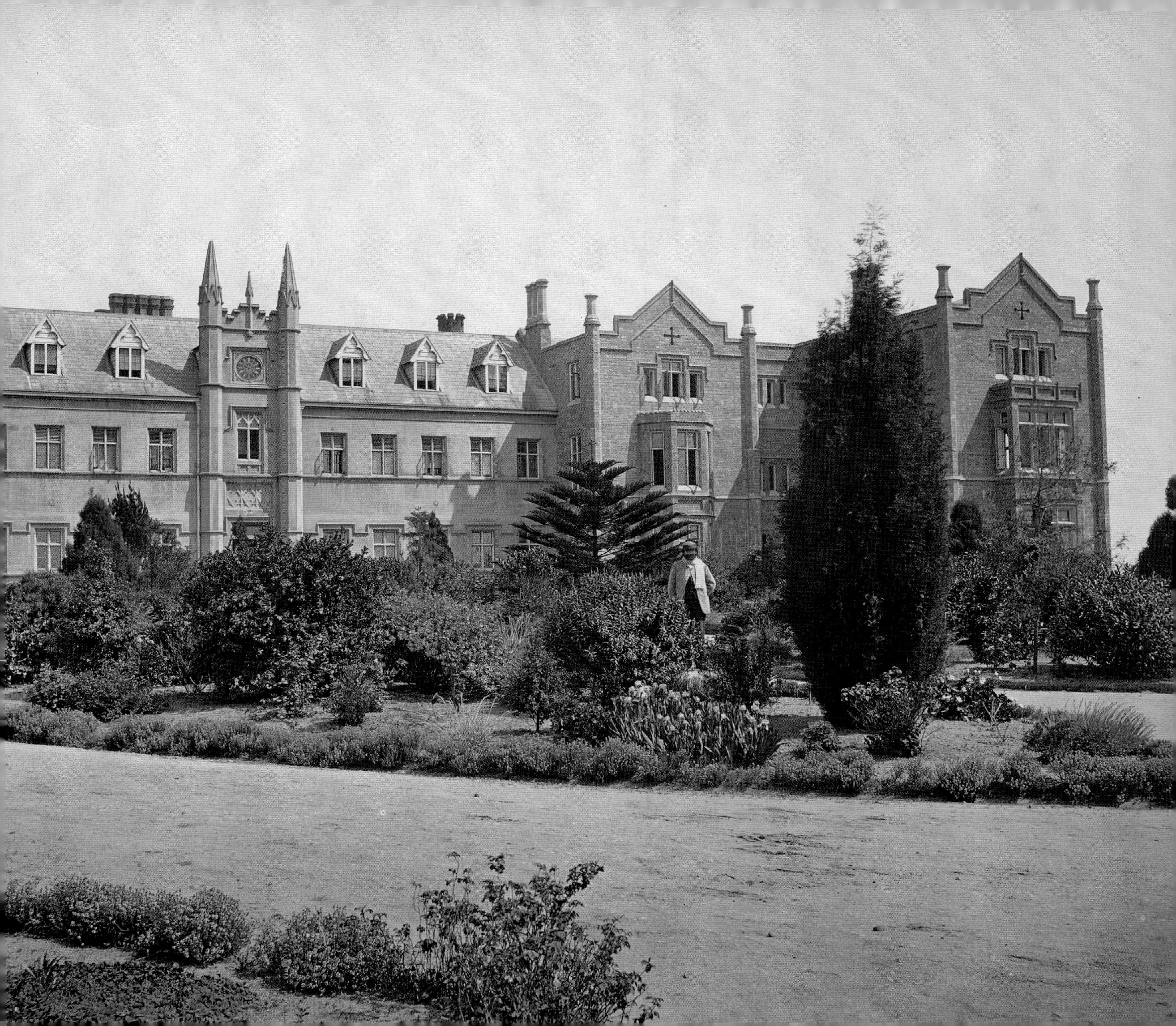

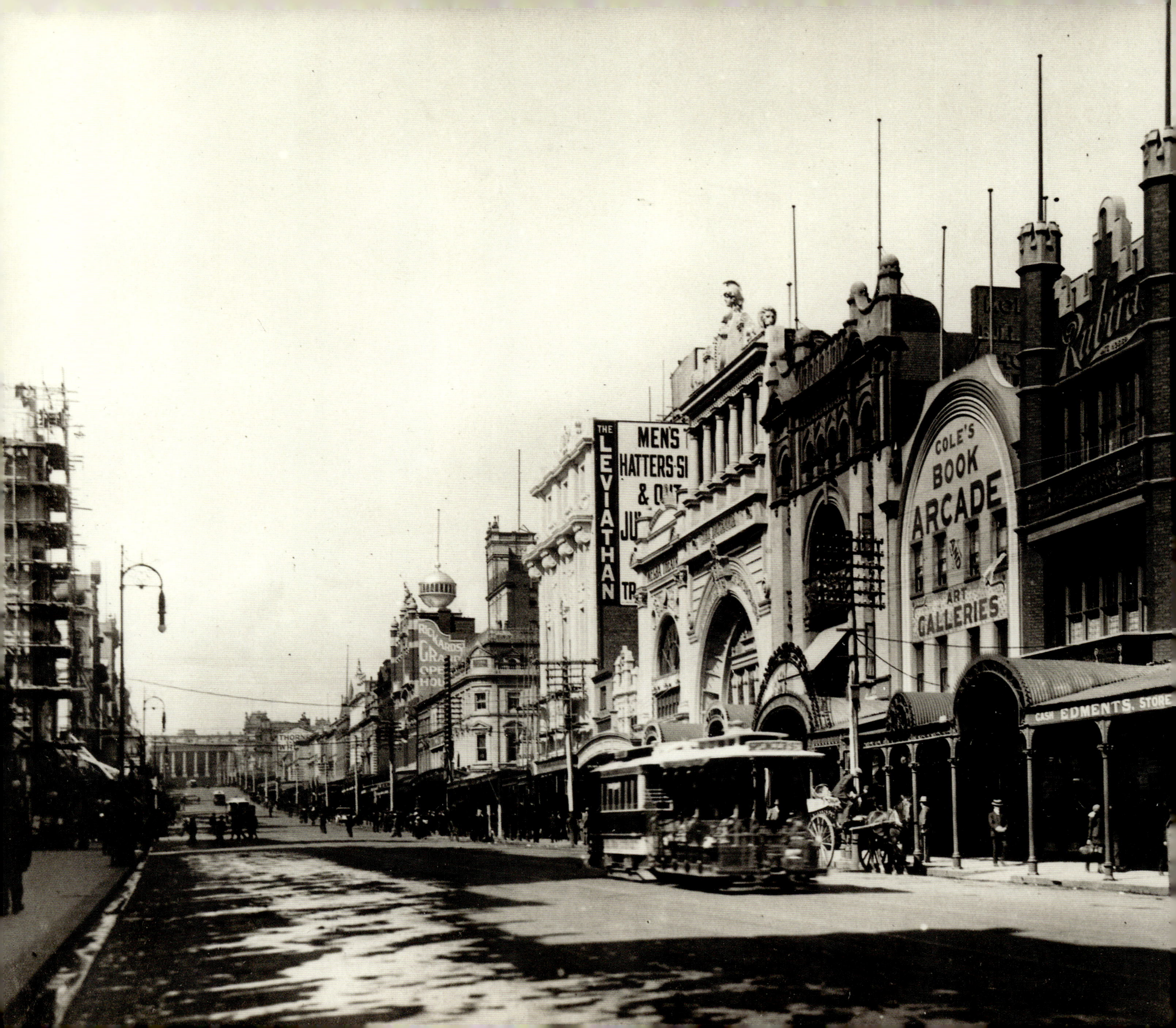
THE LEVIATHAN
MEN'S
HATTERS·
COLE'S BOOK ARCADE
AND ART GALLERIES
CASH EDMENTS STORE

Cole's Book Arcade CLOSED 1928

When Cole's Book Arcade opened in Bourke Street in 1883, its owner described it as the "Grandest Bookshop in the World".

Edward William Cole came to Victoria in 1852 at the age of 20 to make his fortune on the goldfields, having previously failed in South Africa. He had little formal schooling but believed passionately in the value of education. Largely self-taught, he wrote texts and pamphlets on many topics. He petitioned for Wednesday to be a day of leisure and Albury to be Australia's capital, and he published his thoughts on the end of the White Australia Policy and the success of the temperance movement. It was natural that he would open a bookshop. In 1865 he opened a second-hand bookstore in the Eastern Market (Paddy's Market) and by the early 1870s he had taken over the whole Eastern Market site and offered stalls to lots of small businessmen, amassing great wealth in the process.

In 1873 he opened a new shop in Bourke Street near Russell Street that he described as "the prettiest sight in Melbourne". His staff wore red uniforms, there was music for the customers and the mirrors and shiny brass fittings enticed many people through its doors. He was so successful that he was able to move to larger premises in Bourke Street in 1883. These were located near where the second David Jones store is today. Cole set about transforming what had once been a Spanish restaurant into a huge open space where the second floor became an atrium looking down on to the ground floor. Cole's Book Arcade or "Palace of Intellect" was so much more than a bookstore. It contained over two million new and second-hand books, where the public could browse and read all day and not feel compelled to purchase anything.

By 1896 Cole was able to extend his bookstore through to Little Collins Street and in 1906 right through to Collins Street. This store was enclosed with a glass and ornamental gabled roof, still visible today. Customers were entertained with a string orchestra, a clockwork symphonion, a monkey house, a toyland and a funny mirror area for children, an art gallery, a curio shop stuffed with ornaments, and a refreshment room. There were many mechanical devices to fascinate the customers: a hen that clucked and laid eggs when a coin was put in a slot, and, at the entrance, there were two mechanical boys with wise messages telling the public to "Read!" and to "Eat Well". This shop was so well loved and visited that even Rudyard Kipling and Mark Twain were said to have been there.

Cole had many innovative marketing gimmicks, one of which was the deliberate dropping of coin tokens around the streets, which could be redeemed for items in his store. Cole's also produced the *Rainbow Story Book* and *Cole's Funny Picture Book* that today are much sought after by collectors. The *Cole's Funny Picture Book* was full of puzzles, quaint stories, travelogues of exotic lands, drawings and poems, and was the most popular children's book in Australia for 50 years from 1890 to 1940.

Edward Cole died in 1918 and by 1924 the business that had been so financially successful, and a unique place of wonder for all ages, had begun to decline. The "Grandest Bookshop in the World" had its last day of trading in May 1928. Many items from the Book Arcade were saved and can today be seen in the Museum of Victoria. Cole's Book Arcade was sold to G. J. Coles for £200,000 who then demolished it and built the Coles Variety Store on the site. Up-market shops today occupy the glass-roofed arcade, the only aspect of the original shop to be retained, between Little Collins and Collins Streets.

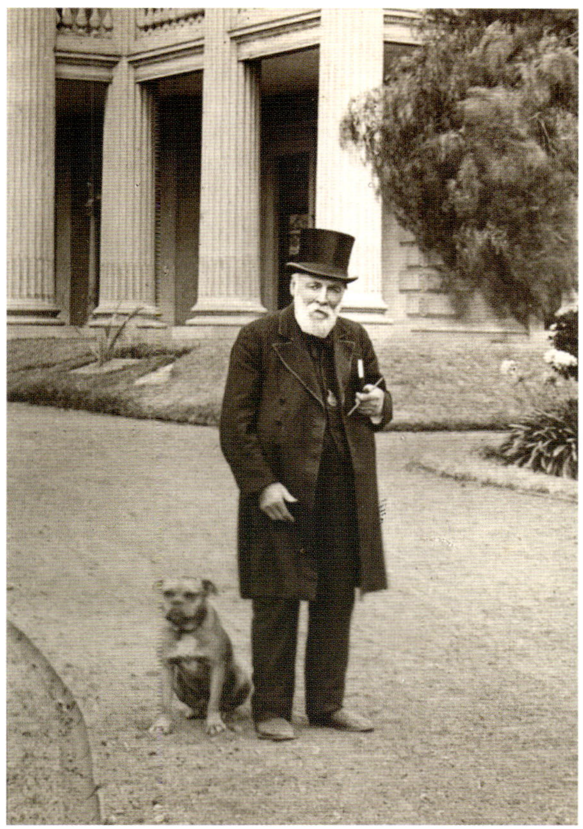

OPPOSITE *Cole's Book Arcade was demolished and replaced in 1932 by an art deco style building for G. J. Coles' (no relation) Large Variety Store.*

LEFT *Edward Cole was one of the most eccentric and fascinating figures in Victoria's history. Failing to make his fortune on the goldfields, he sold food to miners, rowed down the Murray River collecting seeds that he then sold to the Botanical Gardens in Melbourne and he speculated in purchasing land. He even obtained a wife in an unorthodox manner by advertising for one in the paper.*

BELOW *The staff of Cole's Book Arcade pose in the Fancy Goods department for* The Argus *newspaper on the last day of trading.*

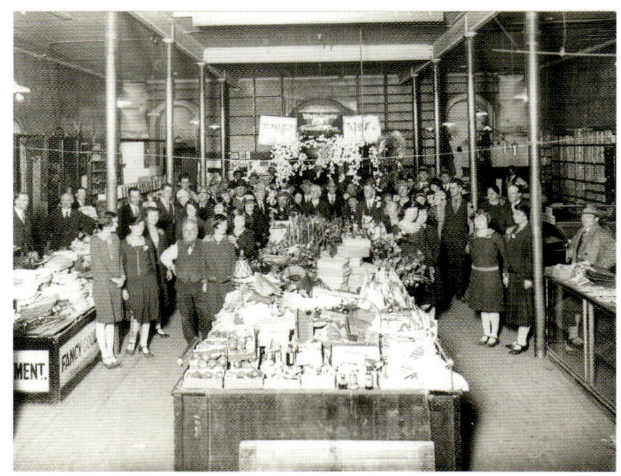

Model School DEMOLISHED 1933

Victoria's National Board of Education was created in 1851 and in 1852 Lieutenant Governor Charles Joseph La Trobe granted land in East Melbourne for educational purposes. This was the start of the Model School. It was designed by A. E. Johnston who had also designed the GPO in Elizabeth Street. But this was the time of the gold rushes in Victoria and men deserted the city in a search of a more lucrative outcome. Building materials became scarce, labour costs increased and construction of the school quickly ran into difficulties. The Model School was built largely by unskilled workers with materials that they could forage from wherever they were available. Though considered an elegant building, it gained a reputation for being badly built and many repairs and alterations were necessary over its lifetime.

The Model School included separate departments for boys, girls and infants, a school for teacher training and administration offices. Arthur Davitt and his wife Ellen arrived in Melbourne on 31 July 1854 from Ireland to take up a joint appointment with the National Board of Education. Davitt became the principal of the school and his wife became the superintendent of the female pupils and trainees. The school opened in September that year. Unfortunately, the Davitts were involved in frequent quarrels with their staff and when Arthur Davitt was dismissed in 1859 it may have been due as much to this as to a reduction of the education grant for that year.

"Model" schools were established as an early attempt to make teaching standards consistent throughout Victoria. When the Common Schools Act of 1862 replaced the National Board of Education, the Model School became known as the Central Common School. In 1872, following the Education Act 1872, it became State School No. 391.

The education department's offices were located at the Model School until 1878 and the teacher preparation (which had ceased in 1859) recommenced at the University of Melbourne in 1889. School numbers gradually declined though, as city residential dwellers decreased. The school closed in 1904 and in 1905 the new Melbourne Continuation School, Victoria's first state secondary school, moved in to the building. In 1912, the name was changed to Melbourne High School with the school becoming co-educational. By 1914 the school was reaching capacity and the idea came to split the school into two single-sex schools. The boys moved to South Yarra in 1927 (the present Melbourne High School site) and the girls (today located at The Mac.Robertson Girls' High School) were left to deal with a cramped and dilapidated building until it was condemned in 1930. Stories of the time talk about girls falling through the floorboards and council workers removing rotting floorings and fallen plaster.

The Model School was the birthplace of universal secular education in Victoria and the site has considerable historic significance. The building itself though was recommended for demolition, which began in 1933. In 1934 construction began on the site for the Royal Australasian College of Surgeons. A plaque there commemorates the demolition of the Model School.

RIGHT *The Model School in about 1880, with staff and students outside.*

BELOW *This view along Spring Street shows the Model School in about 1870.*

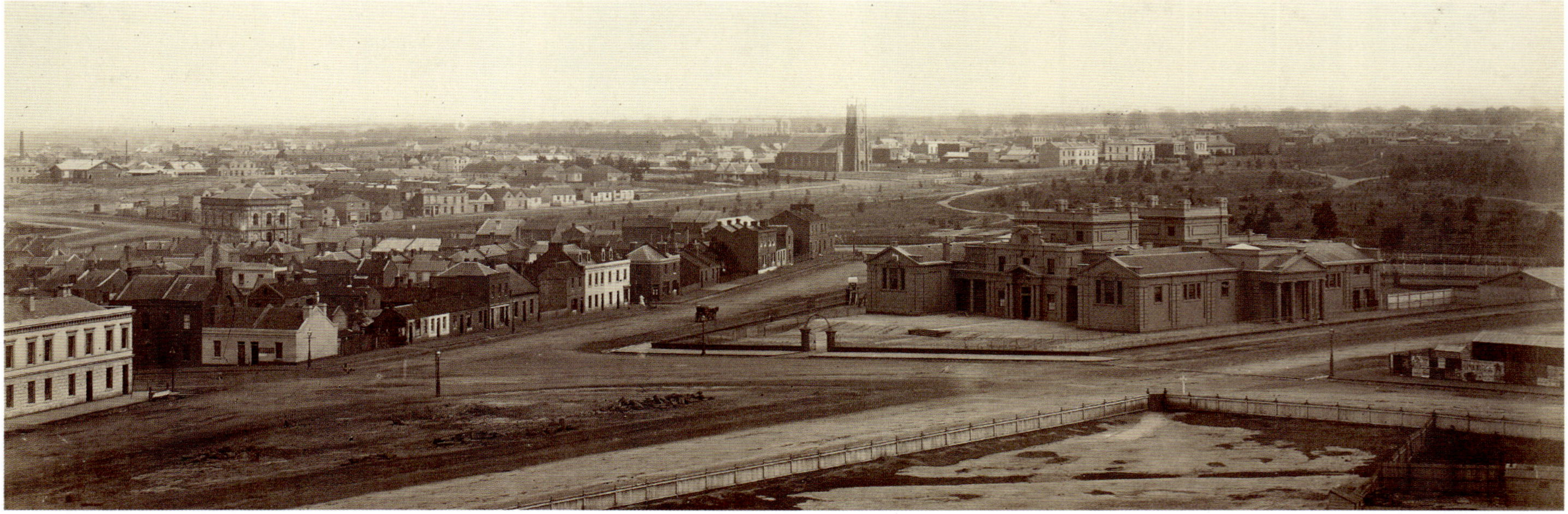

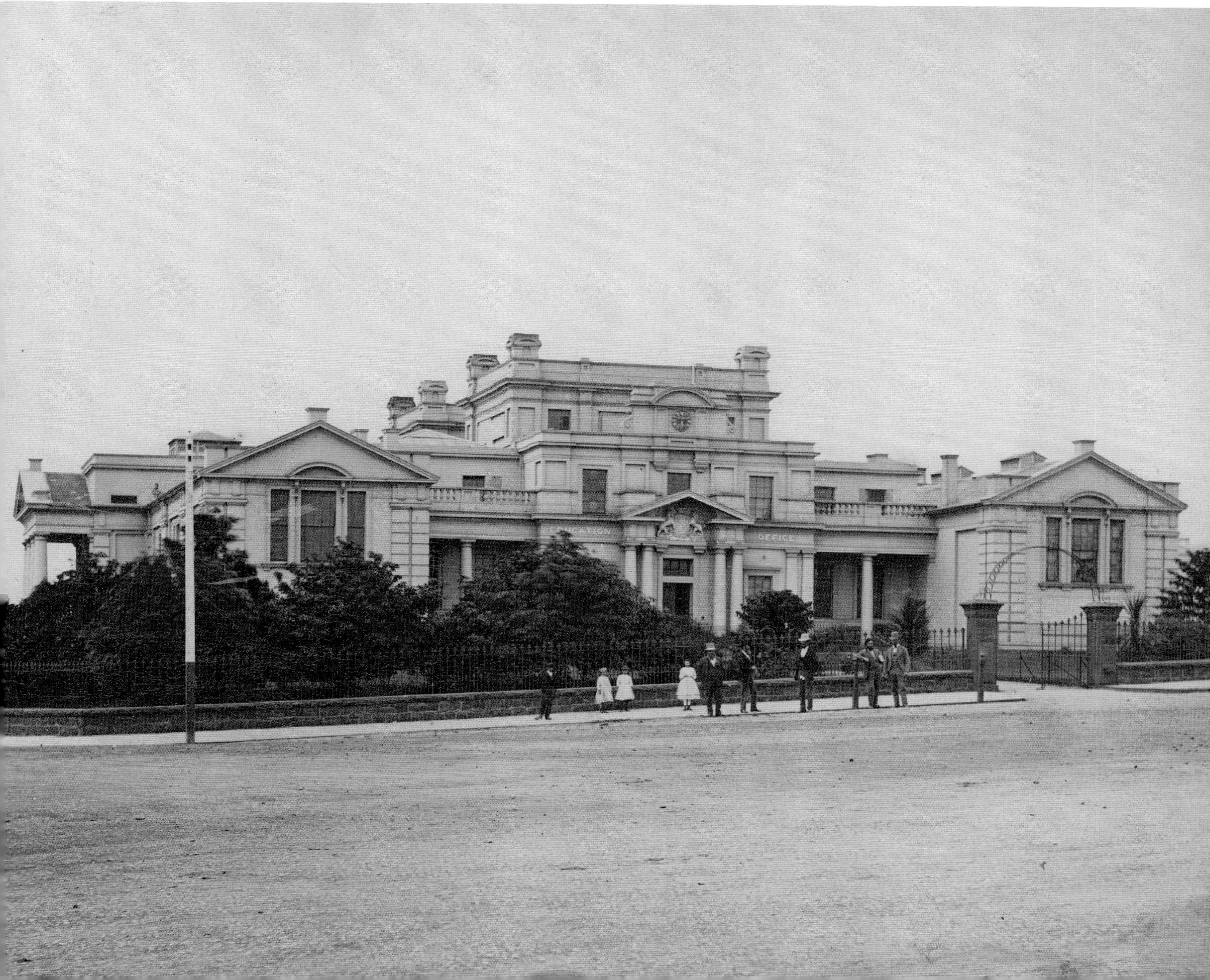
EDUCATION
OFFICE

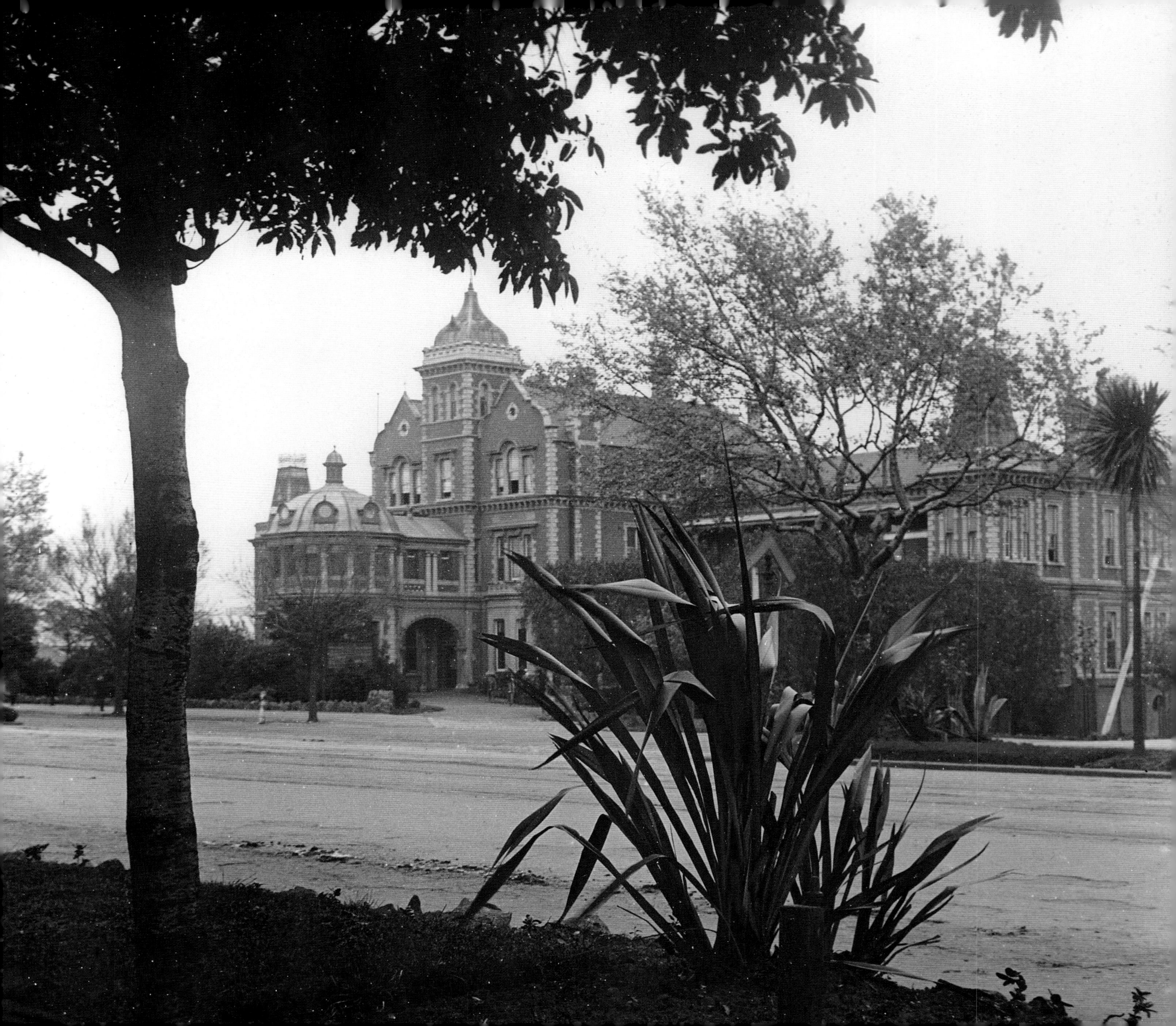

Homeopathic Hospital RENAMED AND REPURPOSED 1934

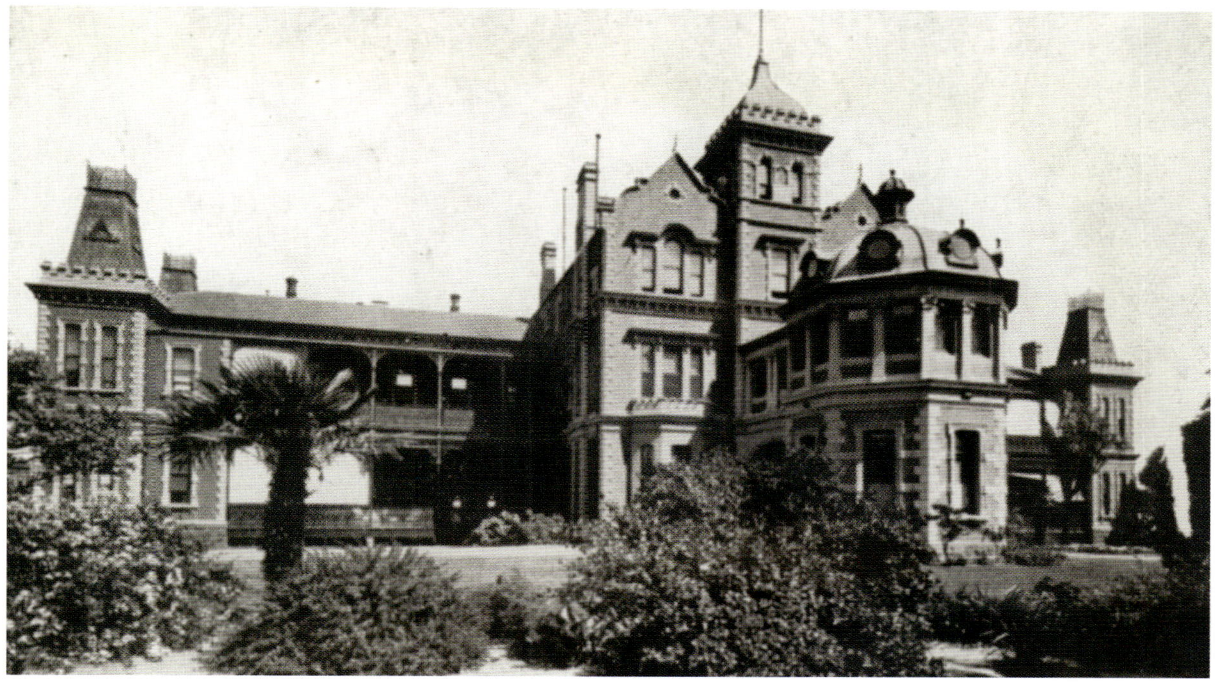

The Homeopathic Hospital, built in St. Kilda Road, had its genesis in the Homeopathic Dispensary established in Collins Street in 1869. Dr J. W. Gunst, one of the founders, actively promoted and published information about the efficacy of homeopathy.

Very quickly the dispensary committee realised that access to inpatient facilities was needed. Unsuccessful overtures were made to both the Melbourne and the Alfred hospitals in 1875 for the homeopathic treatment of patients. Due to the efforts of Mrs Emily Shan, president of the Ladies' Committee, the government granted land for the construction of a new homeopathic hospital in 1875. Unsurprisingly, allopathic medical practitioners thwarted any such venture. A temporary arrangement was made with the opening of an inpatient hospital in Spring Street in 1876. The building was a rundown three-storey structure that once operated as the Sick Children's Hospital. The hospital was soon in dire straits with overcrowding, deteriorating buildings and lack of money.

In 1879, 10 years after the establishment of the Homeopathic Dispensary, at the request of the Homeopathic Committee and preceded by many rejections, a site for a hospital building along St. Kilda Road was granted. The foundation stone was laid in 1882 and the building was opened in 1885.

The building was an elaborate structure facing the unsealed, neglected and rutted St. Kilda Road, and backing onto undeveloped swampy land, flanked on either side by the Victorian Barracks and the Immigrants' Home. It was developed in stages. Crouch & Wilson were the architects for the three-storey administration block, a 25-metre central tower and two square towers on the Northern end. The architect for a further wing added to the Southern side in the 1890s was Mr J. T. Giblins.

The dark red Northcote brick and cream freestone dressings built on solid bluestone foundations were conspicuous for their colour and blending of period styles (perhaps due to different architects at different stages of development). There were parapets and gables and deep verandas spanning the front and rear of the building. Dressed with cast iron lacework popular during the "Marvellous Melbourne" period, they provided an open-to-air protection for the inpatients throughout the seasons. On the right of the front entrance was a 30-bed pavilion style ward with a mirror copy above. By 1891 the hospital had up to 80 beds. The wards were large and bright from natural light with ceilings up to 17 feet high. The interior walls were finished with Keene's cement, which was thought to prevent the accumulation of bug infestations. The St. Kilda Road frontage overlooked what became the Botanical Gardens.

The support for the Homeopathic Hospital waxed and waned in the face of allopathic medical resistance to the philosophy and practice of homeopathy. For example, in 1906 the Victorian Medical Board adopted a code of ethics that forbade any medical doctor from working with a homeopathic practitioner. In 1924, due to shortages of practitioners, medical doctors were again allowed to practise at the homeopathic hospital. The hospital was no longer exclusively homeopathic The allopathic doctors demanded provision and access to laboratories, X-ray equipment and other diagnostic facilities, thus the homeopathic principles and practices were eventually subsumed into allopathic practice. By 1933 the hospital had treated one million patients, but it was now run down and almost unfit for its purpose. Fifty years from laying the foundation stone, and within 10 years of allopathic doctors practising at the Homeopathic Hospital, its name and purpose were permanently changed. In essence it ceased to exist. At a special meeting in 1934, the committee of the Homeopathic Hospital consented to a name change. It became Prince Henry's Hospital, which in turn was demolished in 1994 and replaced by a luxury apartment project.

ABOVE *The Homeopathic Hospital was a blend of styles as it was built in stages by different architects.*

OPPOSITE *The Homeopathic Hospital, seen here around 1885, was built beside the neglected St. Kilda Road.*

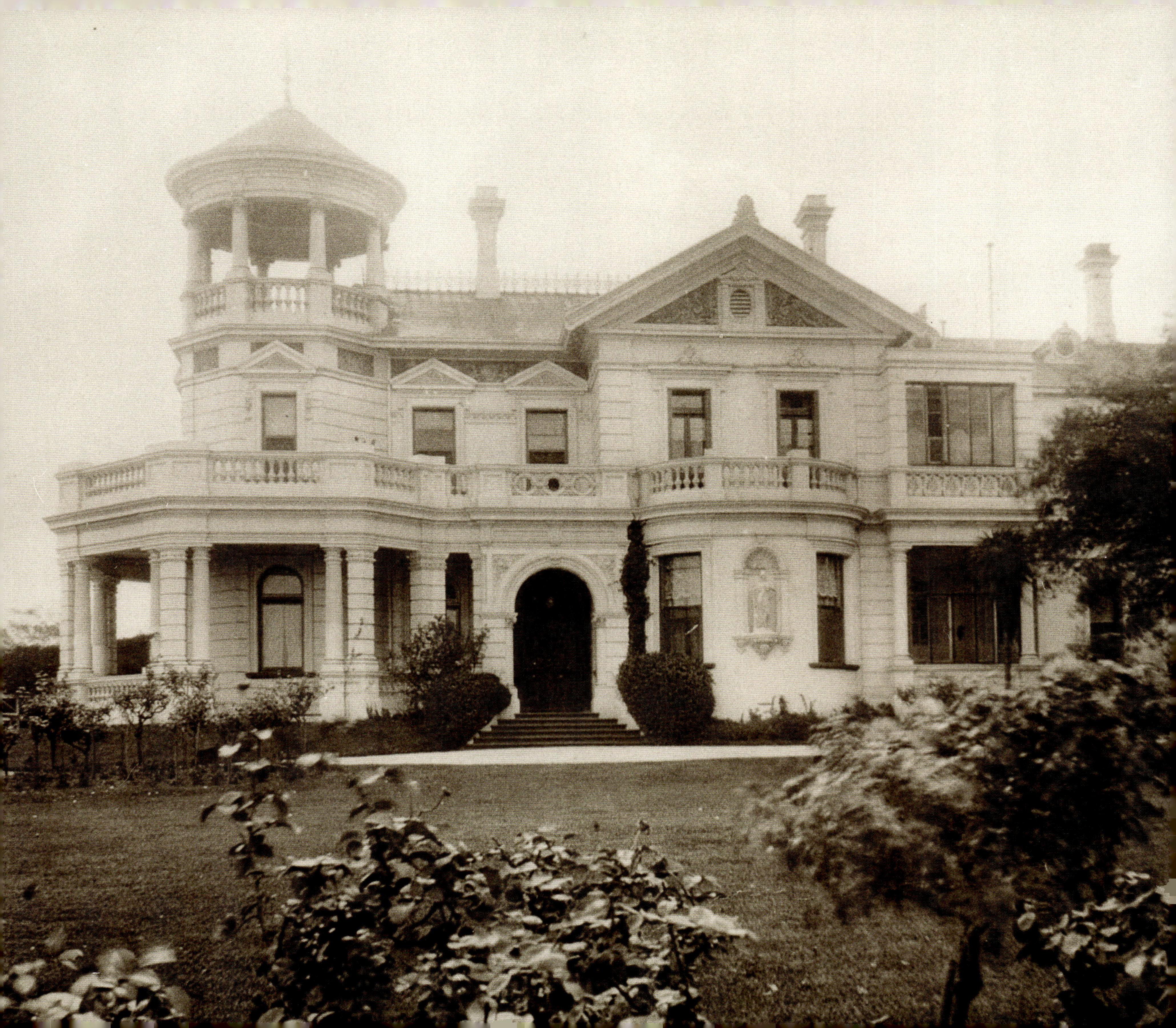

Hadleigh Hall DEMOLISHED 1935

Hadleigh Hall, also known as Gotha, was built for Hugo Wertheim in 1886 and was designed by the well-known architect Charles D'Ebro, designer of Stonington and the Prahran Town Hall. Hadleigh Hall was a very large two-storey mansion in South Yarra that cost £40,000 to build. It had a spacious dining room, drawing room, and servants' rooms. It was said that the drawing room was the most magnificent in Australia and famous musicians such as Paderewski held concerts there, playing on Wertheim pianos. Paderewski favoured the Erard piano while Franz Liszt preferred the Ernst Kaps piano. The drawing room could be opened out to provide an area almost as large as a tennis court. On the first floor were 17 bedrooms, some of which were for staff, a nursery, utility rooms and four bathrooms. Outside there were coal and boot rooms, a fowl house, stable and hothouse, as well as a lawn tennis court. The house was surrounded by sweeping lawns and flower gardens.

Hugo Wertheim, German by birth, came to Melbourne in 1875. He established a sewing machine agency for his uncle Joseph, a successful manufacturer of sewing machines in Germany. In 1882 Hugo became an Australian citizen and returned to Germany to marry Sophie, Joseph's daughter. His sewing machine business flourished and soon he was also selling bicycles, knitting machines, mangles, separators, washing machines, baby carriages and pianos. In 1901 Hugo Wertheim attended the Pan-American Exposition in Buffalo in the United States and met O. C. Beale, a piano manufacturer. Hugo was interested in the manufacture of pianos and eventually came to own 25 per cent of Beale's business. His business was growing and in 1903 new retail premises were opened in Chapel Street, Prahran. In the city, he opened a Bourke Street store and located his head office in William Street, while additional Wertheim stores were established in Adelaide. In 1908 Hugo invested £75,000 in building a piano factory in Richmond. The foundation stone was laid by Alfred Deakin, a prominent Melburnian and the Prime Minister of Australia, who said, " few men with such opportunities in life for ease would have embarked on such an enterprise…the first in Victoria to make pianos."

Hugo travelled widely and advertisements for his pianos and sewing machines could be seen in newspapers from Bendigo to Broken Hill. The newspapers of the day also show that he organised travelling exhibitions, not just showing his machines at agricultural shows in large towns, but in small towns all around Australia. The reports in the local press were invariably complimentary. His sewing machine was described as "beautiful in the extreme…frictionless and noiseless. The machine almost threads and runs itself."

The years of World War I were difficult for anyone of German background and Wertheim was no exception. Despite the fact that he had long ago become an Australian citizen, he was reported several times as being a spy or having pro-German sympathies. Hugo Wertheim died in 1919 and the business passed to his son Herbert, but the Great Depression and the growing popularity of the wireless meant that fewer pianos were sold and the factory closed in 1935. Today Wertheim pianos are still made but ownership is in different hands. Ownership of Hadleigh Hall also changed several times but the cost of maintaining such a large mansion was too great and it was sold for demolition in 1935. The total amount received for 500 lots was £877, and the materials, which had been imported from Germany, sold for a fraction of their original cost. *The Argus* claimed that the amount was more than would have been received had the building been sold in one lot. The site of the mansion was subdivided and flats and maisonettes were built in its place.

OPPOSITE *Hadleigh Hall, also called Gotha, was the home of Hugo Wertheim in Kensington Road, South Yarra.*

BELOW *The Wertheim Piano Factory, designed by Nahum Barnet, was made of red brick and covered a large area of land. It closed in 1935 and then became a Heinz food-processing factory. In 1955 it became the home of GTV9 television production and offices. They broadcasted their last program from this studio in 2011. The building is listed on the Victorian Heritage Register.*

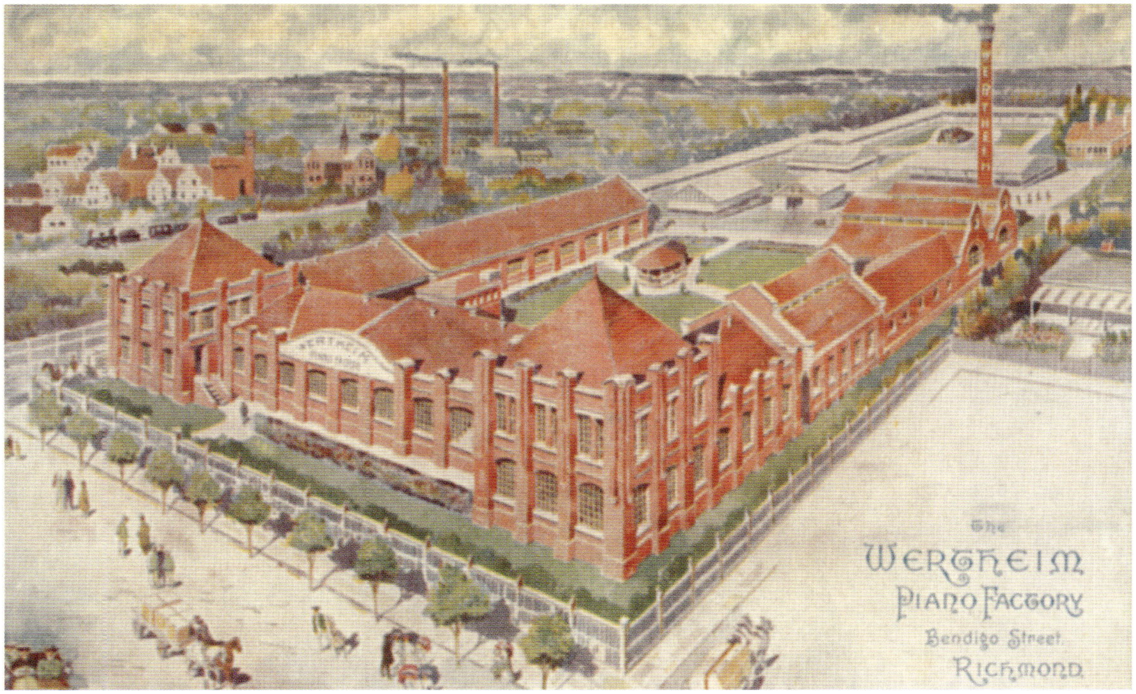

Cable Trams DISCONTINUED 1940

When Andrew Hallidie, a manufacturer of wire rope in the USA, had an idea that the cables he manufactured could be used to pull trams along their rails, he patented his invention and in 1873 the world's first cable tram ran in San Francisco. In Melbourne, Francis Boardman Clapp set up the Melbourne Tramway Company, bought the Victorian patents to Hallidie's invention and the renamed Melbourne Tramway and Omnibus Company operated the first cable tramway on 11 November 1885. It ran from the corner of Bourke and Spencer Street, along Flinders Street, to Bridge Road, Richmond, and Hawthorn Bridge. In time, Melbourne's cable tram network became one of the largest in the world. The Melbourne Tramway and Omnibus Company ran the cable tram routes until 1916.

To place the cables, tunnels had to be dug 1.2 metres beneath the road, sufficiently wide to allow for cables in both directions. These cables were made up of six strands of seven wires twisted around a hemp core. They had to be constantly greased and new wires spliced. The trams weren't particularly heavy, consisting of an open "dummy", which held the driver or grip man, 20 people seated or 22 standing, and a closed car holding 22 people, or 34 standing. A handle mechanism in the dummy enabled the driver to grip the moving cable beneath the road. White lines on the road showed the driver where to engage the grip.

A conductor recorded the collected fares by punching a hole in a long piece of card that was pinned to his uniform. At the end of the day the confetti left behind had to tally with the fares he had collected. It was also his job to call out "Watch the curve!" when the tram approached a corner, and to look out for boys who attempted to avoid paying the fare or tried to put grease on the tracks so that the brakes would have trouble gripping. At the end of the day when the tram had returned to its depot it was hauled in by either man or horse power.

The Melbourne Tramway and Omnibus Act allowed local councils to build the tracks and powerhouses needed to run the system. By 1891 Melbourne had 71 kilometres of track running along most of the city streets and the main arterial roads to Brunswick and Northcote, Toorak, and St. Kilda. There were 11 power stations along these routes. Power stations were dotted across the tram network, supplying power to run the cables. Their tall chimneys distinguished the stations.

The Land Boom of the 1880s encouraged the growth of the suburbs, but the Economic Depression of the early 1890s meant that there were few extensions to the Cable Tram Network after 1891. In 1919 the Melbourne and Metropolitan Tramways Board (MMTB) took over the system and, over time, converted the cable tramways to an electric system. The last cable tram ran from Bourke Street in October 1940. Today's tram network is now thought to be the largest in the English-speaking world.

OPPOSITE *Laying the cable tram tracks in Elizabeth Street, around 1890, with Flinders Street station in the background.*

RIGHT *A cable tram of the Melbourne Tramway and Omnibus Company in front of Flinders Street station, 1900.*

BELOW *Engine houses, where the steam power to run the cables was generated, were usually located in the middle of the line. They were conspicuous in the landscape because of their distinctive architecture and very tall chimneys.*

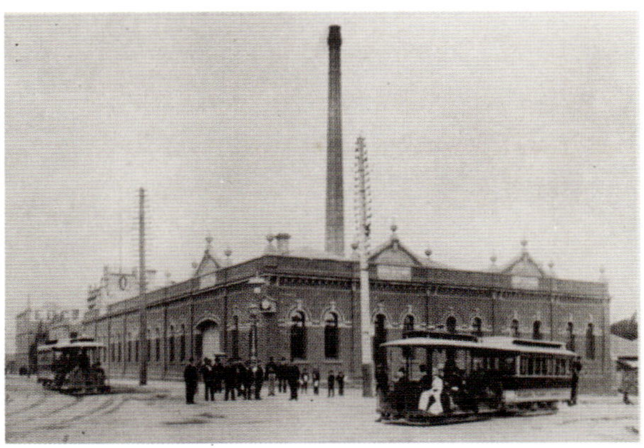

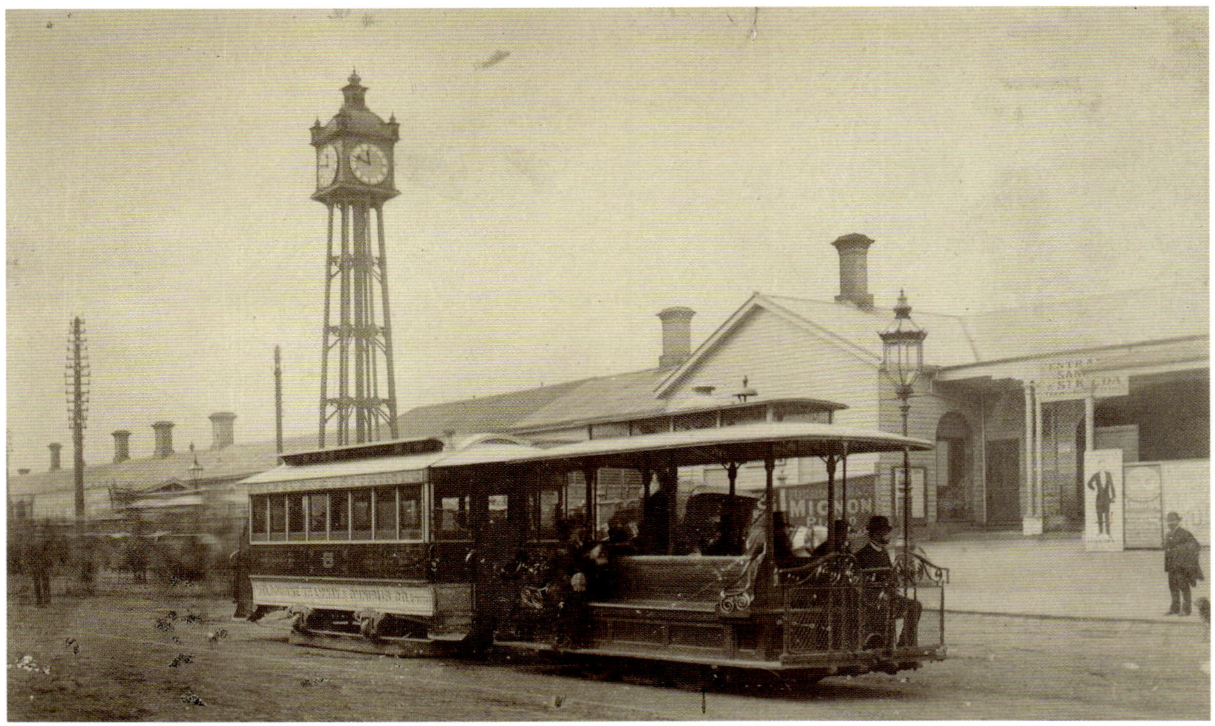

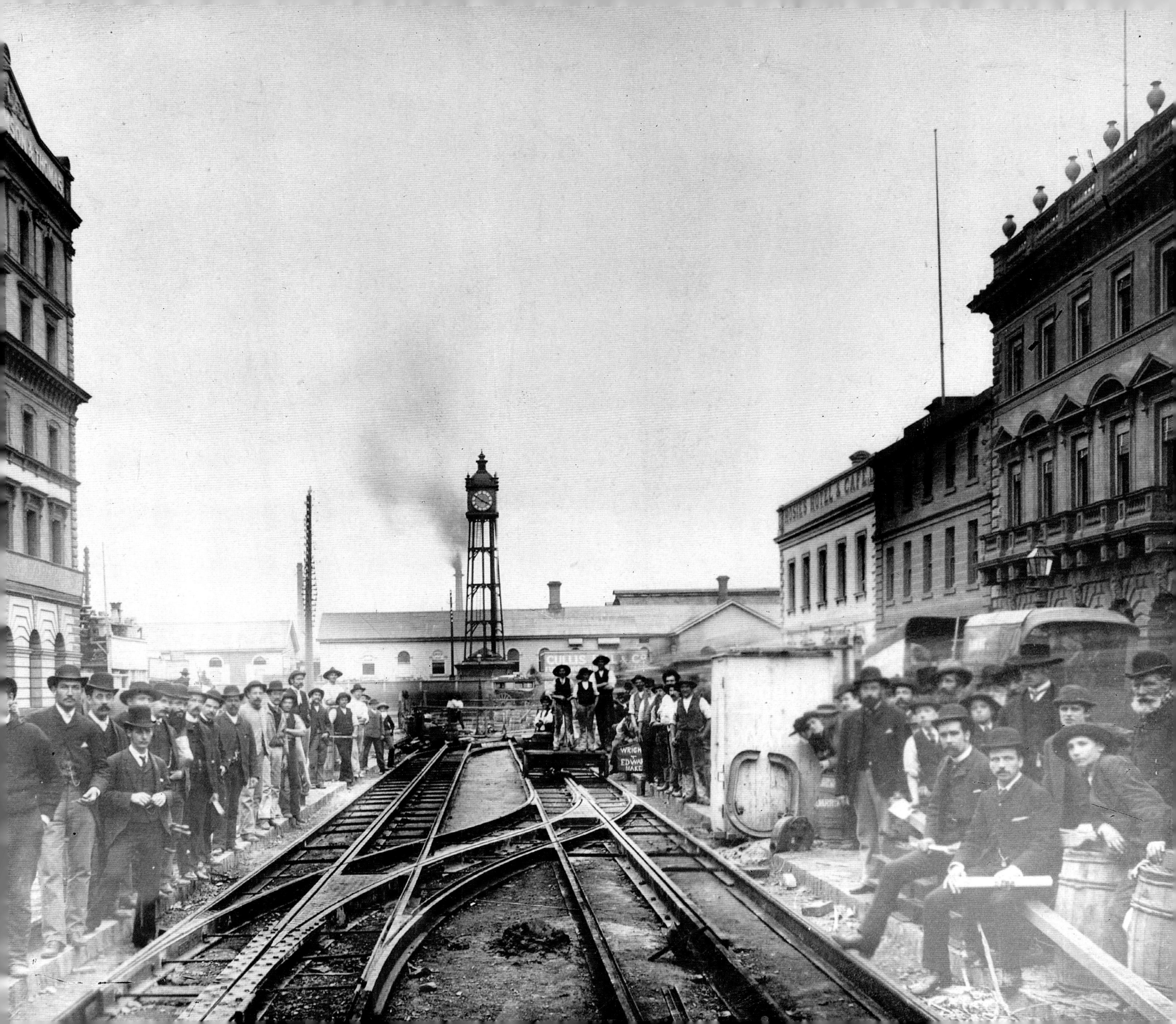
CULLIS

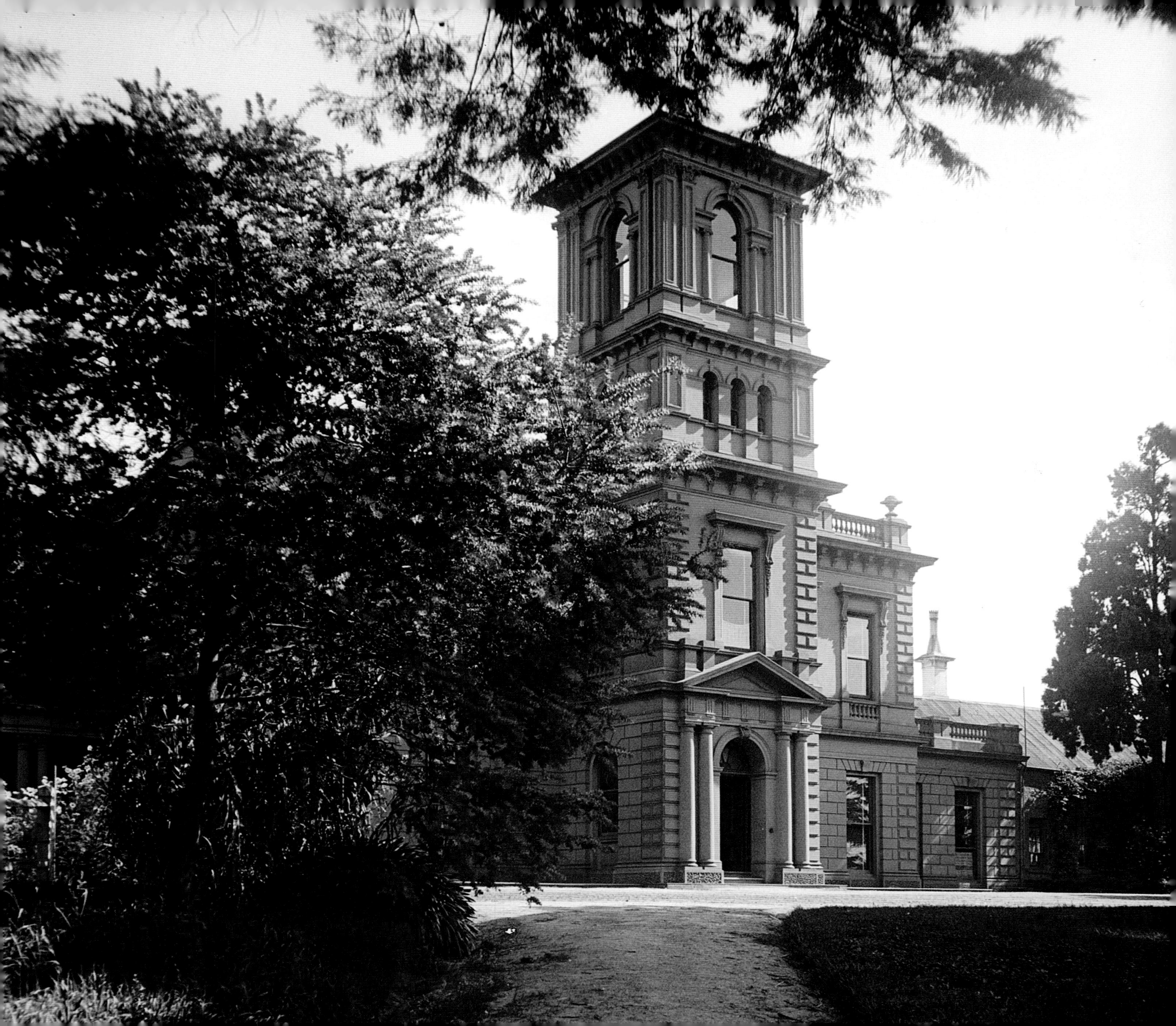

Travancore DEMOLISHED 1940s

The Travancore estate in the 1840s was originally part of a large sheep run owned by James Watson, one of Victoria's earliest squatters. The run had been named Flemington by him in memory of an estate in Scotland managed by his father-in-law. On acquiring the property from Watson, Hugh Glass determined to spare no expense in developing the estate into one of the finest in the region. The original dwelling was quite modest but this was replaced by a mansion known at the time as Flemington House, which subsequently became Travancore. It was built in 1852 for Hugh Glass at the time of his marriage to Lucinda Nash. Glass's brother travelled to England to select appropriate fittings and furniture and many workmen toiled over two years to build the mansion.

The house had a grand ballroom said to be the size of a town hall. It also had two staircases, eight family bedrooms, a library, sitting room, drawing room, two upstairs bathrooms, a kitchen and sewing room. Other buildings included stables, servants' quarters, a summer house, a gatehouse, and a boat house. There were also hothouses, arbours and aviaries, one of which was eventually moved to the Zoological Gardens in Melbourne. At the same time as the house was being erected, and for a number of years after, workmen developed the grounds and landscaped the area. An artificial lake was formed, parklands were created and many acres were regraded. In the large orchard that Glass established, attempts were made to grow many exotic fruits such as banana, pawpaw and sugarcane. He imported trees to grow alongside the Australian ones and brought in brightly plumaged birds. The lake held various species of ducks, white swans and cranes, and glass tanks in the conservatory were home to imported varieties of fish. Suitable enclosures held kangaroo and ostriches, while peacocks and pheasants roamed the grounds. The camels he kept were eventually used by A. W. Howitt in his attempt to find Burke and Wills, the Australian explorers.

Hugh Glass was thought to be the richest man in Victoria and he continued to spend money on his house and land up until the late 1860s, when a downturn in his fortunes saw him rein in his spending. He died in 1870 and Flemington House was later purchased by Henry Madden who, with his brothers, had spent time on the estate as boys. It was he who called the mansion Travancore. He subdivided the property, but kept the mansion and approximately 60 acres until he sold the estate in 1922. The estate was again subdivided before the mansion and the remaining nine acres were sold to the Victorian Government in 1926 at a cost reported to be £11,000. The intention was to create a residential school for disabled children. The house was demolished in the 1940s but the ornate iron gates that marked the entrance to the estate now mark the entrance to Flemington Primary School. The original Travancore estate is today home to almost 2,000 people in flats, houses and town houses. Many of the buildings are on the National Trust's heritage database as classic examples of art deco housing from the 1920s.

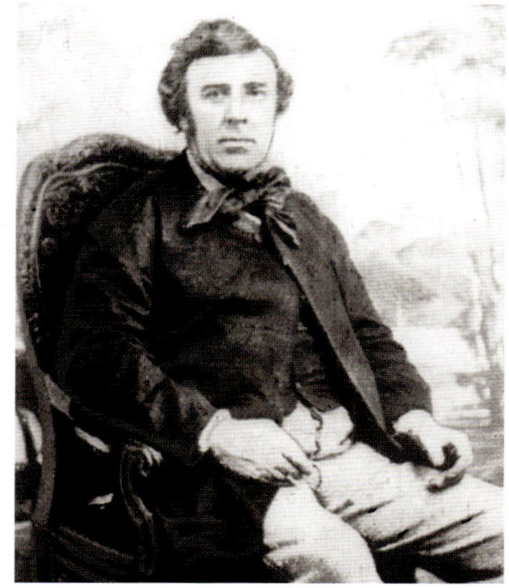

ABOVE RIGHT *Hugh Glass, who converted Travancore to one of the finest estates in Victoria.*

OPPOSITE *This exterior view of Travancore (originally known as Flemington) clearly shows the tower, a distinctive feature of the house.*

RIGHT *One of the two ornate staircases in Travancore.*

BELOW *Travancore estate, originally part of a squatter's sheep run, was developed into one of the finest estates in the region.*

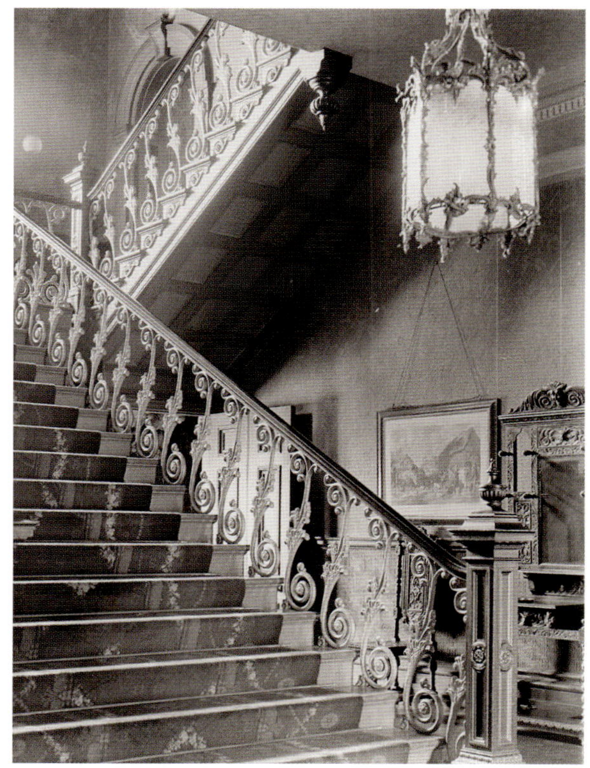

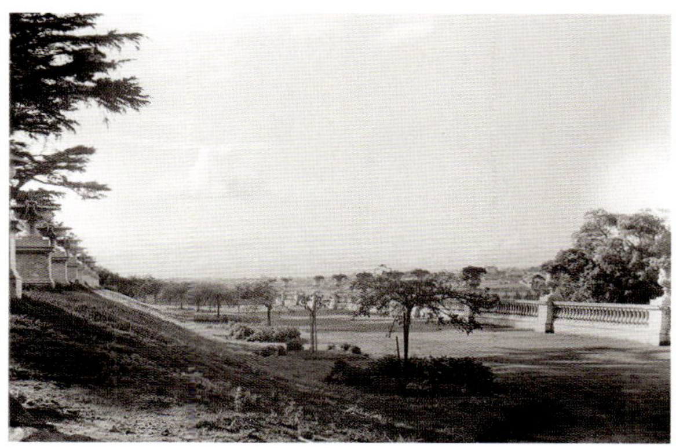

Wharves and Docks on the Yarra

COMMERCIAL USE DECLINED 1950s

In the very early days of Melbourne, boats were able to moor without much difficulty along the banks of the Yarra River, between Queen and Spencer Streets. It was the journey up the Yarra that proved more challenging. There was a sandbar at the mouth of the Yarra that meant only ships drawing less than 2.7 metres at high tide could enter the river. Larger vessels anchored off shore unloaded the cargo on to lighters, which would then transport the cargo upstream. The course of the river downstream from the settlement was a meandering one through the West Melbourne flats to the bay. The confluence of the Yarra and the Saltwater (Maribyrnong) rivers was choked with trees and other debris brought down in floods. "Humbug Reach" was the name given by early sailors to this stretch of water. It was here where their sails lost wind, because of the dense tea-trees that lined the river, and their boats had to be towed to the bank to discharge their cargo at one of the wharves or docks along the Yarra.

The early official wharves near the settlement, like Queen's Wharf, were made of unsuitable timber and were often damaged by floods. Coles Wharf, between King and Spencer Streets, the first private wharf, was erected near the Customs House in 1841. It was very busy and cargo was unloaded straight on to drays and wagons. Next to it was the Customs shed where salvaged goods were held. Although this was a closed and protected area, there were many articles of salvaged clothing that were brought in and then walked out on the backs of workers. In 1848 dredging allowed larger vessels to use the river. By 1850 there were wharves along the banks and one of the busiest was near today's Convention Centre. The Spencer Dock, also called New Dock, or Little Dock, was used between 1854 and 1930. It was particularly useful for the local vessels and for the fish supply to the nearby Melbourne Fish Market. Little Dock was a haven for the mosquito fleet that traded out of Melbourne across the unpredictable Bass Strait or to Sydney, Adelaide, and sometimes New Zealand. Little Dock's wharves projected into the river at an angle, leaving just enough room for ships to enter. The greatest depth of water near the dock was 14 feet, except when the Yarra was flooded. In the Great Flood of 1863 smaller boats were able to travel across country to Sandridge Pier, but some of the larger vessels had to travel downstream stern first, dragging their anchors. In one flood, a ship's captain reported seeing a bridge, complete with lampposts, out in the bay. In 1860 river wharves could house 36 vessels, while the piers at Sandridge (Port Melbourne) and Williamstown could accommodate 43.

The Government set up a Royal Commission to examine the problems that faced the shipping industry. The Melbourne Harbour Trust was finally established in 1877 and a report by Sir John Coode in 1879 made many recommendations: the river was straightened and deepened, new wharves were built, and Victoria Docks were opened in 1892. Throughout the 1880s the river wharves were very busy, but when the Spencer Street Bridge was constructed in 1927 the wharves upstream were effectively cut off. Ship handling migrated downstream to South and North Wharf and to Victoria Dock, which became the most used of the city ports from the 1890s to the 1950s. Spencer Dock was filled in.

New methods of handling cargo – such as containerization, and the bridges built across the Yarra in the second part of the 20th century – meant the death of the Yarra wharves and docks. Today there are still remnants of the old wharves and docking facilities along the Yarra but their use declined from 1950 onwards.

RIGHT *Sailing ships at Little Dock with the Southbank wharves and Teahouse in the background.*

BELOW FAR LEFT *Ships docking along the Yarra River at Melbourne in the 1880s.*

BELOW LEFT *A ferry service to Williamstown ran from Port Melbourne and from the Yarra before the railway was built in the 1870s. Most of these commercial ferry services were finished by the 1930s, and the last cross-river ferry from Spotswood to Fisherman's Bend closed in 1979. Tourist ferries down the Yarra still operate today.*

BELOW *The Spencer Street steam ferry in the 1880s.*

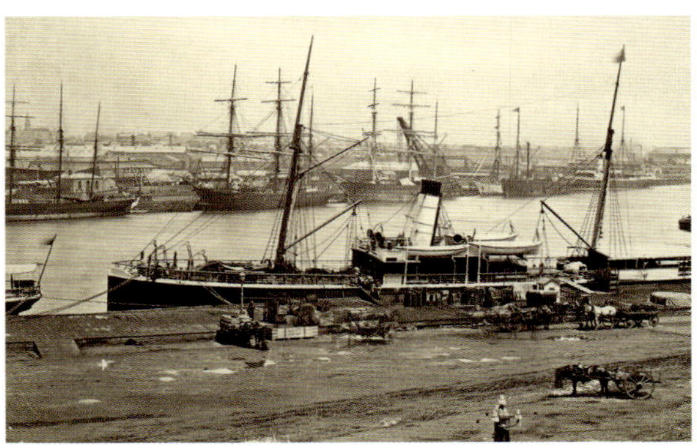

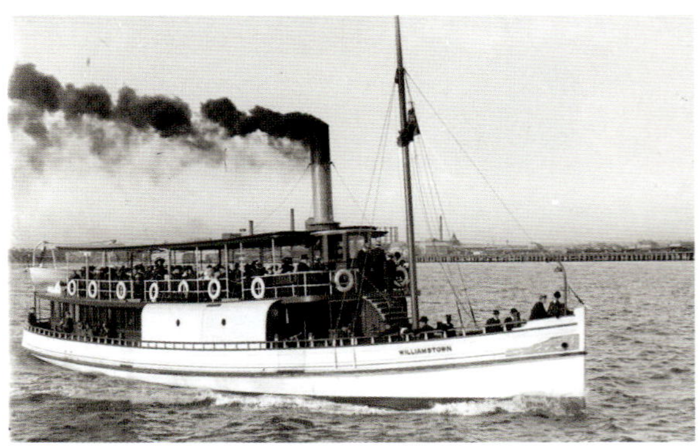

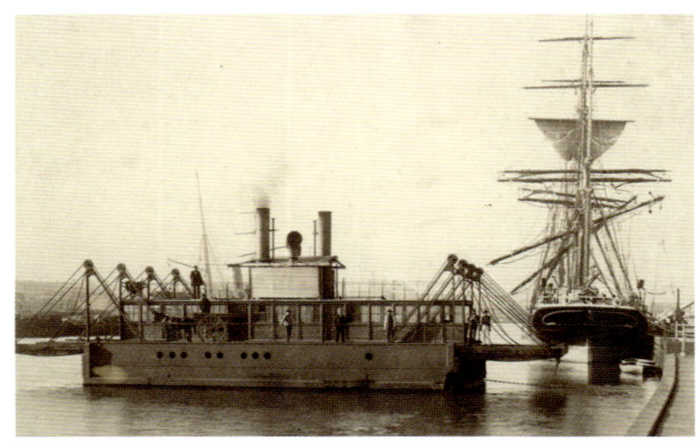

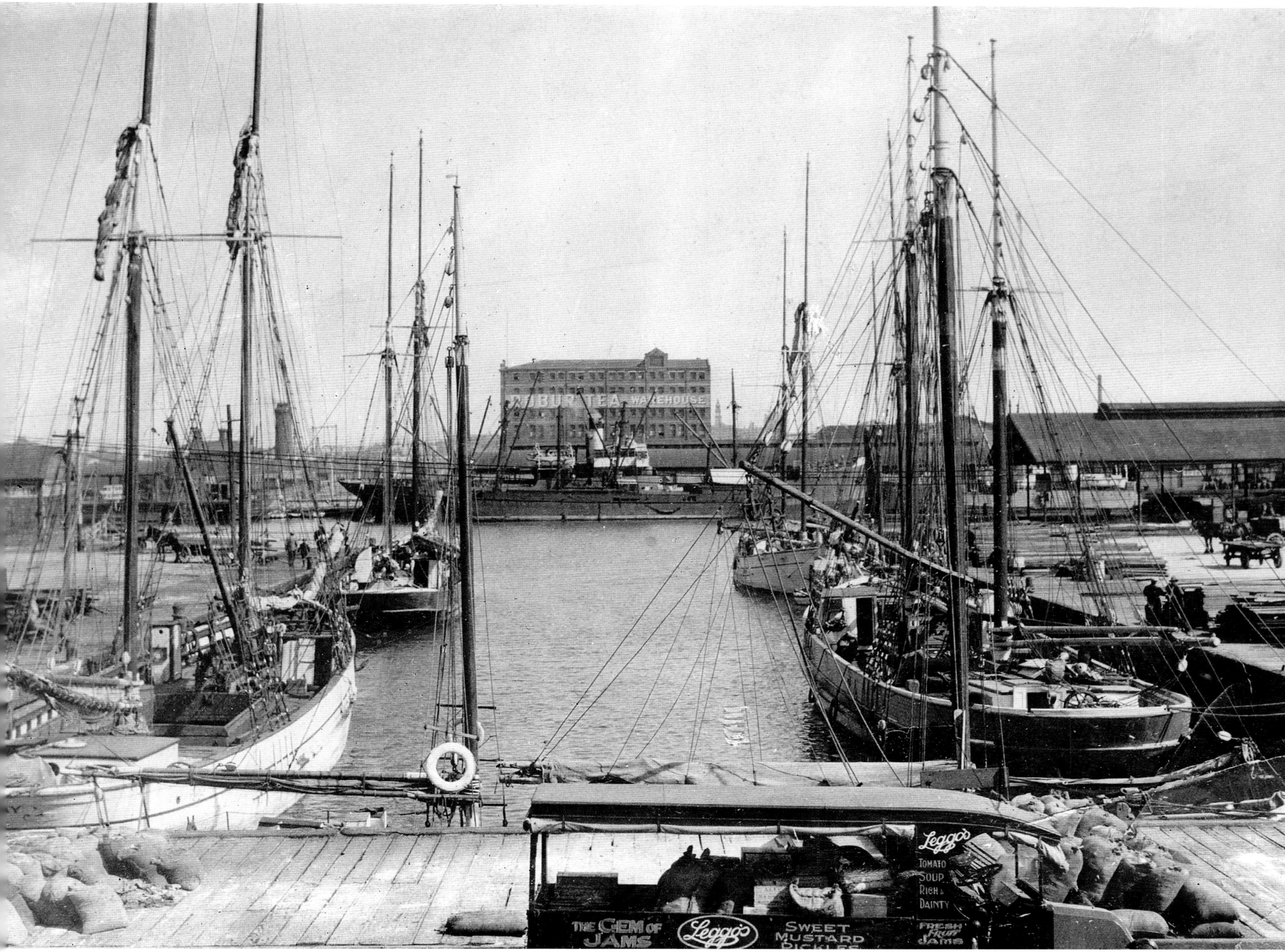
WAREHOUSE
Leggo's
TOMATO SOUP. RICH & DAINTY
THE GEM OF JAMS
Leggo's
SWEET MUSTARD
FRESH Fruit JAMS

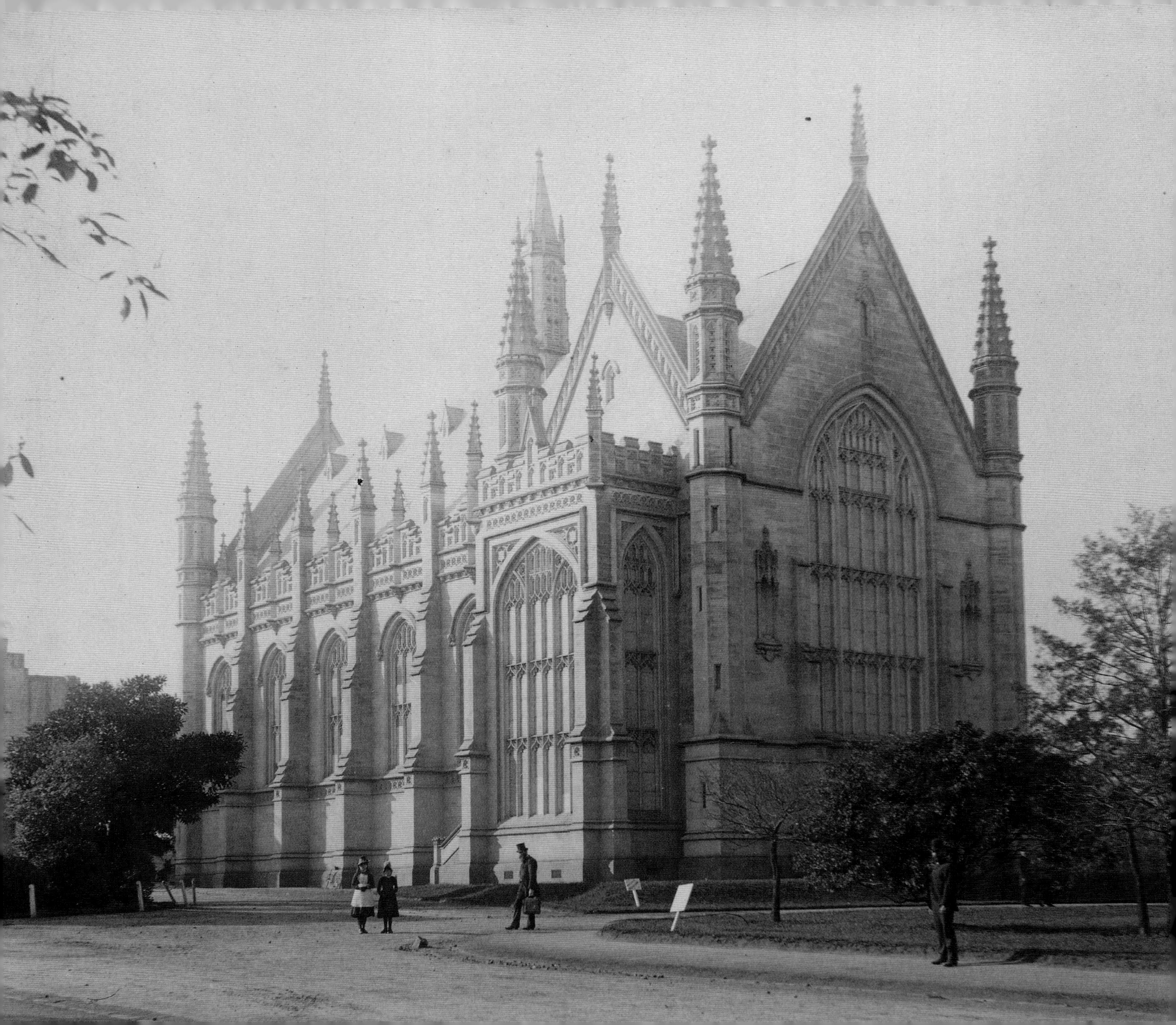

Wilson Hall DESTROYED BY FIRE 1952

The University of Melbourne, founded in 1853, is Australia's second oldest university and the oldest in Victoria. The Quadrangle, designed by F. M. White, was the original university building. It was planned as an enclosed square with the east and west wings completed in 1855. What the university lacked though was a large ceremonial hall. This was funded by a £30,000 bequest in the 1870s from wealthy pastoralist Samuel Wilson, who was also a politician with an interest in higher education. The building was named after him and was to become the university's landmark.

Wilson Hall was designed by Joseph Reed of the architectural firm Reed and Barnes. Built in stone and begun in 1878, it was constructed in the Perpendicular Gothic style. The hall was built as a venue for examinations and to hold grand ceremonies such as the conferring of degrees. Wilson laid the ceremonial stone in 1879 and its completion occurred just in time for the end of year exams in 1882. A newspaper at the time commented, "The new hall is the figure eminent to which all eyes are turned with unqualified pleasure….. It has neither rival nor equal closer than the classic Thames."

Wilson Hall was designed with buttresses, turrets and arched windows. It was 152 feet long by 62 feet wide, with a height of 96 feet to the top of the gables. The foundation walls were of bluestone while the rest of the walls were built of a fine white limestone from New Zealand and the interior from New South Wales. Richly panelled wainscoting and large panelled oak doors were a feature of the building. Most of the windows were finished with historical heads, principally from the Tudor period. The formal promenade and grounds were designed by Edward La Trobe Bateman. The land surrounding the university was public property and visitors were encouraged to wander the grounds. At night the iron gates were closed, then opened again in the morning for students and the public.

Art adorned the interior of Wilson Hall. Portraits and busts depicted the university's founding fathers and later its office bearers. Benefactors commissioned leadlight windows and one of these windows, the Leckie window, survived the fire that destroyed the building. It depicted the growth of civilisation through its biblical stories and figures from classical mythology.

Physically dominating the centre of Melbourne University, Wilson Hall was instantly recognisable, its turrets and size clearly seen from all approaches. Many etchings, photographs, wood engravings and other publications from the time indicate that Wilson Hall was a landmark. It dominated the landscape. As *The Argus* of 1 October 1934 reported, "it is the centre of all the traditional pageantry of University life, and remains in the memory of each University graduate as a symbol both of intellectual struggle and of academic success."

In January 1952, fire destroyed the roof and badly damaged the west wall of Wilson Hall. There was much debate over whether to restore the Gothic ruins or rebuild in a new modernist style. Eventually pragmatism won, as available funds were insufficient for a rebuild. The new Wilson Hall is a modern structure and because of other buildings surrounding it is not the landmark that the original was. Some of the stonework from the original building was recycled at Montsalvat, an artist colony in Eltham, but the Gothic centre of the University was lost.

OPPOSITE *Wilson Hall, named after its benefactor, was to become Melbourne University's imposing landmark.*

BELOW *Land around the university was public property, so visitors, here photographed in the 1880s, were encouraged to wander the grounds.*

BOTTOM *A view across the lake to Wilson Hall at the University of Melbourne.*

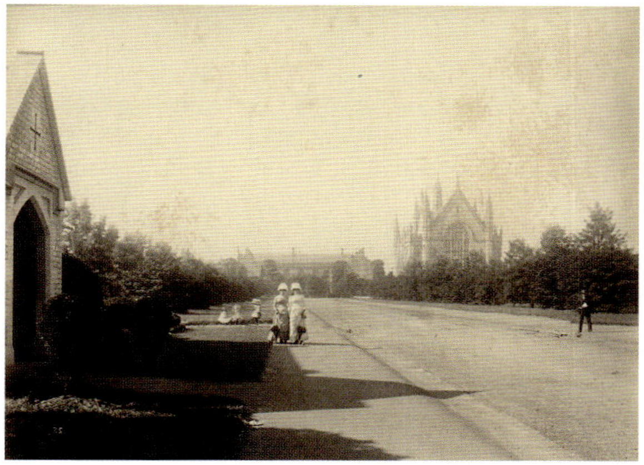

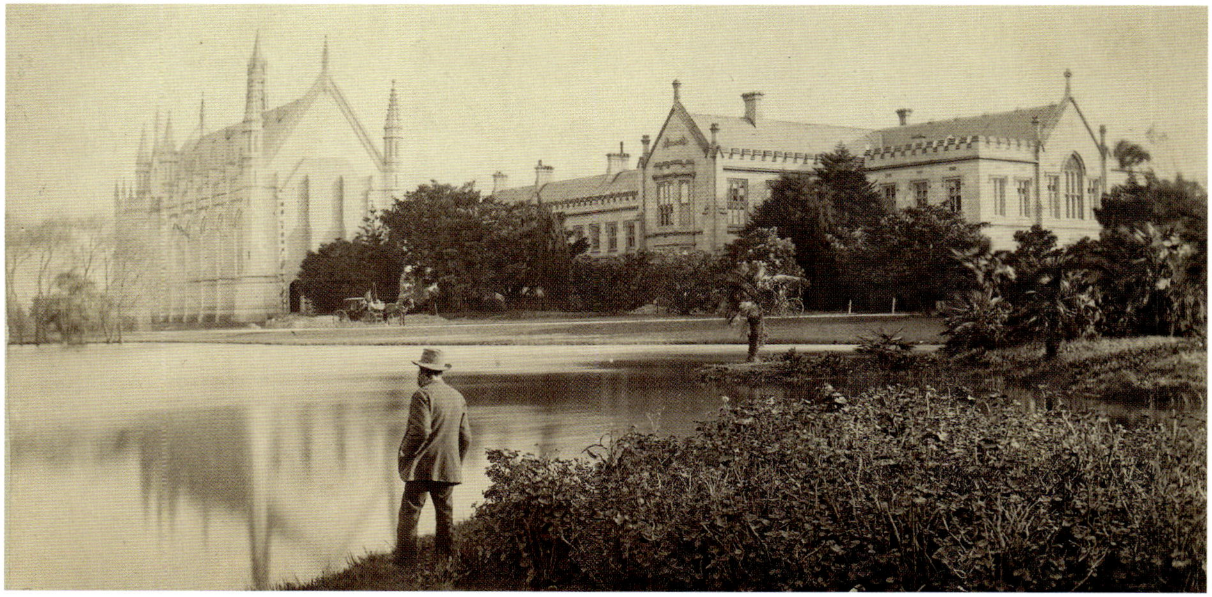

Wirth's Circus OLYMPIA AUDITORIUM DESTROYED BY FIRE 1953

Wirth's Circus was one of the great Australian circuses of the 20th century. The original Wirth Bros., four musical brothers from Bavaria, arrived in Port Phillip in 1855 and travelled the goldfields with their families, entertaining the diggers and others who lived there. In 1882 they established a circus company and in 1887 Wirth's Circus appeared on the Alexandra Stage in Melbourne. The Wirth brothers were all excellent athletes and talented circus performers, the latter skills they learned while travelling with other circuses after their arrival in Australia.

By the end of the 1800s Melbourne was recognised as the circus capital of Australia. Following the failure of the banks in the 1890s, the Wirths responded by undertaking a world tour that lasted seven years. They returned to Australia to find that the FitzGerald Brothers' circus now held the position of being the top circus in Australia. In 1901 the FitzGerald Brothers had leased land close to the Princes Bridge on St. Kilda Road in Melbourne, where they constructed a circus building called Olympia. Bitter rivalry occurred between the Wirths and the FitzGeralds and only ended with the coincidental deaths of Dan and then, in Rangoon, Tom FitzGerald early in 1906. The Wirth brothers' circus premiership of Australia was assumed by default. The land leased to the FitzGerald Brothers in St. Kilda Road was now granted to the Wirths, who wanted to do things on a grander scale than the FitzGeralds. The Wirths constructed a larger and more intricate Olympia and they added both a skating rink and a hippodrome. This new Olympia, the amphitheatre of which was to seat 3,500, was to be so successful that they stopped their year-long touring and their entertainment venue on the Yarra became one of Melbourne's most popular attractions. In the race for profits, the success of Wirth's Olympia near Princes Bridge meant that a number of other funfairs, some located quite close by in St. Kilda, would not survive.

The Wirths brought in many acts from overseas. Some of these acts were represented on the colourful posters produced by the company and these posters provide a wonderful history of Wirth's Circus. There was the "Great Peters" who, during each performance, would perform aerial acts with his head in a noose. Ironically, after he returned to America, he did hang himself when the rope and noose failed to work as expected.

One of the greatest female acrobats on horseback, both internationally and locally, was May Wirth. Adopted by the Wirth family at a young age, the contortionist performed balancing and tightrope acts. May Wirth went on to have a successful career overseas and was inducted into the American Circus Hall of Fame in 1964.

In 1953, the new Olympia was destroyed by a spectacular fire. The galvanised iron building with wooden seats and interior burnt in 30 minutes, with flames leaping 100 feet into the air. Terrified animals had to be rescued by circus hands. Valuable costumes and circus equipment were lost, and though the buildings were insured, the contents were not. The damage bill was £70,000. By this time Wirth's Circus was run by the children of the original brothers and they continued with the business until it was forced to close in 1963. The site where Wirth's Circus was is now occupied by the Arts Centre.

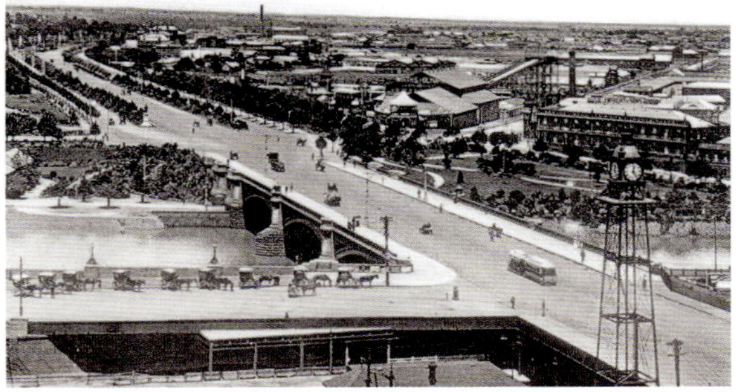

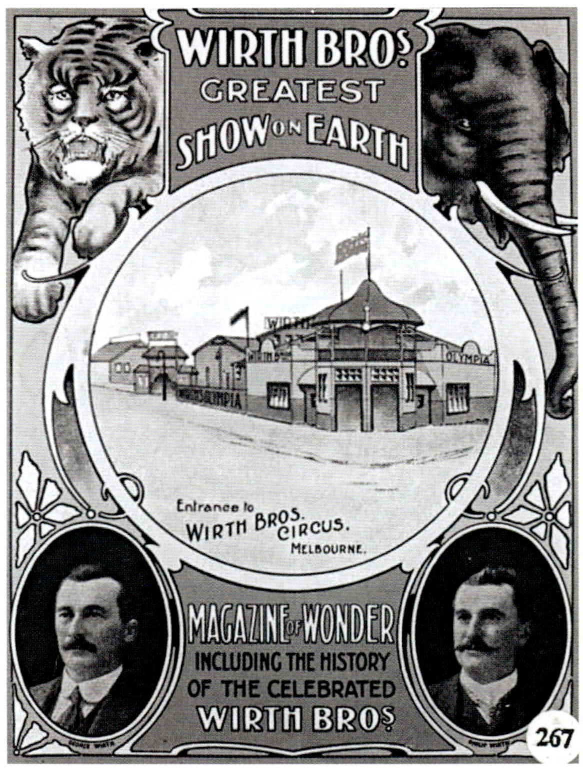

RIGHT *Live animals were a feature of Wirth's Circus in their nightly performances.*

LEFT *The Wirth Brothers used colourful posters and pamphlets to advertise the "Greatest Show on Earth".*

FAR LEFT *Looking along St. Kilda Road in the early 20th century. The "Olympia", on the right, is now the site of the present-day Arts Centre.*

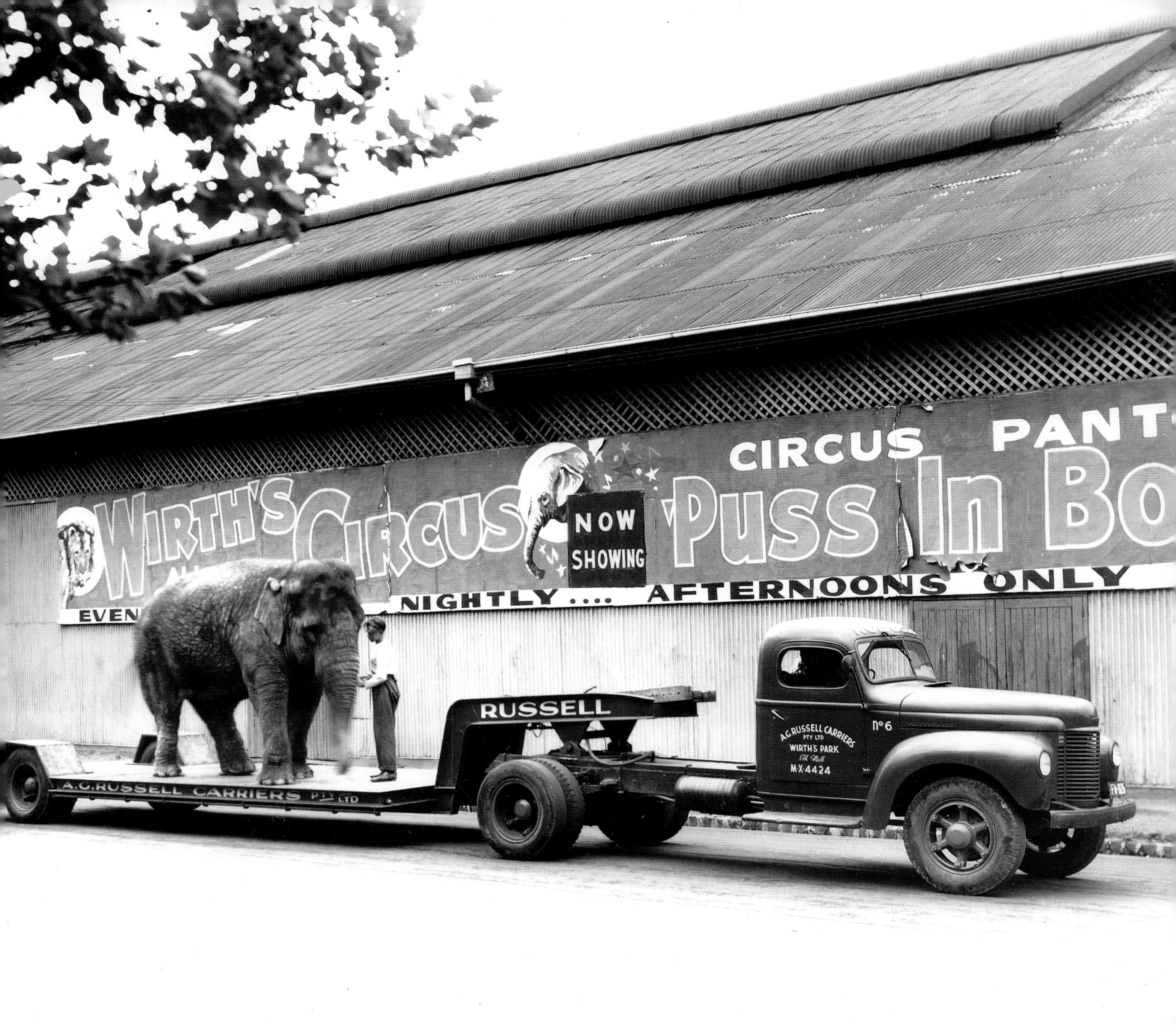
WIRTH'S CIRCUS
CIRCUS PANT
Puss In Bo
NOW SHOWING
EVEN
NIGHTLY .... AFTERNOONS ONLY
RUSSELL
A.G. RUSSELL CARRIERS PTY LTD
A.G. RUSSELL CARRIERS
PTY LTD
WIRTH'S PARK
Sth. Melb
M·X·4424
Nº 6

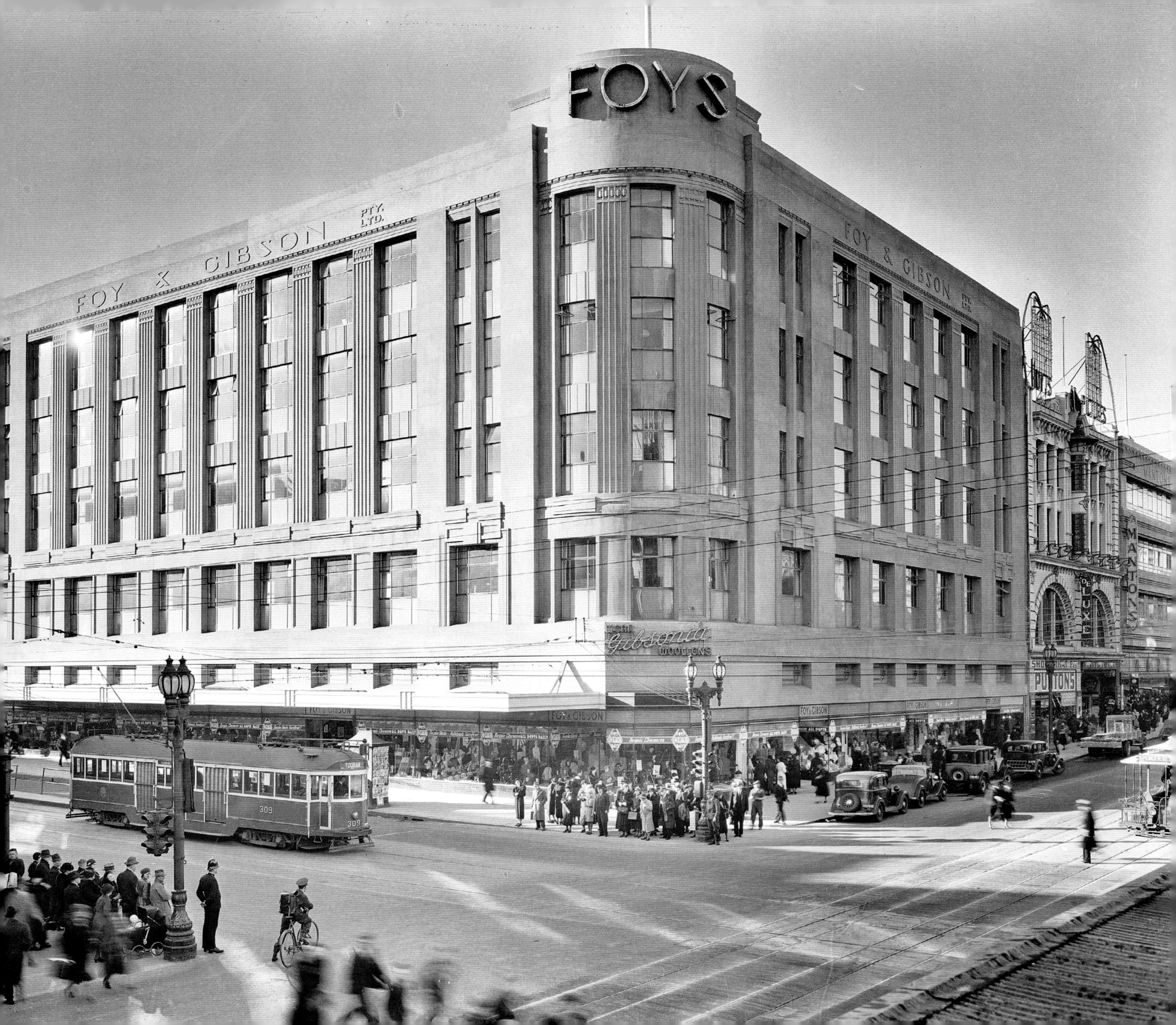
FOYS
FOY & GIBSON PTY. LTD.
FOY & GIBSON PTY. LTD.
Gibsonia WOOLLENS
FOY & GIBSON
TOORAK
309
DE LUXE
MANTONS
PUTTONS

Foy and Gibson's Department Store SOLD 1955

During most of the 19th century, the large stores in Melbourne were drapers selling clothing, clothing accessories, leather goods, manchester and soft furnishings. The department store, as we know it, developed towards the end of the 19th century and into the early 20th century. Myer was an early leader and retailing innovator and the changes they introduced were based on San Francisco's Emporium, while Foy and Gibson's stores were based on the Paris Bon Marché stores.

The new department stores carried a wide range of merchandise, which not only included all that the drapers' stores offered but also everything needed for the home: furniture, floor coverings, white and electrical goods and kitchen hardware. They were places of great excitement for all. Goods were no longer hidden away under the counter but put on display. You could look at items and make your decisions before engaging a salesperson. The department stores had galleries and display halls for fashion parades, fun parks for children, cafés and restaurants, and ladies' lounges where the weary shopper could seek relief. Catalogues announced bargain sales and shop window displays attracted customers.

Many department stores started life in the suburbs and the country towns and Foy and Gibson was no exception. Mark Foy, who had come to the goldfields in 1858, established a drapery business in Bendigo then hired wagons and moved his store, shop front, counters, and stock to Collingwood in 1870. William Gibson was also an enterprising merchant. He arrived in Victoria in 1882, went into partnership with Francis Foy, who now ran his father's business, until the partnership collapsed in 1884. However, the name "Foy and Gibson" lived on.

During the 1880s the business expanded and many improvements were based on Gibson's travels to England and throughout Europe. When the economic depression of the 1890s came Gibson refused to succumb, instead he began his own business in Collingwood, manufacturing clothing, millinery, furniture and bedding. The "Gibsonia" brand became a household name and he became one of the largest employers in Victoria. The Foy and Gibson store in the middle of Melbourne was built in a central location at the corner of Bourke and Swanston Streets on the site of the old Orient Hotel that had been demolished in 1928. The new store was an elegant art deco structure, several storeys high, that curved around the corner of Bourke and Swanston Streets. It was designed by Harry A. Norris, the same architect responsible for the David Jones building and the Nicholas building. This large store was famous for its toy department and for its Christmas fun fair, located at the top of the building, where a Ferris wheel, a big-top tent, a petting zoo, pony and train rides and a merry-go-round entertained children. Most memorable of all was the large Santa Claus high on the outside of the building, beckoning shoppers to enter, spend and have fun.

After the war years the large department stores modernized, improving their counters, escalators and displays. However, discount stores like Coles Variety Stores and specialist white goods and carpet stores started to rob them of customers. While bargain sales, elaborate shop windows, special displays, and new lighting techniques helped to slow their decline, in the end Foy and Gibson sold out to Cox Brothers in 1955, which in turn went into liquidation and sold out to Woolworths in 1967. For some years the building was tenanted by Nike, Billy Guyatt, Apple and, most recently, Telstra. Today the building is owned by ISPT and is currently being refurbished primarily for retail use. The facade of the original art deco building is still recognizable but it is now topped by an extra three floors that were added in the 1960s.

LEFT *This elegant art deco building, the Foy and Gibson department store, was a favourite destination for Melbourne shoppers from 1928 to 1955.*

RIGHT *Newspapers advertised the Foy and Gibson Christmas Toy Fair and thousands flocked to the city store.*

FAR RIGHT *Foy and Gibson's first stores were in Collingwood, stretching along Smith Street, but only their former premises at number 132 remain.*

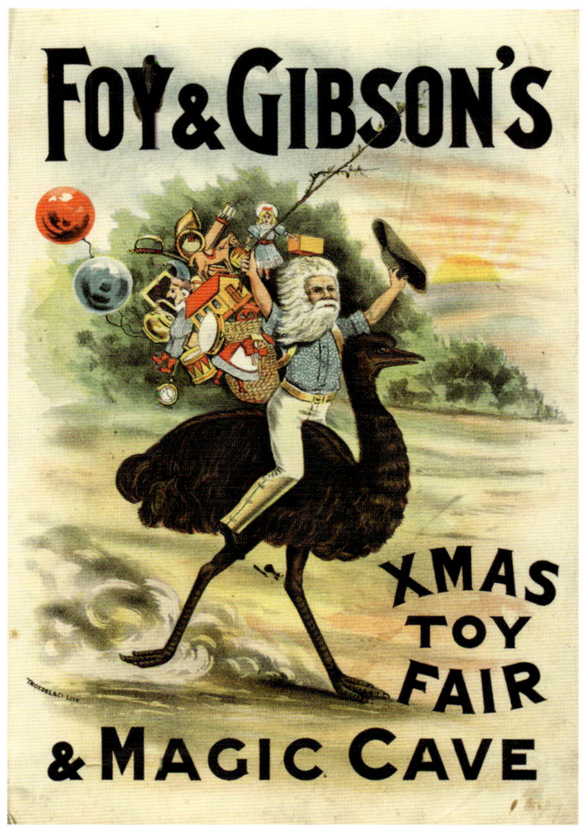

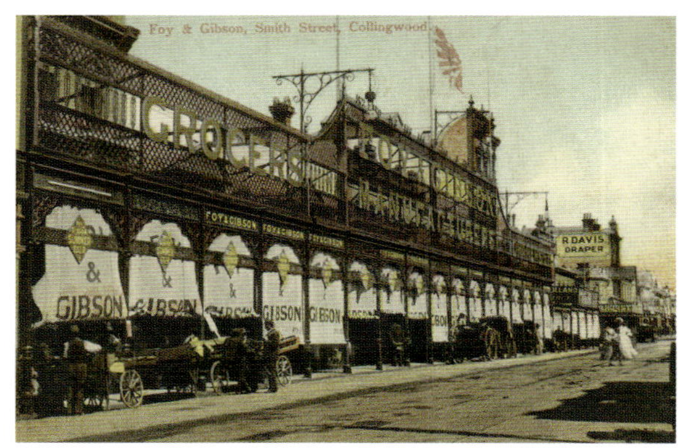

Norwood DEMOLISHED 1955

Melbourne in the 1880s was booming. The population had doubled in a decade and the suburban sprawl encouraged people out of the city centre. The 1880s was a time of speculation, unbridled wealth, overnight millionaires, new land banks and building societies.

The story of Norwood is the story of Mark Moss who had created a thriving business in Melbourne. Like many others, he believed that the boom times would never end. Moss began to invest in his own ventures as he became more successful. He was friends with Thomas Bent, member of the Legislative Assembly, who was responsible for much of the development in Brighton. Moss was to buy the land from Bent in 1883. Brighton was one of the fastest growing areas in the colony, attracting wealthy residents who wanted generous building sites and the prospect of sea bathing. An expanding fortune deserved a better home than Rosebank, the house he owned in East Melbourne. The architect chosen was Phillip Edward Treeby who was already well established in the colony. Treeby was funded to go overseas and come back with ideas for the house.

And so Norwood, named after the home district of Mark Moss's wife Rose, was built. Eclecticism was fundamental to the new style of architecture that appeared at the end of the 19th century. Single buildings combined many styles and so it was with Norwood. No expense was spared and everything was of the highest quality. Norwood was three storeys with 26 rooms built in solid brick. A three-level terrace was crossed to reach the entrance porch. The entrance hall was nine metres high and the upper storeys were reached by three flights of stairs. One of Moss's requirements was colour, and every window contained stained glass of some sort. In the entrance hall was a 35-panel stained-glass window depicting Shakespeare surrounded by the leading characters in his plays. The ballroom was 18 by 7 metres, there were two kitchens (staff and entertaining), servants' quarters, immense bathrooms, a suite of six children's rooms, four main bedrooms and a billiard room. A tower gave magnificent views across Port Phillip Bay. The impressive entrance to the estate would intrigue passers-by for years.

However, Mark Moss was ruined almost overnight when Victoria's boom economy burst its bubble. Norwood was seized by the Bank of Victoria and sold first to Richard White, then John Whitfield and finally E. A. Riches in 1918. By now Norwood sat on only a hectare of land. In 1950 Riches was joined by his niece and family, the Johnsons, who remained in the house after he died in 1953. Norwood was in need of repair, but it was expensive to upkeep and Brighton house prices were increasing. In September of 1955 Norwood was put on the market. The furniture was auctioned over three days and thousands of people queued to see the house. The following month demolition began and the house that was Norwood passed into legend. The land was divided into twelve lots.

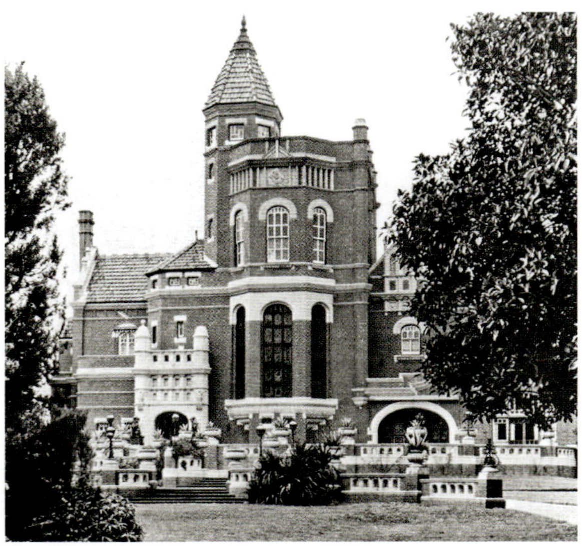

LEFT AND OPPOSITE *Norwood, situated on a two-acre site, was one of Melbourne's most imposing private homes. No expense was spared in building it and everything was of the highest quality.*

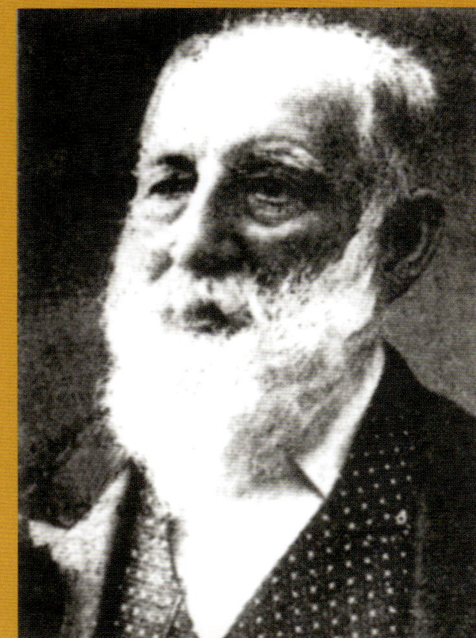

MARK MOSS

Mark Moss was born in England in 1825. He, like many, was attracted by newspaper reports of Victoria's goldfields that were likened to the Californian gold rushes. Moss went first to Ballarat, but unsuccessful there he relocated to Melbourne. Moss put to use the business skills he had learned in England. He established an "Equitable Loan and Investment company" amassing a £500,000 fortune by 1890. He built a small but impressive mansion in East Melbourne called Rosebank which attracted Melbourne society to visit. He later built Norwood in Brighton but was to die almost penniless after Victoria's boom economy burst its bubble.

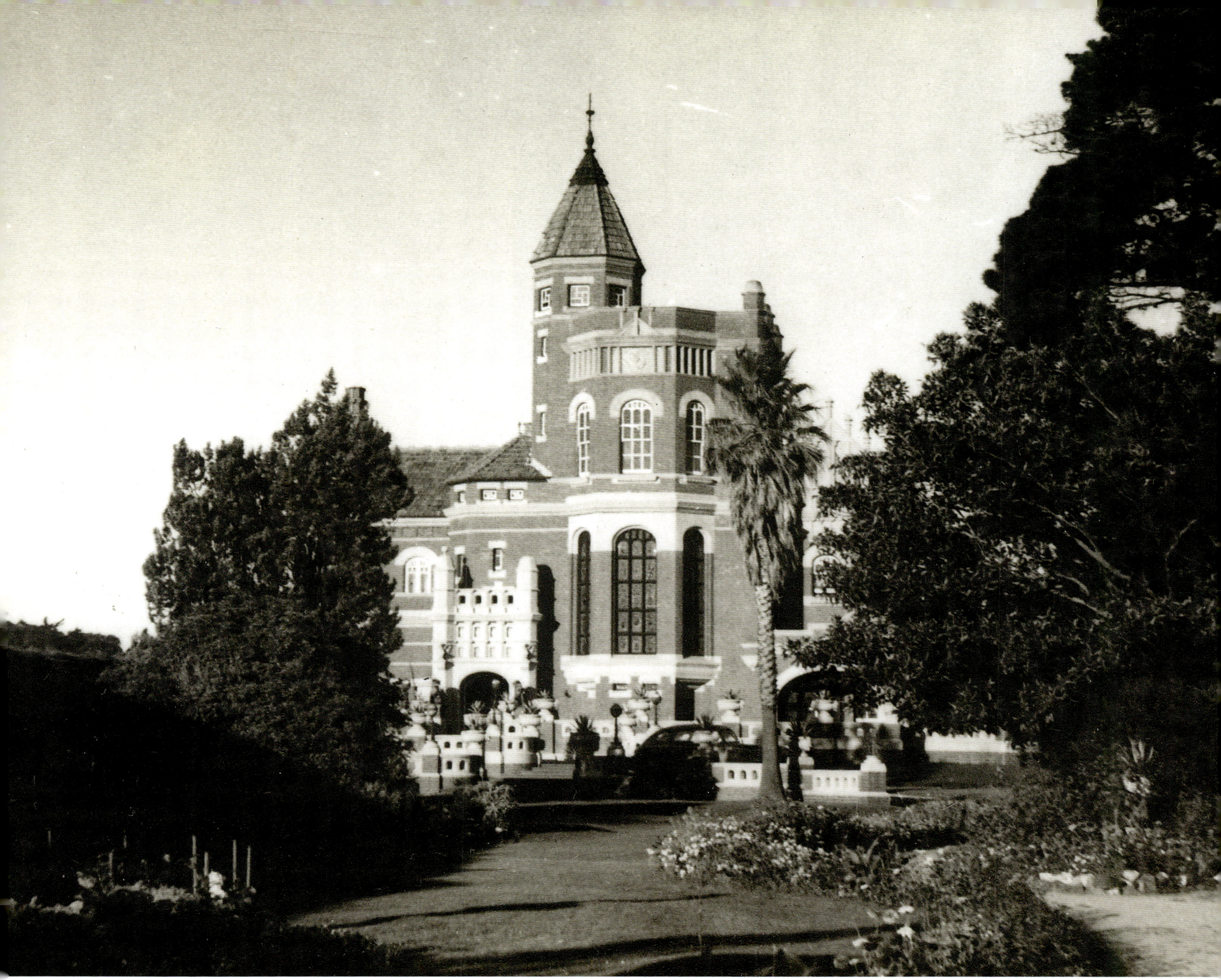

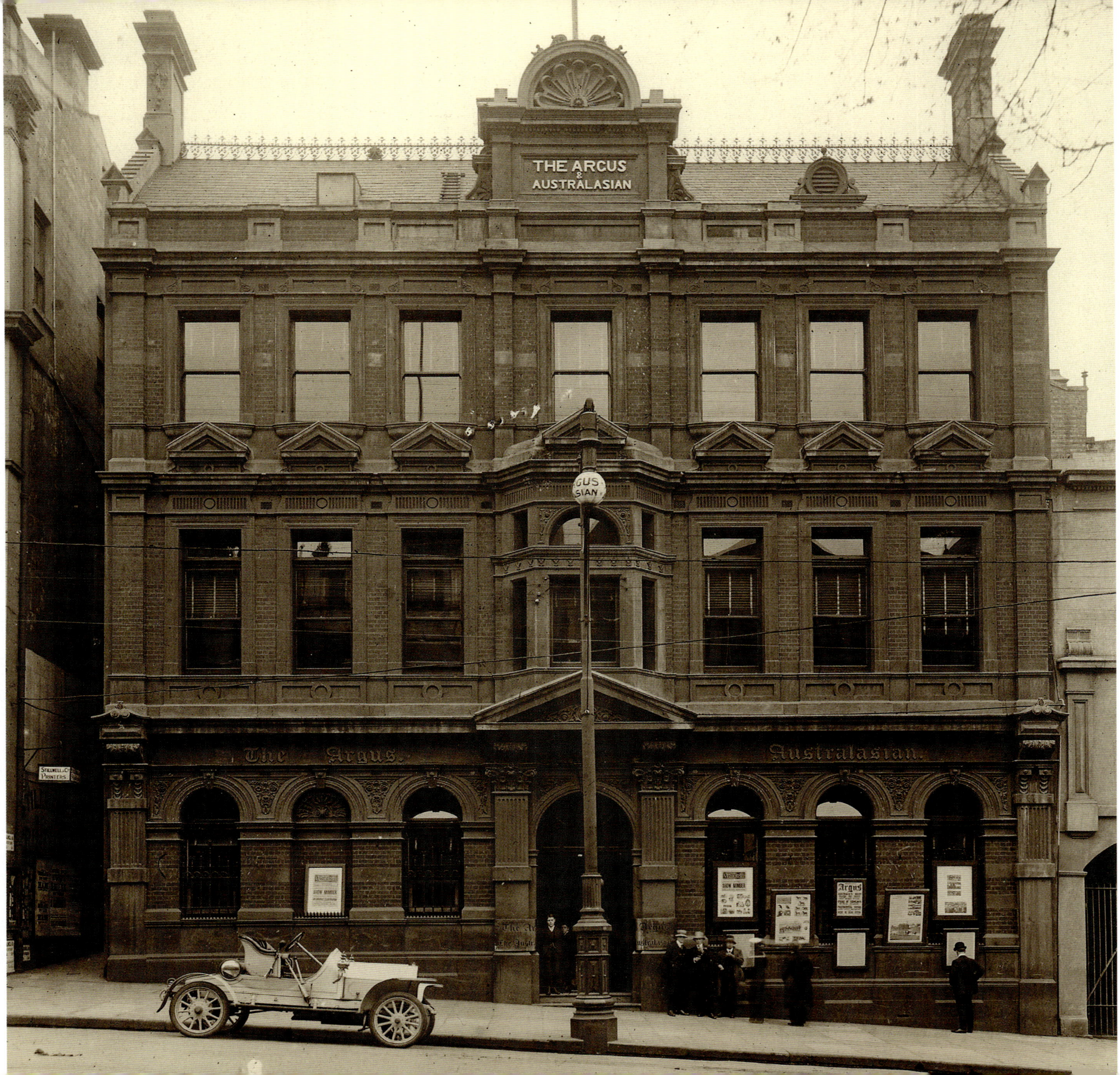
THE ARGUS
&
AUSTRALASIAN
The Argus.
Australasian.
Argus

The Argus CEASED PUBLISHING 1957

Newspapers were a very important part of Melbourne life from the earliest days, supplying necessary information on all aspects of life in the colony. From 1846 to 1957, *The Argus* was one of the most influential and respected newspapers in Melbourne. William Kerr, its founder, was a journalist who had originally come to Melbourne in 1839 to work on John Pascoe Fawkner's paper *The Port Phillip Patriot*, a scurrilous and abusive paper that championed the views of large landowners and early settlers. Under Kerr, *The Patriot* became more of a voice of the urban settlers.

By 1846 Kerr had started his own newspaper, *The Melbourne Argus* and by 1849 it had become a daily. Its offices in Collins Street were a landmark and people queued at the ground floor windows to catch the most recent headlines. When in 1848 Kerr became insolvent, the paper was sold to Edward Wilson and James Johnson, the name "Melbourne" was dropped and Kerr stayed on as editor of the new *Argus*. In 1864 it was joined by *The Australasian*, which later became the *Australasian Post*, the longest running newspaper in Australia, popular in both town and country. Governor La Trobe's attitude to *The Argus* at this time was that it was "quite as discreditable as the *Patriot*". It attacked anyone whom it considered an enemy or rival and libel suits followed.

When Fred Haddon took over as editor in 1867 he took it in a conservative direction, modernised the paper, adopting overseas production methods and insisted on high standards of journalism. He continued as editor until 1898. Newsboys sold *The Argus* on almost every street corner. It was considered to be an excellent daily paper, "the best daily paper published out of England". It remained so until the 1950s. Its readership was largely conservative and its journalists had close links to the conservative politicians who were the source of many leaked stories. *The Argus* moved from its Collins Street home to new premises on the corner of Elizabeth and La Trobe Streets in 1926 and the Collins Street offices were demolished soon after. *The Argus* covered all the areas expected of a newspaper: politics, sport, police reports, accidents, disasters and the activities of the social set. The main rival newspapers were David Syme's *The Age*, and *The Herald* and *The Weekly Times*. Competition between the papers was fierce and because the circulation figures of *The Argus* were much smaller than *The Herald* and *The Sun*, both Murdoch papers, it was vulnerable.

In 1949 it was bought by the London-based *Daily Mirror*. This turned out to be a disaster for all and eventually resulted in the death of a great newspaper. *The Argus* was the first newspaper in the world to publish colour photographs and they expanded their interests into radio and the new medium of television. This was the birth of GTV9. These diversified interests required financing and the new owners were experiencing difficulties. Turning their backs on the traditional readers they moved away from conservatism, alienating both journalists and readers. The British chiefs did not understand Australian society and made little attempt to do so. Those who had previously subscribed to the paper were not interested in girlie pictures and felt that the British owners wanted to produce a replica of *The Mirror*. The talented journalists felt unappreciated and some left. *The Argus* was closed down in great secrecy and the last newspaper rolled off its presses on 19 January 1957.

LEFT AND RIGHT *The impressive Argus and Australasian building was on Collins Street near Swanston Street.*

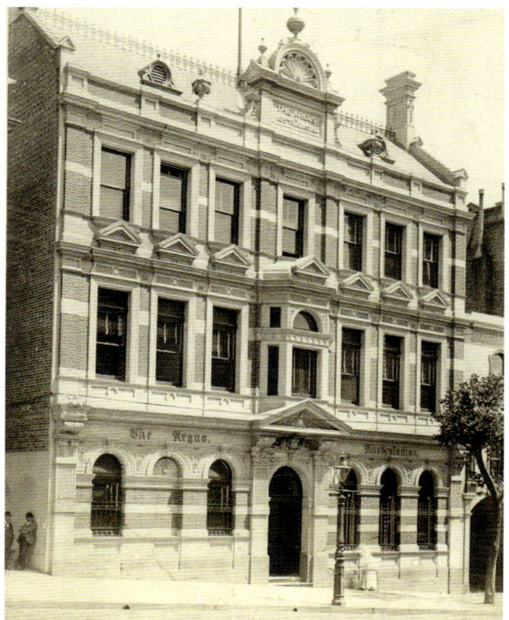

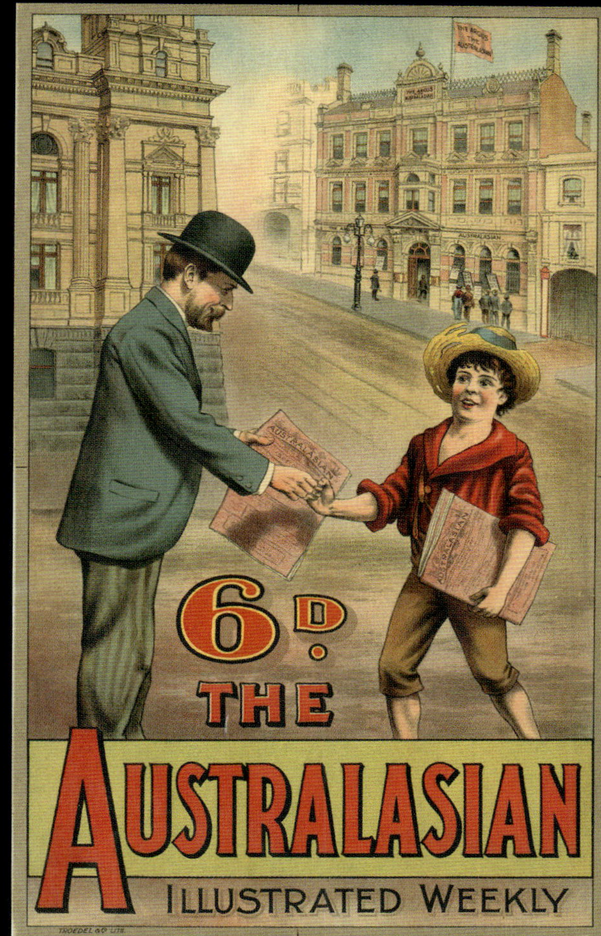

NEWSBOYS

In the 19th and early 20th century small boys could be seen on every street in Melbourne. They might be polishing shoes, holding a horse, or selling fruit, matches or newspapers. Newsboys were known to make up scandalous headlines to convince unwitting members of the public to purchase their paper. The loud behaviour of the newsboys was irritating to some people. They were invariably poor and often exploited. Charitable groups were formed to take care of these children and the annual Newsboys' Picnic was always a great success.

The Fish Market DEMOLISHED 1959

The Melbourne Fish Market was a building unlike any other in the city. Built between 1891 and 1892, it sat on 2.3 hectares squeezed on a narrow strip of land between Flinders Street, the Yarra River and the railway viaduct that had been constructed in 1891. It stretched the entire block from King Street to Spencer Street. The market cost £125,000 to build and replaced an older fish market that had been on the site where the Flinders Street Station now stands.

In a city where the shape of buildings seemed invariably to echo the straight lines of the Hoddle Grid, the Fish Market was an anomaly. The Market was over 200 metres long and three storeys high, the narrow profile of the building curving in line with the railway on the riverside. It was built in brown brick and decorated with cream coloured stone around the doorways and windows. The middle of the building fronting Flinders Street was dominated by an arched entrance with ornate iron gates and topped with a tall clock tower. On the ground floor along Flinders Street were arched entrances to long market halls. On the first floor the windows echoed these arches, while above, the second-floor windows were rectangular, similarly edged in cream. On the roof were a number of conical copper turrets.

The Fish Market had different uses: on the riverside were the fish, game, rabbit and poultry markets, the unique refrigeration and freezing works and the Government Cool Stores. Fish was brought here from the Little Dock at Spencer Street or from the train siding nearby, transported on trolleys that ran noisily along a narrow track. Wholesale fresh produce was in the curved building near and under the viaduct, and warehouses occupied the Flinders Street frontages. The Fish Market was a busy, noisy, smelly place. As early as 4.30 in the morning the air was filled with the shouts of competing fishmongers and hawkers. The hawkers and shopkeepers would purchase their flathead, barracuda and whiting to sell in their shops or on street corners. Here fish could be scaled and gutted, and chickens killed, plucked and cleaned while you waited, the entrails flung to the gulls or expectant dogs. Outside the halls vegetables for sale were displayed, often on the ground. Objections came from nearby traders and the general public who disliked not only the bad smells of rotten fish and vegetables, but also the noise and bad language of the vendors. The Fish Market was dirty and unhygienic. *The Herald* described it as "dingy".

By the 1950s and 1960s Melburnians were looking towards the future, and when the Olympic Games came to Melbourne in 1956, the City Council was bent on cleaning up the city and showing a good face to the world. There was also a plan to build a new King Street bridge, and it was this plan that made the Melbourne City Council decide the fate of the Fish Market. The cleared land was to be used for a much-needed car park. A new fish and vegetable market was built at Footscray and the old Fish Market was demolished in 1959. When the Foundation Stone was lifted, the contents of the time capsule did not fit the inventory. The valuable gold sovereign, put there by the Mayor in 1891, was missing. The gates from the Clock Tower entrance, saved by the wreckers, are all that is left of this Melbourne icon. Today they can be found at the entrance of the Fawkner Cemetery.

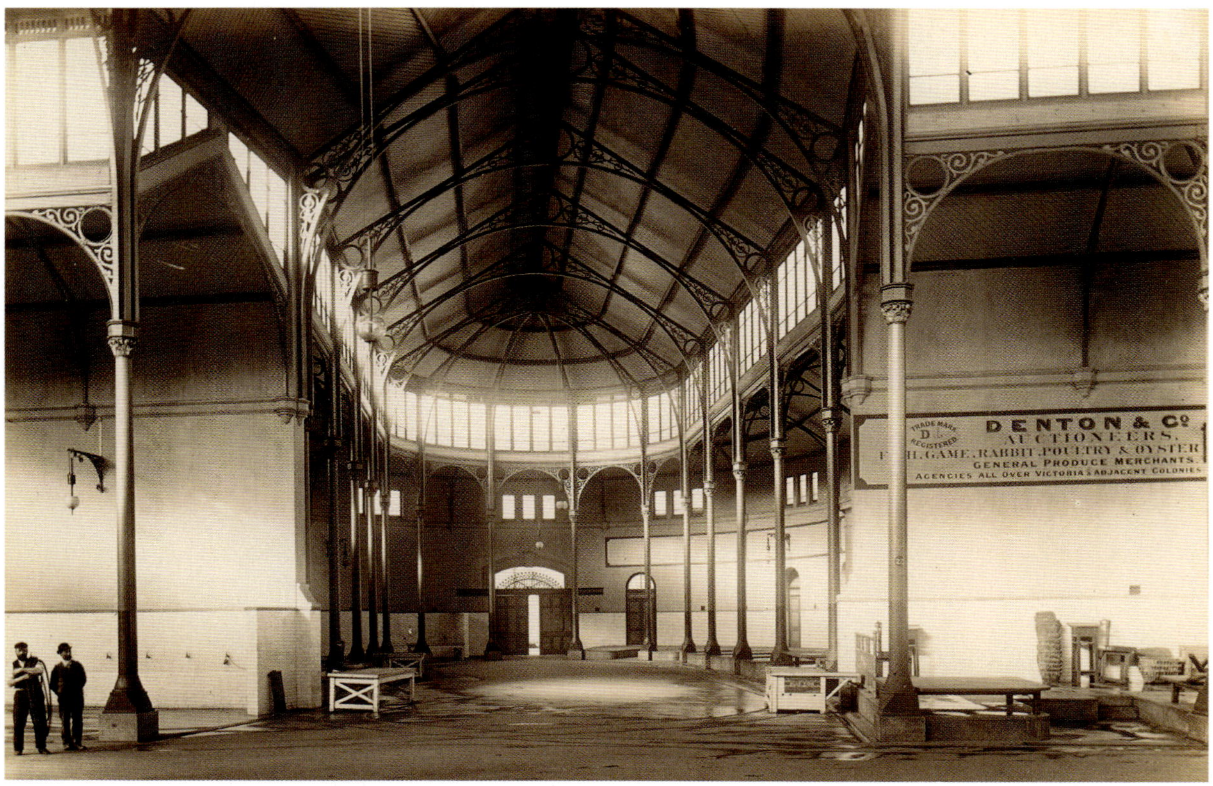

RIGHT *The Fish Market buildings in 1890, with their conical copper turrets and imposing clock tower.*

LEFT *An early 1890s view of the interior of the new Fish Market in Flinders Street.*

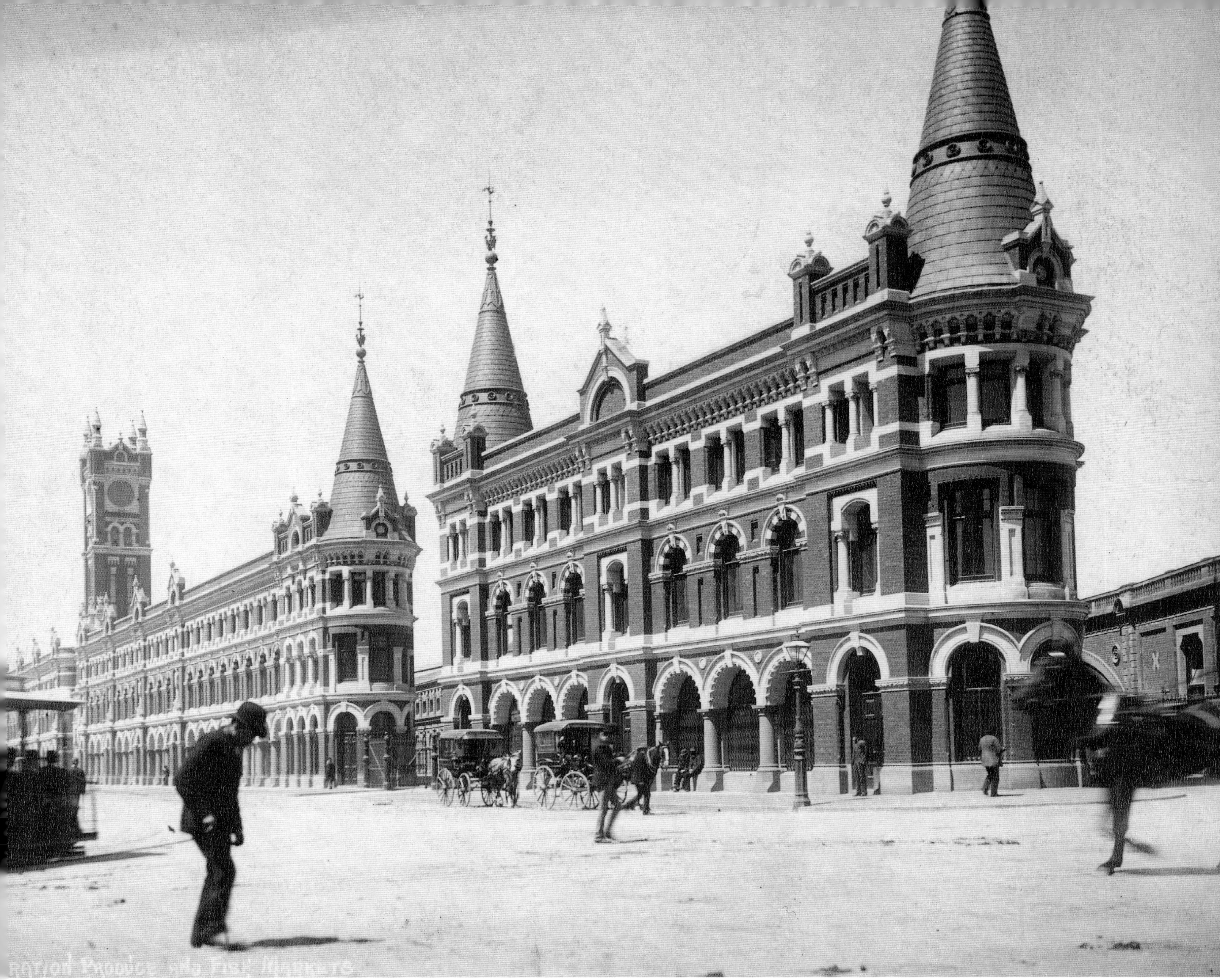
RATION PRODUCE AND FISH MARKETS

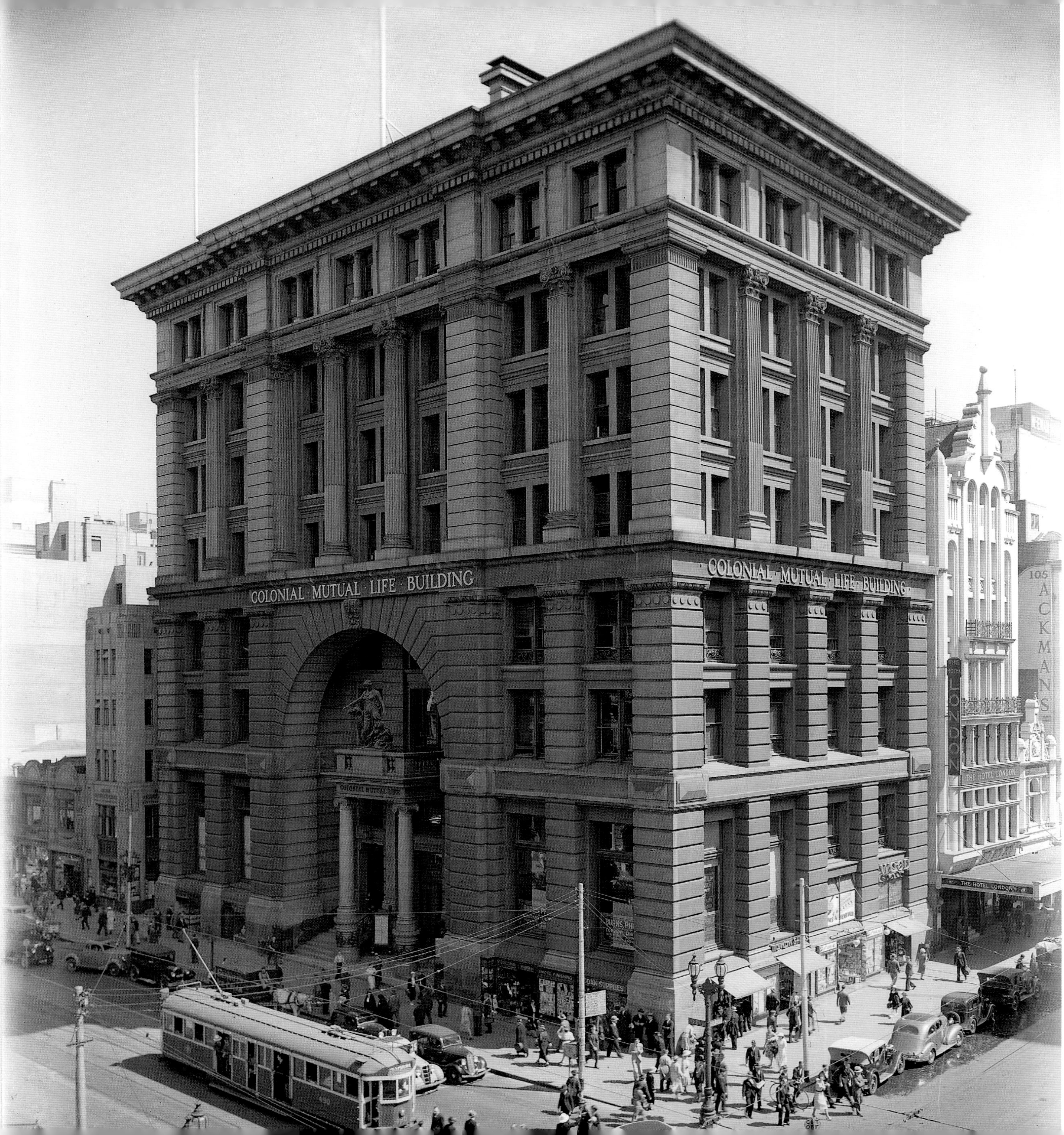
COLONIAL MUTUAL LIFE BUILDING
COLONIAL MUTUAL LIFE BUILDING
COLONIAL MUTUAL LIFE
LONDON
THE HOTEL LONDON
THE HOTEL LONDON

Equitable / Colonial Mutual Life Building

DEMOLISHED 1959–60

The Equitable Building, on the corner of Collins and Elizabeth Street, was built for the Equitable Life Assurance Society of America. It was to be the "grandest building in the Southern hemisphere", designed to "last forever". Certainly the building designed by the Austrian-born American architect Edward Raht probably could have lasted forever, so massive was its size. The project was managed by David Mitchell who had built the Royal Exhibition Building and the foundation stone was laid on 6 March 1893. The Equitable Building was completed in four years and four months. The land purchase price during the Land Boom was reported to be £360,000 and the building costs were £233,000.

Raht's design was reminiscent of some of the buildings in Chicago and New York at the time. This huge building was seven storeys, 132 feet (about 40 metres) high, dominating the streetscape with its bulk and height, but it was pleasing to the eye and was considered to be the best proportioned building in Collins Street. It became the basis of the height restrictions specified in the Building Act of 1916, which stated that building heights could not exceed 132 feet. This height restriction remained in place for many years. Local building materials were used, and some of the massive blocks that had to be lifted and locked together weighed as much as 10,000 kilograms. When a steam engine blew up in the process of lifting one of these blocks the driver was killed and parts of the engine were scattered all over the city. A falling cogwheel also killed one unfortunate man, 200 metres away.

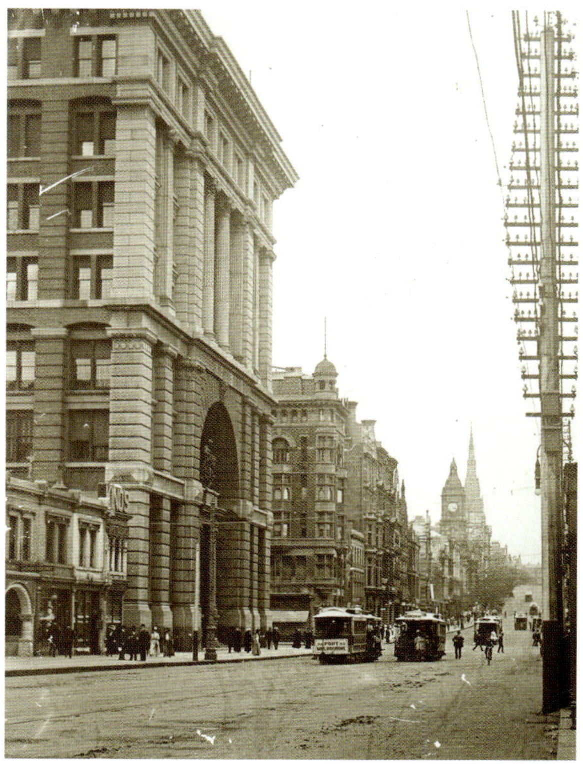

This was a building to impress the public with its grandeur, to reassure them of the wealth and solidity of the insurance industry. Raht wanted it to be "a monument to commercial enterprise of the present age". Corinthian columns soared 41 feet between the fourth and fifth floors and the towering entrance had an archway that reached to the second floor. At this level the columns supported a magnificent bronze statue. This entrance and foyer were lavish, paved in pink granite from Phillip Island and grey granite from Harcourt. Inside the building, the cedar woodwork was so skilfully joined that not one nail was used. Italian and Belgian marble was imported for the walls, skirtings, architraves and floors. The lifts were decorated with bronze bent work.

In 1923 the Colonial Mutual Life Assurance Society bought the building, paying less than half the original cost. By the mid-1950s the Colonial Mutual Life Assurance (CML) had bought and demolished some adjoining buildings and constructed modern office blocks. The Equitable Building was viewed as outdated, too gloomy and ostentatious, and too costly to maintain. The site could be used much more efficiently for a modern building. People no longer wanted marble fireplaces, sweeping staircases and decorative columns. They looked to simpler designs, brighter interiors, clean lines and minimalist furnishings. The National Trust must have shared these views at the time because they did not think it worthy of protection. By 1959–60 the building that was supposed to last forever was gone.

OPPOSITE *The Equitable Building was considered to be the best proportioned building on Collins Street.*

BOTTOM LEFT *Collins Street, looking east, showing the Equitable Building in 1880.*

BELOW *The large bronze statue above the main entrance was designed and cast in Vienna by the Austrian sculptor Victor Tilgner. The angelic woman symbolises the protective insurance company that shields its members from harm. This bronze is now located outside the Baillieu Library at the University of Melbourne, as stipulated in the demolition contract.*

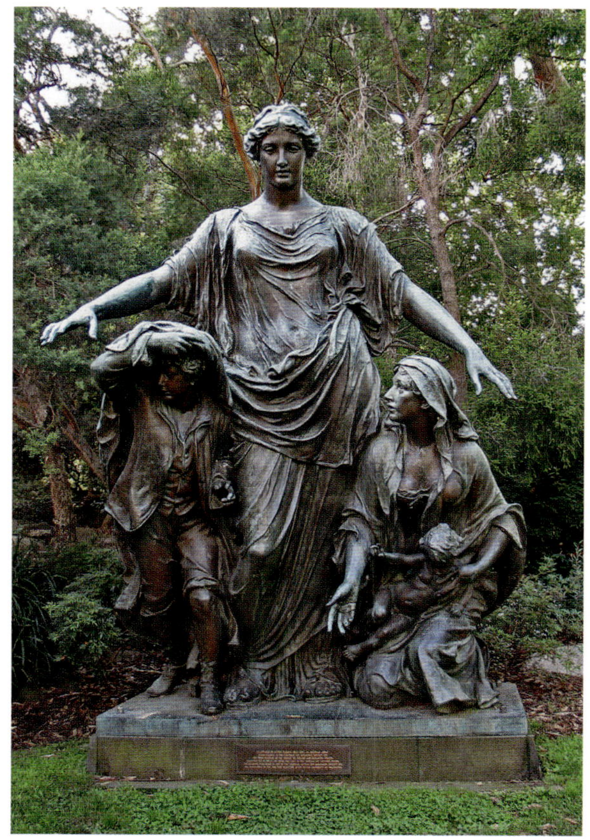

Eastern Market DEMOLISHED 1960

The Eastern Market of Melbourne had a colourful but not always successful history. On surveyor Robert Hoddle's plan for Melbourne there was an area set aside at the corner of Exhibition and Bourke Streets for public use. In 1842 a temporary hay and corn business traded there. It was here that the Eastern Market opened in 1847 as a general market selling fruit, vegetables and poultry up to 9 a.m. It became a hay market after 10 a.m. On Bourke Street, temporary timber shops sold clothes, footwear and books. It was here that Edward Cole (who established Cole's Book Arcade) first sold books and refreshments to the traders. Some of these wooden buildings were destroyed by fire in 1855 and the traders were then forced to sell their goods in the open air from wheelbarrows and carts. Cheap John's stall sold paper, envelopes and sealing wax, and there was a cacophony of sound as vendors sought to outshout each other. On Saturday evening all sorts of traders could move in, paying one shilling for a small area in which to sell their wares. In 1857 a government grant of £3,000 meant that new market buildings could be erected, and when the women's prison site became available in 1858 there was room to build a row of shops on Exhibition Street. In 1859 four long corrugated sheds were opened so that drays could back in. This was "Paddy's Market", a vibrant, noisy place with 224 market stalls.

On Saturday evenings and Sunday mornings the Eastern Market became a Speakers' Forum that attracted large crowds eager to hear discussion, debates and lectures on all sorts of topics. Demonstrations of disgruntled people were also held here, uncomfortably close to Parliament, particularly as the 1860s and 1870s were times of much political agitation.

By the early 1870s tenders had been called for another renewal of the Eastern Market buildings. The notable architects Reed and Barnes won this competition in 1876 and the new building was opened in December 1879. The new market was described in the newspaper as "not lovely to look at but … commodious, with ample room…" but it was a remarkable building in its day. Within a few years the market had expanded and could accommodate 700 drays. It sold over 500 geese and turkeys, 1,000 ducks and fowl, 100 pigs and many other

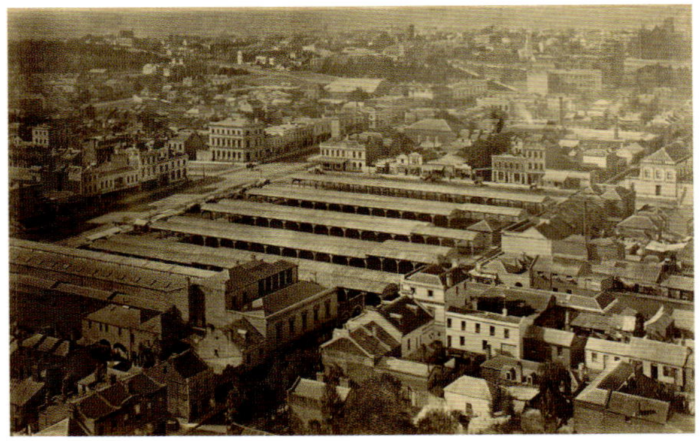

foodstuffs weekly. In 1870 *The Australasian* described some of the food sold there as "cheeses strong enough to waft their odour to Carlton, dried fruits that have been honeycombed with insects…" For the long period it took to construct this building, the stallholders were accommodated at the Victoria Market. Even then there were many criticisms of the building, particularly from the market gardeners. The days of the Eastern Market as a wholesale market were numbered.

When electric light arrived in 1881 there was a revival of interest, especially on Saturday nights when it came to life with entertainers of every type, but there were also other incidents that did not help: a fire, a shooting, a suicide, a multiple murder and several accidents. It was not the success that the City Council had expected. In 1904 revenues from the Eastern Market continued to decline. For some years it operated as a flower and general merchandise market. In 1960 it was demolished and the coins in a copper box under the foundation stone placed there by the Mayor in 1878 were retrieved. A hotel was built on the site.

ABOVE *A bird's eye view of the Eastern Market in 1875, seen from the top of Scots' Church spire in Collins Street.*

OPPOSITE *The Eastern Market was a fruit and vegetable market, a general market, the site of public meetings and protests, and the centre of a vibrant nightlife in the second half of the 19th century.*

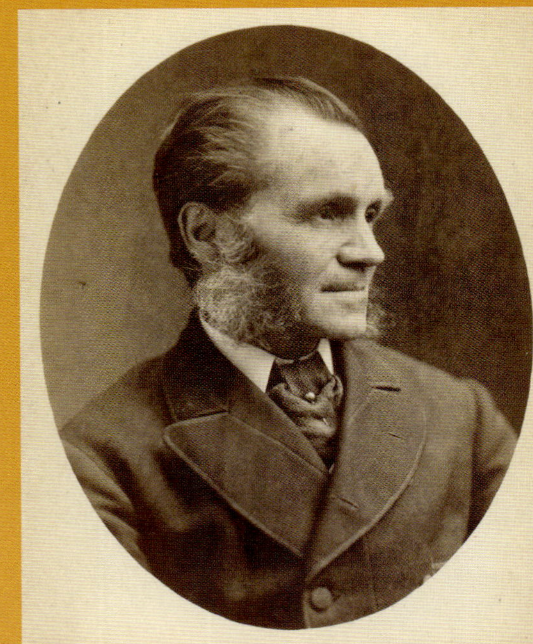

JOSEPH REED (1823–90)

Joseph Reed was an English architect who came to Victoria in 1853 at the age of 30. In 1854 he won a competition to build a State Library, and over the next 37 years, in partnership with Frederick Barnes and others, he designed many of Melbourne's public buildings. His legacy includes the Exhibition Buildings, St Michael's Church, the Town Hall, Wilson Hall and St. Paul's Cathedral, completed to William Butterfield's design. His practice with Frederick Barnes, which was established in 1862, was the beginning of what is believed to be one of the oldest continually operating architectural practices in the world. Today Reed and Barnes is known as Bates Smart.

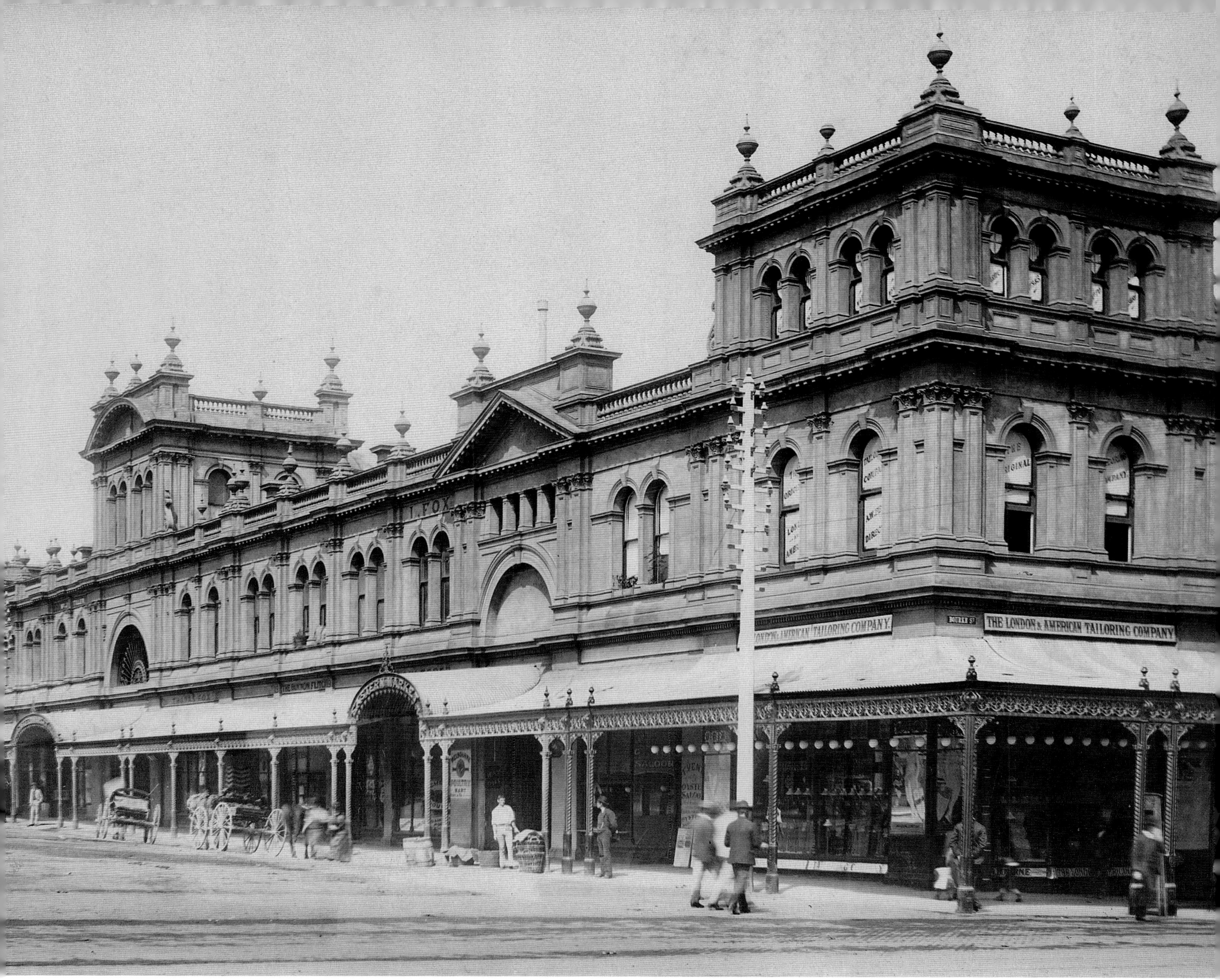
I. FOX
LONDON & AMERICAN TAILORING COMPANY.
THE LONDON & AMERICAN TAILORING COMPANY

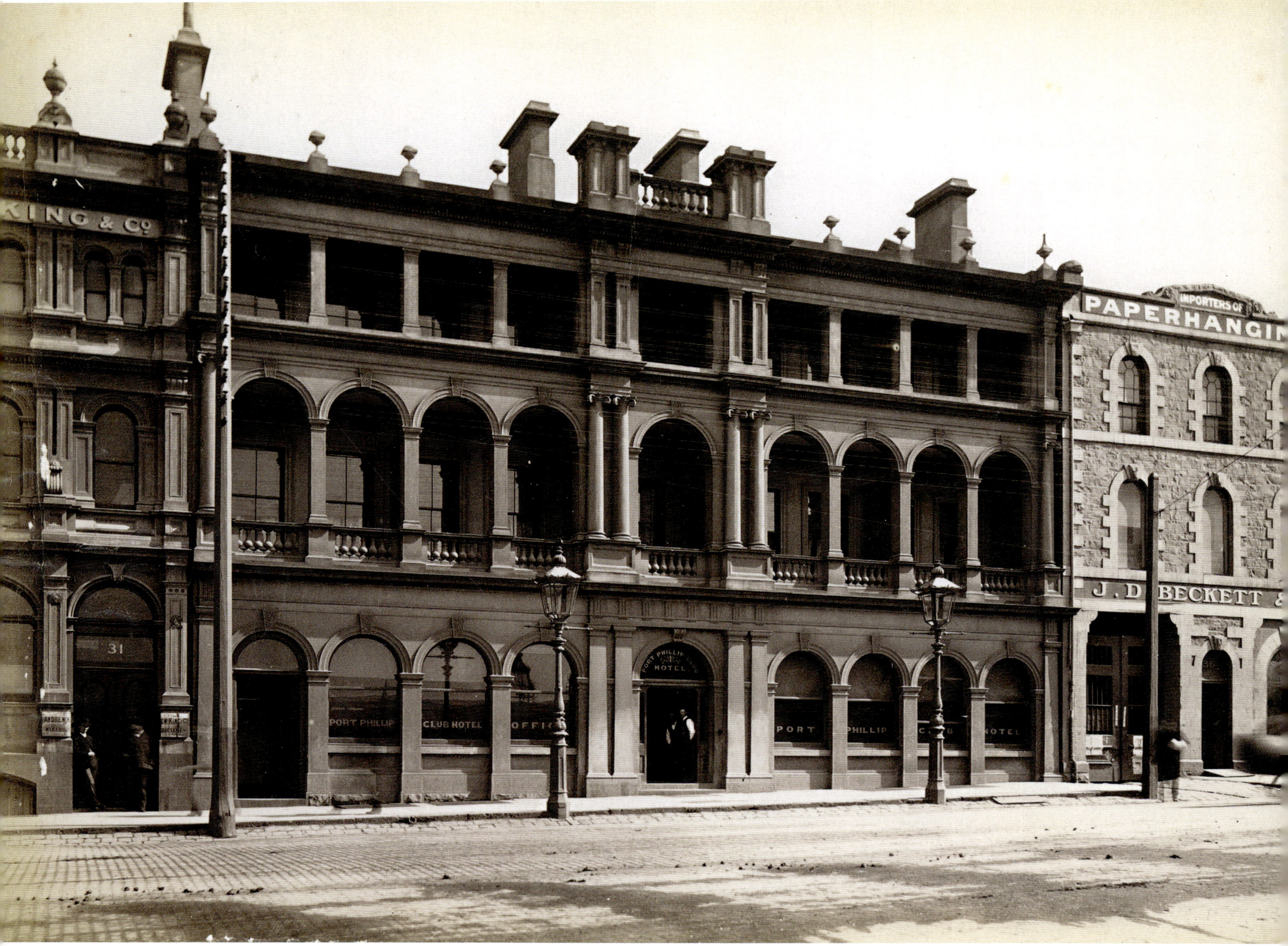
KING & Co
31
PORT PHILLIP
CLUB HOTEL
HOTEL
PORT
PHILLIP
CLUB
HOTEL
IMPORTERS OF
J. D BECKETT

Port Phillip Club Hotel DEMOLISHED 1960

In 1838 Melbourne was just three years old, and of the roughly 10,000 population in the Port Phillip area, 70 per cent were men. The previous year, Robert Hoddle lay out the streets in the central business district of Melbourne in what was to become known as the Hoddle Grid. John Hodgson, later a Victorian politician and Mayor of Melbourne, owned one and a half of Hoddle's "allotments" in section one of the new city. The land was set between Flinders Lane, Flinders Street and Queen Street. It was in his half-acre block, on Flinders Street, that Hodgson built the town's most substantial dwelling. This dwelling was called Yarra House and was for a time the centre of social life for the newly developing village, while the garden attached to the house achieved colonial fame.

Unfortunately, following the building's completion, falling prices left Hodgson bankrupt and, as such, his elegant house came to be known as "Hodgson's Folly". On 11 February 1841, Hodgson became the second person to be registered as insolvent in the Port Phillip district. In the settlement of Hodgson's affairs, John Pascoe Fawkner acquired the "Folly", renamed it Yarra House and leased it for £600 per year, as a meeting house to the Port Phillip Club, which was formed in 1840. The main reason given for the formation of the club was to provide decent accommodation in the city. However, other reasons suggest it was for Port Phillip gentry to separate themselves from the other classes and that it was in response to the 1838-formed Melbourne Club's propensity to blackball prospective members. In any case, the Port Phillip Club had strict rules about behaviour and received much less negative publicity than the Melbourne Club. Despite having one hundred members, the Port Phillip Club was not able to survive Melbourne's first depression and folded in 1843. An attempt to amalgamate with the Melbourne Club was rejected, though Port Phillip members were free to apply for membership of the Melbourne Club.

Yarra House went on to become a rooming house for young women until, in 1850, it was bought by Edward Scott who named it the Port Phillip Club Hotel, after its former occupants and acquired its first licence. Much of the original 1838 house was included in the renovations for the new hotel and in 1861 an impressive three storey frontage was added. Edward Scott retained the hotel until he relinquished it to purchase the Old Lamb Inn. He took the name of the Port Phillip Club with him but after renaming the Old Lamb Inn after himself (Scott's Hotel), the name Port Phillip Club reverted to its former site. In 1897 the hotel was fortunate to escape being burnt by the large fire that destroyed almost an entire city block close by. In 1923 *The Argus* reported that the Port Phillip Club Hotel, in Flinders Street, the oldest hotel in Melbourne, had been sold to a syndicate for £130,000. And so it remained as the Port Phillip Club Hotel over the years, despite a few other changes in the holders of the licence.

The Port Phillip Club Hotel survived until 1960, when it was demolished after being delicensed. It was replaced by the Port Phillip shopping arcade that opened in 1961.

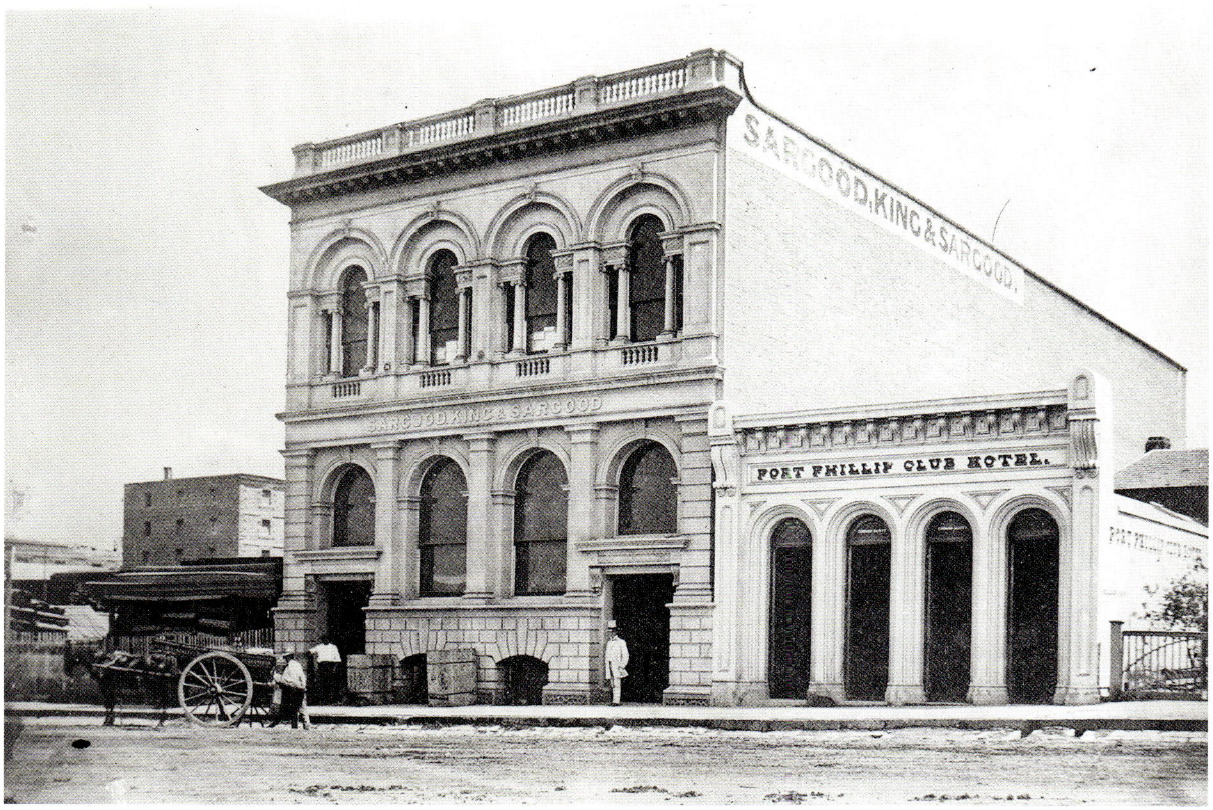

LEFT *The wholesale clothing merchants, Sargood, King & Sargood, next to the original single-storey Port Phillip Club Hotel, circa 1860.*

OPPOSITE *The Port Phillip Club Hotel in the 1880s, showing the upper two storeys with arcaded verandas.*

Royal Mail Hotel DEMOLISHED 1960

Edward Bernard Green, born in England in 1809, came to Australia as an officer in the King's Own Regiment. After resigning his commission, he was successful in winning the contract to supply mail between Melbourne and Sydney in 1840. This journey was arduous and Green at first made the journey alone, then with a dogcart and passengers, and later as part of a stagecoach line. He kept this contract until 1850, making his fortune in the process. The suburb of Greensborough, 17 kilometres northeast from the Melbourne central business district, is named after him, as he held the mail contract in that district.

In 1848 Green purchased a corner site at Bourke and Swanston Streets and in the same year the Royal Mail Hotel was built as a terminal for his coach line. The three-storey hotel at 251 Bourke Street took up a considerable part of the street frontage and with its wide verandas it enabled pedestrians to walk the streets there without fear of inclement weather. It was also well placed to view the parades that passed down Swanston and Bourke Streets.

The second licensee was William Sugden. He was the founder of the first plain-clothes detective force in the city. In order to become the licensee, he was obliged to resign his position as Melbourne's Chief Constable, but he did keep his position as the first chief of the publicly funded fire brigade. W. Sugden acquired a night licence – both difficult to obtain and highly prized at that time – which enabled the Royal Mail to stay open after 9 p.m. Sugden was to have an area of the city named after him. Sugden Place (also known as Sugden Alley) is located between Elizabeth and Swanston Streets and in 1860 was a very busy place with merchants, billiard rooms, tobacconists and other business activities. In 2002–3 it played an important role as part of the City of Melbourne's Laneways commission program.

The third licensee was Paddy Reynolds. During his time at the Royal Mail the custom began of presenting the gold-mounted whip to the winning jockey on Melbourne Cup night. Around this time too, the Royal Mail became the headquarters for the hansom-cab drivers. They stationed a time-keeper there with a clock and whistle to alert the drivers when a customer appeared.

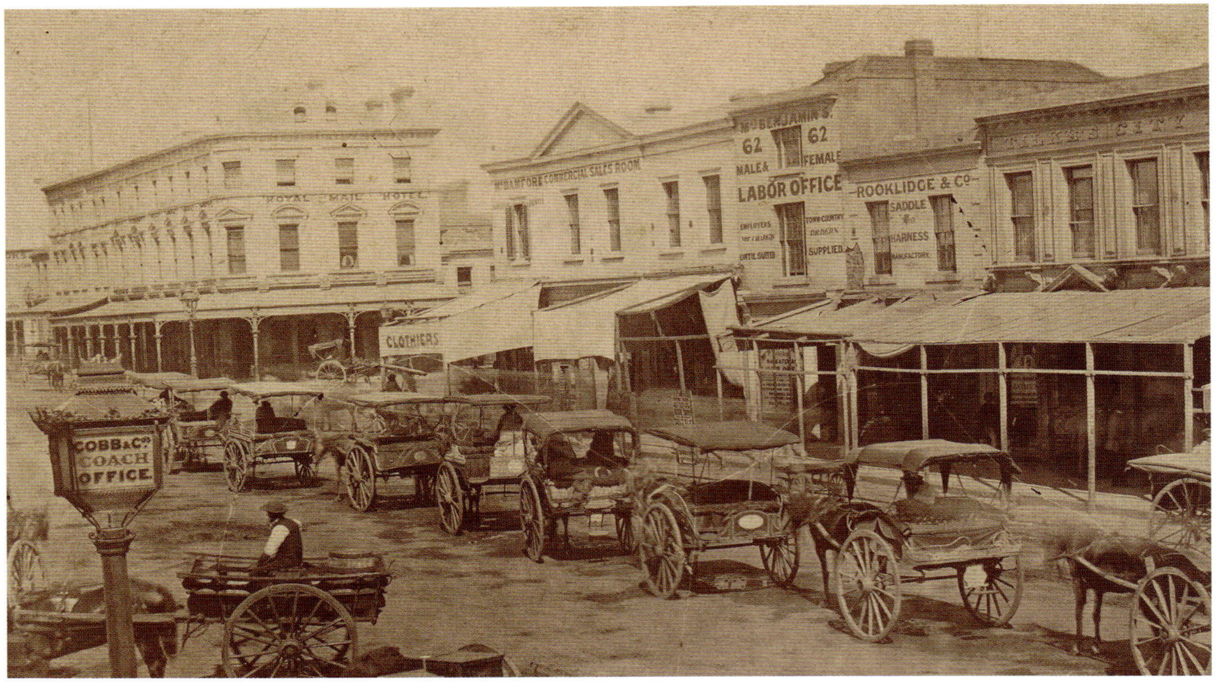

ABOVE *Cobb & Co. Coach Office and a line of horses and carts, with the Royal Mail Hotel behind, circa 1860.*

RIGHT *Prominent advertising on the Royal Mail Hotel as people wait to cross the road in this 1938 photo.*

BELOW *An Army contingent march past the Royal Mail Hotel, at the corner of Swanston and Bourke Streets, around 1900.*

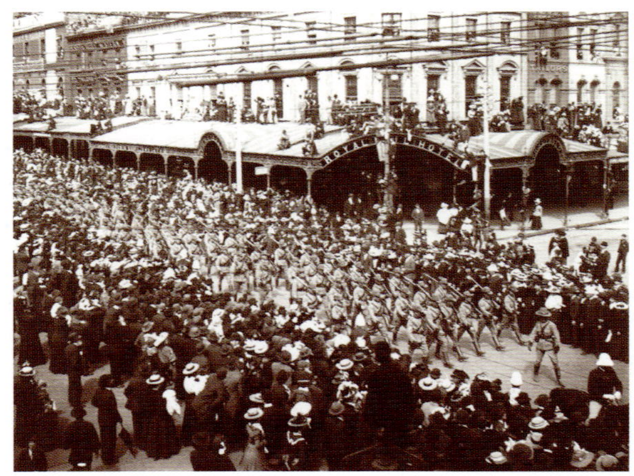

The Royal was reported in the newspapers a number of times. In 1874 a young former employee of the Oriental Bank committed suicide in the hotel and in 1912 a former bartender, now armed, entered with the intention of robbing it. There were a number of building changes at the Royal Mail Hotel over the years. In the 1930s there was a partial demolition for renovations to add a luncheon room. Bricks located during this demolition bore thumb prints that seemed to indicate convict manufacture. They were later identified as being of Port Arthur origin and therefore recognised as among the city's oldest bricks.

The Royal Mail was in existence for well over a hundred years but its valuable location was eventually earmarked for redevelopment. Thus, in late 1960 it was demolished. Its replacement, an office and retail block, was known as Royal Mail House for many years.

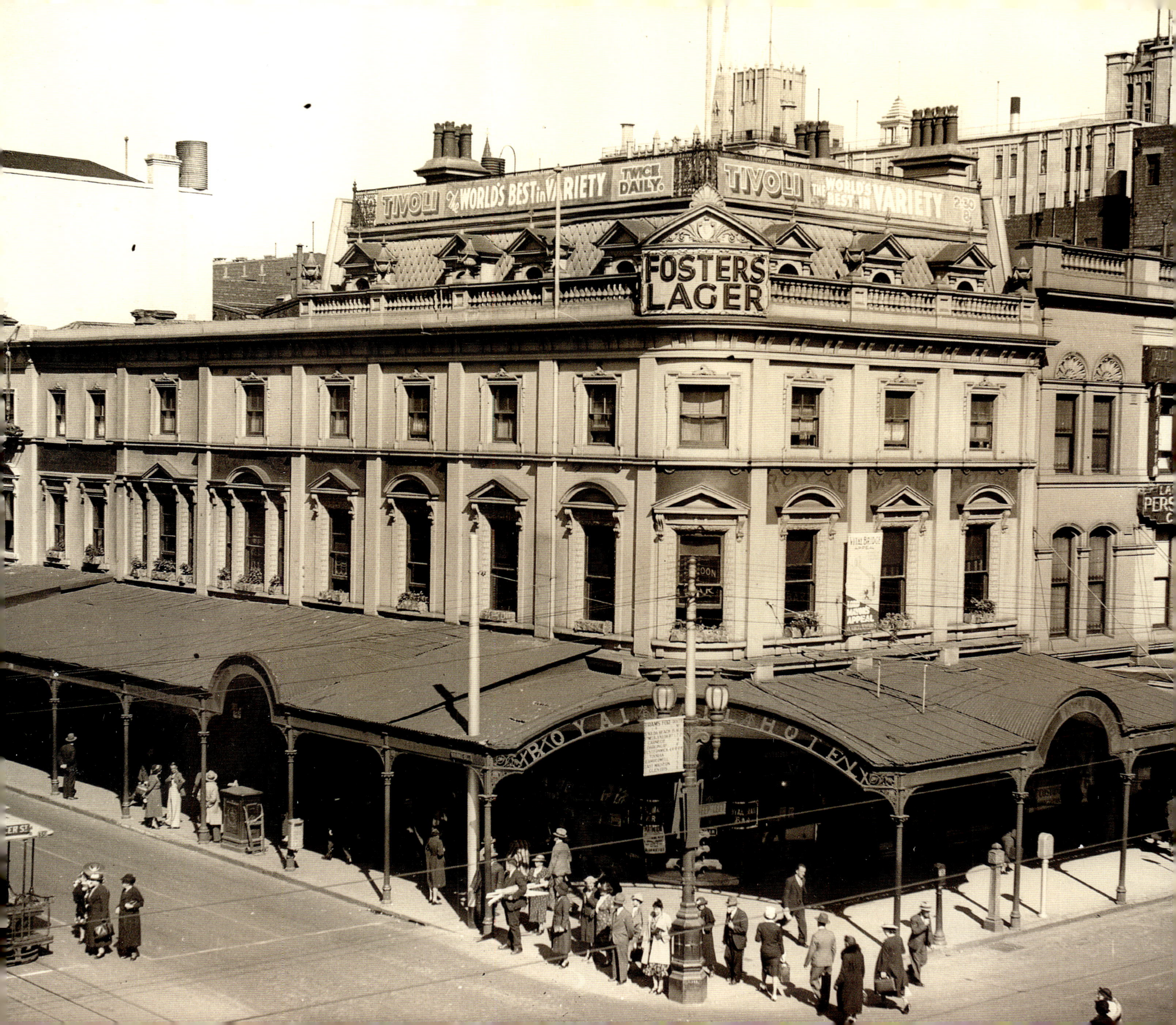
TIVOLI
the WORLD'S BEST in VARIETY
TWICE DAILY.
TIVOLI
THE WORLD'S BEST IN VARIETY
FOSTERS LAGER

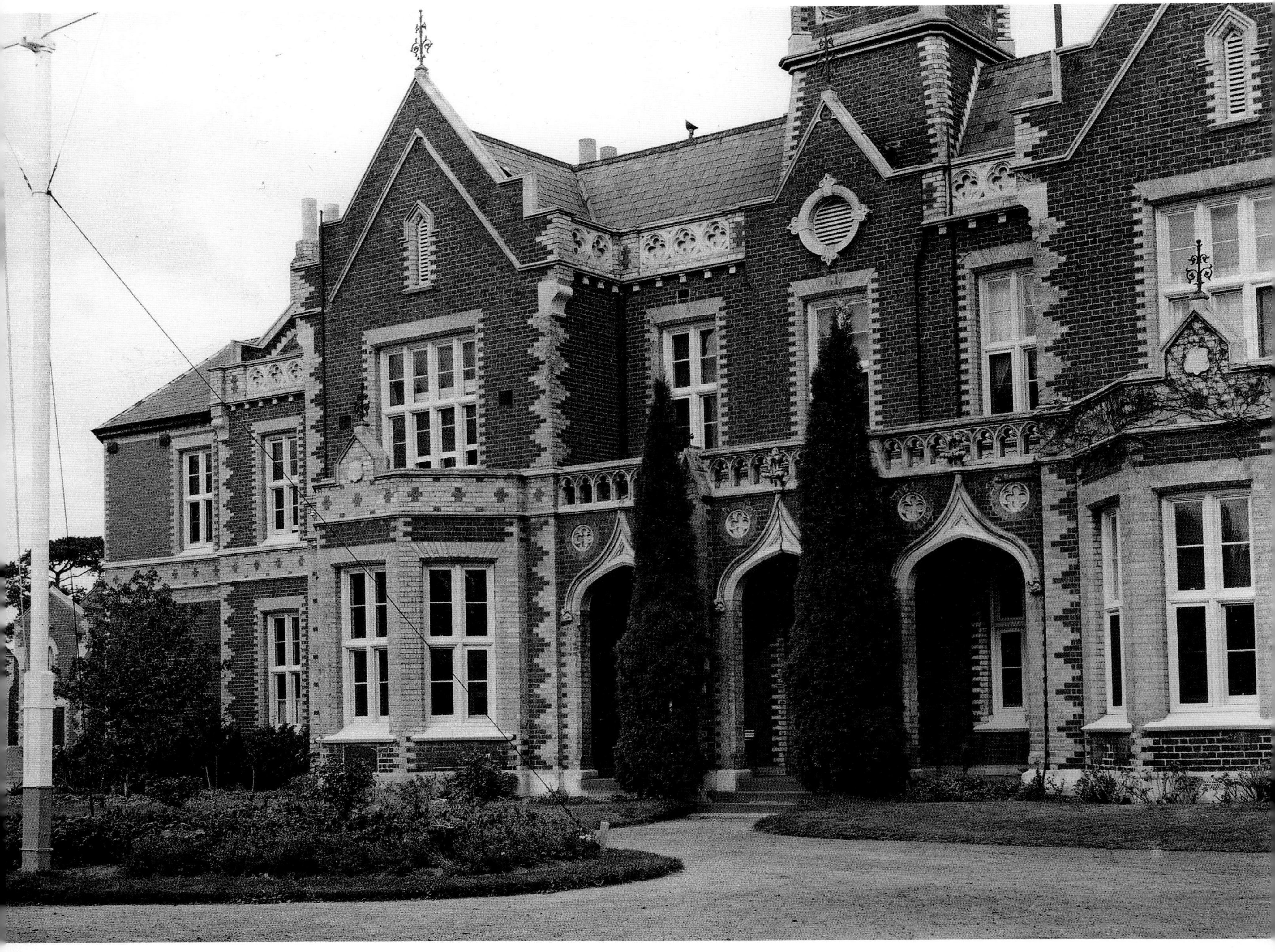

Melbourne Orphanage DEMOLISHED EARLY 1960s

In 1853 the Melbourne Orphan Asylum was established in Emerald Hill to provide residential care for children without parents. It evolved from the Dorcas Society (1845), the first women's organisation to begin in Melbourne. It had as its aim the assistance of the most vulnerable members of society. Emergency support was provided for families and this developed into residential care for children up to the age of 14.

The asylum was conducted on the Christian principles of the Protestant church and orphans were admitted no matter what their parents had believed or where they came from. The first site opened in 1856 in Emerald Hill, but the decision was made in 1876 to sell this site. Several new sites were mentioned but Brighton became the most suitable option, offering access to the sea, a railway line, cleaner air and more space. By 1879, following several purchases of land there, the Melbourne Orphan Asylum was to own 20 acres of property, which could provide milk, vegetables, poultry and eggs. By 1883, the address for the Melbourne Orphan Asylum was "Windemere", Butler Street, Brighton.

The intention was to build barrack-style accommodation at the new asylum, and plans for a three-storey brick building to house 300 children were drawn up. Before this could occur, however, questions were raised regarding the benefits of building cottage style accommodation that would introduce more of a family feel into children's lives. This idea was adopted and in 1877 Charles Webb was instructed to prepare plans for 150 children to be accommodated in five cottages with 30 children per cottage. Each cottage would have a Cottage Father and a Cottage Mother. A school and a hospital were also to be built. The foundation stone for the first building was laid on 22 July 1877 and nine months later, in horse-drawn vans, children, staff and furniture moved from Emerald Hill to Brighton.

In 1926 the Melbourne Orphan Asylum changed its name to the Melbourne Orphanage. Over the following years there were several additions to the orphanage, including a recreation room for senior girls, a chapel, improvements to the kitchen and a piano in each cottage. In 1943 the age for leaving the orphanage was raised to 16, to better equip each child in readiness for the outside world. After World War II, the orphanage began to accept children from broken homes in addition to orphans. Brighton Beach State School was located at the Melbourne Orphanage and children from the local community attended alongside those from the orphanage. The school was able to access the orphanage's facilities and many friendships were made at this time.

In its first one hundred years, Melbourne Orphanage helped over 7,000 children. However, in the early 1940s running costs increased and by the 1950s the orphanage had moved from a credit to a deficit financially. The decision was made to accept child endowment payments from the government. In 1954 a social worker was appointed and in 1956 the Melbourne Orphanage was declared an approved children's home under the Children's Welfare Act of 1954. The 1950s also saw a change in the arrangement for the welfare of children. In line with overseas trends, the move was to embrace the family group rather than the child alone. By 1956 a decision was made to leave the Brighton site and move into family group homes located in Glen Waverley. Fourteen family group homes were established between 1959 and 1963. The orphanage building was demolished in the early 1960s and the site is now occupied by the Brighton Beach Primary School.

OPPOSITE *Front facade of the Melbourne Orphanage at Butler Street, Brighton in about 1925.*

BELOW *A group of young girls at the orphanage, photographed for the* Illustrated Australian News *in 1895.*

BOTTOM *A panoramic view of the Melbourne Orphanage, with formal lawns and gardens in the foreground.*

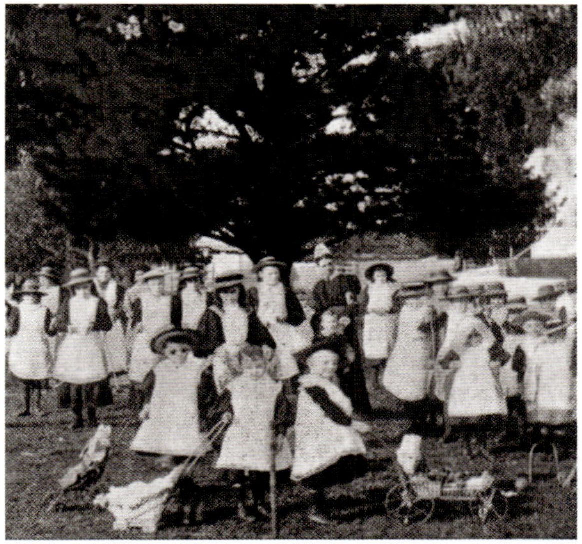

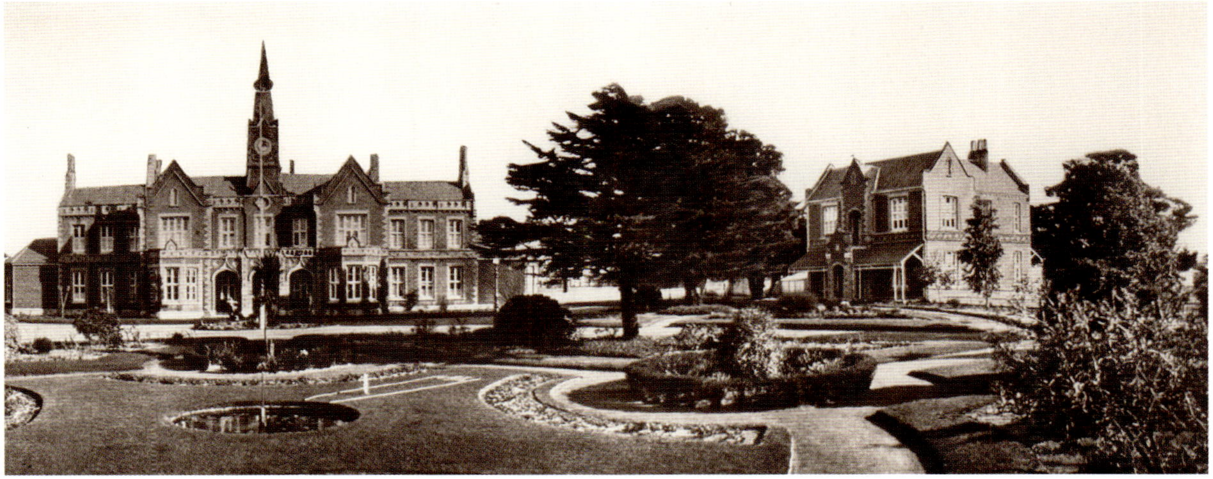

Western Market DEMOLISHED 1961

The Western Market was opened in December of 1841, only six years after the beginning of Victorian settlement. Robert Hoddle drew up the grid plan for Melbourne's streets in 1837 and the government kept the block between Market and William Streets for the Western Market. This area was in a central location and close to the ships that docked at the end of Market Street. It took up a city block that encompassed Market Street, Flinders Lane, William Street and Collins Street. The area was originally a reserve and a petition was drawn up to establish a public market. As Melbourne was still governed by Sydney, a public vote was held to appoint commissioners to manage the market. This was the first act of self-government by the citizens of the Port Phillip district, and a year later the town council took over the responsibility for the market.

The first market was held in the open air, but by the 1840s more permanent structures had been erected. Within a few years the Western Market had to contend with the increasing popularity of the Eastern Market. In 1853 there was a fire at the Western Market and the fruit and vegetable growers were forced to move to the Eastern Market. This looked to be the end of the Western Market but trading recommenced in 1856, beginning as a general market. In 1863 new legislation allowed the council to lease out the Western Market site for 21 years to private operators. The city fathers held a design competition for new buildings at the venue. The idea was to combine a market with commercial premises. The council sought the services of the architect J. M. Barry who divided the site into 29 parts, each to be leased to a developer who would build in accordance with the overall design. Few of these leases were taken up, though the council took three and built at the Western Market in accordance with the design. Despite many leases being available, money was in short supply, and most were eventually leased by one man: Henry "Money" Miller. He retained control of the complex until 1889 when it returned to the council. It is difficult to believe that the Western Market was a market. It was an imposing building with many of the tenants having a relationship with the sea. There were shipping and custom agents housed in the building and they provided much of the revenue for the Western Market.

The market ran for six days each week and in 1904 it was reported as being the chief wholesale fruit supply centre for the city and suburbs. In time, though, it became a victim of its own success. There was insufficient space for the carts and trucks of the buyers and sellers and they were forced to park some distance away. With the Queen Victoria market enlarged, patrons increasingly moved there and many of the Western Market traders moved into the 60 new brick stores. An idea that the Western Market site would be a general market failed. The government handed control to the Melbourne City Council who used the site as a carpark from 1934. During World War II some of the buildings were used as an Air Force hostel, but after the war, building restrictions meant that very little use was made of the site. Finally, in 1960–61, the wreckers moved in and between 1962 and 1965 the £4 million, 22-storey National Mutual Centre was built.

RIGHT *Horse cabs wait outside the Western Market, at the corner of Collins and Market Streets, in the 1870s.*

BELOW LEFT *A truck loads goods outside the Williams Street end of the market in the late 1950s, not long before its demolition.*

BELOW *The Collins Street front of the market in the 1870s.*

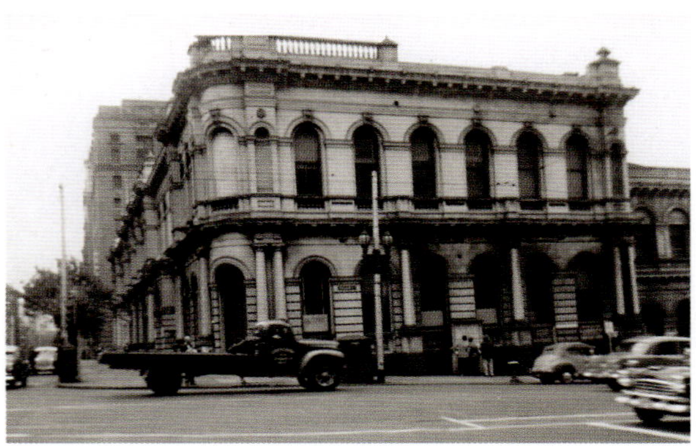

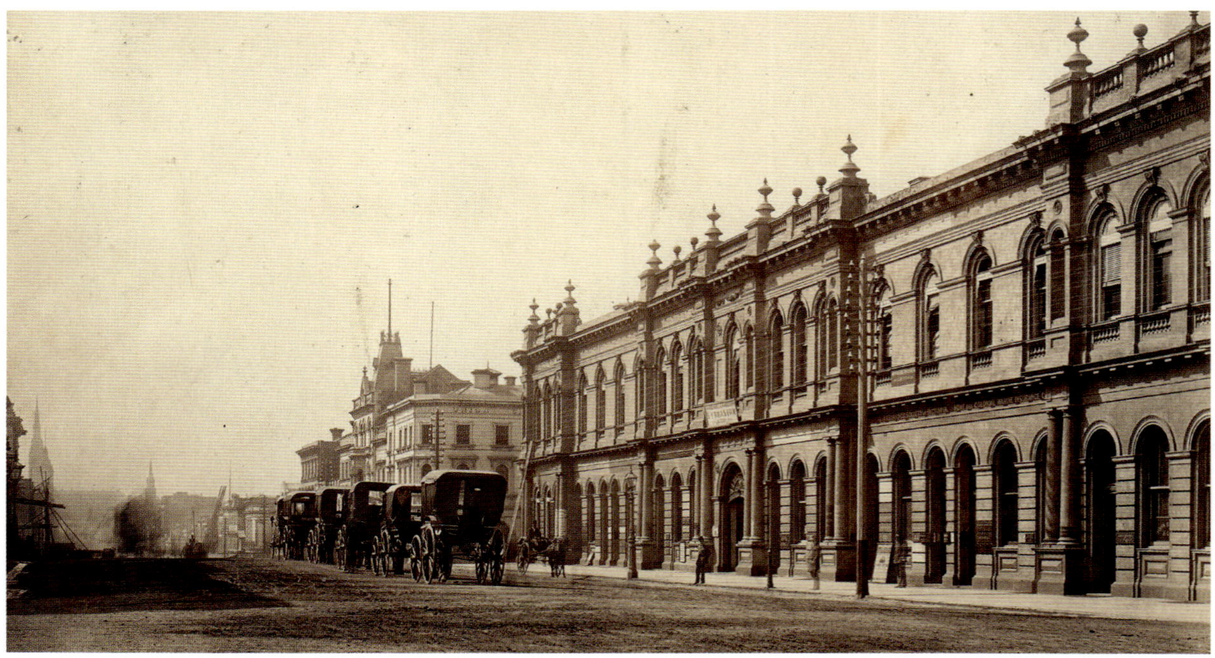

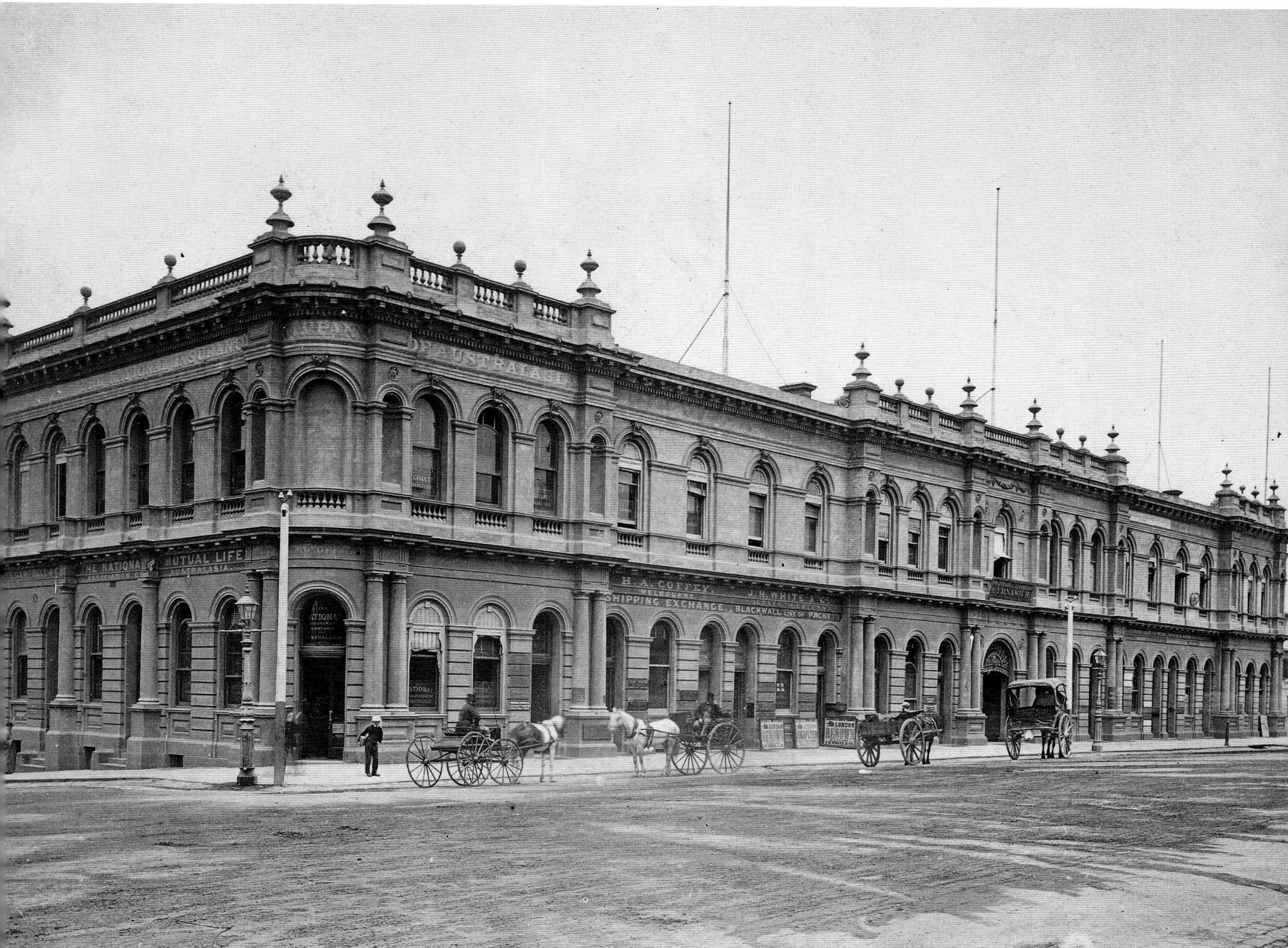
OF AUSTRALASIA
MUTUAL LIFE
H. A. COFFEY
MELBOURNE
SHIPPING EXCHANGE.
BLACKWALL LINE OF PACKE

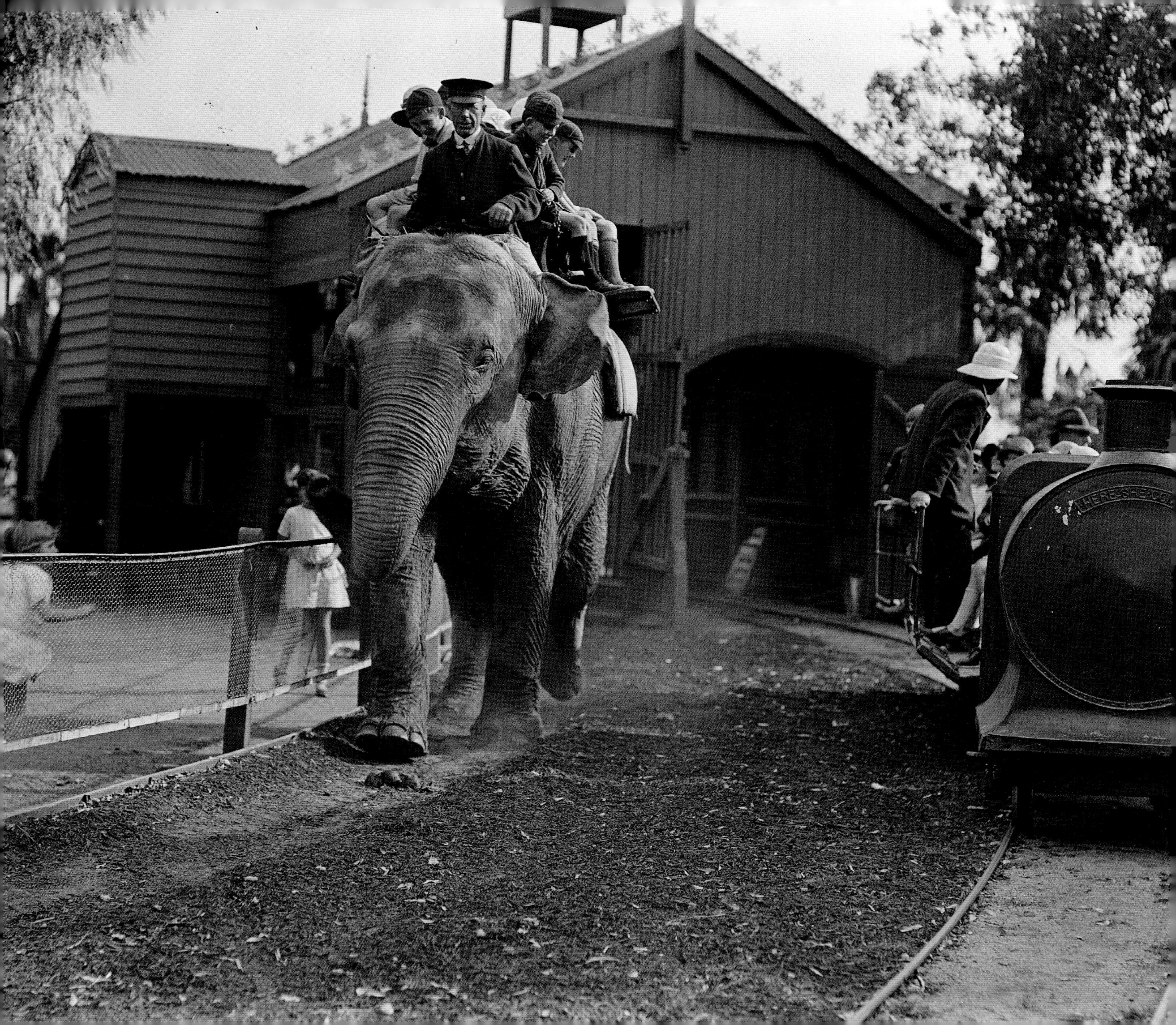

Elephant Rides at Melbourne Zoo CEASED 1962

Melbourne Zoo, the oldest zoo in Australia, began in October 1862, located on 22 hectares in Carlton. It was built for the Acclimatisation Society of Victoria to house animals recently brought from England that needed to recover from the long sea voyage. The zoo also bred exotic animals like rabbits, deer and pheasants for release into the bush, perhaps in an attempt to make Victoria more like England. After 1872 more exotic animals were displayed and for almost 90 years the zoo paid hunters in Africa to supply tigers, lions and monkeys.

Between 1930 and the 1950s many animals were kept in small cramped spaces that were unsanitary and smelly. By the 1960s the idea of zoos without bars was becoming popular, and with better financial help zoos were able to establish lion parks and import larger animals. The treatment of animals in zoos was changing, and international breeding and exchange programs were being established. The public was becoming more interested and the growth of societies like Friends of the Zoo helped promote zoos as tourist attractions.

The first elephant, Ranee, came to the Melbourne Zoo from Calcutta in 1883, a period of great wealth and change in "Marvellous Melbourne". Soon after arrival, Ranee began giving rides to children around a special track. The passengers climbed steps up to a platform and then took their seats on the howdah, the special saddle on the elephant's back. This was an enormously successful development and crowds flocked to the zoo.

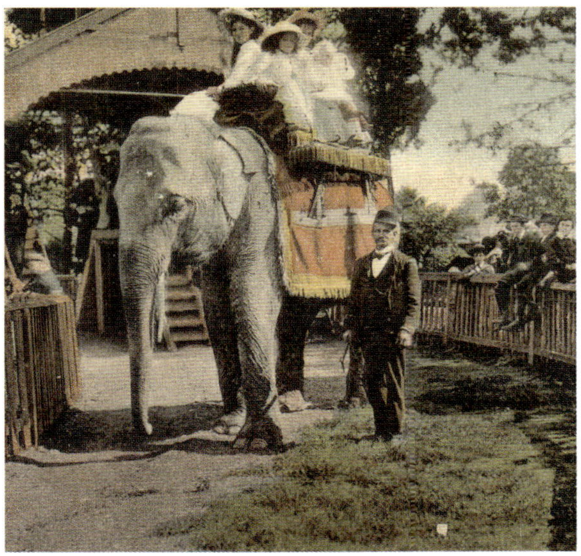

Queenie, one of the most well-known elephants on which children could ride, came to the zoo from India in 1901 when she was six years old. She refused to leave the ship without the accompanying bull elephant, but in 1901 no one understood what social animals elephants are. Queenie started carrying as many as 500 children a day from 1905 and did so for the next 40 years, covering more than 165,000 kilometres along a special route. A miniature train carrying 10 children travelled beside the elephant. A ride on Queenie was a highlight of a child's visit to the zoo and there are many stories of children who placed peanuts and apples on posts for her to eat. Some people recall that she would toss annoying boys into the dust or spray them with dirty water. It cost two pence to have a ride on Queenie and children queued for long periods. When the first merry-go-round arrived at the zoo children were worried that Queenie would be deserted and they wrote her many letters to reassure her.

In 1944 Queenie crushed her keeper, Wilfred Lawson, and he was found dead next to her. There was an inquest into his death and Queenie was declared guilty. Contradictory reports of the keeper's handling of Queenie abounded. A nephew said that Lawson hit Queenie with a stick but others said that he loved the gentle animal. There were no witnesses to his death. The zoo no longer allowed rides on Queenie and she was kept for another nine months then destroyed. The reason given was that feed was expensive and in short supply during the war years and the zoo could not afford to keep Queenie despite the past contribution she had made to their coffers.

Elephant rides ceased at Melbourne Zoo by 1962, and at most Australian zoos by 1980, but elephants are still an important attraction for many visitors to the zoo. Discussion continues about the desirability of keeping such large animals but Zoos Victoria argues that they are no longer just exhibitors but valuable researchers and conservationists of a species that is under constant threat in their natural environment.

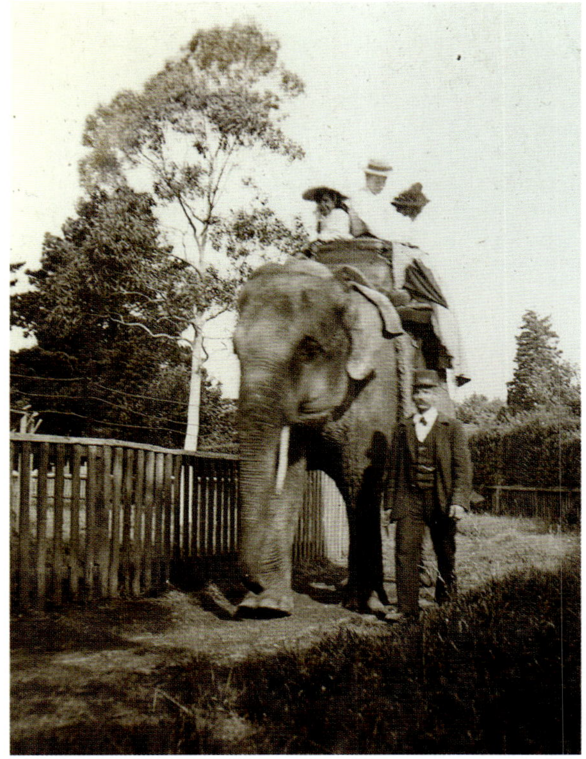

ABOVE *The elephant ride took children along a defined route. In her almost 40 years of service, the popular Queenie walked more than 165,000 kilometres.*

LEFT *Queenie and her keeper in 1907. A ride on Queenie was a highlight of a child's visit to the zoo.*

OPPOSITE *A small train carrying 10 children was introduced to run alongside the elephant track.*

Scott's Hotel DEMOLISHED 1962

Scott's Hotel was considered a landmark in the city but it was also the first of Melbourne's top hotels to be demolished.

Scott's Hotel had its beginnings in the Lamb Inn built in 1837 in Collins Street. Within three years the Lamb Inn had attracted the younger sons of good families who were called Waterfordians (after the Marquis of Waterford, then at the height of his depravity). In 1838, these young men were to form the Melbourne Club, an institution that continues to this day. The Lamb Inn changed owners in 1840 but within a few years had lost most of its clientele. In 1852 William Morton partly demolished the Lamb Inn and remodelled it as the Clarendon Family hotel. It, in its turn, was purchased by Edward Scott in 1860 who constructed a much grander hotel on the site, naming it after himself. Scott, an aristocratic man, built up the reputation of the hotel then sold it to William C. Wilson in 1868. Wilson was a man similar in demeanour and manner to his predecessor. His family were to own the hotel for the next 80 years, retaining Scott's name until it was demolished in 1962.

In 1903 the hotel was modernised and expanded. Between 1910 and 1914 it was substantially remodelled, the architect being Arthur Henry Fisher. Its ornate rooftop featured a twin cupola atop an elaborately composed early palazzo. It was opened as a new five-storey hotel complete with private phones connected to the front desk. A 1924 update added a bathroom to every suite, making it more modern than the other 19th-century Melbourne hotels. It was claimed that Scott's Hotel supplied the finest food and wine, rivalling that of the Menzies Hotel. It also provided the Melbourne accommodation for international cricketers such as W. G. Grace and it was said to be opera singer Dame Nellie Melba's favourite hotel. Scott's Hotel was the place where local racing personalities came to stay and where pastoral property auctions were held. In December 1949, it was used to auction Foilacleugh mansion in Brighton.

Till the 1950s, Scott's was one of the three top places to stay in Melbourne, along with the Menzies and the Oriental. The difficulty with being a top hotel though is there aren't enough of the upper class to go around and the hotels set about trying to win the patronage of the middle classes, or at least those with healthy bank balances. To this end, Scott's was refurbished again in the 1950s with new bars on the inside while maintaining the Edwardian exterior. But beginning in 1955, Scott's was to change hands three times in six years. The first new owners planned to upgrade the hotel and the second to incorporate it with a department store and office block. But there was much interest in office construction and when the Royal Insurance Company bought the hotel in 1961, Ellen and the Two Shilling School – a group of businessmen who drank at Scott's daily – advertised for elbow room in a similar bar. They even brought their own barmaid. Scott's was demolished in 1962 and Royal Insurance built their new headquarters on the site in 1965. It was claimed that Scott's was the oldest continuously licensed establishment in Victoria.

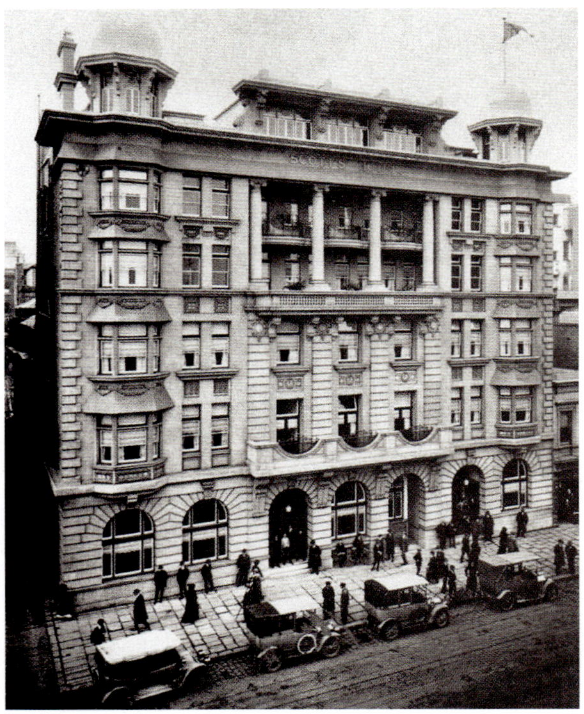

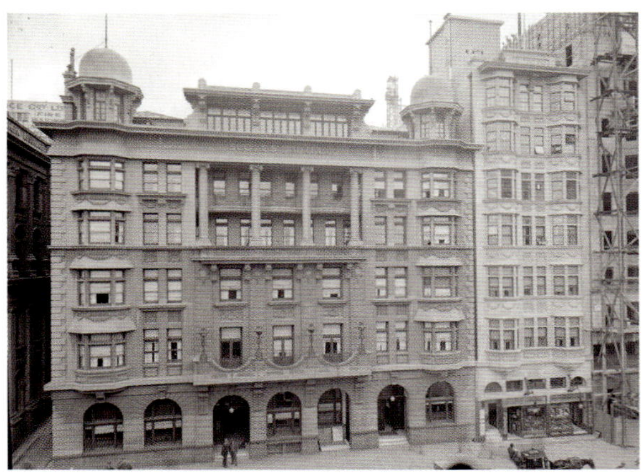

RIGHT *An elevated view of Scott's Hotel in 1957. To the right is the Scott's Hotel Building, home to Bernard's Florists and Scott's Hairdresser & Tobacconist.*

BELOW LEFT *Exterior of Scott's Hotel in the early 20th century.*

FAR LEFT *Taxis wait for their upper-class passengers outside the hotel in this 1920s photo.*

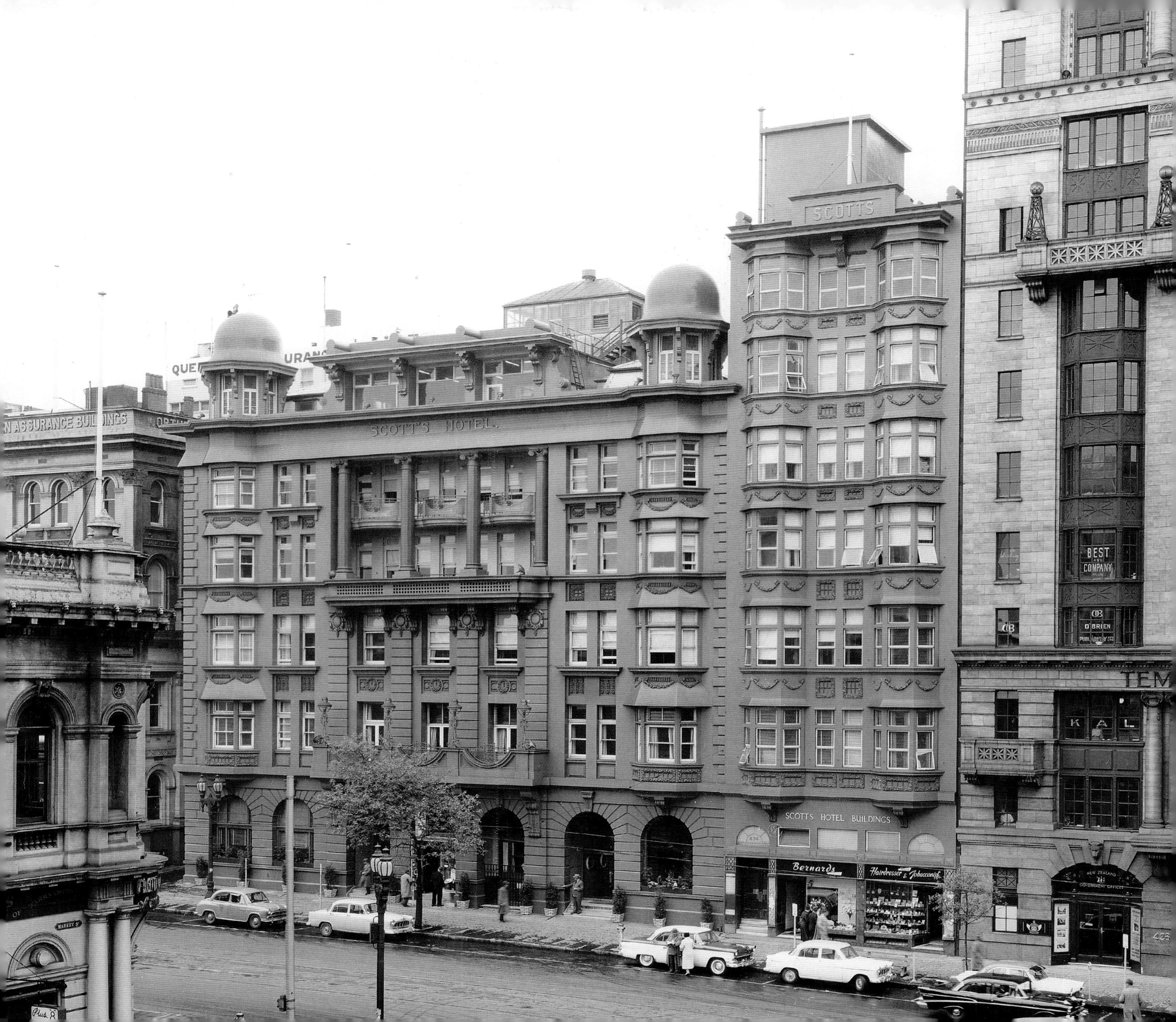
SCOTT'S HOTEL.
SCOTTS
SCOTTS HOTEL BUILDINGS
Bernards
Hairdresser & Tobacconist
BEST AND COMPANY
ASSURANCE BUILDINGS

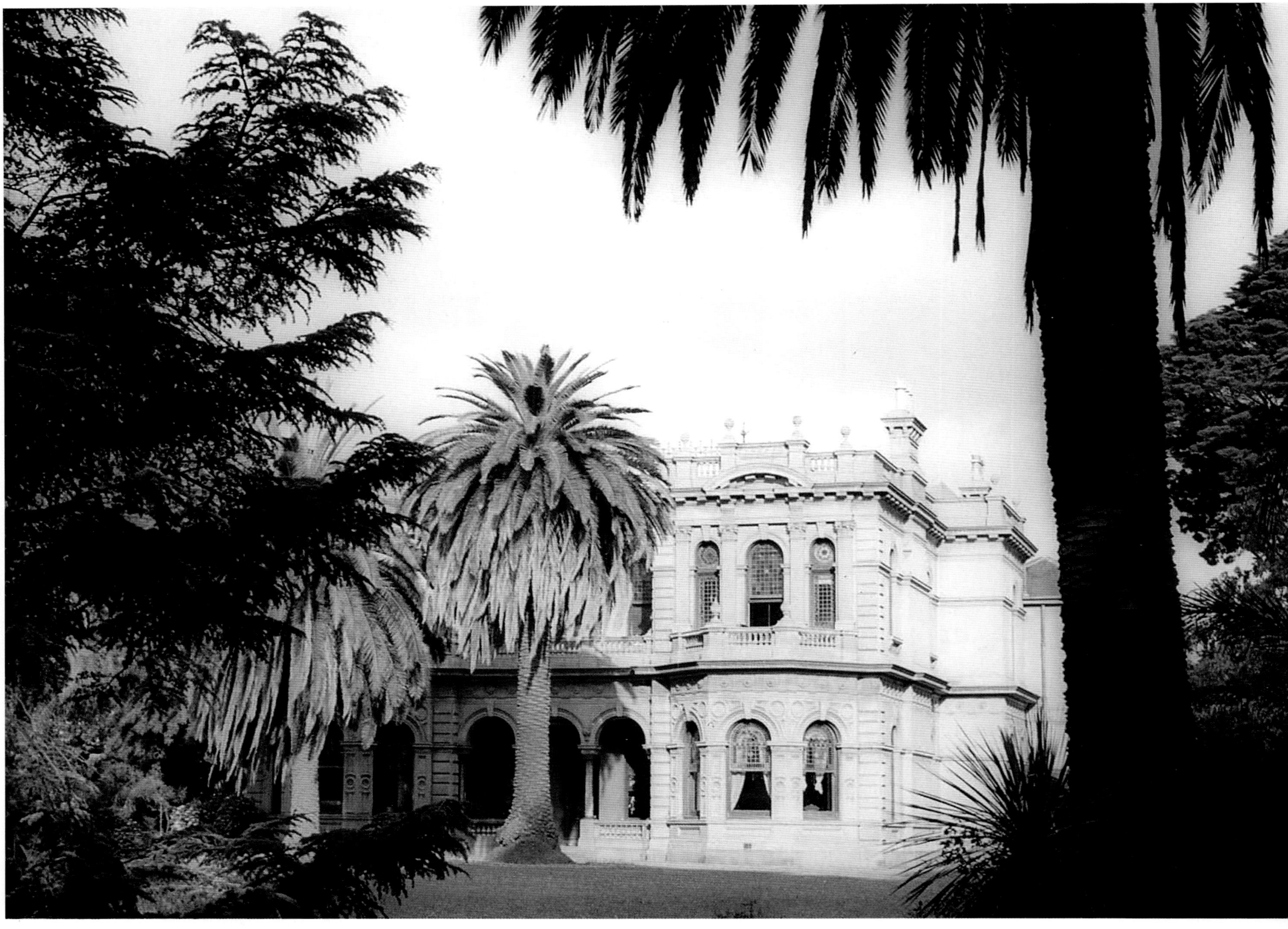

Nareeb / Oma DEMOLISHED 1964

Nareeb, or Oma, as is was originally called, was located in Kooyong Road, Toorak. It was built for Octavius Charles Beale, his wife Elizabeth and their 13 children in 1888. Octavius Charles Beale was born in Ireland and came with his family to Van Diemen's Land in 1854. He established the Beale Piano Factory in 1893, which was thought to be the largest piano factory in the British Empire. The architect of Oma was William Salway, who also designed Raheen, one of the few grand mansions to survive destruction in the name of progress. Salway also designed the Alexandra Club and the facade of the Meat Market, both of which still exist today. Oma was a two-storey Italianate style mansion with red granite pillars. It had 34 richly decorated rooms, with a grand entrance and main hall with first floor balconies. There was also a smoking room, music room, servants' quarters, bedrooms, drawing and dining rooms and a bathroom with an unusual fold-up urinal in the cupboard. The majority of the furniture was imported from England, though there was a stunning 16-piece Australian blackwood dining suite. The grounds were extensive and there was a serpentine drive with elaborate scroll-work entrance gates. These gates were constructed in England and bequeathed to the National Trust of Australia by the mansion's last owner Miss Gertrude Simmons. These gates are now at entrance D of the Royal Botanical Gardens in Melbourne.

James Grice purchased Oma in 1890, perhaps attracted by the extensive stables also designed by Salway. Grice, who became chairman of the Victorian Amateur Turf Club, used Oma as his town house, when he wasn't at Moondah, his main residence near Mornington. In 1906 Oma became the home of Walter and Alice Simmons who renamed it Nareeb. The house was to host many parties and balls to mark special events such as the Spring Racing Carnival. The house and those in it were often featured in the society pages of the newspapers.

Nareeb was sold in 1964 after the death of the remaining Simmons heir. At that time the house was still powered by gaslight. The lamps and chandeliers were quite stunning, as were the exquisite stained-glass windows in this stately home. Because there was no electricity a huge fire stove in the kitchen was lit once a week for bath time. More than 1,000 people viewed the house and gardens over two days before it was sold and the queues to enter snaked along the drive out into the main street. Many were in awe of the extent of the property, particularly as it was located in Toorak, arguably the most expensive suburb in the city. The marvellous collection of antiques, original gaslights, two pianos and fine arts were crowded into the rooms for the auction, and the Simmons' 1920 Rolls Royce was also auctioned prior to the sale of the house. The 5.5 acres of the property were subdivided after the property's sale and Nareeb was demolished. Nareeb Court was created and several residential properties now occupy the site.

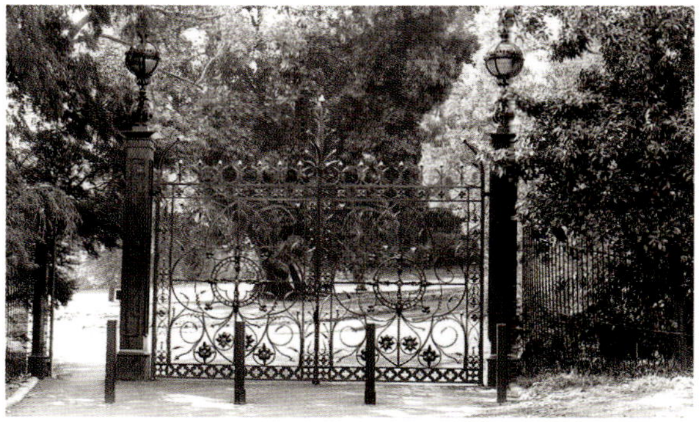

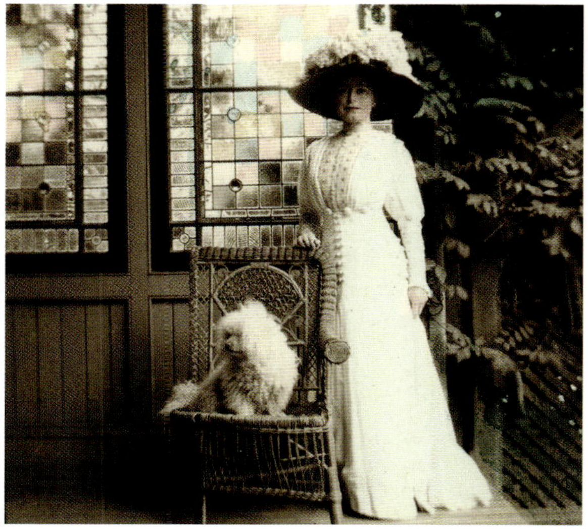

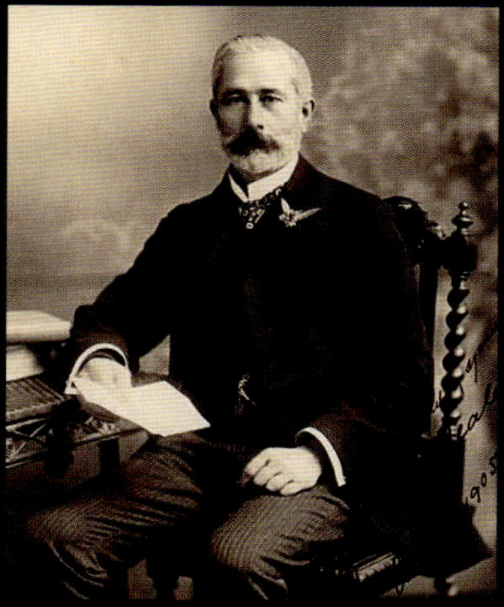

OCTAVIUS CHARLES BEALE (1850–1930)

The Irish-born piano manufacturer Octavius Charles Beale was a prominent business and public figure who became a fellow of the Royal Historical Society and of the Royal Society of Arts. In 1918 he was made a freeman of the City of London and in Sydney he was a trustee of the Australian Museum and of the New South Wales Savings Bank. He established Beale & Co in Sydney in 1884 and opened his first piano factory in 1893. It was thought to be the largest piano factory in the British Empire. Beale was killed in a motor vehicle accident at Stroud, New South Wales, in 1930.

LEFT *A young woman on the back veranda of Nareeb, Kooyong Road, Toorak, around 1910.*

FAR LEFT *The front gates of Nareeb are now in the Royal Botanical Gardens, Melbourne.*

OPPOSITE *An exterior view of Nareeb showing the gardens and mansion shortly before its demolition.*

Swallow & Ariell DELISTED 1964

In the 1880s, Swallow & Ariell was the fifth largest biscuit company in the world and manufactured more than a hundred types of biscuit. One of these, the meat biscuit, was apparently taken by Burke and Wills on their ill-fated expedition to cross Australia from the south to the north. The company, which also made cakes and ice-cream, was known for its patriotism and held fund-raising campaigns during both World Wars. During World War II, most of its biscuits and plum puddings were diverted to the Australian and U.S. services.

Perhaps it is the name "Swallow" that appeals to consumers, but the brightly coloured posters and tins also advertised the Swallow & Ariell brand very effectively. The labels were designed to be glued to the front of the metal biscuit tins used by grocers in the days when biscuits were stored loose. They were sold by weight to customers and placed in brown paper bags. Later, Swallow & Ariell moved into chocolate-coated and cream-filled biscuits in packets to save time in the kitchen. These were aimed at housewives who appreciated their lives being made a little easier and who could provide their family and guests with such attractive biscuits at the same time.

The Swallow & Ariell factory extended over three acres in Sandridge (now Port Melbourne) and the company owned flour mills and sugar plantations throughout the country. The factory in Sandridge was built in several stages: the three-storey section was the first in 1858 and there were two-storey additions in the 1870s and 1880s as the company needed to expand. A malt house in Stokes Street was purchased in 1876 and refaced to match what already existed.

Originally the building was constructed of face brick with rendered dressings, but later it was totally rendered. Further work occurred in 1911 with a building designed by Gordon McRae in Stokes Street. In 1922 the architectural firm of Bates, Peebles and Smart designed the adjoining building at the corner of Beach Street. A loading bay dating from the 1940s filled in the area between these two buildings. Extending the factory complex even further, a Rouse Street site was completed with a three-storey building that came to dominate the area because of its size and its unified facade that stretched around the block.

The Swallow & Ariell factory was the first industrial complex of its type and was the oldest and largest biscuit manufacturing factory in Victoria. However, after World War II, there was a downturn in manufacturing and many of Australia's major biscuit companies came together under the same umbrella to counteract takeovers from foreign companies such as Nabisco. Swallow & Ariell was the last, but in 1964 it was delisted after 95 per cent of its capital was acquired by the Australian Biscuit Company. It now operates under the name of Arnott's Biscuits. The factory itself, after some years of neglect, was registered by the National Trust. The Swallow & Ariell factory is considered historically important because it is largely an externally intact industrial complex and it has a strong relationship with the development of manufacturing in Victoria. The factory was converted into residential units in the 1990s.

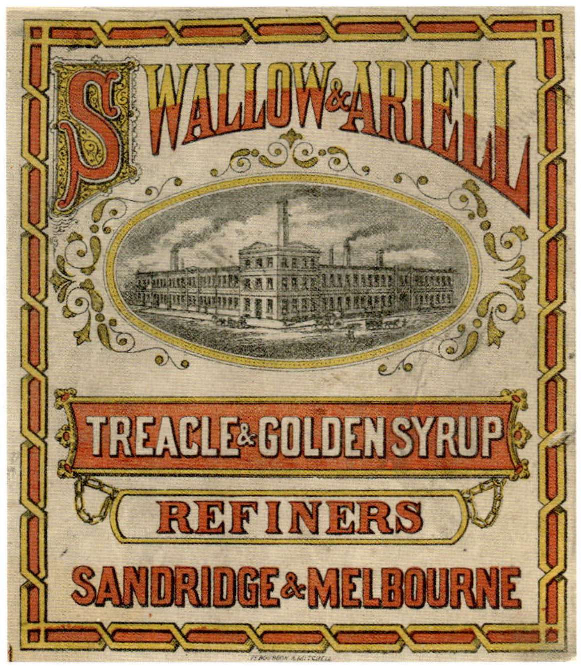

ABOVE *This circa-1890 Swallow & Ariell Treacle and Golden Syrup Refiners poster includes an illustration of their impressive factory complex.*

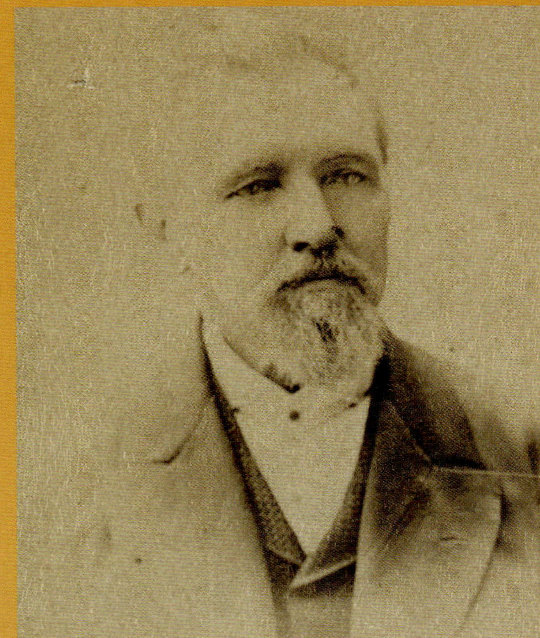

THOMAS SWALLOW (1823–90)

Thomas Swallow came to the Victorian goldfields town of Ballarat in 1853. Finding there was more money to be made in supplying products to the miners than in digging for gold himself, he settled on sea biscuits, which were both tough (the weevils made little impact on them) and nourishing. In 1854 he opened a factory manufacturing and selling ship's biscuits in Sandridge (Port Melbourne) and took a partner, Thomas Ariell. Despite Ariell's death in 1875 the firm continued to operate as Swallow & Ariell for several generations.

RIGHT *An early 1960s view of Swallow & Ariell Steam Biscuit Manufactory in Rouse Street, Sandridge (now Port Melbourne).*

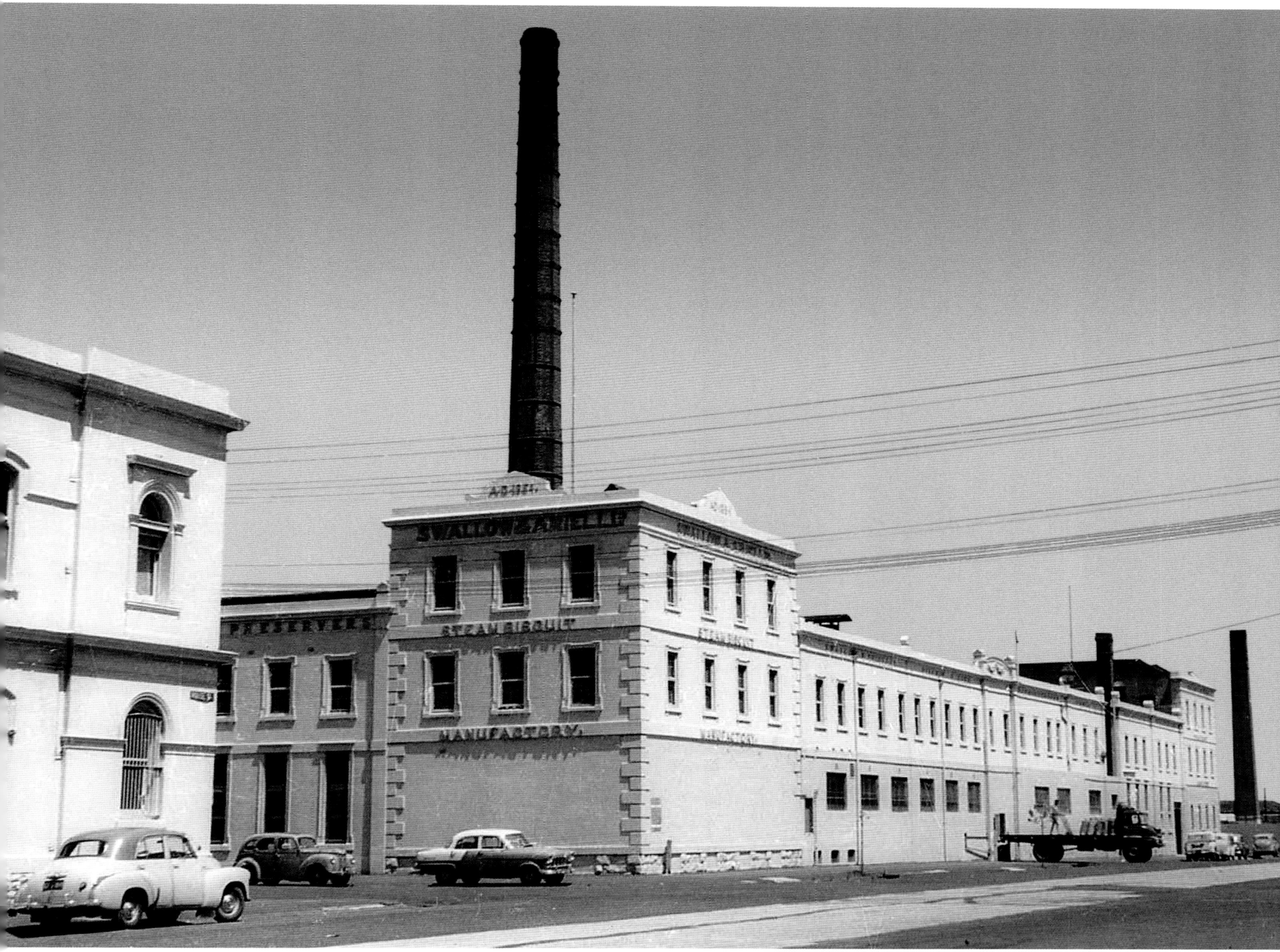
PRESERVERS
STEAM BISCUIT
MANUFACTORY.

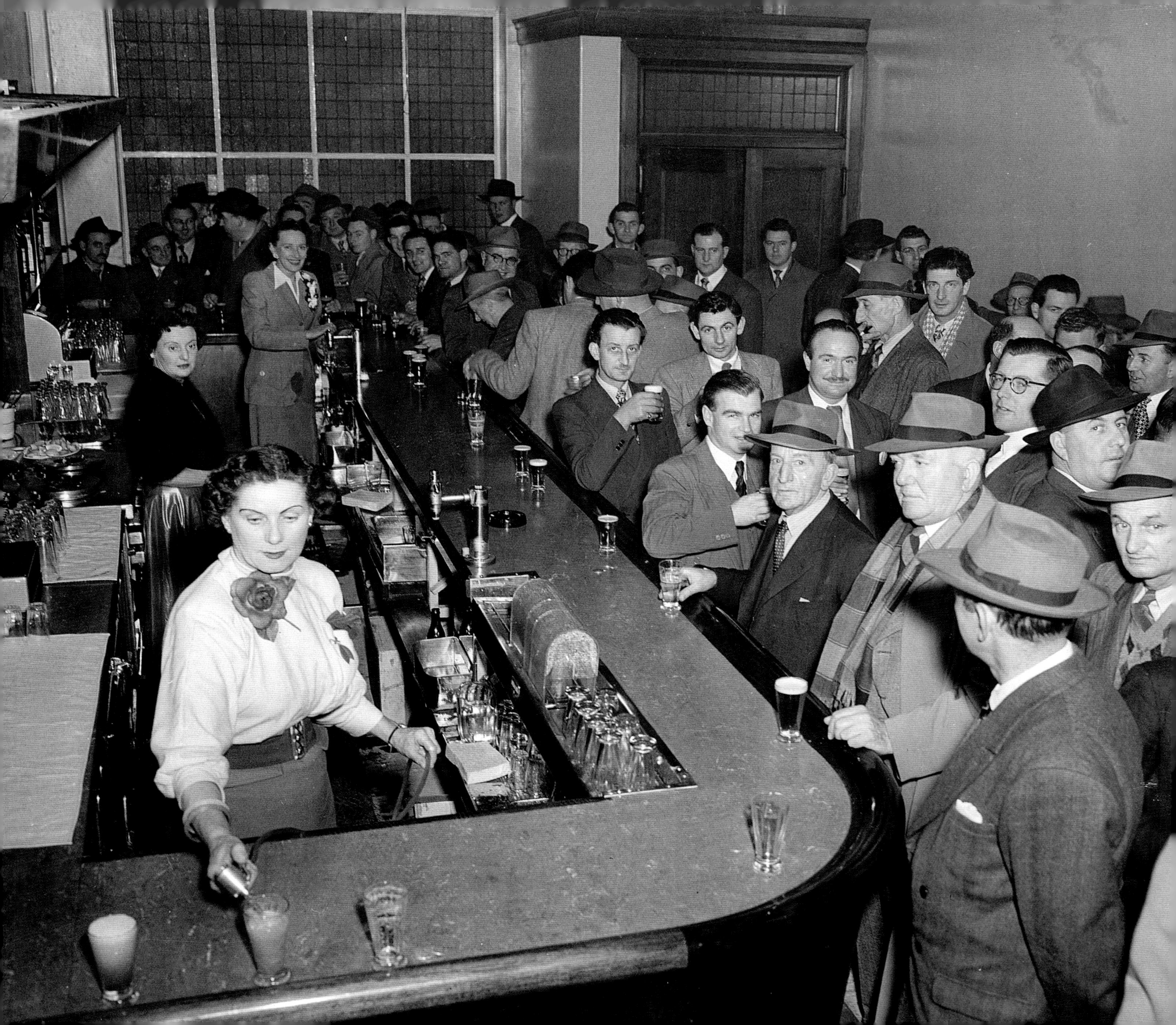

"Six O'Clock Swill" ENDED 1966

Alcohol was etched in the Australian psyche from early colonial days, when convicts were recompensed in part with rum. Attempts in the 1850s to prohibit alcohol were a failure leading to the establishment of and increase in sales from "sly grog shops" (unofficial outlets). Before 1916, most public houses (a place licensed to sell alcoholic drinks) and hotels in Australia closed closer to midnight. The temperance movement though had been active since the 1870s. It opened temperance hotels or coffee palaces and gathered momentum with the turn of the century. After the introduction of six o'clock closing for the retail trade, the argument went that public houses should not be kept open when the retail shops were not.

Under wartime and multi-denominational temperance pressure, the licencing laws were changed to move the closing times of hotels from midnight to 6 p.m. Introduced as a temporary measure in 1916, it became permanent in Victoria in 1919. The intention behind six o'clock closing was twofold: to control the consumption of alcohol and as a war austerity measure. Neither worked.

The amount of alcohol consumed steadily increased, despite the shortened drinking hours. The law allowed licensees to conduct billiard rooms and temperance bars on the premises and, though it was difficult to prove, they were often used for the illicit sale of intoxicating liquor. More worrying for the patrons was the fact that the difference between "knock off" time and six o'clock closing allowed less than an hour of drinking at the end of a work day. Hotels catered to this short heavy drinking period by extending their bars. In these bars, pushing, shoving and crowding all occurred in the effort to get to the counter, purchase beers and get as drunk as possible in the limited time available. This orgy of drinking became known as the "six o'clock swill" because it reminded observers of a pig swill. The cry "Time, gentleman, please!" would occur just before 6 p.m. and the patrons would jostle and shout to get served. Some groups would position one man at the bar 20 minutes before closing, while the rest were interspersed through the crowd. Beers would be lined up on the bar and then passed from man to man to rest on ledges at the back. The beer would be quickly consumed when time was called. It was a common sight to see men being ill in the gutters or brawling as they made their way home. Half a dozen beers in half an hour on an empty stomach was difficult to handle. It was noted that car crashes and domestic violence was far more prevalent in the hours between 6.30 and 8 p.m. Women were excluded from public bars, the idea being that they were at home preparing dinner for their family. Thus, the six o'clock swill was conducted in an all-male environment. During the 1956 Olympic Games, the sight of men in business suits shouting and pushing to get served at the bar caused great amusement to overseas visitors. By the early 1960s it was recognised that the six o'clock swill was a demonstration of the failure of the early closing hours. In 1966, six o'clock closing ended and trading hours were extended to 10 p.m. At the same time the 0.05 blood-alcohol limit with regard to driving was introduced. With women now entering the previously male-only bars, the six o'clock swill was ended.

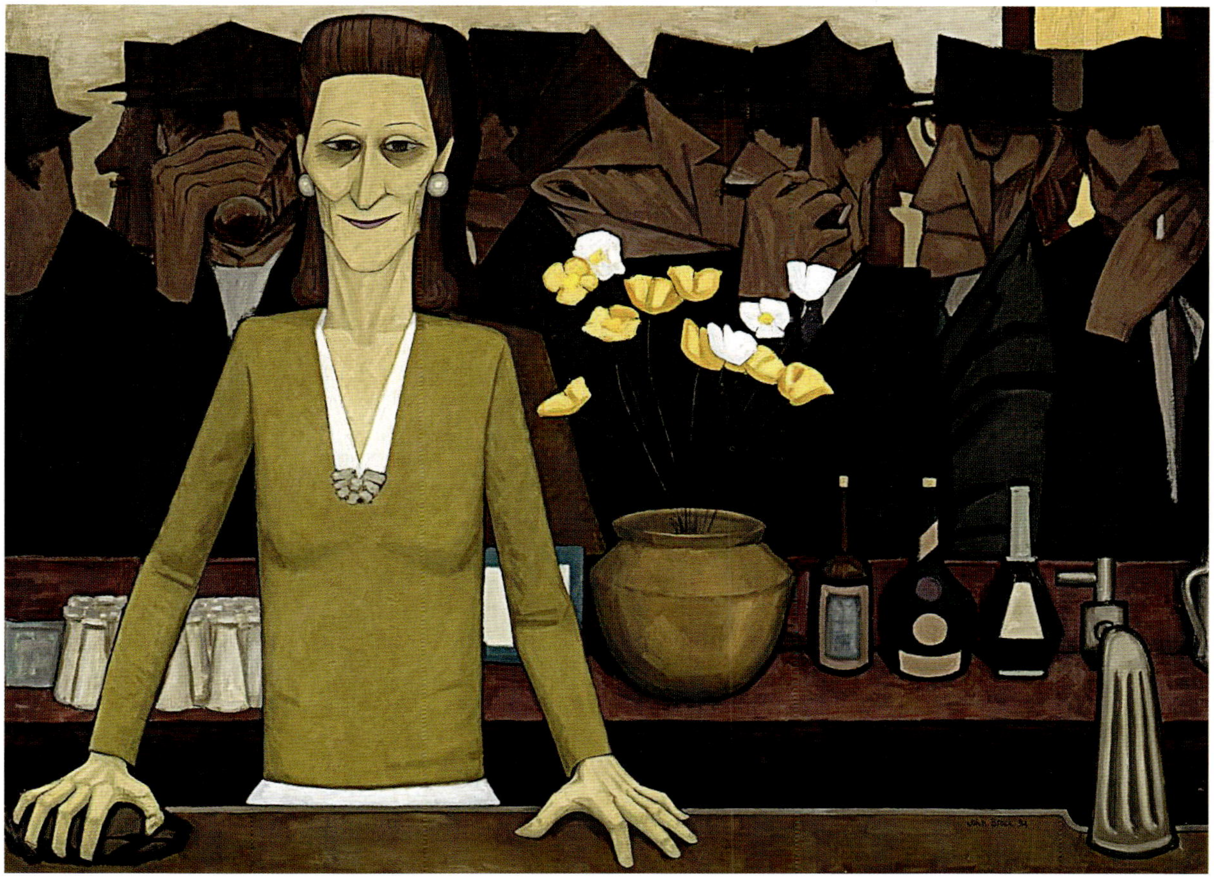

LEFT *John Brack's depiction of the "six o'clock swill" (The Bar, 1954) is part of the National Gallery of Victoria collection.*

OPPOSITE *Men crowded the bar to be served before the six o'clock closing time. Women were excluded from the bars but not from serving as bartenders.*

Verona and Fitzroy Terrace DEMOLISHED 1966

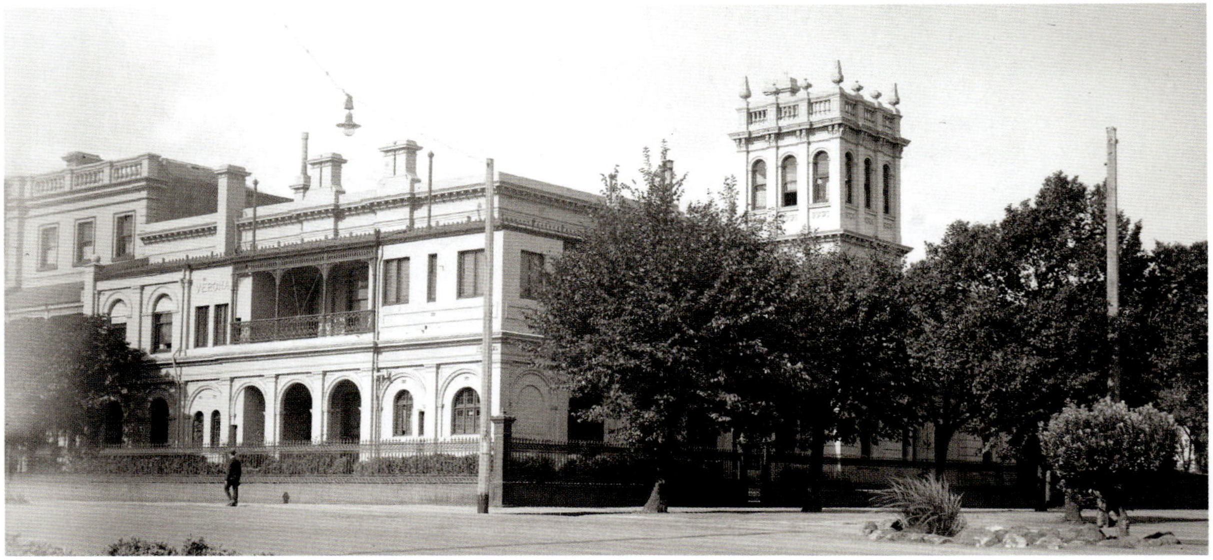

Multi-storey terraces were prevalent in a number of Melbourne suburbs dating from the 1850s. It is notable that in 1851 there were no iron railings or balconies in the city, yet by the 1870s light, intricate iron work was to appear on many of the balconies of these terraces, and in the wrought-iron fencing that protected some of them from the street. In the 1920s though, terrace housing fell out of favour and there was even a move to ban them. The problem was seen to be the small size of the inner city allotments, which were associated with an increase in slums where terrace housing existed. There was now a shift to larger block sizes and many terraces were converted into flats. During the 1950s and 1960s widespread slum reclamation programs favoured high-rise public housing and many of the complete rows of terraces were lost. Gentrification of Melbourne suburbs also saw many terraces lost. Today, there are strict overlays to preserve those remaining terraces and Melbourne has one of the best collections of Victorian terrace homes in the world.

Unfortunately, Fitzroy Terrace and Verona were not to be as lucky. Situated along Clarendon Street in East Melbourne, Fitzroy Terrace was a row of six three-storey terrace houses. Verona, a magnificent mansion with an impressive tower, occupied the block on the corner with Grey Street. In 1855 Samuel Ramsden built Fitzroy Terrace and in 1864 indicated that he wanted to build another four houses. Verona appears to have been the seventh unit of Fitzroy Terrace and remained Ramsden's family home until his death in 1877. Although part of the terrace, it was designed to stand alone. The balcony was decorated with cast iron lace of the filigree style very typical of the boom years in Melbourne. The fencing too was cast iron. Indeed, it was said at the time that Melbourne had more decorative cast iron than any other city in the world. But by the 1950s the formerly grand terraces of Fitzroy Terrace were in need of repair. Many of the verandas had been filled in to provide extra accommodation and this further detracted from their appearance. Renovation was not seen as an option and Victorian architecture had lost its popularity as people sought more modern residences. The houses were all demolished in 1966 and replaced by the Mercy Hospital for Women, which has now been converted to apartments. The name of this gracious mansion is at least retained in Verona Lane, East Melbourne, which is home to Mercy Place, a residential aged care facility.

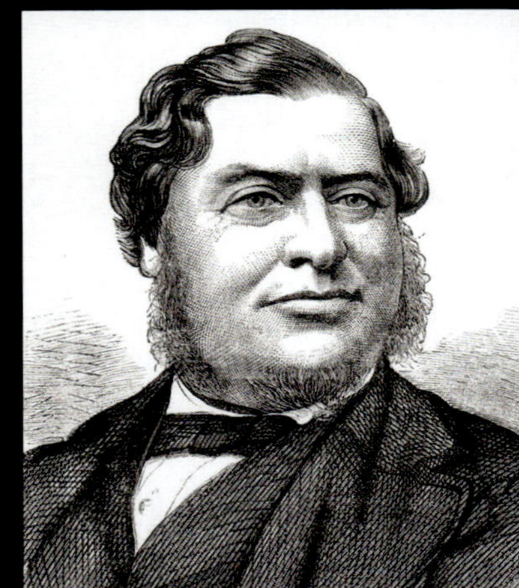

SAMUEL RAMSDEN

Samuel Ramsden arrived in Victoria in the early 1840s as an assisted migrant. He came with his bride with the aim of making his fortune. At the time of building Fitzroy Terrace and Verona, Samuel Ramsden was a flour miller and his fortune was to be built on milling. He began a partnership in the 1850s with David Aitken and together they developed the Carlton Flour Mill. The partnership lasted until 1857 when Ramsden became sole owner. In the same year he purchased Thomas Kenny's paper making machinery, gained a government grant of land on the south bank of the Yarra near Flinders Street Station and opened the Melbourne Paper Mill, which, merging with others, eventually became the Australian Paper Mills Co. Ltd. The family remained at Verona until his death in 1877.

ABOVE LEFT *Verona, seen here in the early 1900s, was the seventh unit of Fitzroy Terrace in Clarendon Street.*

RIGHT *An 1880s view of Verona on the northeast corner of Clarendon and Gipps Street, East Melbourne.*

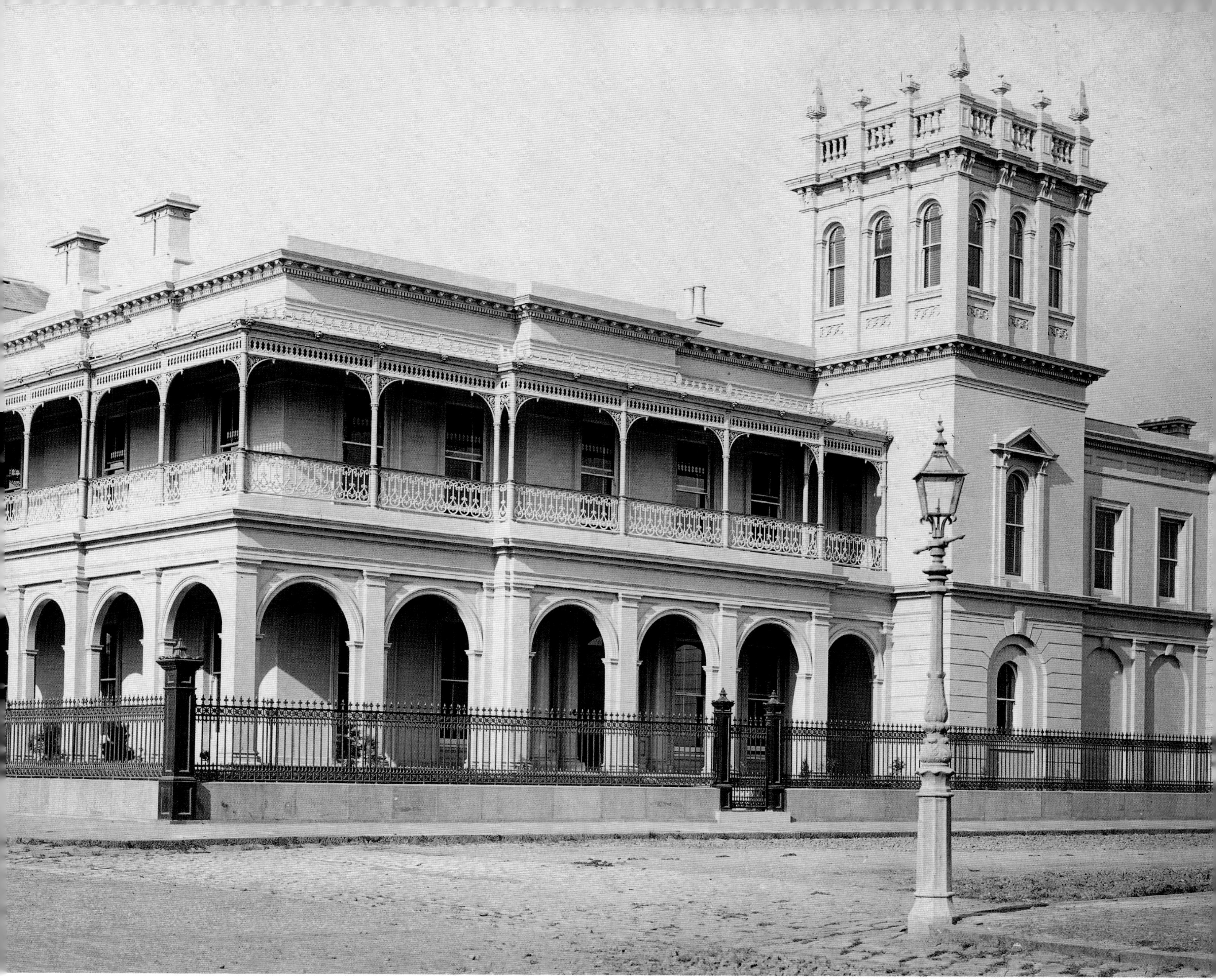

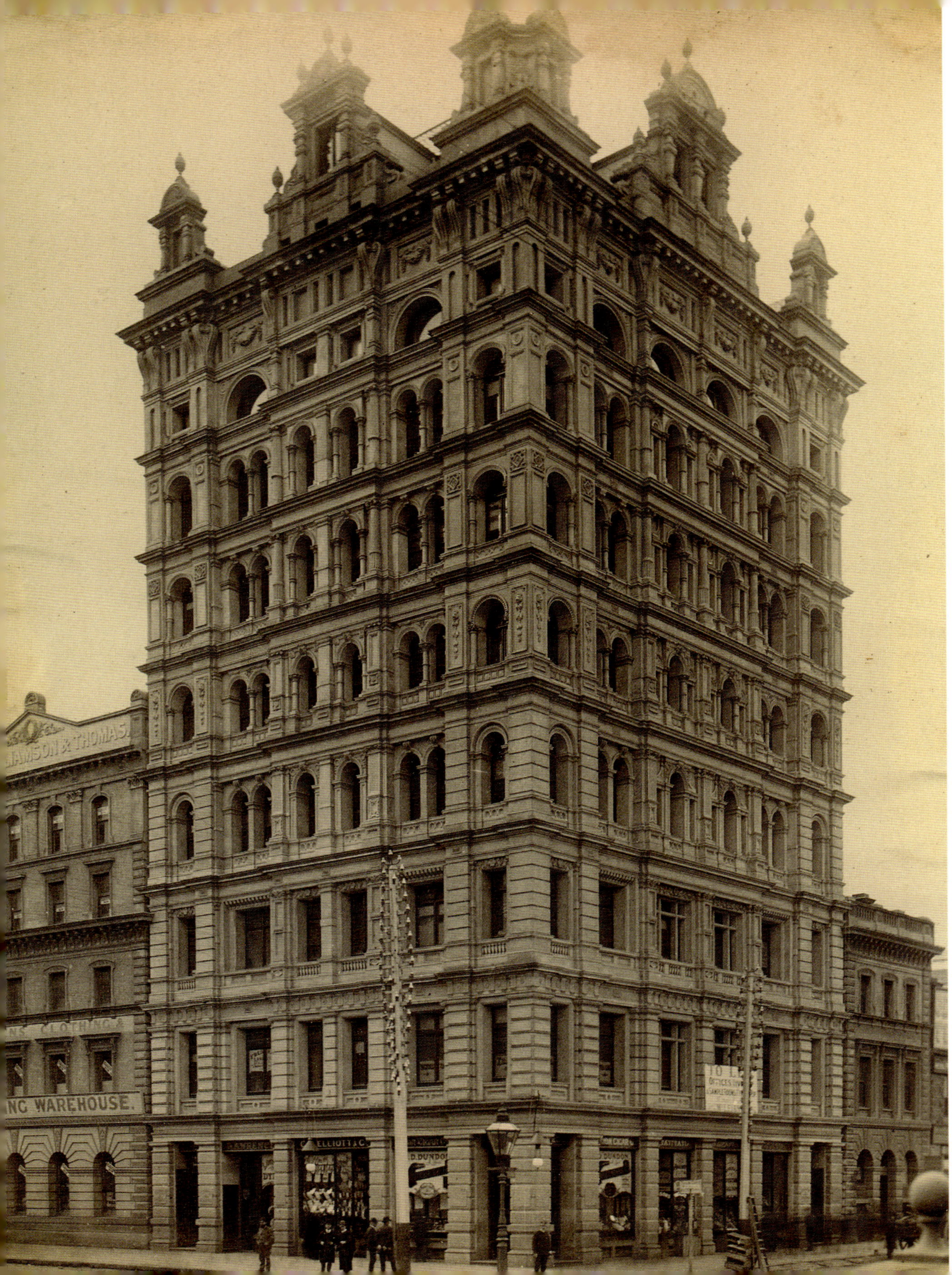

Fink's Building

DEMOLISHED 1967

The building at 276 Flinders Street was constructed for Benjamin Josman Fink, a prominent financier, politician, land speculator and developer during the boom years of the 1880s. The Fink's Building was designed by architects Twentyman & Askew, who also designed the Block Arcade. This building, constructed in 1888, became a landmark building not only for its Mannerist design with its complex facade and picturesque roofline but because at 10 storeys it was almost as tall as the 12-storey Australian Building, the tallest building in Melbourne at the time. It was built for commercial use at a time of extraordinary growth and optimism. Unfortunately, it was engulfed by the Great Fire of 1897 that had started in the nearby department store of Craig, Williamson and Thomas. This conflagration burnt almost an entire block of city buildings. The wonderful Renaissance facade of Fink's Building was still intact and the building was rebuilt but finally demolished in 1967.

Benjamin Josman Fink was born in Guernsey in the Channel Islands and came with his parents and siblings to Melbourne in 1861. In 1865 he started work as a clerk in the Wallach Brothers Elizabeth Street furniture emporium and by 1874 he was a part owner in the business. By the 1880s he not only owned this store but two others and had investments in gold, coalmines and in pastoral property. He was a hardworking, astute businessman and he expanded his interests to include the City of Melbourne Bank, which became the biggest buyer of gold in the colony. He borrowed heavily from this bank and subsequently lost most of it when land prices plummeted. His financial affairs were deliberately complicated and almost impossible to unravel. But he was not alone. There were many Melburnians of comparable education and social class who had similar stories.

In 1884 his purchase of the furniture store W. H. Locke meant that he had a monopoly on the supply of fine furniture. He formed the Mercantile Finance Company that became one of the most

LEFT *The Fink's Building was remarkable, not just for its complex facade and roofline but because it was almost as tall as the Australian Building.*

important Land Boom companies. By 1888 he had built Fink's Building, on the corner of Flinders and Elizabeth Streets, the Block Arcade, rebuilt Georges department store and bought Cole's Book Arcade. His land on which the Stock Exchange was built made him a profit of £55,000.

When the building boom collapsed so apparently did his assets, and his investors were only able to recover one halfpenny in the pound. He left massive debts of £1,520,000 behind when he and his family left for England. He was declared insolvent in 1892 but by this time most of his assets were transferred to his wife. She was able to make this money grow by subdividing and selling her husband's land in partnership with the politician Thomas Bent.

Benjamin Josman Fink must have been a shrewd businessman but many members of the public, including his lawyer and politician brother Theodore, suffered through his actions.

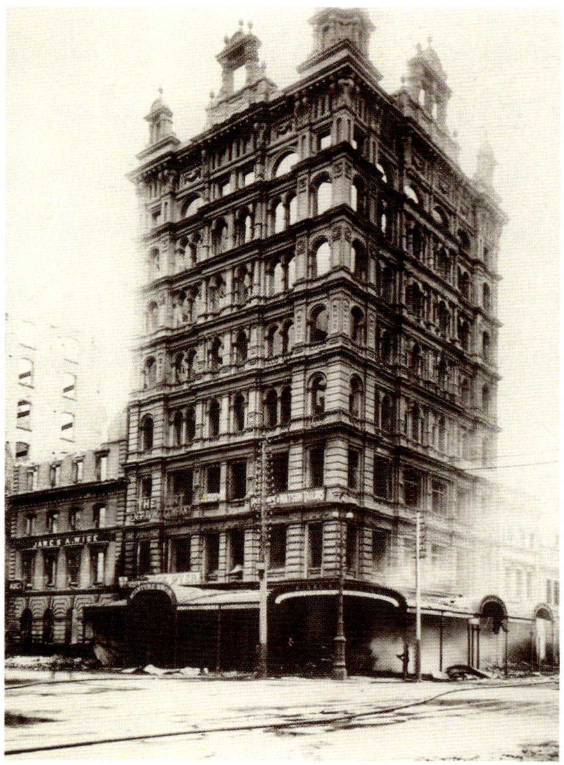

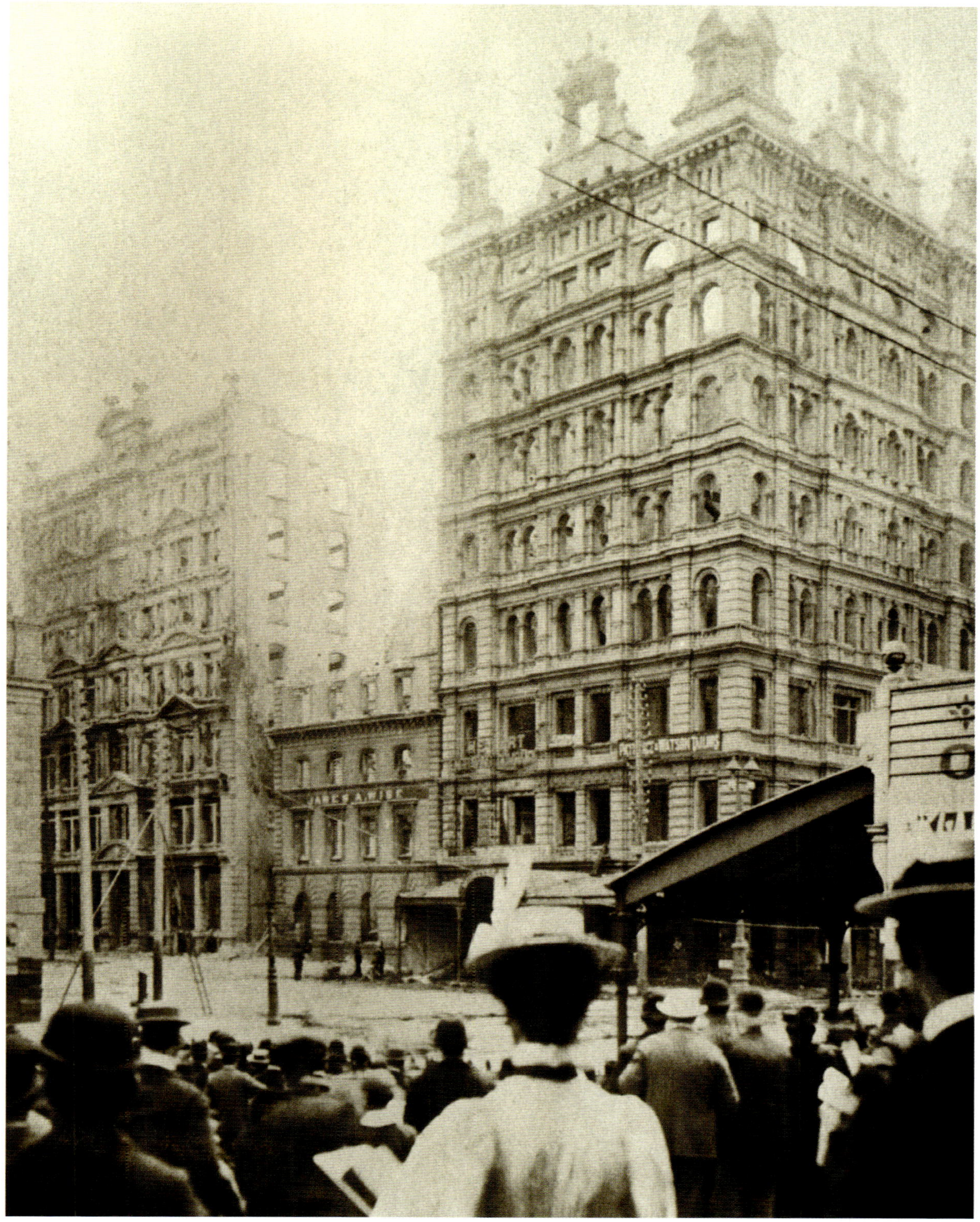

ABOVE AND RIGHT *In 1897, 50,000 people travelled into the city by train to see the damage. The fire was even reported in the* Los Angeles Herald.

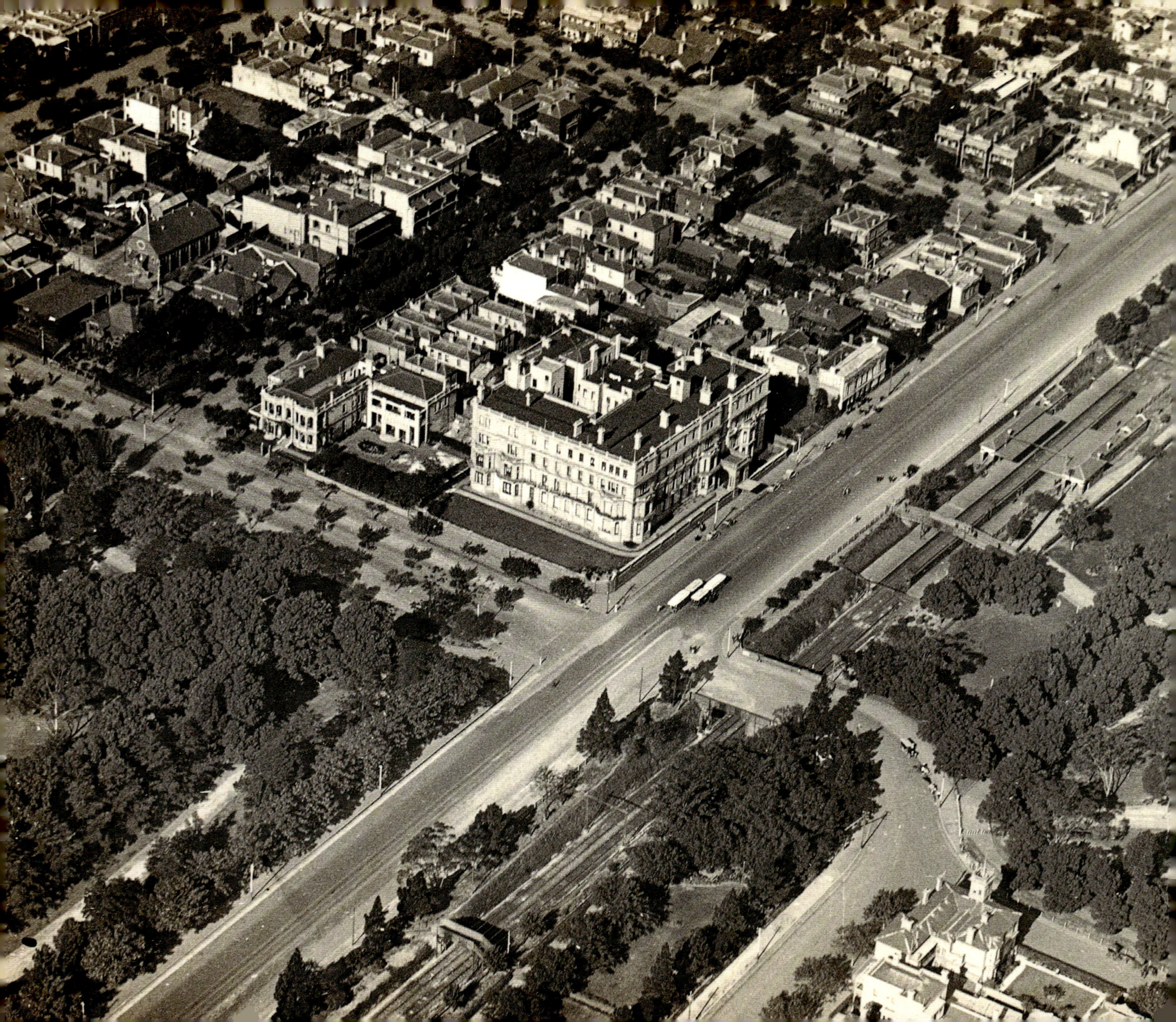

Cliveden DEMOLISHED 1968

East Melbourne was one of the city's earliest suburbs, first planned by surveyor Robert Hoddle in 1837 and settled about 1840. It became the preferred place for politicians, businessmen, professionals and government officials to live from the early 1850s. Cliveden was built here in 1887 for William Clarke, a wealthy landowner and politician whose parents had amassed great wealth. The mansion was positioned on the most valuable site in East Melbourne and was the city's largest residential building at that time. William Wardell – the architect of St Patrick's Cathedral and Government House – and W. L. Vernon were the architects.

Cliveden was built in the Italian Renaissance style on the corner of Wellington Parade and Clarendon Street, opposite the Treasury Gardens. This huge house had 28 bedrooms, five bathrooms, a billiard room, 17 servants' rooms and a ballroom that could hold 250 people. The oak panelling that lined the walls came from England, and Italian craftsmen installed the stained glass from Italy. One stained-glass window featured a plump Renaissance woman surrounded by servants and cherubs with the words "You are as welcome as the flowers in May". The total cost of the mansion was £182,000.

This mansion became the centre of Melbourne high society life and the Clarkes entertained generously and lavishly. A small dance might have as many as 150 guests. Both Clarkes had many interests and Lady Clarke is remembered for her charitable work. She supported hospitals, educational and cultural institutions, and in the hungry 1890s she fed many Richmond and Collingwood inhabitants from the kitchens at Cliveden. When Janet Clarke died in 1909, the mansion was sold to the Baillieu family for £44,000. The Baillieus added another floor in 1910 and eventually divided it into many luxurious apartments called Cliveden Mansions. The apartments had no kitchens and meals were prepared by a French chef and served in a communal dining room. It was not uncommon for large mansions to be turned into apartments or boarding houses in the 1920s, as they were very costly to maintain and repair.

By the 1960s the building had fallen into disrepair and it was no longer a desirable place to live. Apartment owners no longer wanted to share kitchens and bathrooms with other owners. In 1967 the Baillieus sold it for £444,000 and it was demolished in 1968. The interior fittings were sold off and some were later displayed in the Hilton Hotel that was built on the site.

OPPOSITE *Built on a wonderful site opposite the Treasury Gardens, Cliveden was the largest residential building in Melbourne for many years.*

BELOW AND BOTTOM *The exterior of Cliveden Mansions and a drawing room from one of its suites, photographed for a late 1920s real estate brochure.*

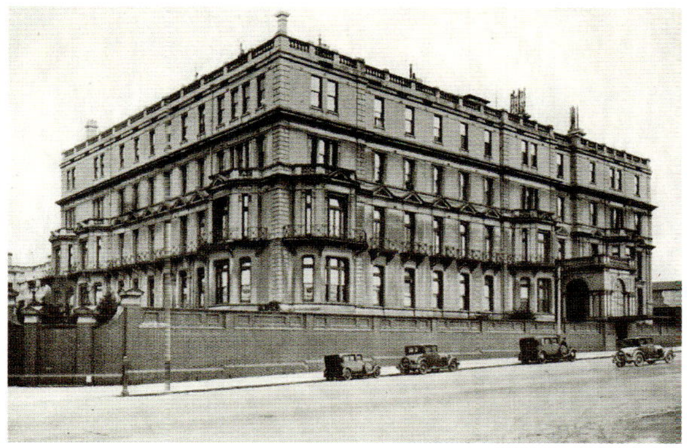

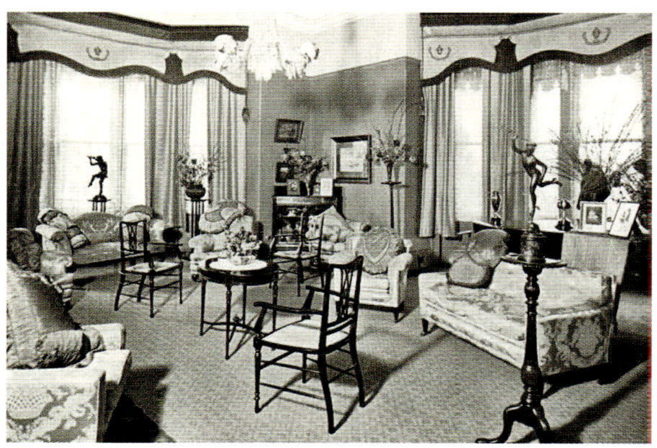

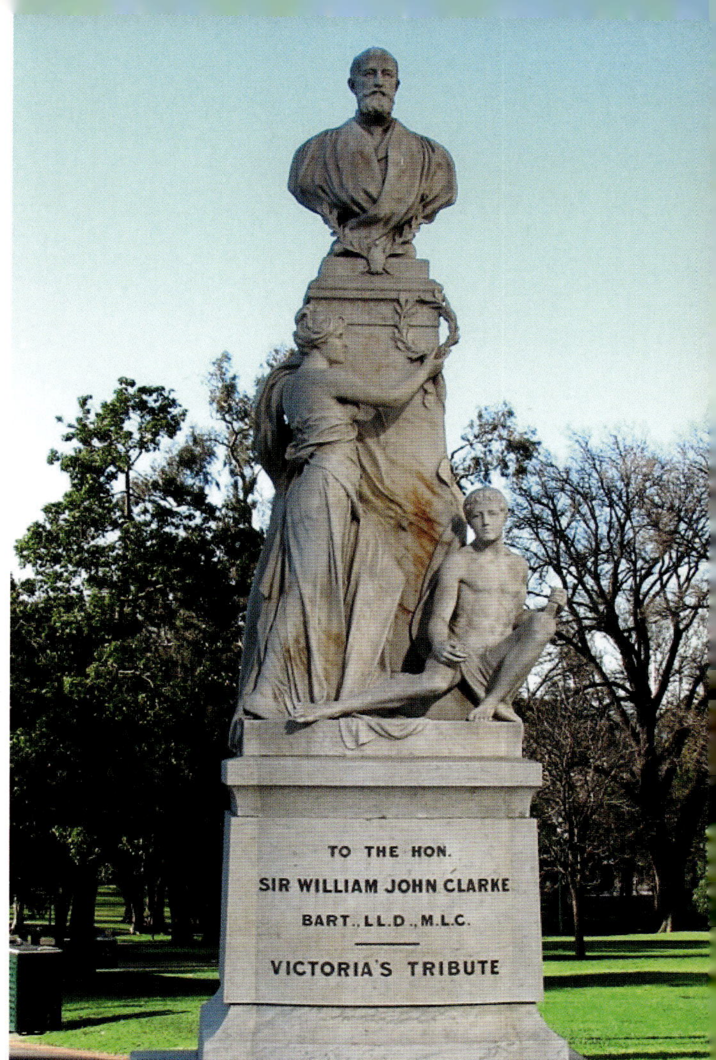

SIR WILLIAM CLARKE (1831–97)

William Clarke, the son of English migrants, took over the family's landholdings and businesses in 1860 and within 15 years he had become one of the largest landholders in Victoria. He was a landowner but also a philanthropist, a State politician, president of both the Melbourne Cricket Club and the Victorian Football Association, and a director of the Colonial Bank. When the bank collapsed in the economic depression of the 1890s, Sir William is said to have repaid the depositors out of his own pocket. He was made a baronet, the first Australian to receive this honour, in recognition of his community work and generosity.

Palais de Danse, St. Kilda DESTROYED BY FIRE 1968

The people of Melbourne have always been attracted to the seaside and the large bayside area has been accessible to all. Fortunately, the St. Kilda beachfront is Crown land and, in 1906, the St. Kilda Council decided to use this land for the entertainment and amusement of the people.

The first structures built for this purpose were a merry-go-round, the Luna Park funfair and the large timber Palais de Danse, built by the Americans Leon and Herman Phillips in 1913. In 1915 this became Palais Pictures. It was eventually dismantled in 1919 and set up next door, and it was this building that the American architects Walter Burley Griffin and his wife Marion Mahoney extensively renovated in 1925 as another incarnation of the dance hall.

In 1926, just as the Griffins were completing their work for a new entrance, there was a fire, which destroyed some of their work. The artist Sidney Nolan remembered the fire and "that people climbed up the white girders of the Luna Park funfair to get a bird's eye view of the fire." The Phillips brothers decided to build a much bigger building next door, so a fourth Palais Pictures was designed by Henry E. White, the theatre architect who had also designed the interiors of the Princess, the Athenaeum and the Palace theatres in Central Melbourne. This grand building is the Palais Theatre we see today. The Palais de Danse fire damage was repaired and once more it became a popular dance hall. Dance halls were considered to be refined entertainment. They were lavishly decorated, provided lemonade and ice creams and, although more expensive to enter than some other entertainment establishments, attracted enormous crowds. Excellent dance bands like Ern Pettifer and the Rhythm Boys drew large crowds. The Palais de Danse was considered to be the place to go above all other dance halls, and it had a wonderful dance floor. Many patrons and musician who had been to the Palais Pictures would move on to the Palais de Danse to complete their evening. The Australian Dancing Competitions were generally held in the Palais de Danse.

During World War II the Palais de Danse was frequented by large numbers of American GIs, bringing with them the latest American music and dance practices. Long after they had departed, their influence lived on in square dancing, the dirndl skirts and blouses of the women, the check shirts and string ties of the men, and the hit songs. Between 1944 and 1945 the Palais de Danse was requisitioned and became a Post Office, and hobnail boots and postal carts ruined the beautiful floors. The Palais never quite recovered from this period and did not reopen as a dance venue until 1953. The Phillips brothers spent a lot of money repairing the dance hall and then the 1956 Olympic Games came to Melbourne and television was introduced. People stayed home, not just to watch the televised Games but also to soak up the new form of entertainment. Many venues, including cinemas and dance halls, were adversely affected and struggled to survive.

Then the disastrous fire of 27 December 1968 occurred. It started in the ceiling of the kitchen and quickly engulfed the timber and stone building. Despite the efforts of over a hundred firemen, within half an hour the Palais de Danse was gutted and collapsed. Four years after the fire, in 1972, the Palace Nightclub was built on the site of the Palais de Danse, continuing the live music tradition until it too closed, was burnt down and then demolished in 2007.

RIGHT *The Palais de Danse was considered to be the best dance hall in Melbourne.*

BELOW LEFT *The Palais de Danse with the Palais Pictures and Luna Park in the distance, circa 1920.*

BELOW *The interior was modern in style with geometric design elements dominating. Umbrella-like branches above vertically patterned columns supported the arched ceiling. This large building seated as many as 2,870 people. The ceiling of stars was up-lit and many remember the wonderful atmosphere this created. St. Kilda can be very hot in summer and the louvred walls of the Palais could be opened to let in the sea breeze.*

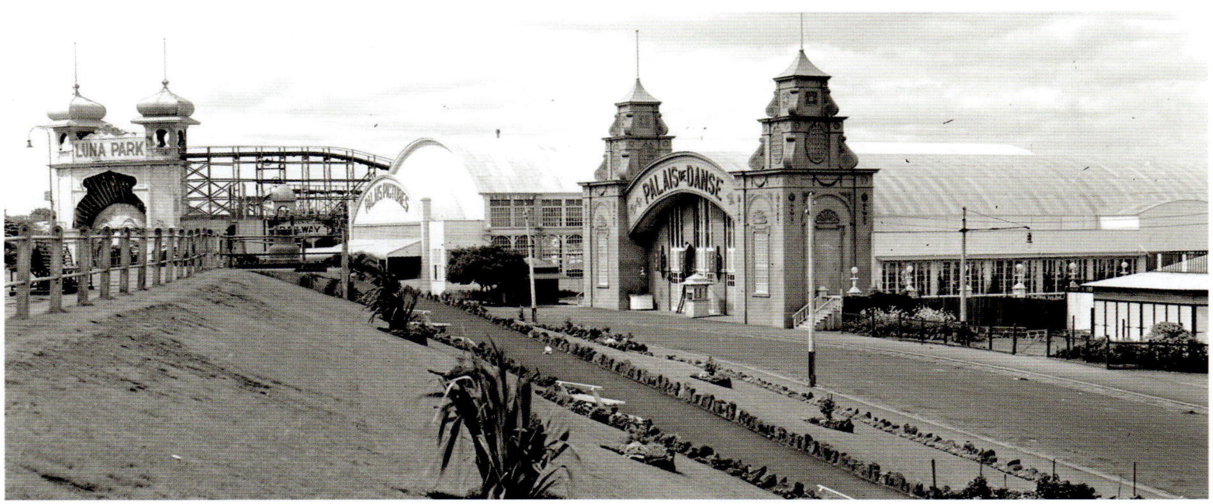

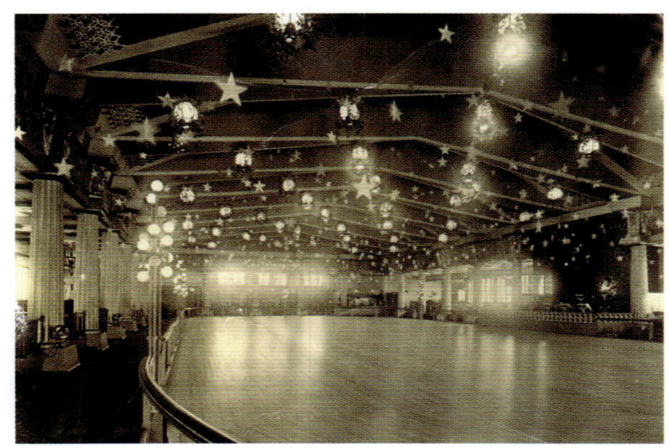

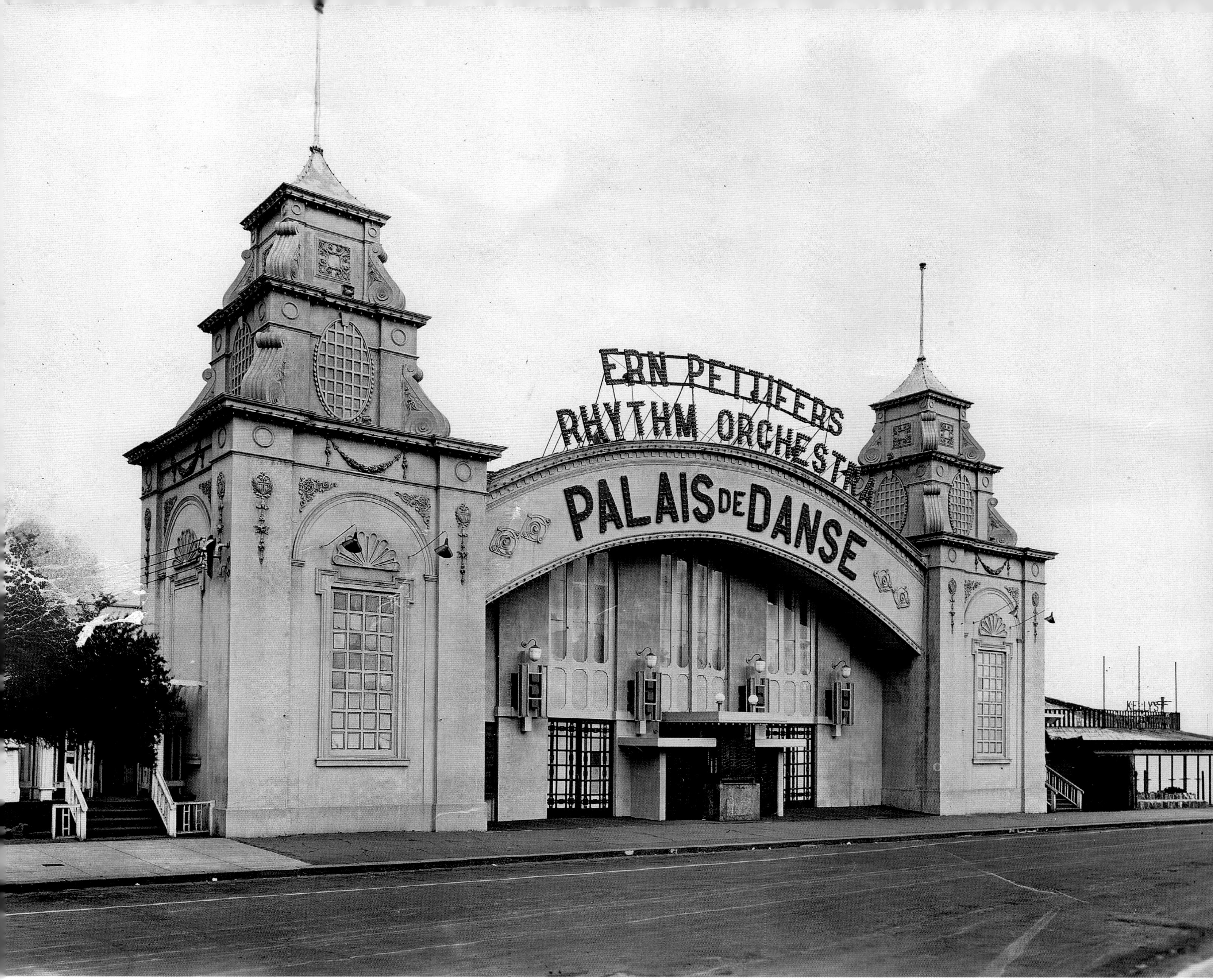
ERN PETTIFERS
RHYTHM ORCHESTRA
PALAIS DE DANSE

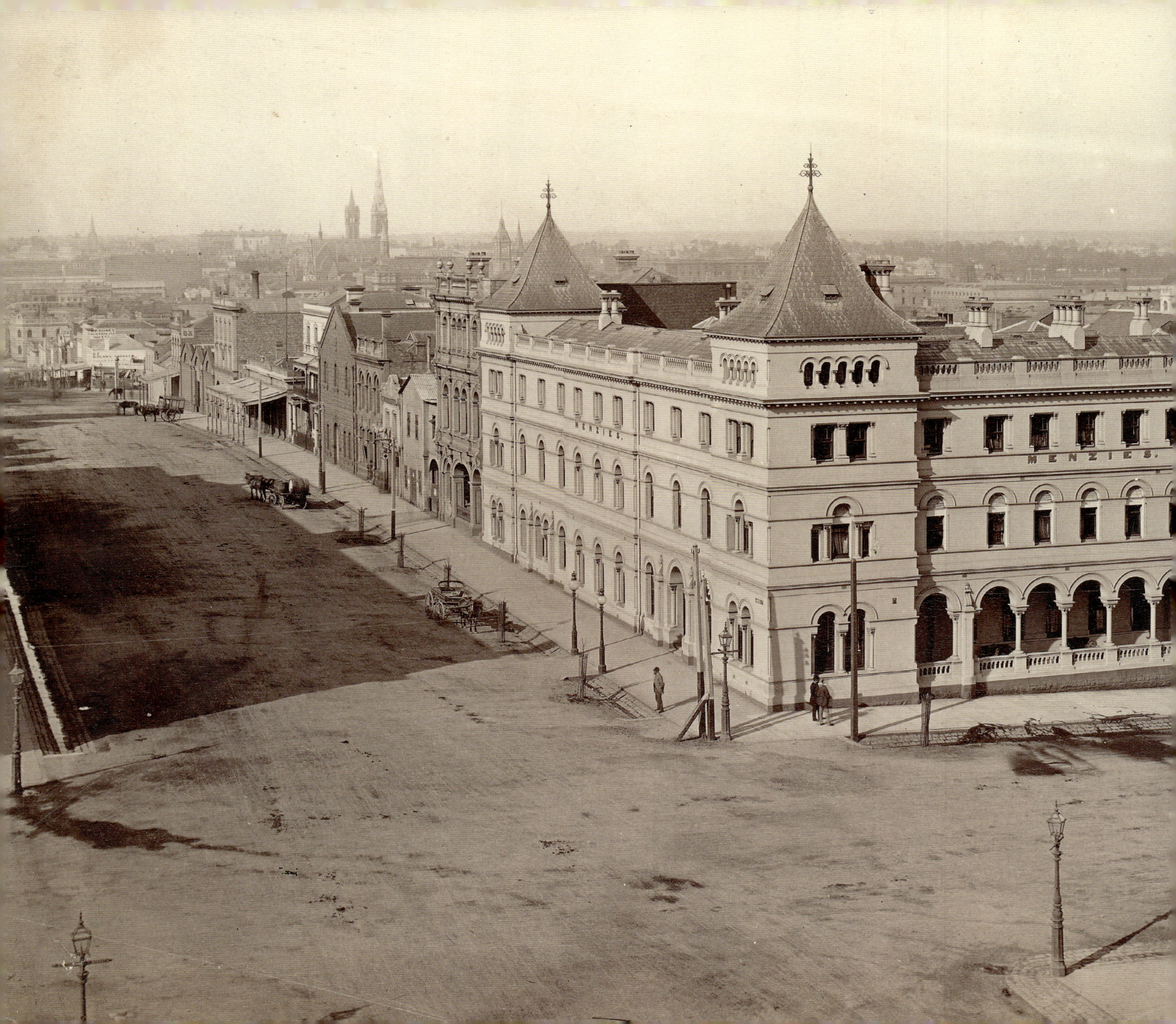
MENZIES.
MENZIES.

Menzies Hotel DEMOLISHED 1969

When English author Anthony Trollope visited the Menzies Hotel in 1872, he said that he had never stayed "at a better inn in any part of the world". The Menzies was the first of Melbourne's grand hotels and one of its best. Archibald and Catherine Menzies arrived in Victoria in 1852 and in 1853 they opened a boarding house on La Trobe Street that became known as the Menzies Family Hotel. Waiters wore the Menzies' clan tartan and service and comfort of the guests was very important. Following their success, both on the goldfields and with their current hotel, the Menzies purchased land at the corner of Bourke and Williams Street to build a new hotel. It was designed by Reed and Barnes with construction by David Mitchell (father of singer Dame Nellie Melba) at a cost of £32,000. Trees felled on the site were used in its construction. The site was claimed to be on the highest ground in Melbourne, close to the business centre but far enough away to ensure the quietness of the country. While Archibald Menzies had the head for business, it was his wife Catherine who set the standard of hospitality that was to last for a century.

The new building was three storeys high with 25 suites on the ground floor and 25 bedrooms above. The opening of the hotel coincided with the visit of the Duke of Edinburgh. When not encouraging return visits from royalty, the Menzies catered to Victoria's wealthy landed families and international visitors such as Mark Twain, Herbert Hoover, Noel Coward, Anna Pavlova and Alexander Graham Bell. It became a tradition for Melbourne society to lunch at the Menzies on the day the English mail was delivered. Although other grand hotels were to be built, the Menzies was considered to be one of the finest and it was the only hotel south of the equator permitted to use the Royal crest on its napery. Two floors and a corner tower were added in 1896, with telephones, electric lights and a lift installed. In 1924 the dining room was added, which coincided with the Menzies becoming a publicly listed company. In 1936 the last of the Menzies' family interests were bought out, first by Norman Bede Rydge and afterwards by the Federal Hotels Ltd (later the Federal Pacific Hotels Group), who reintroduced top-hatted doormen.

In 1942, General Douglas MacArthur commandeered the top floor of the Menzies as the headquarters of the Allied Pacific forces. After the war, changes were made in an attempt to attract overseas visitors. But as time passed it seemed that the Menzies was too staid for the "jet setters" and too changed for its traditional clientele. The latter preferred the Windsor, which had refused to embrace the changes of the 1960s. Ironically, the Windsor was the only grand hotel to survive the wrecker's ball. In 1967 Federal Hotels placed the Menzies, which stood on very valuable land, up for sale. In 1968 it was announced that it would be demolished, and in 1969 the contents were auctioned off in the hotel's Chandelier Room. The building was demolished in 1969 to make way for BHP Plaza.

OPPOSITE *An elevated 1870s view of the Menzies Hotel.*

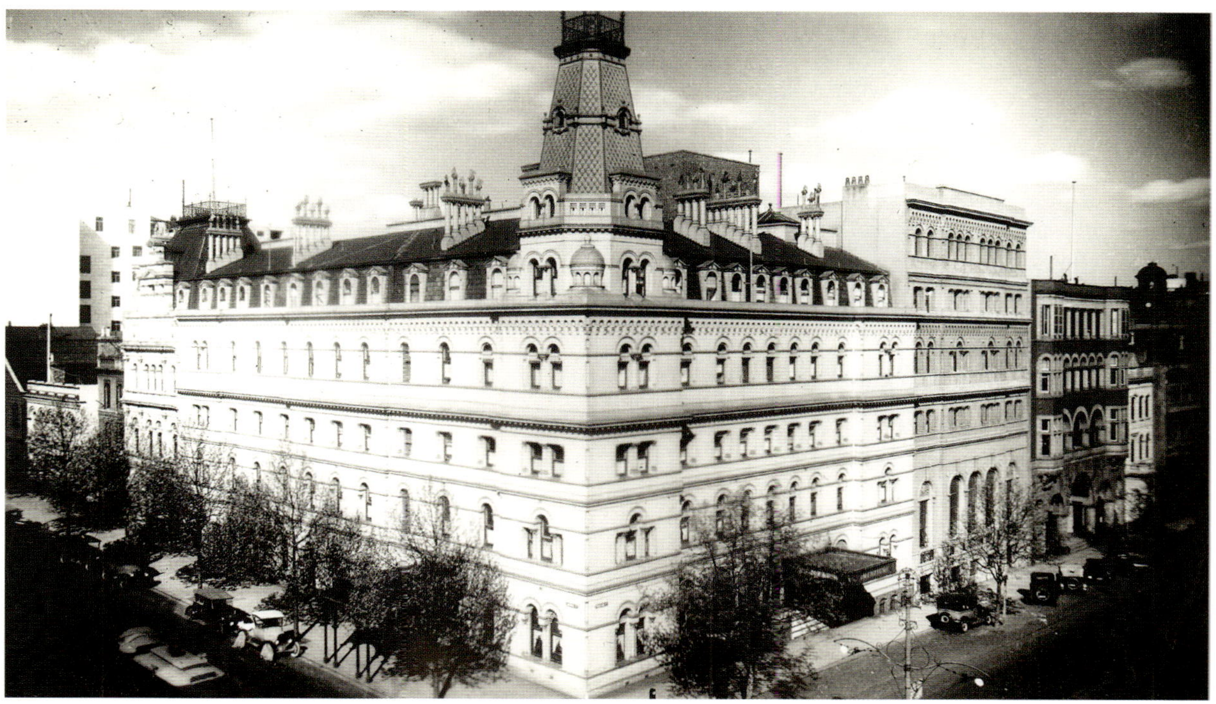

LEFT *The Menzies Hotel in the mid-1930s, dominating the corner of Bourke and William Streets. Two extra floors and a tower had been added in 1896.*

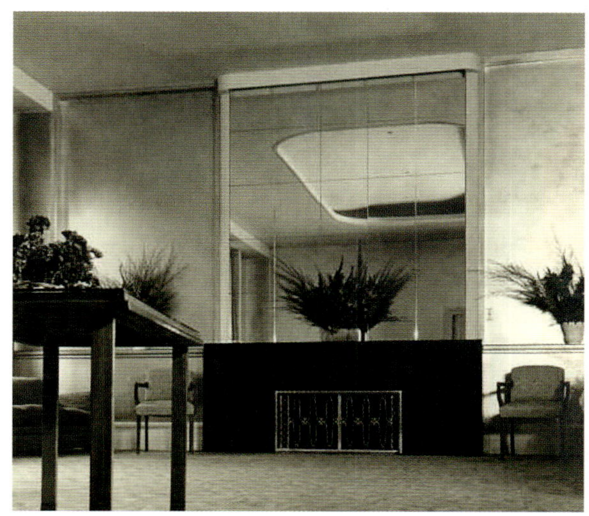

BELOW *The reception room at the hotel in the late 1930s.*

Opera House / Tivoli Theatre

DEMOLISHED 1969

For 65 years, the Tivoli (locally known as the "Tiv") was the home of vaudeville in Melbourne. The site of the theatre was historically significant though as it began life as a timber yard and stables in the mid-19th century. In 1866, a hall built over the top of the stables became known as the Varieties and it was here that the can-can was first performed in Australia.

Despite having a capacity of over 2,000 people the Varieties was poorly ventilated. In 1872 a name change occurred, though not much else and the theatre became the Prince of Wales Opera House. The Opera House produced a variety of popular entertainments in order to entertain the diverse theatre audiences in Melbourne. Harry Rickards, who toured as a singer and comedian at the Opera House in its early days, was to lease the Opera House in 1894. The first screening of motion pictures in Australia occurred in 1896 when Rickards engaged the American illusionist Carl Hertz to project his "Cinematographe".

By 1897 the building was condemned as unhealthy and dangerous and in 1899 it closed. Harry Rickards was then able to negotiate a 50-year lease in return for spending £35,000 on rebuilding. The new Opera House designed by William Pitt was made of red brick with a seating capacity of between 1,500 to 2,000 people. It had a three-level auditorium comprising a dress circle and gallery tier. Some of the columns that supported these levels hampered the vision of patrons in certain seats. The stage was large with a fly-tower and a proscenium etched with gold and silver leaf. The interior was lit by electricity, and ventilated through a heavily ornamented sliding shutter in the roof. The facade was an interesting amalgam of styles and featured Moorish arches and filigree cast-iron balconies. Access was from Bourke Street through wide and decorated corridors that opened onto twin marble staircases leading to the next level. The theatre opened in 1901 with the British music hall performer Marie Lloyd. Later stars were Houdini, Chico Marx and W. C. Fields.

In 1912, after Rickards sold the Opera House to Hugh D. McIntosh, it was renamed the Tivoli to reflect the fact that the theatre was part of the "Tivoli circuit" of venues throughout Australia. From the 1930s elaborate revues became the standard fare at the Tivoli. At Christmas there were pantomimes and on occasions musicals. One of the local favourites was Roy "Mo" Rene. During World War II the Tivoli did much to maintain the spirits of the population. From 1946 many of the stars and acts were from overseas: Shirley Bassey, Nelson Eddy and the Folies Bergère being some of them. In 1956 the theatre's auditorium was rebuilt but live entertainment was no longer as popular. Jimmy Edwards starred in the theatre's final show in April 1966. He told the audience, "I don't relish the distinction of being the man who closed the Tiv. Music hall's dead in Britain. Now this one's dead, there's nowhere to go. I'll either become a character comedian or a pauper." The "Tiv" became a cinema, but its interior was destroyed by fire in 1967. It was later used as a flea market but was sold for redevelopment in 1969. A tall office block, Tivoli Court, replaced it in 1970.

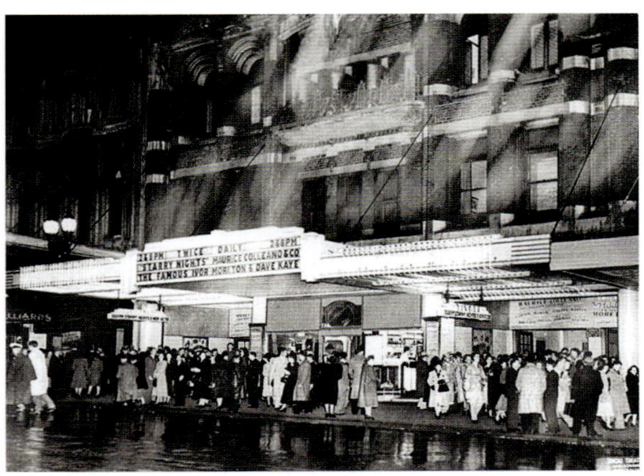

LEFT *Crowds queue at the "Tiv" in 1949 to see the musical* Starry Nights.

OPPOSITE *The building opened as the Opera House on 18 May 1901; it was renamed the Tivoli in 1912.*

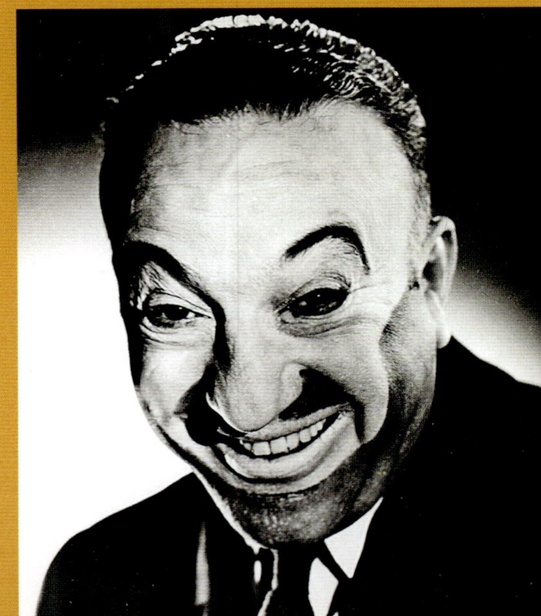

ROY RENE (1891–1954)

As Mo McCackie, Roy Rene was one of the most well-known and successful Australian comedians of the 20th century. Some of his expressions, such as "Strike me lucky!" and "Cop this, young Harry!" have become part of Australian language. In 1916 he teamed up with comedian Nat Phillips ("Stiffy"). They became the famous Stiffy and Mo, renowned for their larrikin comedy until they finally split in 1928. Mo was to appear in many of the theatres throughout Australia and the letters "MO" outside a theatre guaranteed the success of the show. During World War II he followed the Tivoli circuit, alternating between Melbourne and Sydney. Since 1975, the Mo Awards have been presented annually for excellence in live performance.

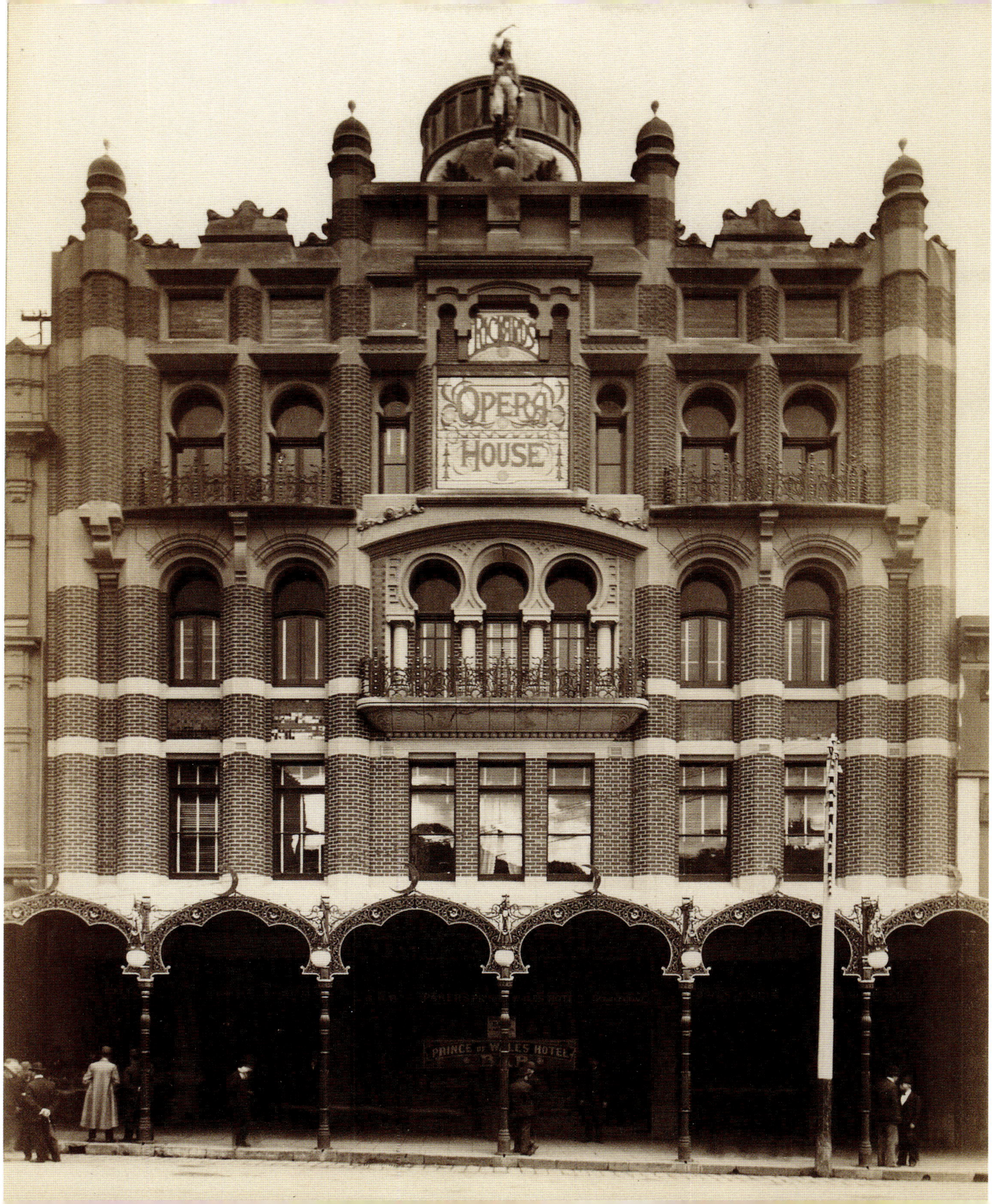
RICHARDS
OPERA HOUSE
PRINCE OF WALES HOTEL

Craig, Williamson, and Thomas DEMOLISHED 1969–70

Craig, Williamson, and Thomas was a very large commercial building strategically located in Elizabeth Street, very near the Flinders Street Railway Station. Wood engravings of 1883 show Craig, Williamson, and Thomas occupying several different premises along Elizabeth Street. The work rooms were quite separate from the sales areas and people were being served from behind long counters, quite different from what we know today.

The Craig, Williamson, and Thomas store was one of Melbourne's most popular shopping destinations in the second half of the 19th century. They described themselves as "importers and manufacturers, carpet and furniture warehousemen" that sold a huge variety of "drapery and napery, woollens, clothing, mantles, costumes, boxed robes, silks, satins, plushes, velvet and velveteens." Here gentlemen could buy their hats, tweeds, ulsters, portmanteaus, railway rugs, collars and Saratoga trunks. A tin trunk for storing or transporting such goods was also available. All floors of the store could be accessed by a hydraulic lift "comfortably seated and cushioned for passenger traffic".

By the 1880s the owners of the business were wealthy men. William Craig bought "Linda", a mansion in Camberwell. Craig died in 1899 and in 1928 the mansion became the Presbyterian Babies' Home. The firm's growing success was also reflected in the plans for a new building, an elegant structure of seven storeys, classical in style with decorated lintels and long windows. Then came a disastrous fire in 1897, so large that it was reported in newspapers overseas.

On the morning of 22 November 1897 a huge fire consumed almost an entire city block. The fire started in the Craig, Williamson building and wasn't discovered until 1 a.m., by which time the "building presented the appearance of one vast pyramid of fire". Many of the smaller premises were reduced to ashes and the larger Fink's Building and the cavernous Sargood warehouse were also alight. The Mutual Stores Building had a miraculous escape while all the surrounding buildings were completely destroyed; "an island in a sea of desolation" was the description in *The Brisbane Courier*. Closer to Swanston Street, the Port Phillip Club Hotel and Young and Jackson's Hotel escaped, the patrons of Young and Jackson's rolling the beer barrels across Swanston Street to the safety of St. Paul's Cathedral. Craig, Williamson's building was full of highly flammable goods and the Metropolitan Fire Brigade had no way of stopping it. Fortuitously, there was a change of direction in the wind, or the damage would have been much worse. The Duke of Rothesay Hotel on one side was reduced to ash, as was the vacant warehouse on the other side of Craig's. Additional danger to firemen was caused by the partial collapse of the walls of the building. Craig, Williamson's stock loss was valued at over £100,000, mostly covered by insurance, while the overall damage bill was in excess of £1,500,000. Three firemen were found in possession of three bottles of whisky and fined three pounds each by the magistrate.

After the fire, the original facade was extended on both sides, and over the site of the former Duke of Rothesay Hotel. The new Craig, Williamson's building had a longer terrace with verandas over the footpath, extending right to the street. Later, the graceful verandas with their arched roofs and wrought-iron posts were removed and replaced with a straightened and cantilevered veranda.

In 1937 the building was put up for sale, but it was not until 1946 that it was successfully sold to the Federal Government for £370,000. The Commonwealth Bank of Australia opened a branch there and in 1969–1970 demolished what had once been "the largest retailer in Australia".

RIGHT *The massive Craig, Williamson, and Thomas warehouses and drapery store.*

BELOW *Elizabeth Street, near Flinders Street, showing the arched verandas of the Craig, Williamson building and the tall Australian building on the left in 1900.*

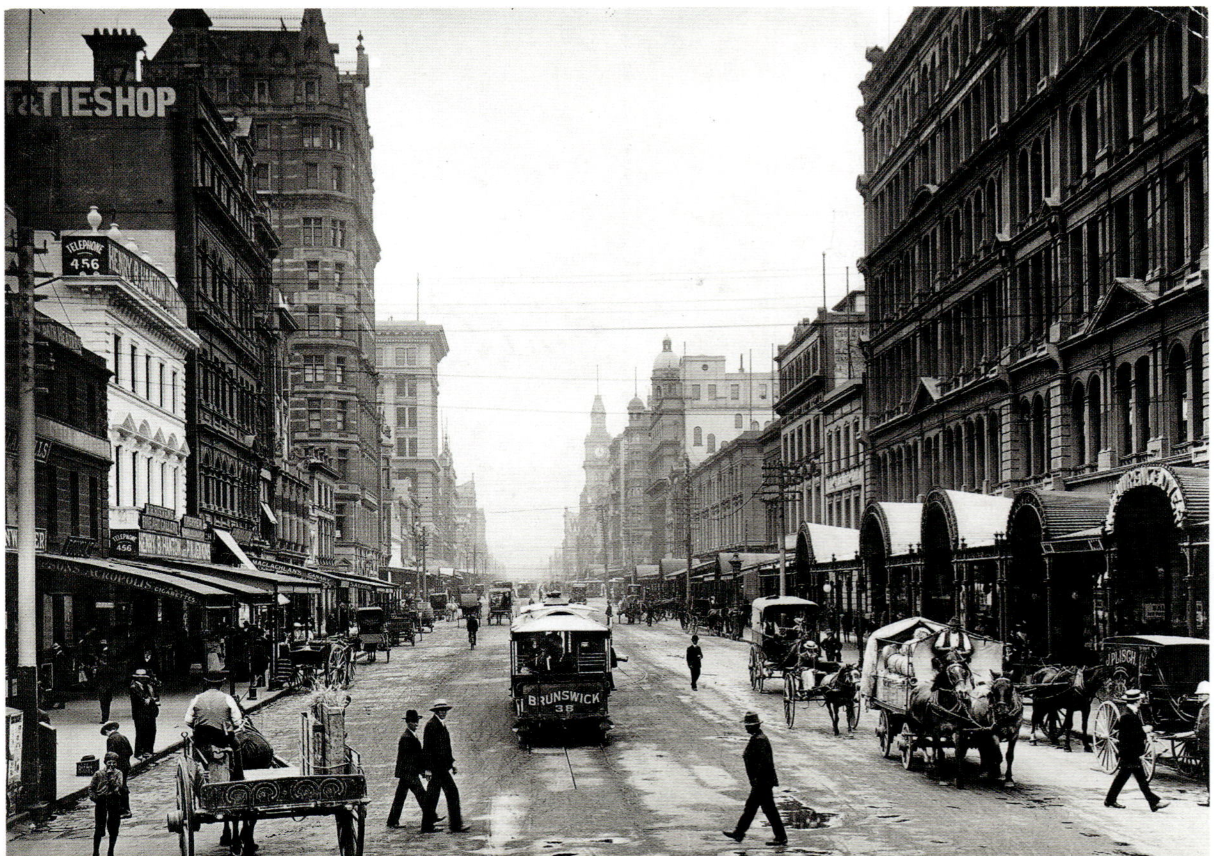

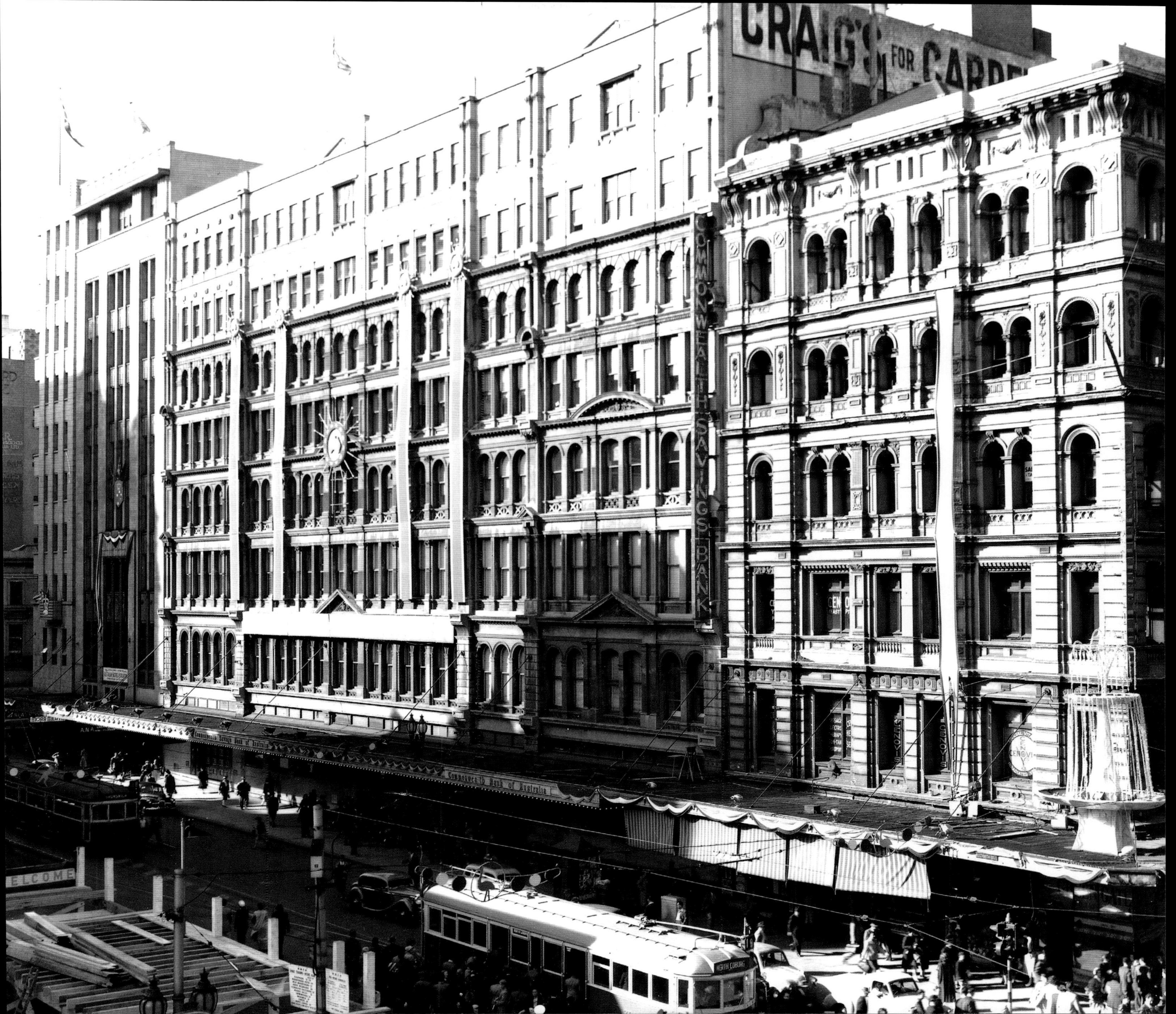
CRAIG'S FOR CARPE
COMMONWEALTH SAVINGS BANK
Commonwealth Bank of Australia
NORTH COBURG

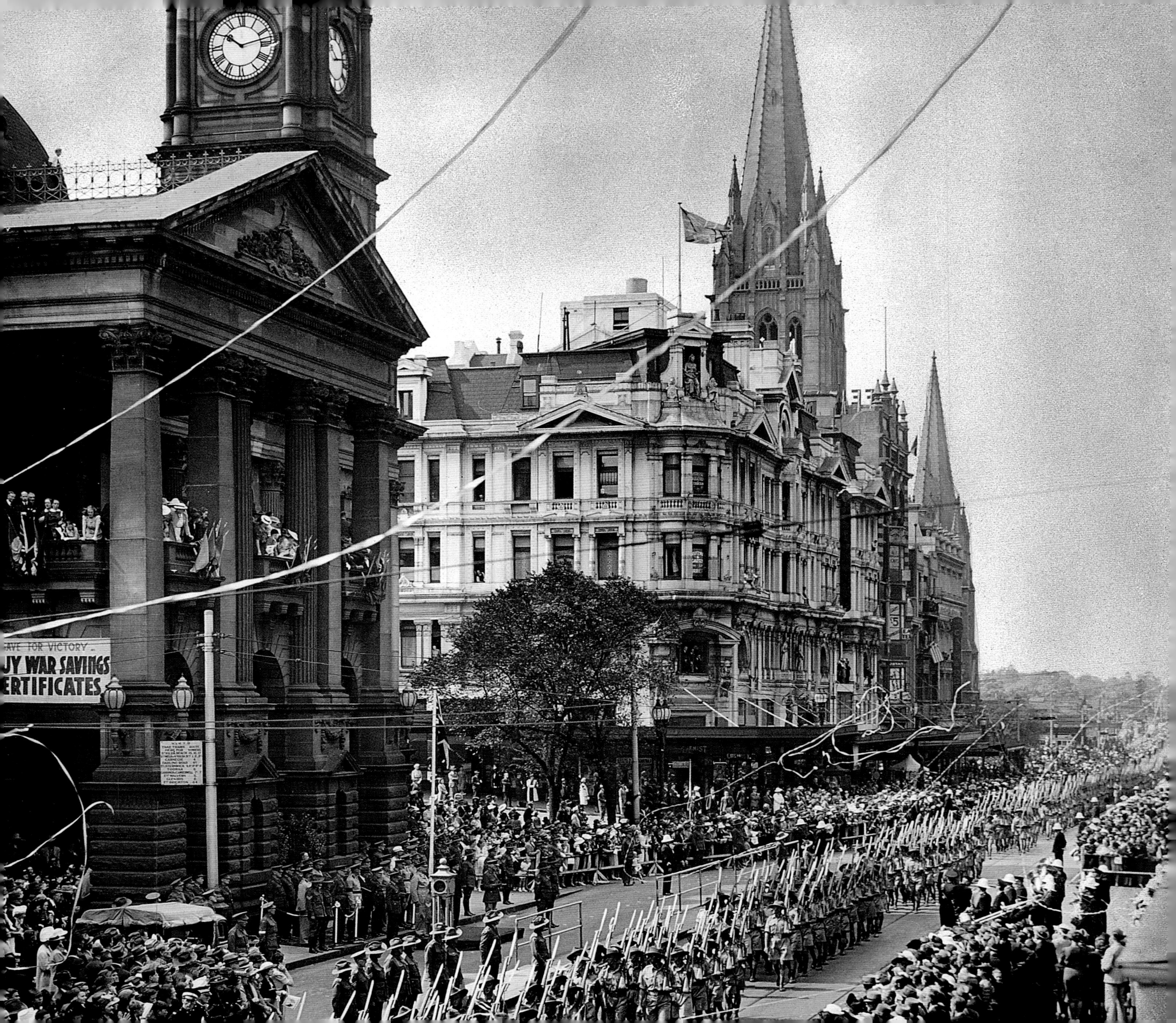
UY WAR SAVINGS
ERTIFICATES

Victoria Building and Queens Walk Arcade

DEMOLISHED LATE 1960s TO EARLY 1970s

The Victoria Building was designed by the architect David Wormal and built in 1888 by the Freehold Investment and Banking Company – one of the many land banks built during the boom years in Melbourne. Once a landmark in Melbourne, running the length of the block on Swanston Street, the Victoria Building was a combination of the French Second Empire style with Mannerist and Baroque detail and was located on the corner of Collins and Swanston Streets. The original design featured a large corner mansard spire which was removed in the 1950s. A gilt statue of Queen Victoria sat on the corner and the building housed many high-end retail shops and offices, including the Victorian Government Tourist Bureau that occupied the corner shop from 1908 to 1940. There was also an L-shaped, glass-topped arcade known as Queens Walk.

When Melbourne was being planned, the idea was to have a number of open spaces around the business district. Partly to deter a spirit of democracy that seemed to arise when there were public spaces available, and to maximise land sale revenue, these plans were ignored and large buildings filled most of the available spaces. Proposals for a city square began in the 1920s but largely went unheeded or were bogged down in the arguments about the various locations suggested. It wasn't until the 1960s that the idea of a city square firmed and the city council determined to find a site. A site opposite the Town Hall was chosen, with the idea that this central meeting place would bring people back to the city to shop and would also be in harmony with the Town Hall and St. Paul's Cathedral. Unfortunately, all the buildings on the site chosen were in private hands and it took many years for the council to acquire, at no small cost, all the buildings needed to build a city square. In 1965 the Victoria Building became part of this proposed development site and, with the City Club hotel, was bought in 1966 when they came on the market. Demolition of the area began in the late 1960s. In the next few years, union bans, protests and rising costs dogged the plans for Melbourne's city square but gradually familiar landmarks, alleyways and shops were removed. Eventually the square was emptied, but it wasn't until 28 May 1980 that it was opened as Melbourne's city square. The square was never a complete success with Melburnians and in the late 1990s half of the site was sold for a new city hotel.

LEFT *Australian soldiers marching past the Victoria Building during World War II. The Town Hall is in the foreground.*

BELOW *The Cavalier Tea Rooms in Queens Walk Arcade.*

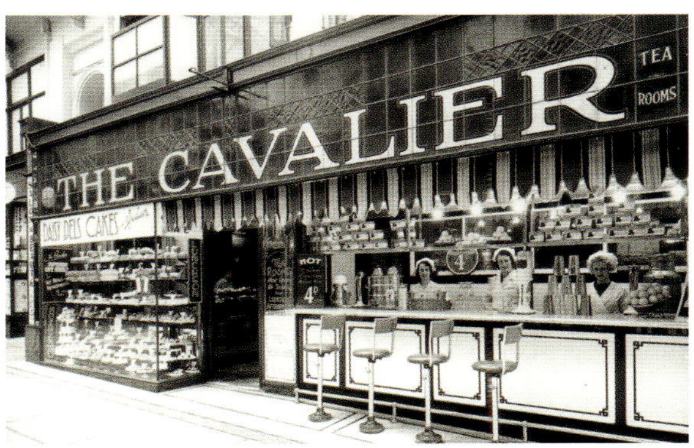

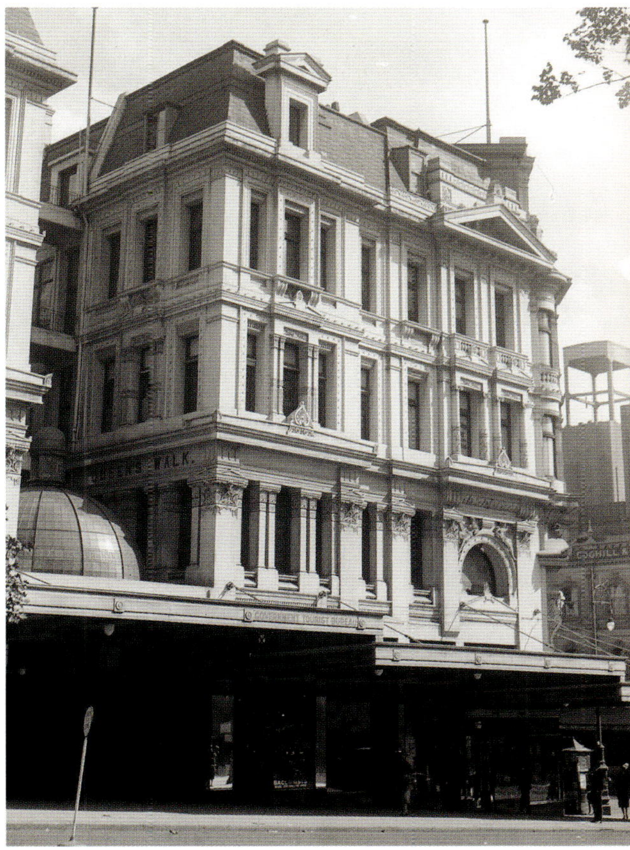

QUEENS WALK ARCADE

Queens Walk Arcade was constructed in 1889 and was a glass-roofed shopping arcade, one of a number built around this time in Victoria. It cost approximately £30,000. These arcades, which included the Victoria Arcade in Lonsdale Street, demonstrated the modernity of Victoria as they followed styles found in Europe. Queens Walk Arcade, which connected Swanston Street to Collins Street, was distinguished by the cupolas over the entrances. Despite being rather grand, in the late 1800s it faced problems of poor sanitation resulting in foul smells and was regarded as a health hazard. Numerous complaints were received by the City of Melbourne's Inspector of Nuisances. Once these were overcome, the Queens Walk Arcade became home to important Melbourne institutions such as the Savage Club until 1925, menswear specialist Henry Bucks in the 1950s and the Cavalier Tea Rooms. Queens Walk Arcade was purchased by the Melbourne City Council in the 1960s and demolished in the early 1970s.

State Savings Bank **DEMOLISHED EARLY 1970s**

The Port Phillip Savings Bank opened in 1842 and when the colony of Victoria came into being in the early 1850s it was proposed that it should be renamed the Savings Bank of Victoria. Each branch of the Savings Bank was to operate as a separate institution and it wasn't until 1896 that the unifying Savings Bank Act came into effect. In 1897 the Post Office Savings Bank merged with the Savings Bank and in 1912 the various savings banks merged by legislation and became the State Savings Bank (SSB).

The State Savings Bank gradually grew to become the major bank in Victoria, with 500 branches across the state. As the Savings Bank, it had opened its head office on the corner of Market and Flinders Street in 1858. This was to stay until 1912, when a suitably impressive headquarters for the now State Savings Bank was begun on Elizabeth Street. It was to be built in three stages. The first, the southern five bays, was designed by Grainger and Little. John Harry Grainger was an architect and engineer who at the age of 25 designed the Princes Bridge in Melbourne, a swinging bridge in Sale (the first to use this technology), the Masonic Hall in Lonsdale Street and several mansions and buildings throughout the country. He is largely forgotten as an architect, instead remembered as the father of the Australian composer and concert pianist Percy Aldridge Grainger. The style of the headquarters of the State Savings Bank was described as restrained Renaissance Revival.

In 1925 two further floors were added and in 1933–34 the building was extended up to the Bourke Street corner. These second and third stages were designed by Stephenson and Meldrum. Sir Arthur George Stephenson was, in time, to develop what was described as "the colossus" of Australian architectural practices. The State Savings Bank building, with a combination of palazzo and art nouveau details, had now more than doubled in size. This new facade fitted seamlessly into the earlier building.

The State Savings Bank had a huge influence throughout the State of Victoria. In the 1920s it created a housing estate in Port Melbourne, to encourage home ownership. After World War II it began lending on overdraft to the co-operative housing societies. By 1954 nearly £16 million had been lent to approximately 50 societies as overdraft facilities. In order to encourage saving, nearly every Victorian school child had an account with the SSB and each week at school were encouraged to deposit money into their passbook. In 1970 the bank issued a medal to commemorate the bicentenary of the arrival of Captain James Cook.

In the early 1970s the headquarters were demolished and replaced by the State Bank Centre office tower (now the Commonwealth Bank Tower), and a shopping "galleria" completed in 1981. In 1980, the bank's name was changed to the State Bank. A series of bad loans following banking de-regulation in the mid-1980s and the stock market crash of 1987 left the bank unable to survive. In 1991, after almost 150 years of operation, it was sold to the Commonwealth Bank.

RIGHT *During World War I, the State Savings Bank used large advertisements to encourage people to buy war bonds. This shows the original Elizabeth Street building, before it was enlarged and extended to the corner of Bourke Street.*

BELOW *The State Savings Bank headquarters, on the corner of Elizabeth and Bourke Street, in the late 1930s. This building was to appear on children's money boxes in most Melbourne homes.*

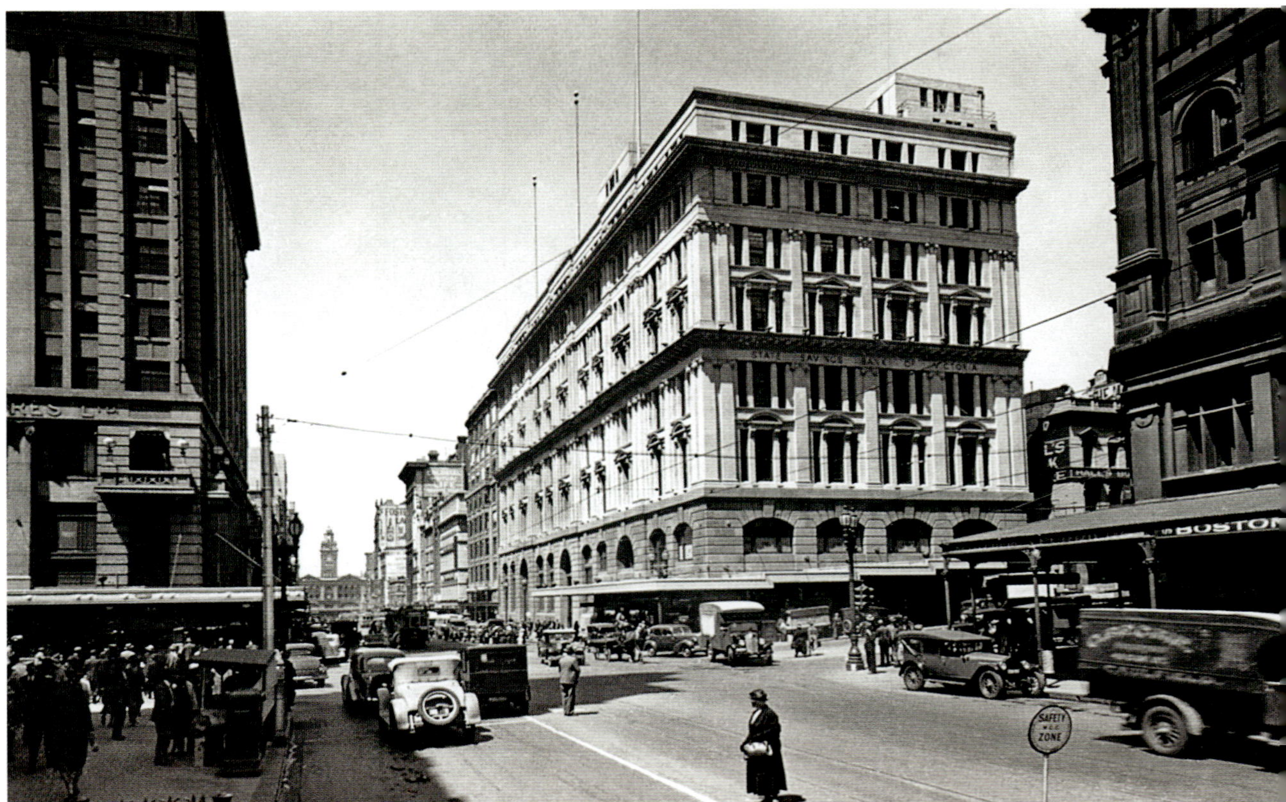

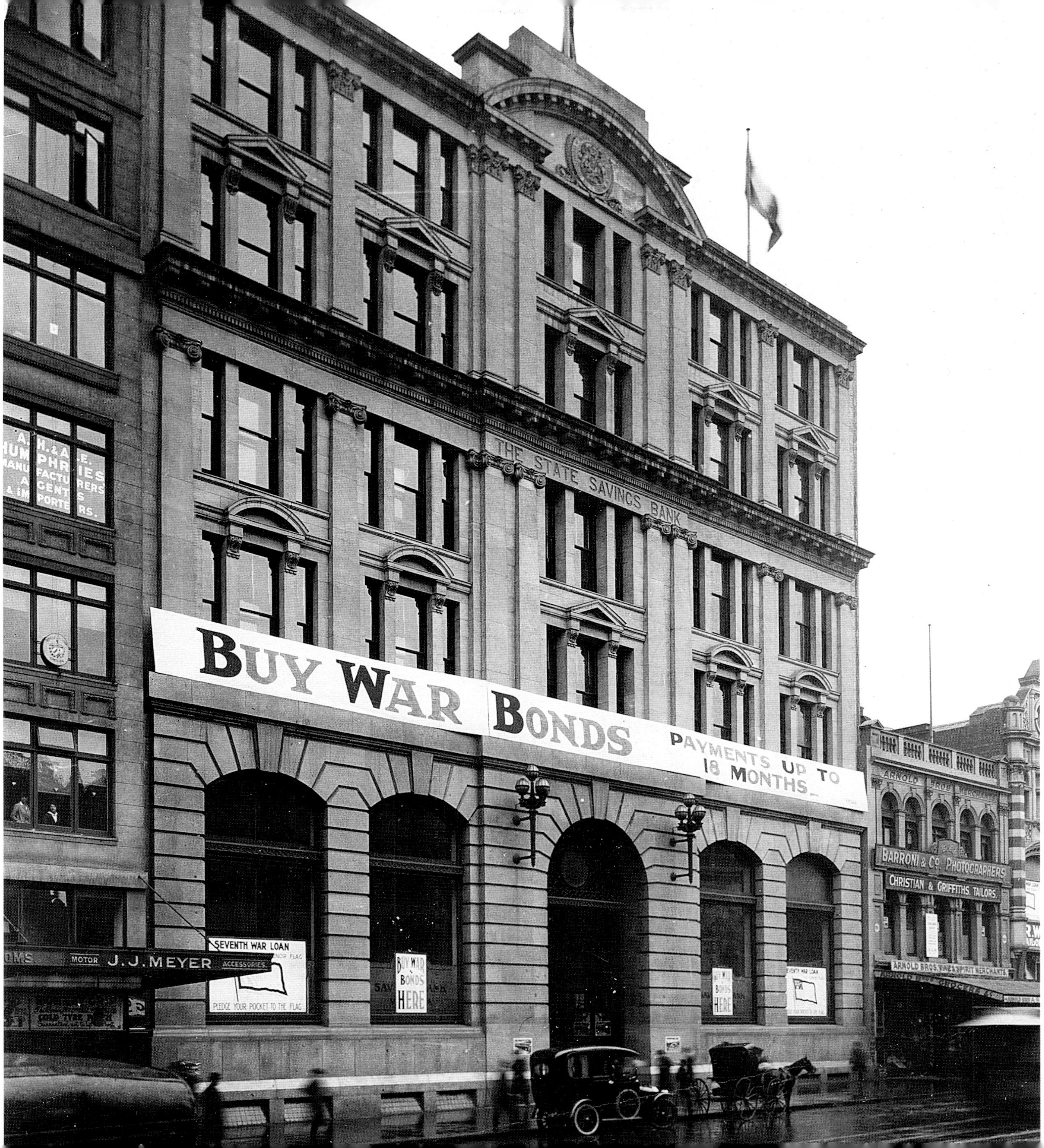
THE STATE SAVINGS BANK
BUY WAR BONDS
PAYMENTS UP TO 18 MONTHS
MOTOR J.J. MEYER ACCESSORIES
SEVENTH WAR LOAN
PLEDGE YOUR POCKET TO THE FLAG
BUY WAR BONDS HERE
BARRONI & Co PHOTOGRAPHERS
CHRISTIAN & GRIFFITHS, TAILORS.
ARNOLD BROS WINE & SPIRIT MERCHANTS

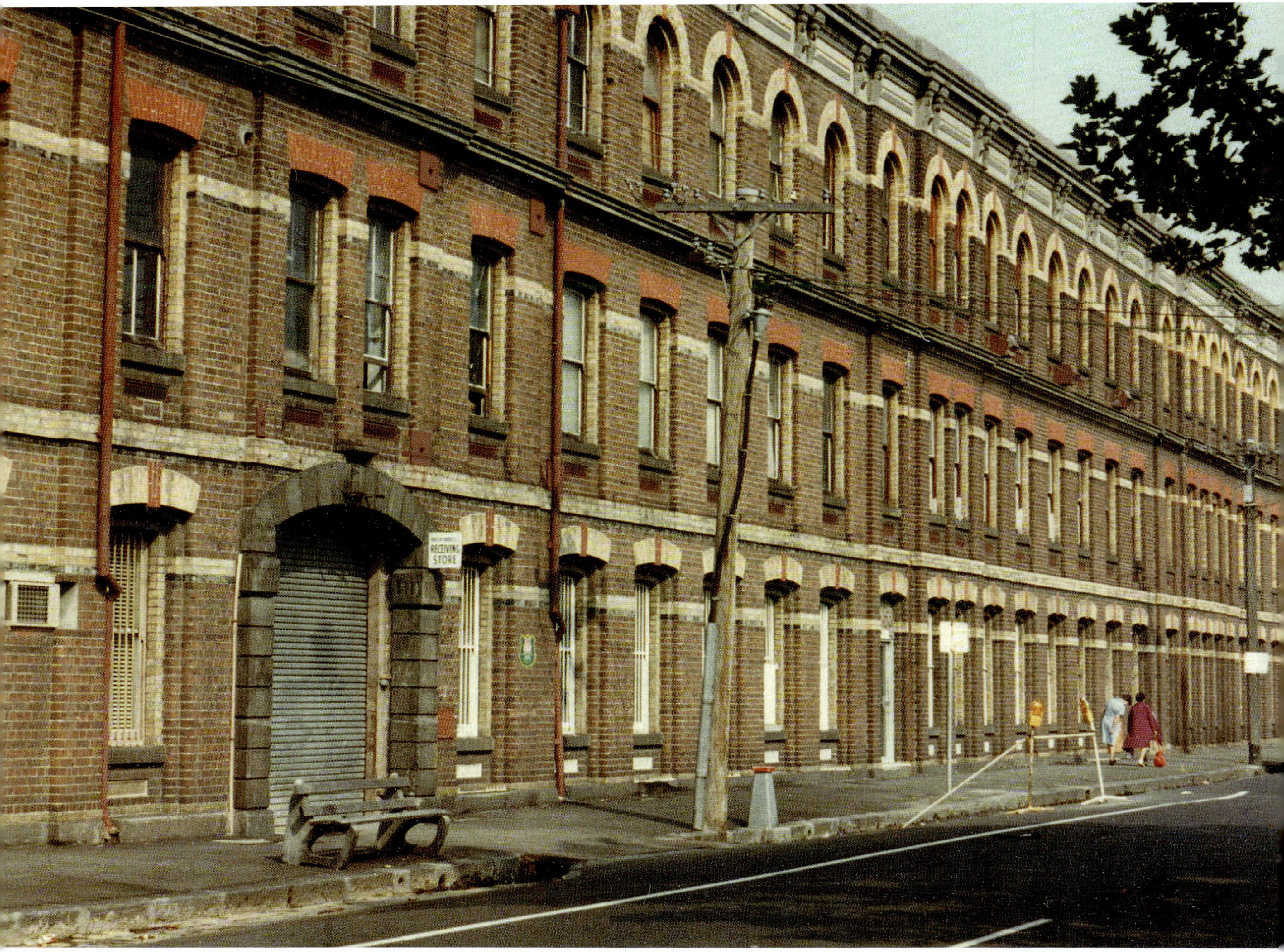
RECEIVING
STORE

Denton Hat Factory MANUFACTURING CEASED 1971

Hat making started on the site beside the Yarra River in the early 1870s. James Hobson Turner had established a large tannery in Collingwood and in 1870, together with James Miller, a rope manufacturer, he purchased the land opposite his tannery. A brick-built hat mill was constructed in 1877 and Turner named it the Fayrefield Hat Factory.

Felt manufacturing and hat making were industries allied to the tanning industry, as they made use of the by-products of fur, hair and wool. Both required large amounts of water and it was natural that they would seek waterfront locations to set up these industries. This could be found upstream from the main settlement of Melbourne on the winding course of the Yarra around Abbotsford and Collingwood, and along the low-lying parts of the Maribyrnong River near Flemington. They were also helped by the fact that the price of land was lower in these areas.

Rabbits had been introduced in 1859 by a Winchelsea landowner and the original 24 rabbits, having no natural predators, multiplied to such an extent that by the 1920s there were estimated to be 10 billion rabbits spreading across Australia and wreaking havoc on the fragile environment. These rabbits represented the basic raw material of the hat industry. During the manufacturing of felt, short animal fibres are subjected to heat, water and pressure, and they interlock in a number of different directions. This matting process makes felt almost impervious to water and gives it great strength. Animal fur does not tend to soak up moisture. It is this felt that is then blocked and made into hats.

James H. Turner's Fayrefield Hat Factory was managed by Thomas Shelmerdine (the son of a Lancashire hat manufacturer), Thomas Davison and Robert Simon. Under Shelmerdine's management the business grew. In 1879 the business was bought by George Stevenson, a merchant and importer, and renamed the Denton Hat Factory, presumably after the hat-manufacturing town of Denton in Lancashire, England. Denton's was Australia's first felt hat manufacturer, one of the few clothing industries using a mechanized plant, and comparable in size to the large factories in England.

Between 1881 and 1916, the original hat factory buildings were replaced by the brick buildings with the Italianate polychrome facade and tall chimney that can still be seen today. William Pitt, the well-known architect of the Rialto and Olderfleet buildings, the Princess Theatre, the Federal Coffee Palace, Foy and Gibson's department store, Bryant and May's factory in Richmond, and the Victoria Brewery, designed the factory.

By 1887 the factory was employing over 200 workers, turning thousands of rabbit skins and hundreds of wool bales into hats that were sold to all the Australian colonies, and employing over 200 workers. Denton's was able to buy out the London and Paris Hat Company in North Fitzroy, owned by Victoria's leading soft-goods firm, Paterson, Laing and Bruce. There are still hat manufacturers in Melbourne, but no longer is the hat an obligatory item of clothing. The factory ceased manufacturing hats in 1971 and the building is currently being converted into apartments. The factory building is of historical interest, not only because of its association with William Pitt but because it was Australia's first steam-powered hat factory, and an example of the early Victorian clothing and hat-making industry in the Collingwood area, set up by men of enterprise and vision.

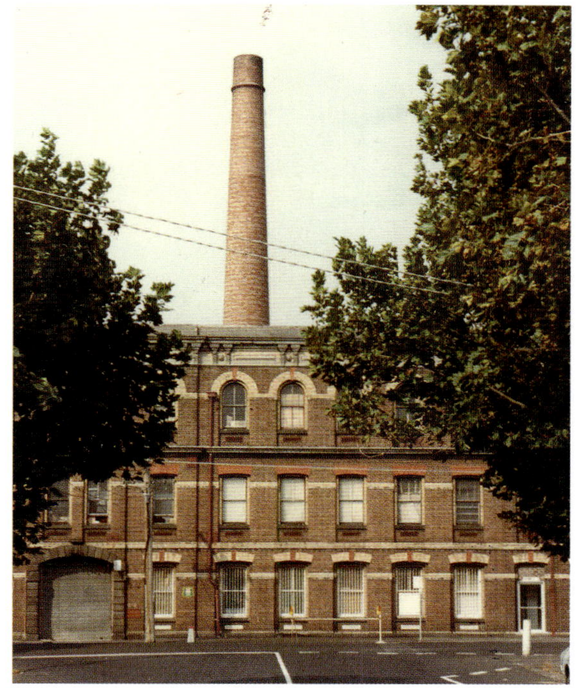

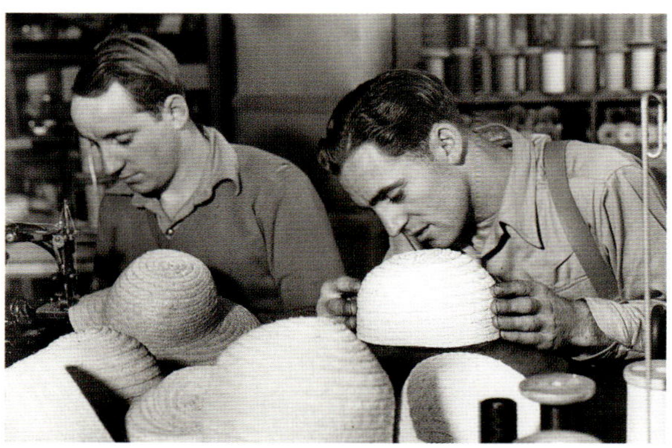

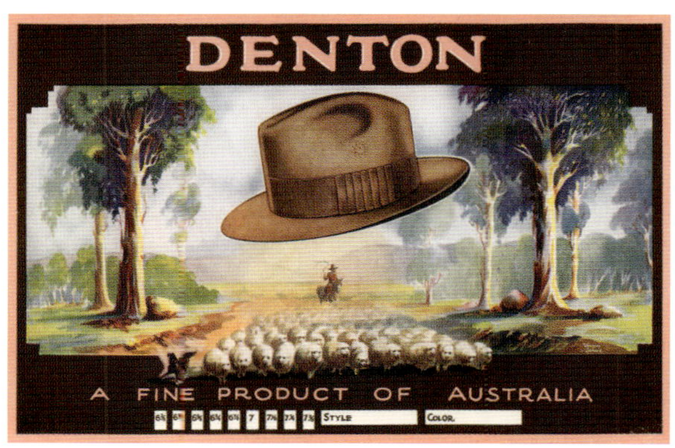

ABOVE AND OPPOSITE *The William Pitt-designed Denton Hat Factory remains a reminder of the importance of such industries in the Collingwood area.*

LEFT *When James Turner and James Miller first started their hat factory most hats in the colony were imported from England. This advertising poster, showing an easily recognizable image of Australia, was designed to appeal to Australians' patriotism and make a bold statement about the origin of the Denton hat.*

FAR LEFT *Sewing and filling women's hats at the factory in 1946.*

St. Patrick's College DEMOLISHED 1971

In 1848, Bishop Goold, appointed as the Bishop of Melbourne, wanted to strengthen the Catholic Church against what he saw as a strong Protestant colony. St. Patrick's College came into being because Goold wanted to create a school and seminary for his community. The college would cater to the increased number of Catholics living in East Melbourne while supporting another school that he had established in Lonsdale Street. The creation of Melbourne University also meant that more affluent parishioners would need a school to send their sons to, and Goold did not want to lose them to other denominations.

The opportunity came when the Victorian government initiated a public schools' scheme. The Catholic share was £2,500 of the £20,000 the Legislative Council voted for out of the public purse. Subscriptions were taken up by parishioners and St. Patrick's College was designed and built between 1854 and 1855. The architect was Patrick Scanlan. The building, situated on Eastern Hill, overlooked the northern end of the developing city. Two storeys high with a tower at either end, it had an impressive bluestone facade and was a companion piece to the impressive St. Patrick's Cathedral.

Bishop Goold hired the best educators to develop the best curriculum. The school offered a selective but extensive classical education. Unfortunately, the bankers were neither impressed nor generous and the school went bankrupt twice in 10 years. The bankruptcy was solved by Bishop Goold inviting the Jesuit Order from Ireland to take over the running of the school and its debt. In September 1865 the school had approximately 30 pupils. In late 1866 it had 105 and by 1878 there were 170. The solution was so successful that more land was bought in Kew to house more students who wanted to board. This was to become the modern day Xavier College.

St. Patrick's remained an average sized school, but its size meant it was unable to field a regular sporting team. Despite the lack of sporting teams, the school remained popular. The students achieved good results and the school turned out what the local community saw as good, upright Catholic citizens.

Following World War II, there was a huge expansion of education in Victoria. Part of the charm of St. Patrick's was that it had retained its small size and its results were outstanding. But plans to change were afoot. Changing requirements of the diocese and rising real estate prices both played a part. The plan was to create modern diocesan offices to bring together the various organisations which served the Catholic Church within Melbourne. Demolition of St. Patrick's College would also allow a better view of the cathedral. Over 5,000 students had been present at St. Patrick's by the time that Archbishop Knox decided in 1968 that the school should close. The National Trust called the destruction of St. Patrick's "the greatest loss of any historic building" since its formation 15 years earlier. It is ironic that St. Patrick's College was considered to be so important that it was safe from any destruction. It was not to be and in 1971, despite vocal objections, meetings, petitions and the greatest heritage protest up to that time, the college was demolished.

Today, all that remains of the building is the bluestone East Tower. The St. Patrick's Old Collegians' Association (founded in 1911) survives.

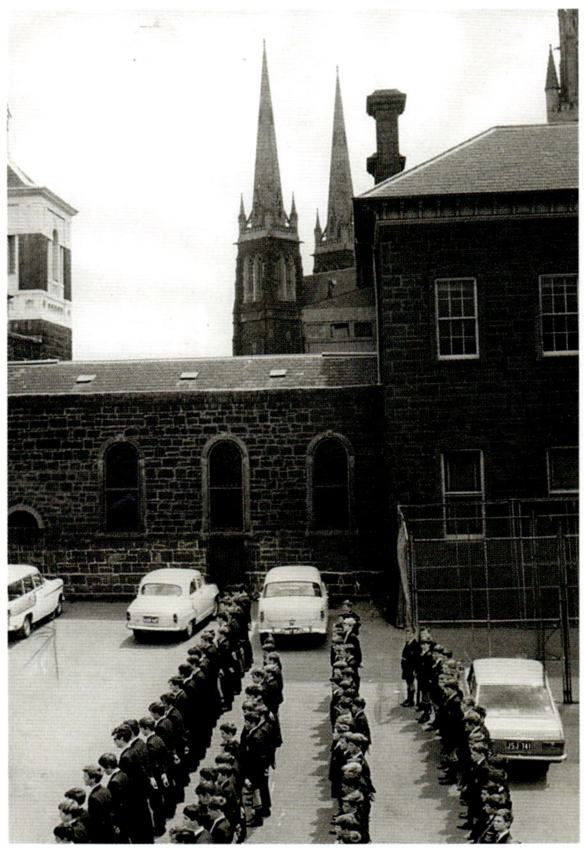

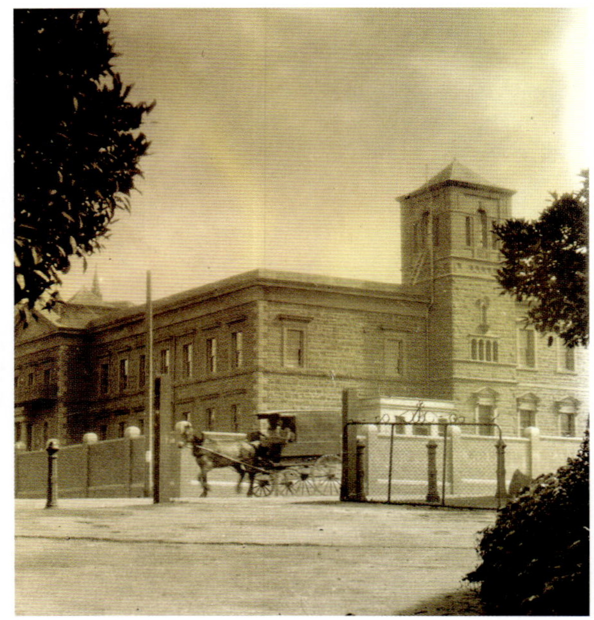

ABOVE AND RIGHT *The impressive bluestone facade of St. Patrick's College with towers at either end.*

LEFT *The spires of St. Patrick's Cathedral are in the background as the boys line up for the final assembly at St. Patrick's College, East Melbourne.*

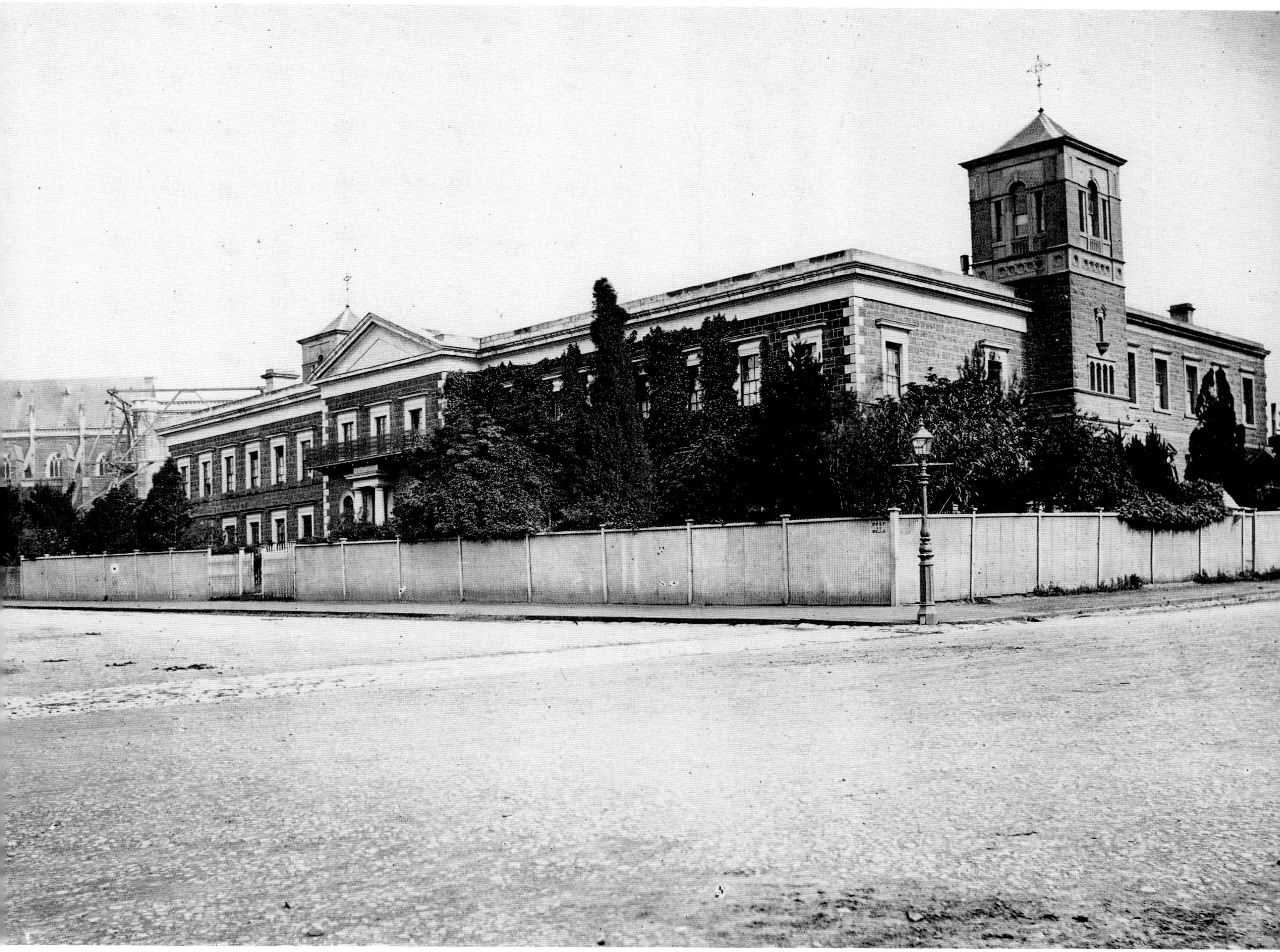

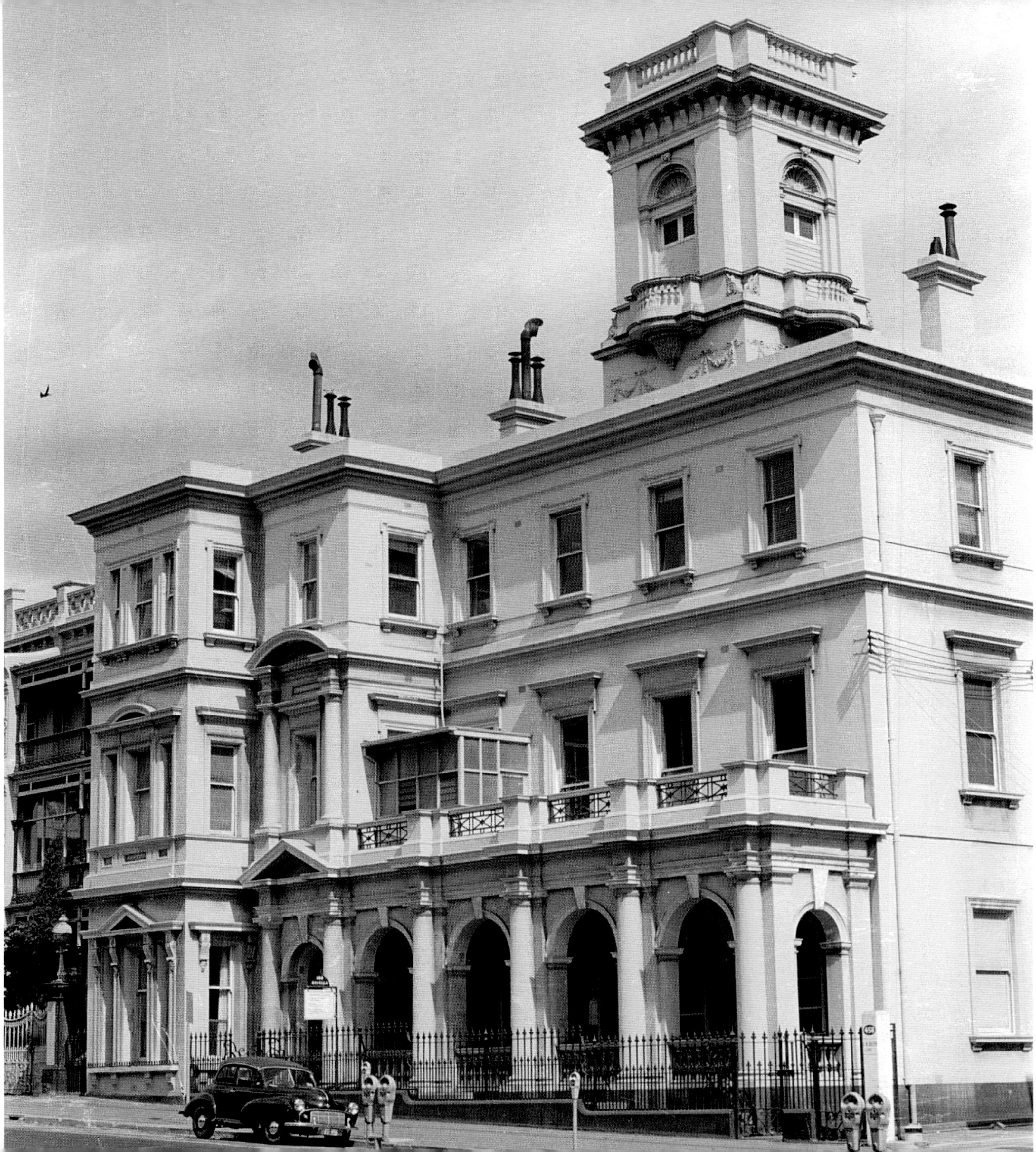

Rostella DEMOLISHED 1972

This three-storey Italianate mansion at 146 Lonsdale Street, known as a place of "gracious hospitality", was commissioned by Sir Thomas Naghten FitzGerald in 1869. Sir Thomas was born in Ireland and came to Melbourne as a ship's surgeon in 1858. He later became the acting house surgeon at the Melbourne Hospital and went on to open a private practice on land he'd purchased nearby. Elected an honorary surgeon to the Melbourne Hospital in 1860, he held that post until 1901 and in 1902–7 was consulting surgeon. Rostella was designed by Irish architect John Michael Barry, who also designed the Western Market. In 1887, Sir Thomas purchased the adjoining property from the Presbyterian Church and built two three-storey terrace houses to be used for his private hospital. The mansion had a tennis court and in his active years FitzGerald always played there before breakfast. The tower at Rostella provided the opportunity for lovely photographs of Melbourne to be taken, for the tower was once one of the highest points in Melbourne, with 360-degree views of the city. From there it was possible to see down Lonsdale Street, along William Street, and to view the saltwater Blue Lake. The mansion contained FitzGerald's fine and extensive collection of paintings. Amongst these was Lefebvre's *Chloe*. He bought the painting for 850 guineas after it featured at the Melbourne International Exhibition in 1880. The nude was the cause of much public outrage during its sojourn in the National Gallery when FitzGerald returned to Ireland for three years. After a period of time in Adelaide, it was returned to FitzGerald who was forced to hang it in a rear room of Rostella where it would not be visible from the street. *Chloe* now resides in Young & Jackson's Hotel, Melbourne.

In 1884 FitzGerald held the first clinical lectureship in surgery created by the University of Melbourne at the Melbourne Hospital. He died in 1908 and Rostella was leased by the Australian Navy. Later the building was used by the Commonwealth Court of Industrial Arbitration. The mansion was demolished in 1972 to create a car parking space for the Australian Broadcasting Commission. A pair of pillars and gates is all that remain from the original house. Once part of the gated entrance to his private residence, the pillars, which are topped with the word "Rostella", sit at the side of the two three-storey terraces, also on Lonsdale Street, that were built for his private hospital.

OPPOSITE *Exterior view of Rostella in 1963. The colonnade, pediment and tower made the house a landmark on Lonsdale Street.*

BELOW *A partial view of Rostella, also from 1963, taken from a narrow lane off Lonsdale Street.*

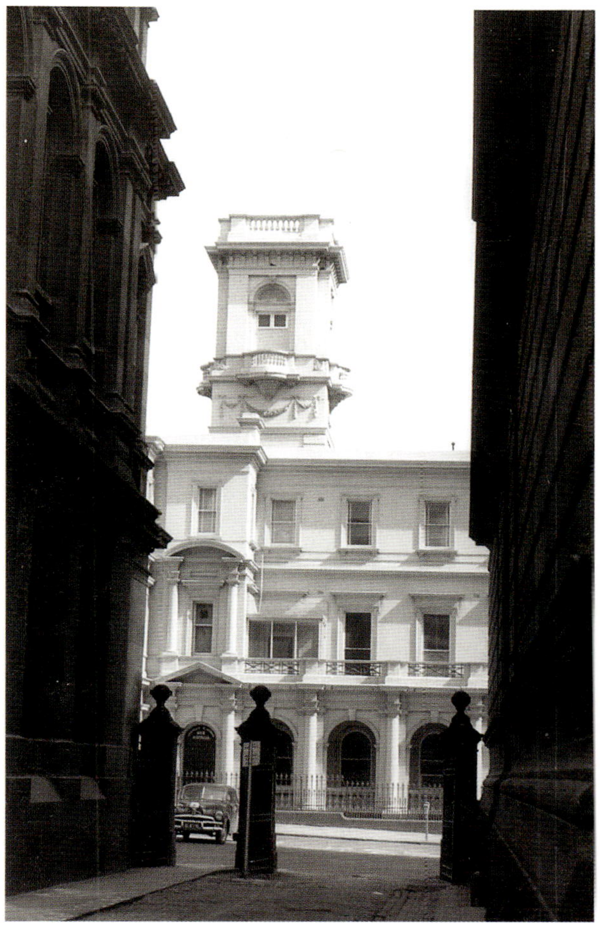

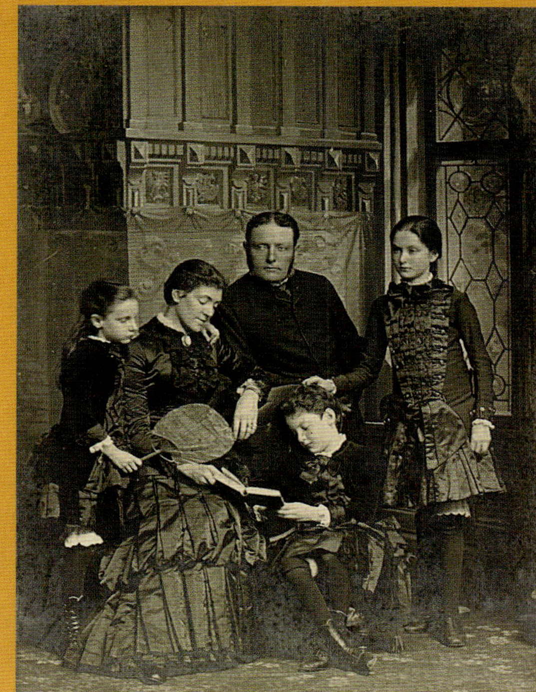

SIR THOMAS NAGHTEN FITZGERALD

The eminent surgeon, Sir Thomas FitzGerald (1838–1908), was held in high esteem by his colleagues and widely admired for his technical skills and diagnostic abilities. It was said that FitzGerald was a distinguished person in any company, but it was acknowledged also that the spoken and written word was not his strength and that his students learnt more from what he did than what he said. In May 1897 he was knighted, the first Australian to be so honoured for eminence in the medical profession. One of his three daughters, Kathleen, upon her death in 1951, bequeathed to the University of Melbourne, her residual estate for the founding of the Sir Thomas Naghten FitzGerald Scholarship in memory of her father.

Federal Coffee Palace DEMOLISHED 1973

Of all Melbourne's lost buildings, the Federal Coffee Palace is one of those most mourned and many consider that its demolition was an example of urban vandalism. At the time of its construction *The Age* newspaper called it "one of Australia's most splendid". It might not have been the most beautiful of Melbourne's land boom buildings, but it was certainly one of the most impressive.

The first temperance societies appeared in Melbourne in the 1830s and many temperance hotels were built during the 1880s in the city and suburbs to provide much-needed accommodation. They did not serve alcohol but they did offer accommodation, meeting rooms and leisure facilities. They were often given grandiose names like Grand and Royal. The 1880s was a period in Melbourne's history of great wealth and optimism following the gold rushes. There were many investors, influential landholders, businessmen and property owners interested in investing in property. James Munro and James Mirams, politicians, property developers, and temperance campaigners, commissioned the building of a grand temperance hotel which, when opened in 1888, was to be one of the largest hotels in Australia, and one of the largest Second Empire Style buildings in the world. It was opened in time for the Centennial Exhibition that brought visitors from around the world.

A competition to design the Federal Coffee Palace was won by two different architectural firms. The exterior design was won by architects Ellerker and Kilburn, and the design for the interior by William Pitt. At a cost of £150,000, the seven-storey Federal Coffee Palace was an impressive building. Its exterior was decorated with statues and ornaments over a metre tall, including sea-horses, chariots, and griffins. The Collins Street corner of the building was crowned with a tall tower 165 feet high, topped by a large dome with a blue light. This light could be seen down the bay and was a helpful landmark for ships. An enterprising, wealthy and imaginative racing car driver, Peter Jansen, saw the potential of the tower, extensively renovated it and lived there from 1967 to 1971.

The interior was no less impressive. There were five floors of bedrooms, almost 400 of them, and, on the ground floor, there were entertainment rooms, a billiard room, smoking and reading rooms, a dining room, offices and shops facing the street. Under this floor was a basement that housed all the hotel services, a kitchen 18 metres square, and even an icehouse. No expense was spared in the construction of the grand interior spaces. A beautiful white and red marble staircase reached the first-floor dining room, bridal chamber, drawing room, ballrooms and other entertainment rooms. There were fireproof staircases, lifts that were guaranteed not to break down, 7 kilometres of bell-wire, 8 kilometres of gas piping, and a rooftop promenade providing a marvellous view of the city and bay.

During the Depression that followed the 1880s land boom it became more and more difficult for the hotel to fill the rooms, so many were let as office space and the hotel applied for an alcohol licence. It became the Federal Palace Hotel in 1897 and in 1923 it was renamed the Federal Hotel. By the middle of the 20th century the cost of constant renovation of these grand buildings, and the public preference for modern American style hotels, spelled the death of older establishments like the Federal Hotel. Despite public outcry and petitions, the building was demolished in 1973.

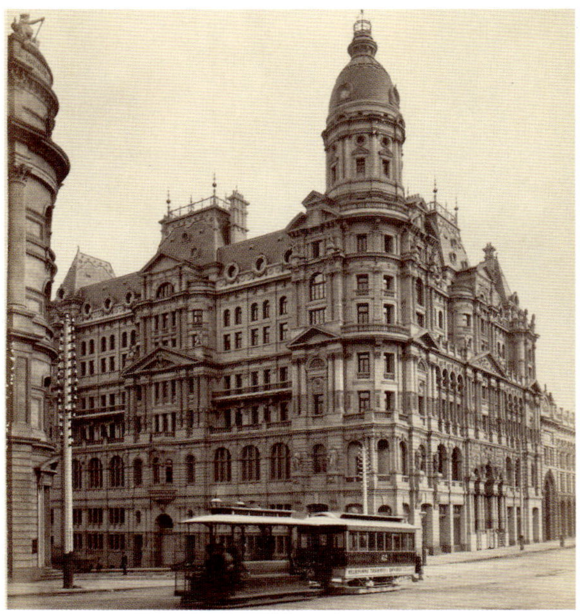

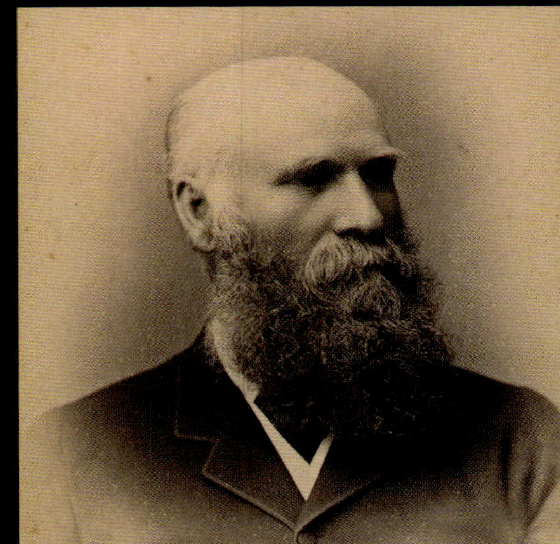

JAMES MUNRO (1832–1908)

James Munro migrated to Victoria in 1858 and soon established himself in business, particularly in banking and building societies. He became very wealthy during the real estate boom of the 1880s. Like so many others, he speculated in land and property. When the crash came many investors in his companies lost all their savings. At the time Munro was Victoria's 15th Premier, so he appointed himself Victorian Agent-General in London. He resigned as Premier and retreated to London in 1892. His reputation as a leader in the temperance movement and as a man of integrity was damaged. His business partner James Mirams was imprisoned for fraud.

RIGHT *The Federal Coffee Palace was one of the largest and most opulent hotels in Australia when it was built in 1888.*

LEFT *A cable tram passes the Federal Coffee Palace in this view from the 1890s.*

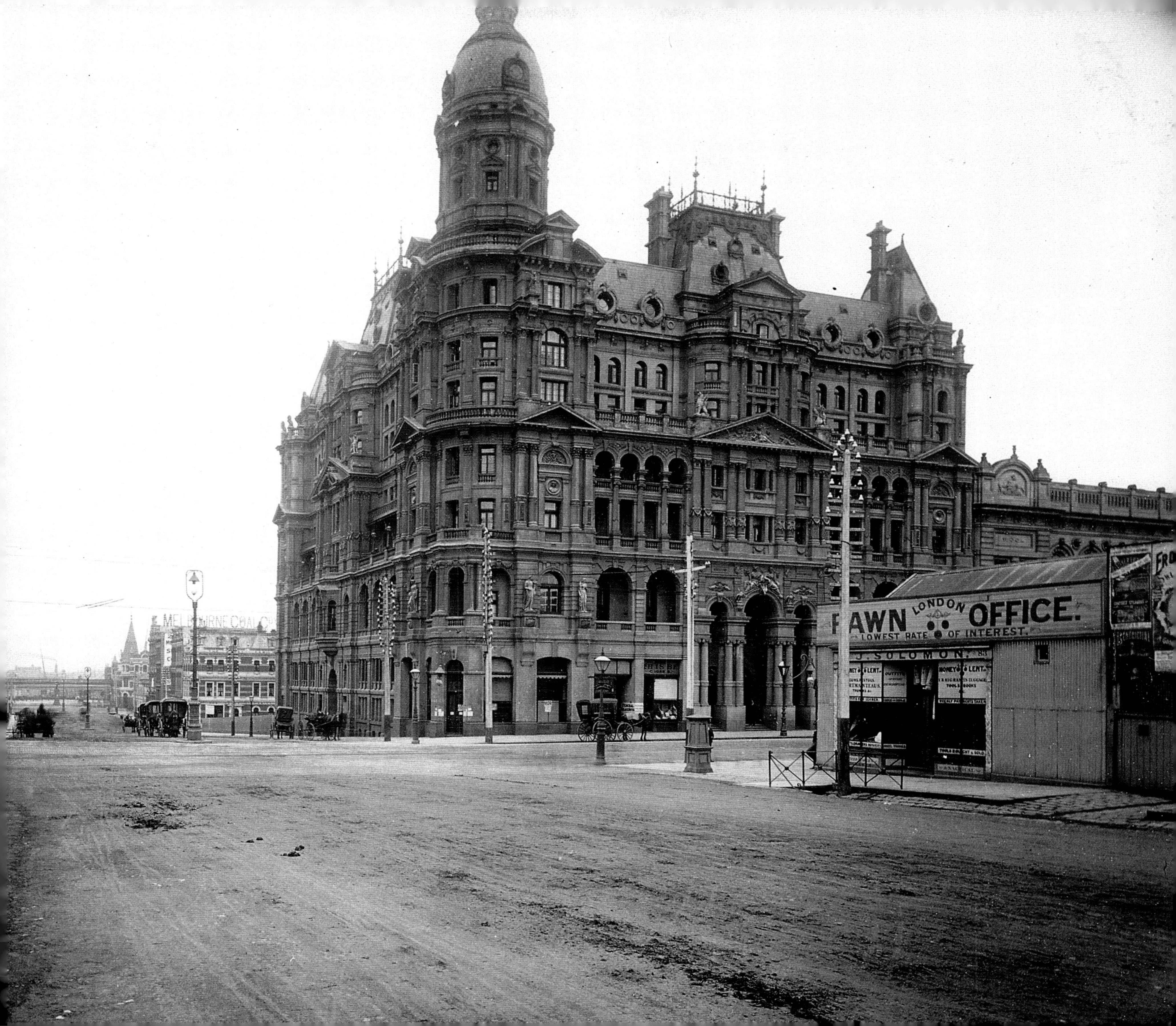
PAWN
LONDON
OFFICE.
LOWEST RATE OF INTEREST.
J. SOLOMON. 83
MONEY LENT
TOOLS & BOOKS
WEEKLY PAYMENTS TAKEN
TOOLS BOUGHT & SOLD

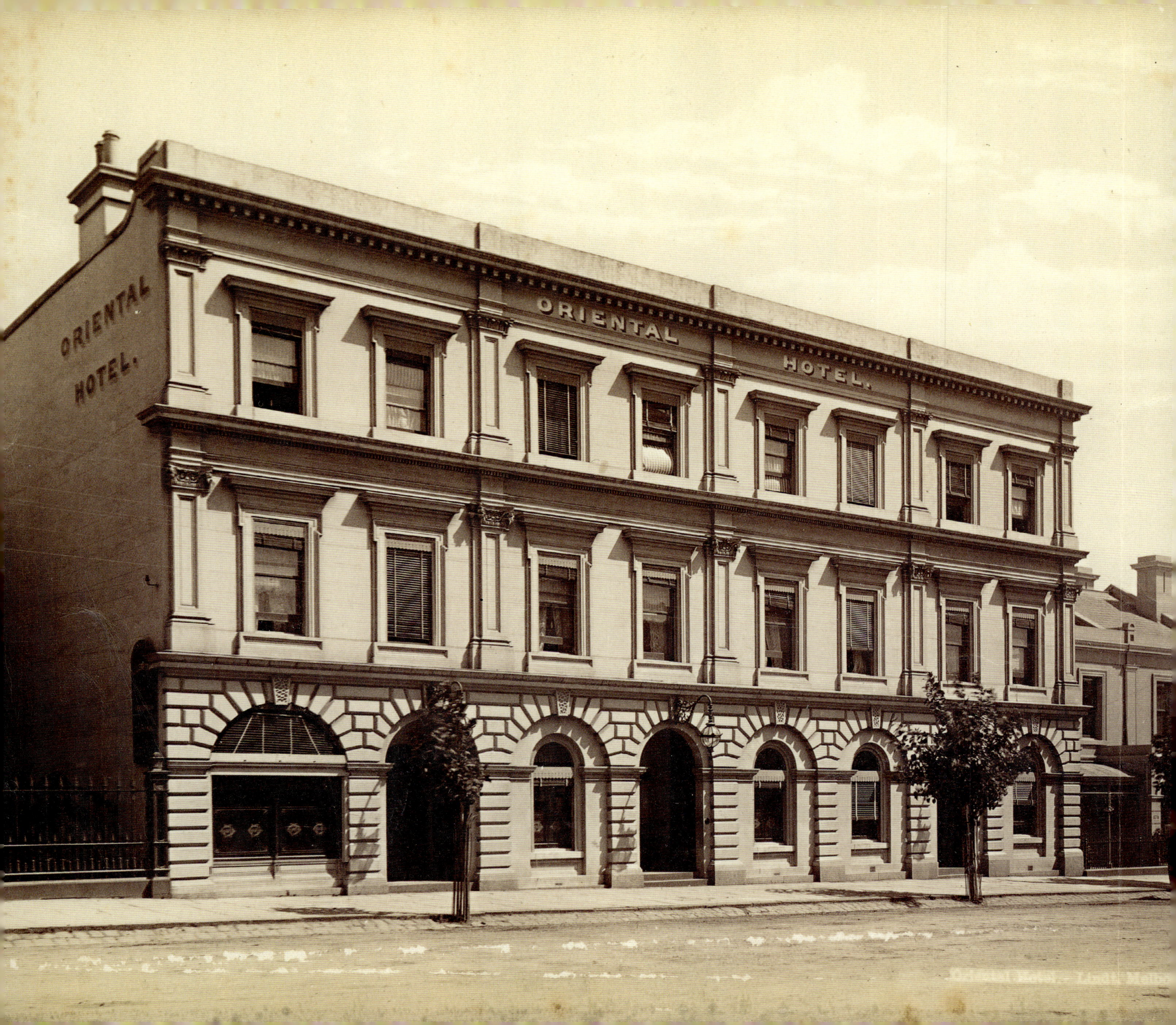
ORIENTAL HOTEL.
ORIENTAL
HOTEL.

Oriental Hotel DEMOLISHED 1973

In 1856, 136 inns and taverns were to be found in an area bounded by Flinders, Spencer, Spring and La Trobe Streets. The Oriental Hotel was built in 1878, replacing the Bedford Hotel, which was built in the 1850s on the site of a former sawmill. Its address was the fashionable end of Collins Street and was opposite the Melbourne Club and close to Parliament House. It soon became a favourite of the landed gentry.

In the 1880s the Oriental Hotel ranked as one of Melbourne's best hotels and was famed for the quality of its food and drink. Even until the 1950s, the Oriental, together with the Menzies and Scott's, was considered one of the top three places to stay in Melbourne.

The Oriental was bought by Pearson Tewkesbury, a wealthy gold dealer. When the Tewkesburys first moved to Melbourne, they made their home in a suite at the Oriental, but after an argument with the owner over poor service they moved to the Grand (later the Windsor Hotel). Not satisfied with this solution, Tewkesbury bought the Oriental, sacked the manager and moved back in.

A number of renovations immediately occurred. He added a new wing, by purchasing and pulling down the house next door, and he established the City Motor Service behind the Oriental, which offered chauffeur driven cars. Pearson Tewkesbury travelled regularly overseas and always came back with new ideas for the hotel. In the late 1930s the ground floor was altered and the entrance moved eastward. He also proposed sidewalk dining, as he felt Melbourne's mild and pleasant climate was suited to this, but the Melbourne City Council refused to consent to his idea.

Tewkesbury's plans to extend the Oriental to 13 storeys failed to materialise, and following his death the hotel was sold to the Ress family. They too transformed the Oriental, adding luxury suites in time for the 1956 Olympics and revamping the hotel's dining facilities. Unlike Tewkesbury, they were successful in introducing sidewalk dining. They managed this in 1958 and Mrs Ress commented that it was "just like the Champs-Élysées back in Paris." Her description caught on and today Melburnians still refer to the "Paris end" of Collins Street. The cosmopolitan look engendered by the sidewalk café lasted for two years, until it was forced to close in 1960 when it was decided that the tables caused an obstruction to traffic.

In the 1960s further changes were made. The dining room became a restaurant–discotheque called the Persian Room. Renamed the Casbah in 1966, it became a venue for live music. But the days of the Oriental were numbered. The hotel was sold to the ANZ bank in March 1969, ending 90 years of operation. In 1971 came the proposal for Collins Place with its twin towers, each of 47 storeys. All buildings in the vicinity were to be razed and the newspapers dubbed 1972 as "the year of the wrecker". So it was that in 1973 the Oriental, one of many classic Collins Street buildings, was demolished as part of the Collins Place development.

OPPOSITE *Looking across the street towards the three-storey Oriental Hotel around 1890.*

BELOW *A late 1880s view showing the Oriental Hotel and the Grosvenor Chambers.*

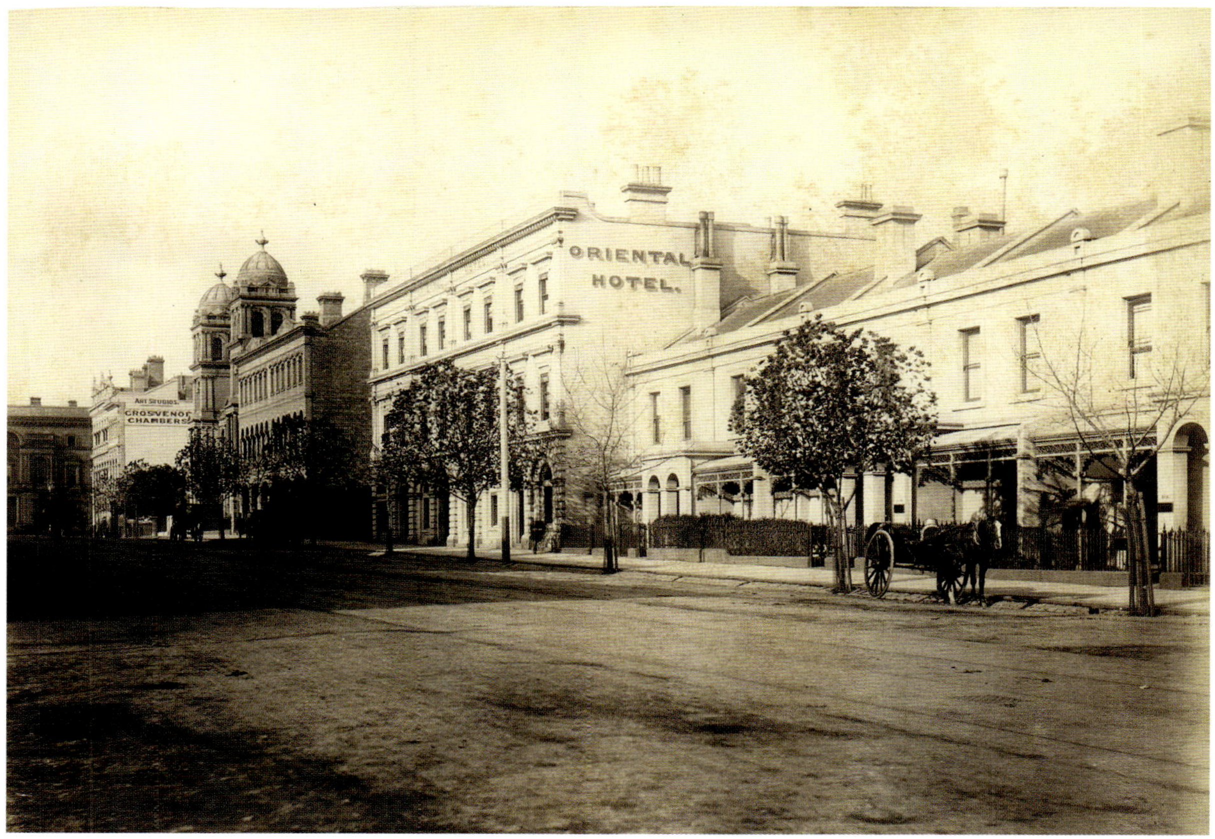

St. Kilda Junction and the Junction Hotel

JUNCTION REROUTED EARLY 1970s / HOTEL DEMOLISHED 1973

The Junction Hotel was located in the triangle that was St. Kilda Junction and it had a long history. In 1857 the St. Kilda Council held their first meeting in a room beside the Junction Hotel. George Sparrow, the licensee, changed its name to the Grand Junction Hotel in 1864 but it was not until 1887 that the hotel was redesigned. This was the period of the land boom and during this time the St. Kilda population more than doubled. Palatial hotels and mansions were built and the Grand Junction was one such example. A three-storey, elaborate wedge-shaped building, the hotel was designed to fit its corner location. Its Italianate Mannerist spire encouraged the viewer to look up. Despite the wealth in St. Kilda at that time, by 1917 the then licensee, N. Splatt, was requesting a rate decrease because of a decline in business. In 1929, further renovations occurred: an additional saloon bar (on the Barkly Street side) and a lounge and bottle shop (on the High Street side) were added. There was also an application to allow a sign to be built for advertising on the front of the building. In time, St. Kilda Junction became well-known for its advertising.

The completion of the King Street Bridge in 1961 increased markedly the traffic through St. Kilda, and of major concern was St. Kilda Junction. By 1966 the junction was a giant roundabout with eight streets intersecting it. As well as cars using the roads, trams crossed the junction before breaking off onto one of three paths. At peak hours traffic was at a standstill, as cars jockeyed to change lanes or move along one of the roads. Accidents were common and this area regularly became gridlocked. Some country drivers would wait for a tram to come so they could follow it in order to safely negotiate the traffic.

In the late 1960s the State Government proposed to overhaul the intersection. In the first stage, roads were rerouted, new streets came into being, roads were widened and some were lowered and built under the rest of the intersection. Trams too were realigned and the tramline lowered. In all, over 150 houses, 52 business premises, 42 shops, three service stations and three hotels were demolished to make way for an underpass and bypass road construction. One of these was the Junction Hotel. Bulldozers ran through its main bar, once lined with photographs of famous sportsmen. The hotel had been known for flying the flag when St. Kilda won the football but flying it at half-mast when they lost. Now the flag would fly no more. The Junction Hotel, used variously as a coffee palace, club and hotel, was demolished in 1973. What was saved in the vicinity was the Corroboree Tree. A plaque there read "Aborigines of early settlement days congregated and held their ceremonies under and in the vicinity of this tree." A 20-metre stretch of St. Kilda Road was realigned so that the tree's root system was not damaged. The completed junction was expanded slightly, taking in 12 streets but allowing traffic to move far more easily through the area.

RIGHT *A late 1890s elevated view of St. Kilda and Punt Roads, from the tower of the Junction Hotel. The city of Melbourne is in the distance.*

LEFT *St. Kilda Junction and the Junction Hotel. A tram and horse-drawn vehicle share the street in this circa-1900 view.*

BELOW *The Junction Hotel, just prior to its demolition, appears isolated by the overhaul of St. Kilda Junction.*

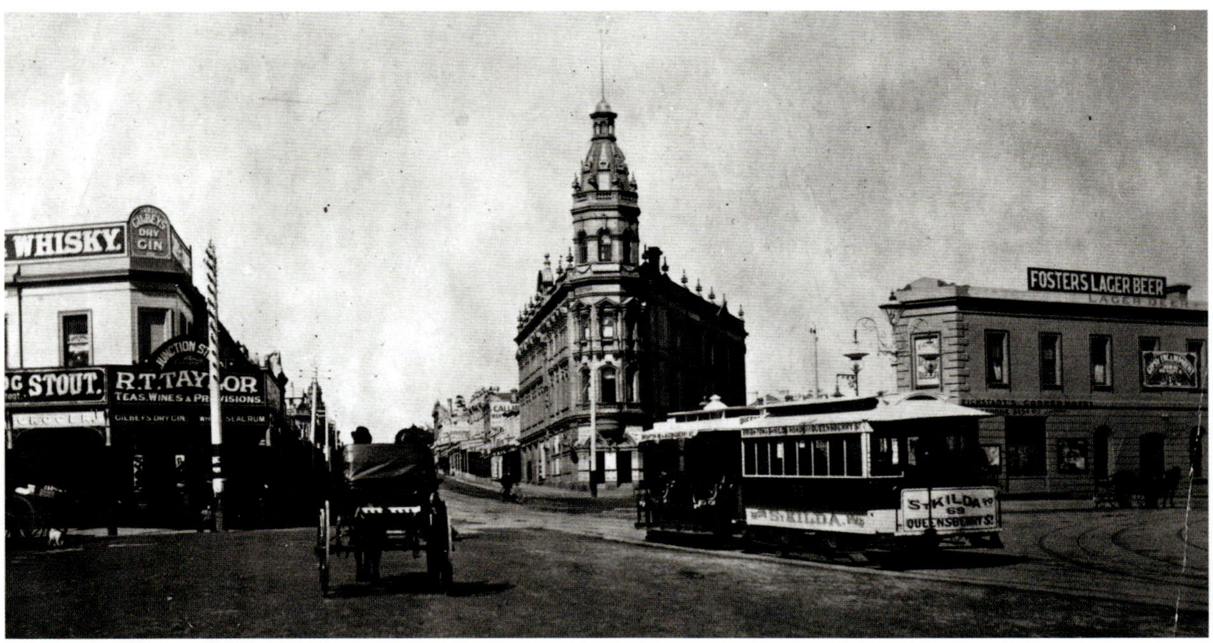

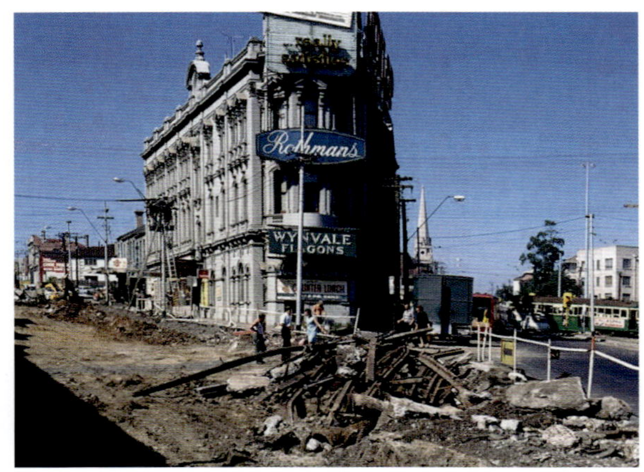

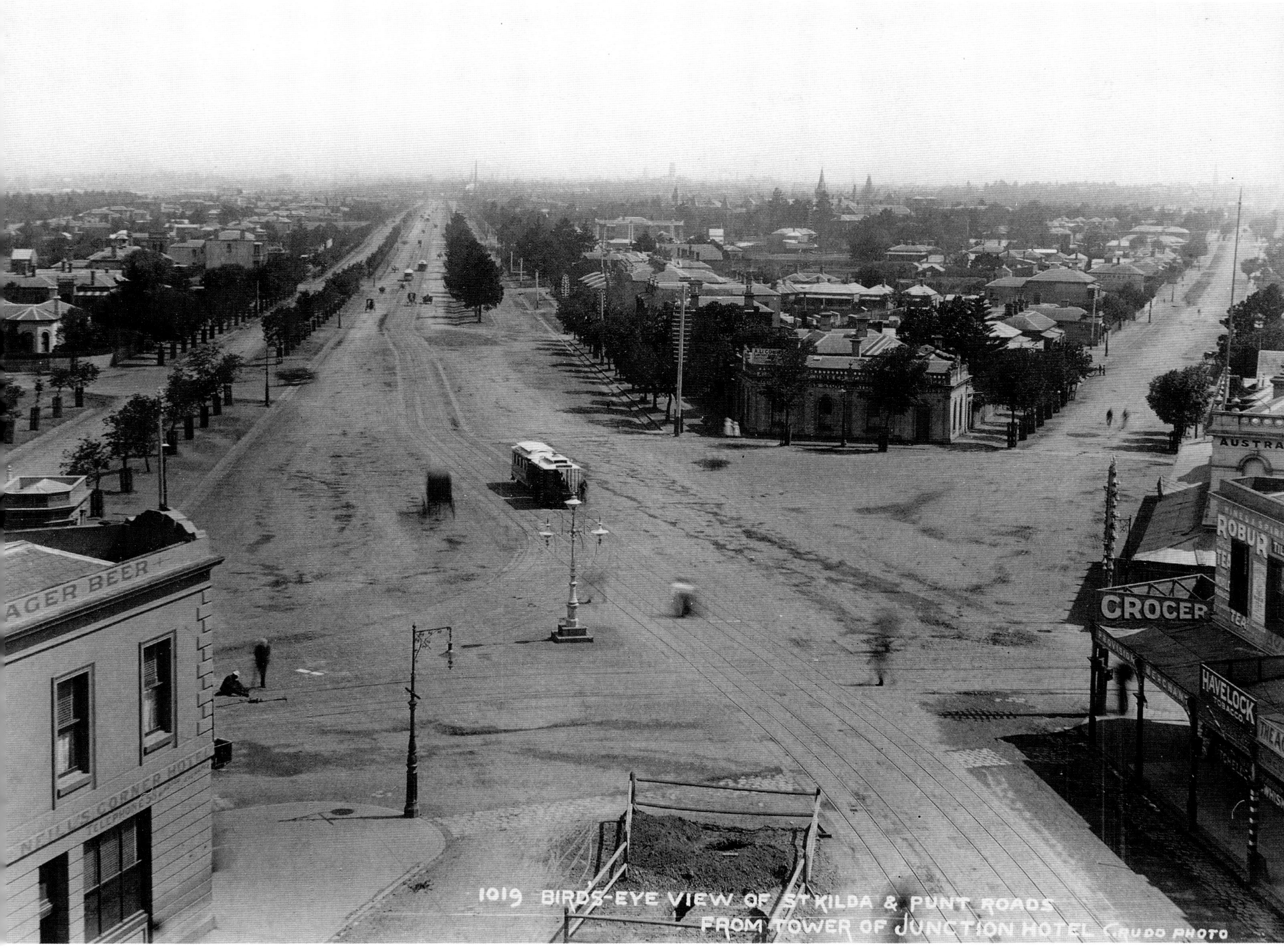
1019 BIRDS-EYE VIEW OF ST KILDA & PUNT ROADS
FROM TOWER OF JUNCTION HOTEL CAUDO PHOTO
AGER BEER
CROCER
ROBUR
HAVELOCK
TOBACCO
AUSTRA

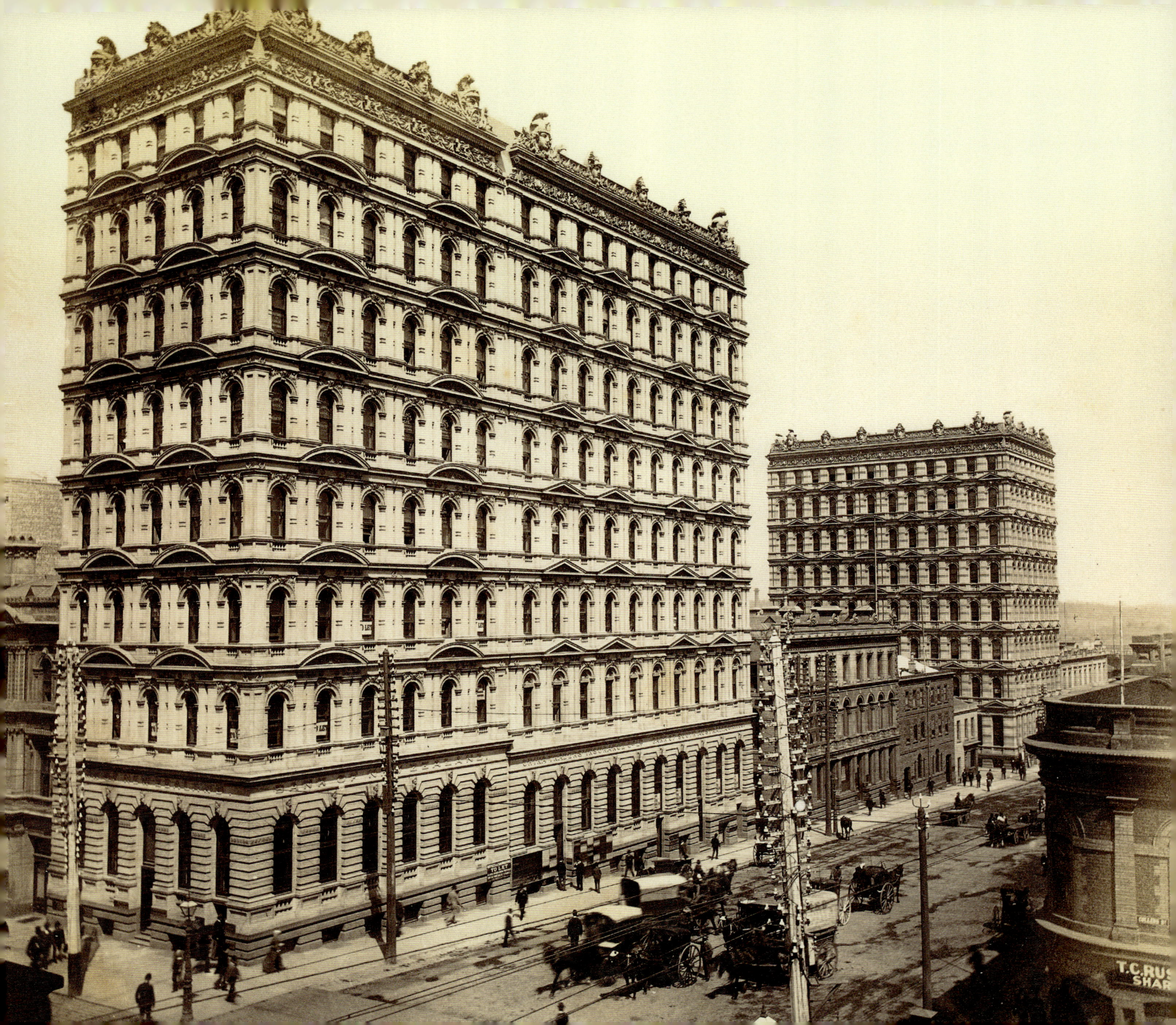
T.C.RUS
SHAR

Prell's Buildings and the APA Tower

TOWER DEMOLISHED 1967; FIRST PRELL'S BUILDING DEMOLISHED 1975

The 1880s was a time of great wealth and optimism in Melbourne, and it was during this property boom that speculator and developer Friedrich Wilhelm Prell was commissioned to construct buildings in the City of Melbourne. Prell was born in Hamburg and migrated to Australia at the age of 21. He was a very physically active man, with an interest in billiards, chess, walking, rowing, athletics and horse racing. In business he was energetic, well respected and astute. He founded the firm of F. W. Prell and Company Limited that was engaged in both export and import of goods at a time when there were great changes taking place in world trading methods. He readily adapted to these changes and was particularly active in the development of the wheat trade.

In 1886 the vice-president of the American Otis Elevator Company, W. F. Hall, visited Melbourne. In conversation with Prell he remarked upon the fact that Sydney had six Otis lifts in operation but Melbourne had none. Hall pointed out that "the gentleman who had to climb four flights of stairs would probably reach the top floor with aching legs, fluttering heart and a firm resolution to do business elsewhere." Prell added two more storeys and installed Victoria's first passenger elevators.

Between 1888 and 1889 he constructed three 11-storey buildings in Queen and Collins Streets. During the 1880s there were other buildings constructed that were eight to 10 storeys high, but Prell's buildings, which resembled Lego blocks in the streetscape, dominated the southern section of the city. Only the Australian Building on the corner of Elizabeth Street and Flinders Lane was taller. The introduction of hydraulic lifts made Prell's buildings more attractive to potential tenants. People no longer wanted to climb 11 floors of stairs and these technologically advanced lifts meant that tenants no longer had to be frightened that ropes and cables would break. Water-driven pistons pushed the elevator to the required height and this meant that the lift shafts needed to be as deep as the 11 storeys the elevator had to travel. The installation of these lifts not only attracted tenants, but the public as well, who travelled into the city just to ride in these marvellous inventions. Prell's building in lower Bourke Street was the first of the new iron-framed skyscrapers.

Prell's buildings, designed by F. M. White and Son were described as being built in the "Modern Renaissance" style. They were also called "Towers of Babel of the elevator type" and were made of brick or stone with ornamented cornices. The lower floors had walls that were almost a metre thick in order to support the structure. Most of the floors were used for commercial offices. In 1929 one of Prell's buildings became the home of the Australian Provincial Assurance Company and was extensively altered. A large art deco tower was added to the Collins Street front of the building, a model of engineering excellence at the time. The facade of the building itself was modernized to blend with the art deco tower, which dominated the skyline for the next 40 years. The tower was demolished in 1967, apparently for no sound reason. The first of the Prell's buildings was demolished in 1975 although nothing was built on the site until 1983. Today only the Felton Building on Queen Street survives as an example of Prell's vision for Melbourne.

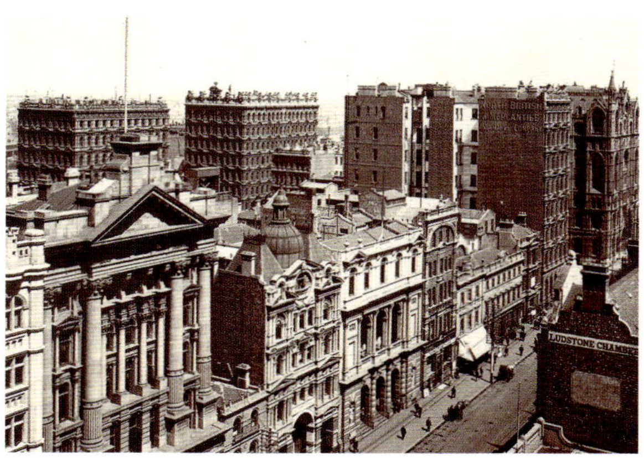

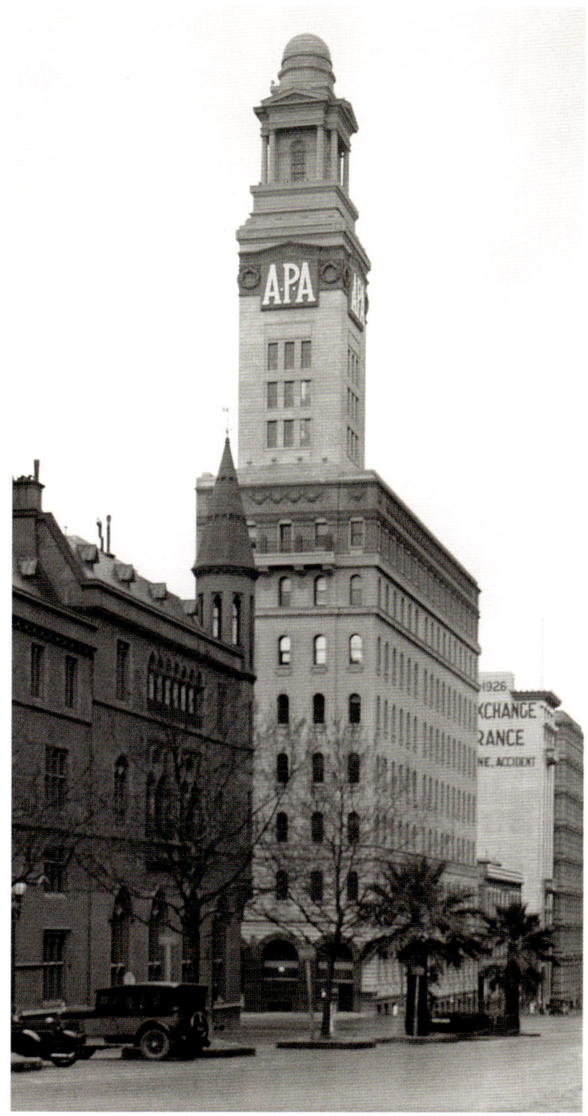

OPPOSITE *Two of Prell's buildings on Collins Street. Prell constructed several 11-storey buildings in the modern renaissance style in Queen and Collins Streets between 1888 and 1889.*

LEFT *The Prell's buildings dominated the skyline in the southern part of the city.*

RIGHT *The exterior of this Prell's building was modernised to match the art deco tower that was added in 1929.*

Milk Bars DECLINED EARLY 1980s

The earliest milk bars were a far cry from the functional, almost identical, convenience stores of today. Milk bars had their origins in the United States and Australians first saw them featured in movies or in the conversations of the thousands of American servicemen who were stationed in Melbourne during World War II.

Glossy Laminex and chrome counters displayed new delights for all-comers. Large wall mirrors reflected these temptations, while on the floor linoleum, often threadbare in front of the counter, was a testament to the popularity of the milk bar. Behind the counters, on shelves on the wall, were glasses and tin drink containers, the like of which had never been seen before. Milk shakes were always served in tall metal containers and other drinks in long glasses with short flat stands. Often behind the high counter stood the glass syrup bottles with their familiar and sometimes more exotic flavours. The syrup was dispensed from a rubber stopper and sometimes via a long-handled measure that dribbled its stickiness over the counter top.

A milkshake consisted of cold milk poured into the tin container followed by flavouring and ice cream. This concoction was whipped within an inch of its life by a very noisy beater. By this time the container would be chilled and frosty. The most common flavours were strawberry, vanilla, chocolate and caramel. The exotic flavours of Blue Heaven, sarsaparilla, mint and creaming soda were more often used in the making of a spider or floater. A spider was probably an Australian invention that visiting Americans had not known. A spider was lemonade with mashed ice cream in it, whereas with the floater the ice cream was not mashed.

A mouth-watering array of sweets was stored in lidded glass lolly jars, safely out of reach from small fingers. There were gob-stoppers; conversation lollies with messages on them; buddies and freckles of chocolate; black cats and liquorice blocks to turn your tongue black, and redskins to turn it red; mint leaves; false teeth; sherbets; snakes; bananas; musk sticks; and kisses. For three or six pence, pocket money could be spent on mixed sweets placed in a white paper bag. It was no wonder that milk bars became the new social centre of the adolescents' life.

In many cases these milk bars were family concerns and all in the family were expected to contribute. Deliveries arrived very early in the morning and often closing time was 10 o'clock at night, or later if the milk bar was near a cinema. The cinema patrons would buy refreshments from the milk bar before the film and then stock up again at half time.

Gradually the milk bar of the 1950s and early 1960s morphed into something else, and most of the original establishments had changed by 1980. They started to sell newspapers, sandwiches, hot meat pies and sausage rolls and canned soft drinks in special refrigerators. Eventually the milk bars were unrecognisable, with shelves stocking household necessities like detergents, toilet rolls, sweet and savoury biscuits, tinned food and even soap. In Victoria there had been a law about selling groceries after 9 p.m. but that law had long gone.

There are still milk bar signs around but the once-familiar Sennit's ice-cream signs have gone, as have most of the bars themselves, replaced by 24-hour convenience stores, mini-markets and supermarkets. Our greater mobility, longer shopping hours, better food-storage and food preservation, rising rents and land values have all changed our shopping habits and meant the demise of the milk bar as we once knew it.

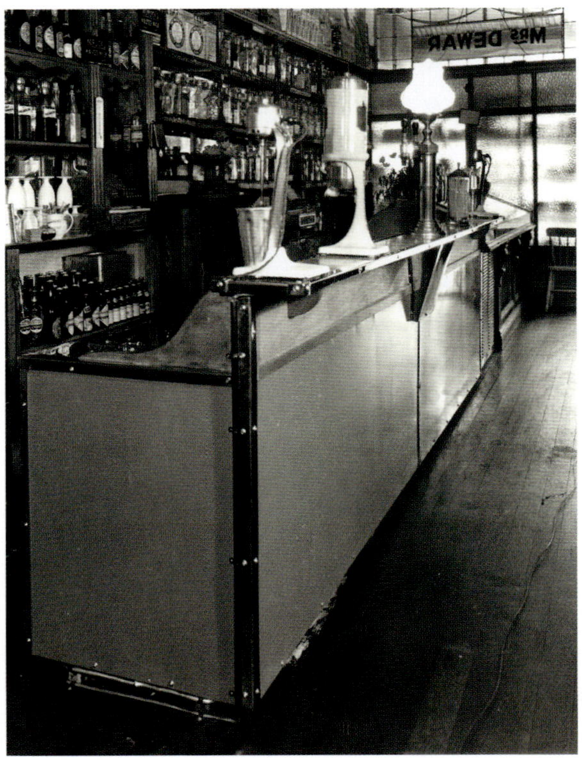

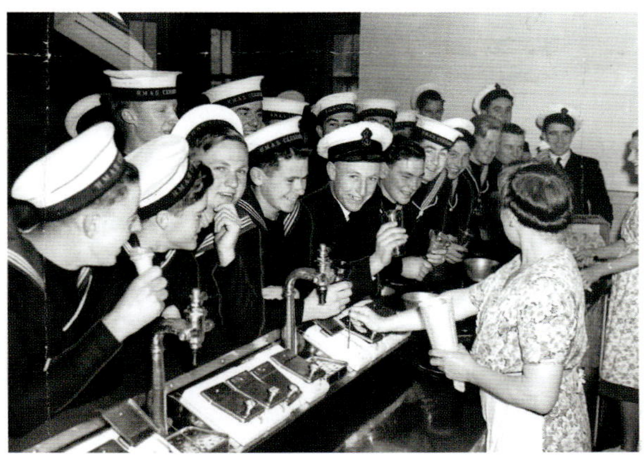

RIGHT *Staff pose for the camera behind a Melbourne milk bar in this 1950s photo.*

LEFT *Young sailors enjoying the milk bar at the Flinders Naval Depot in 1948.*

FAR LEFT *Mrs Dewar's milk bar (1929–1937) in Sydney Road, Brunswick. The menu lists cordials and flavourings, Horlicks malted milk, Tarax soft drink and Elliots' lemonade.*

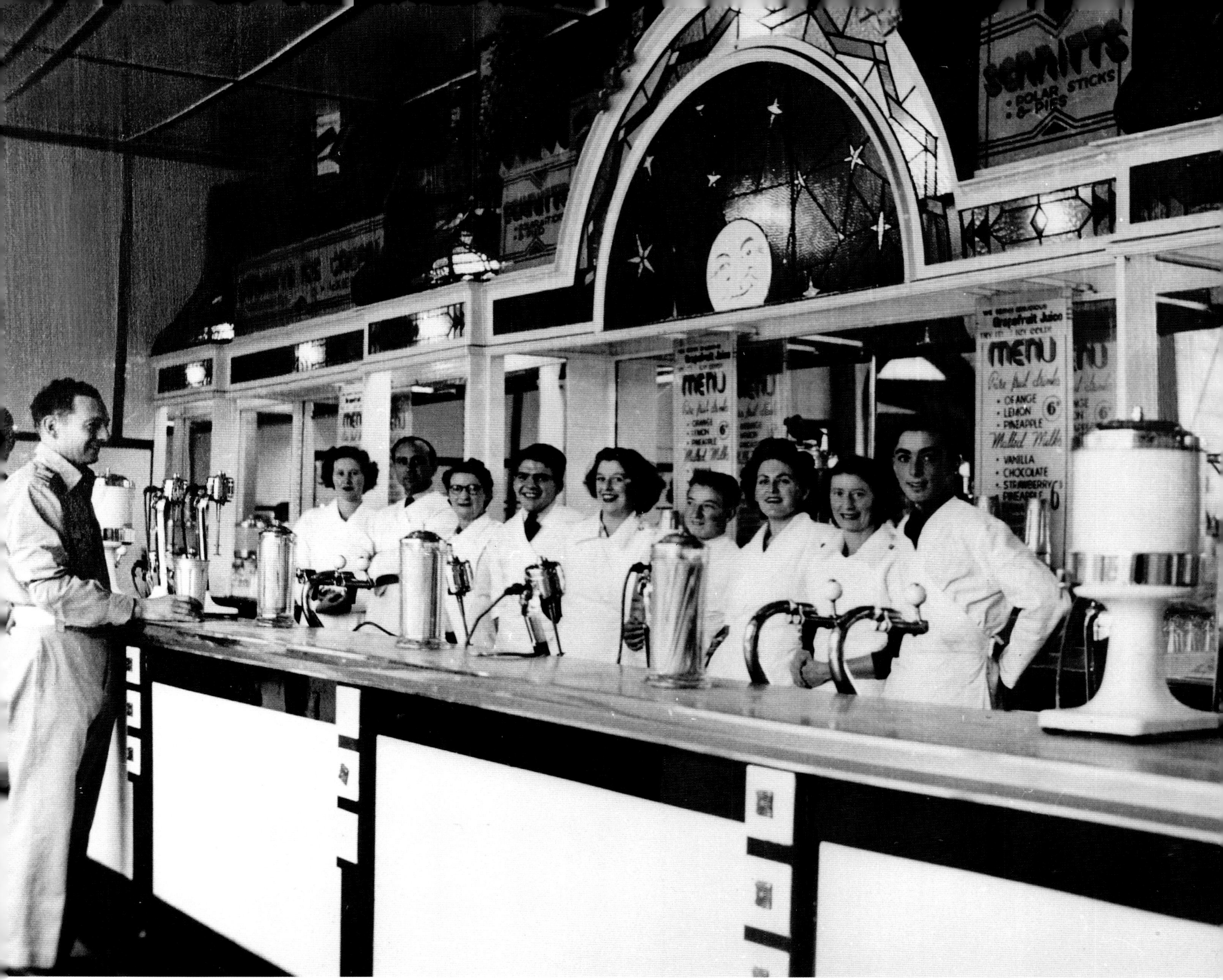
POLAR STICKS
& PIES
Grapefruit Juice
MENU
ORANGE
LEMON
PINEAPPLE
6d
Malted Milks
VANILLA
CHOCOLATE
STRAWBERRY
PINEAPPLE

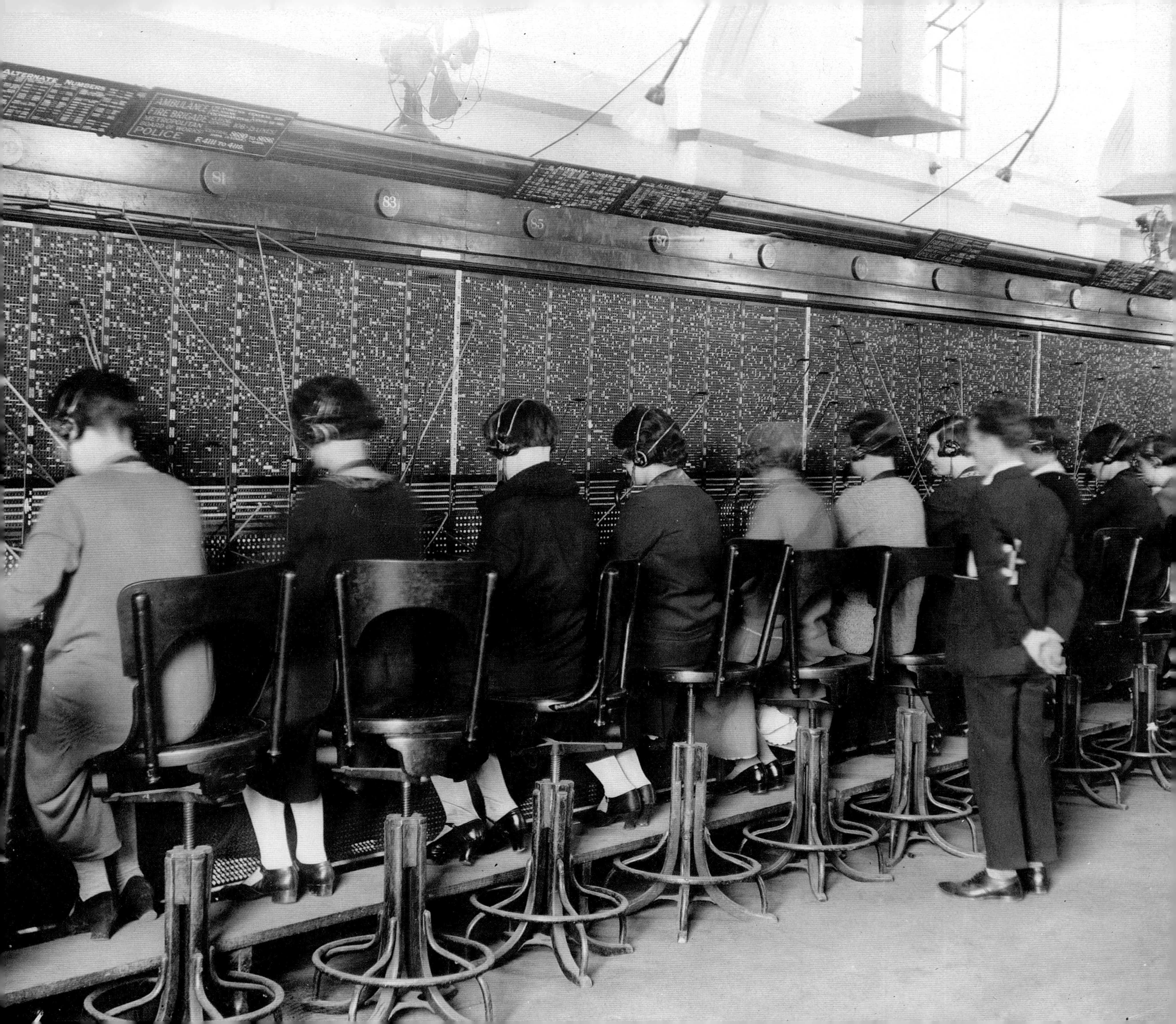
ALTERNATE NUMBERS
AMBULANCE
FIRE BRIGADE
METROPOLITAN
BOARD OF WORKS
POLICE
F.4111 TO 4119
81
83
85
87

Telephonists PHASED OUT 1980s

Australia's first telephone connection was installed in Melbourne in 1879 and the country's first exchange opened in the city in 1880. Located on Collins Street, the exchange was operated by the Melbourne Telephone Exchange Company, the private business of Henry Byron Moore, who bought the Melbourne rights to Bell's 1874 invention of the telephone. At that time there were few subscribers, but the number was to grow rapidly. Each subscriber had a small box with an ear and a mouth piece while at the central exchange the subscriber's number was placed on a board and two young ladies were employed to connect (or switch) the two people who wanted to talk to each other. By the time of the government takeover of the Victorian Telephone Exchange Company (as it was then called) in 1887, there were 887 subscribers and 21 employees. At that time Melburnians made 8,000 calls each day, mainly from banks, importers, insurance companies, merchants and brokers.

The *Town and Country Journal* of 10 September 1887 explained the role of the switchboard operators or telephonists:

> There are, in all, twenty-four lady operators employed in the Exchange, the time-table being so arranged as to provide eleven always in attendance at the switch board.... Place yourself in the middle of the room and gaze upon the delicate hands in magic confusion playing as it were upon metal switches, plugs, and switching cords. There is no shouting or even excitement – no apoplectic strain into the machine's mouth. The young ladies rarely turn their heads. There is a soft sighing murmur in the room; and one could easily imagine the spare forms to be automatic figures.

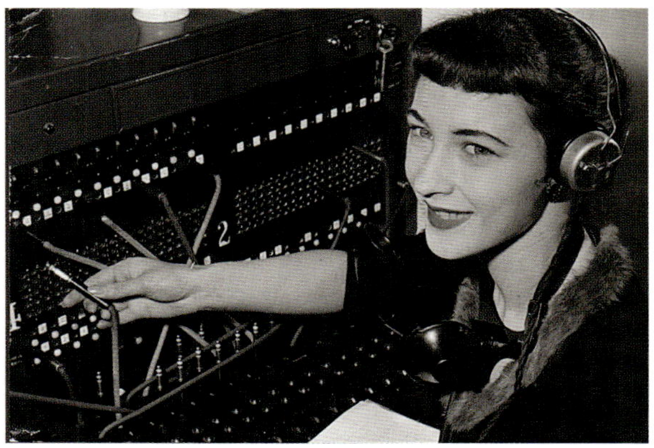

Most of the telephonists were female. Women were paid less than men – there were not the same career choices for women – and the job tended to attract women of a better class and education. Telephonists were rarely acknowledged for the important role they played within the communications industry. Of course engineers, linesmen and managers were important but it was the reliability of service offered by the telephonists that was the first point of contact for customers. Switchboard telephony was a particularly successful employment field for visually impaired or blind workers. At the Royal Victorian Institute for the Blind, specially adapted switchboards and other equipment were used for training purposes.

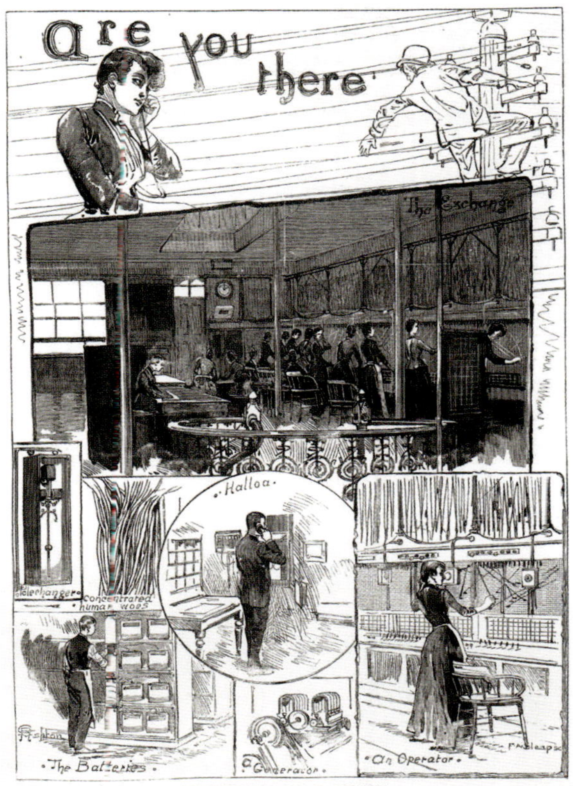

For a telephonist, the first requirement of the job was to give service to the customer, to connect them quickly and efficiently to the desired number. They were closely associated with the business, social and domestic life of the community. The caricature of the city telephonist was a disembodied voice aiding the telecommunication process. For country telephonists it was the one-dimensional gossip and eavesdropper. The voice was always characterised as female, thus failing to recognise the male minority who also worked in this field. As an occupational group, telephonists made a substantial economic and social contribution to the community. Despite the early image of the telephonist being less-than-human disembodied voices, telephonists during the 20th century became more assertive as they fought to retain their jobs or improve their career prospects.

From the 1980s, the privatisation of telephone services, the take-up of mobile phones and the use of telephone infrastructure meant the demise of telephonists as part of a Telecom rationalisation program. Today, even the fixed-line local calls are disappearing because of the take-up of mobile phones and broadband. Perhaps, in time, the contribution of telephonists to commercial and national growth in Australia will be fully recognised.

LEFT *An illustration of Melbourne's telephone system from around 1890, showing operators, batteries, generator, switchboard and the recipient of the calls.*

FAR LEFT *An operator at the console of a switchboard in the late 1940s.*

OPPOSITE *Female workers with a male supervisor at Melbourne's Central Telephone Exchange, around 1930.*

Australian Building DEMOLISHED 1981

The Australian Building (also known as the APA Building) was, for a brief time, one of the tallest buildings in the world. It was certainly much taller than any office building in Europe when F. T. Derham built it in 1888–89. During the period of 1883 to 1889 many speculative companies were started, often with little secured finance, collapsing with disastrous results after a very short time. In central Melbourne land values were very high and vast amounts of money were spent constructing large buildings for insurance companies, mortgage lenders and banks. In 1884, Derham, then Post Master General and a director of the biscuit manufacturing firm of Swallow and Ariell, floated the Australian Property and Investment Company near the end of the Land Boom and attracted to its board some notable figures, such as politicians Alfred Deakin and James Munro. Derham bought the E. S. & A Bank in Elizabeth Street, on the corner of Flinders Lane, for £65,000. Here he intended to build a 15-storey office block, but in reality it only reached 12 storeys. Nevertheless, at 164 feet (53 metres) high, it was still taller than any other building in Melbourne at the time.

This massive structure was constructed in the Victorian period in the Queen Anne style, with a gabled roofline, walkway, pinnacles and decorative masonry. It was built in red and cream horizontal bands, and the bands, together with the long windows, broke up the mass of the structure and gave it a more elegant, lighter appearance. At the base, the granite walls were more than 3 feet (1 metre) thick. Much pink and grey marble was used in the interior. Shops occupied the ground floor and in the upper storeys there were 220 offices. These offices were connected to the ground floor by speaking tubes and an electric indicator showed whether or not the tenant was in the office.

Hydraulic lifts were used and the total cost of installing these elevators was supposed to be one twelfth of the £80,000 total building cost. The lifts were powered by high-pressure water and on the day they were to be opened by the Premier, Alfred Deakin, something went badly wrong. As reported by Henry Kemp (the building's architect), the official party was in the lift when "… as the rope was pulled, the cage shot up like a rocket…. Fortunately the safety springs brought the flight upwards to a not too violent conclusion, the lift recoiling a mere ten or twelve feet."

By the time the building was finished in 1889, Melbourne's land boom was starting to collapse into an economic depression that took the city decades to recover from. It became increasingly difficult to lease the office space and, with small financial reserves, the Australian Property and Investment Company was in trouble. Derham was saved by Munro's Real Estate Bank, which bought Derham's assets at many times their market value.

The building was demolished in 1981, supposedly because it was a fire hazard and the owners refused to pay the £2 million for the necessary fire insurance. In 1916 a mandatory height limit of 132 feet (40 metres) was introduced and, until the ICI Building was constructed in 1957, the Australian Building remained the tallest in the City of Melbourne.

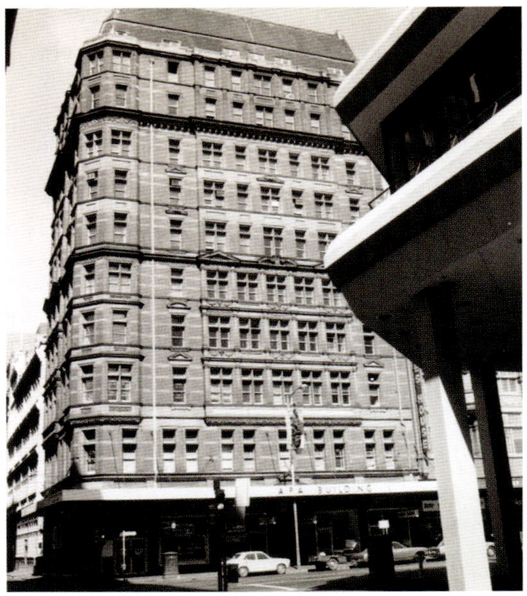

ABOVE *In the 1950s the top floor and pinnacles of the Australian Building were removed.*

OPPOSITE *The distinctive red and white Australian Building with its ornate roofline was the tallest building in Melbourne for many years.*

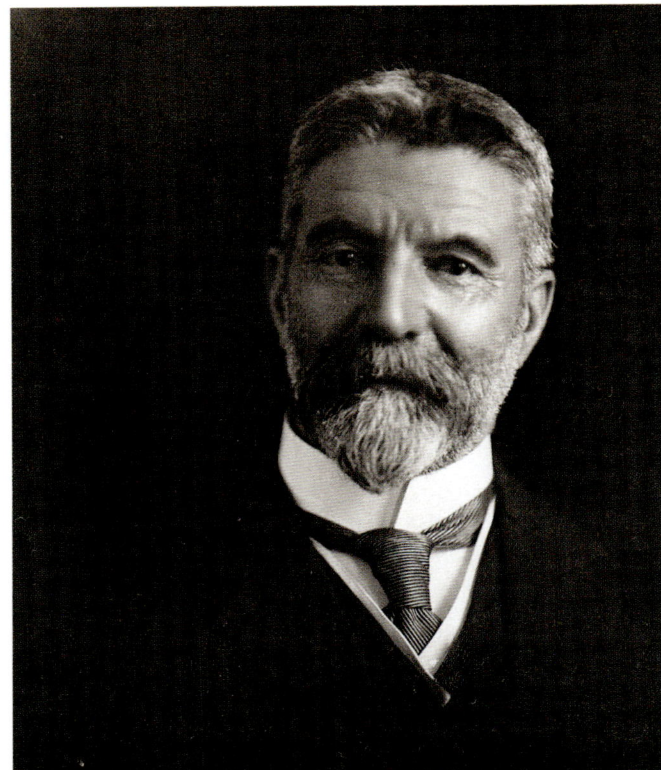

ALFRED DEAKIN (1856–1919)

Alfred Deakin was a very important figure in Australian history. He was a barrister, journalist and politician, and three times Prime Minister of Australia. Like many others of his education and position, he was an investor, director or chairman of some of the companies formed during the 1880s land boom, the most notable of which were those of James Munro and F. T. Derham. He lost his savings and those of his father in these speculative investments. He is best remembered for the part he played in the Federation Movement, which culminated in 1900 in the Royal assent to an "Act to Constitute the Commonwealth of Australia".

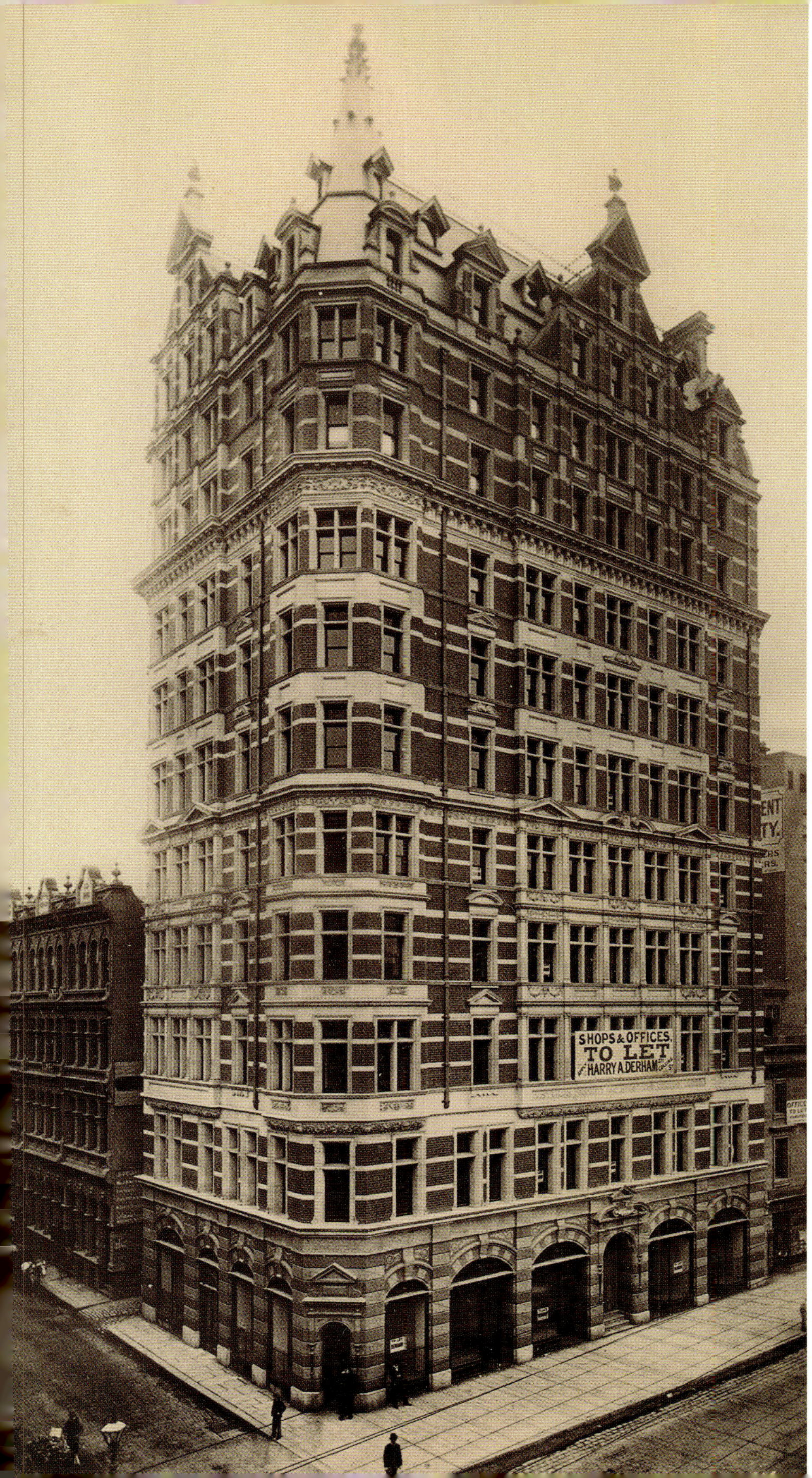
SHOPS & OFFICES
TO LET
HARRY A. DERHAM

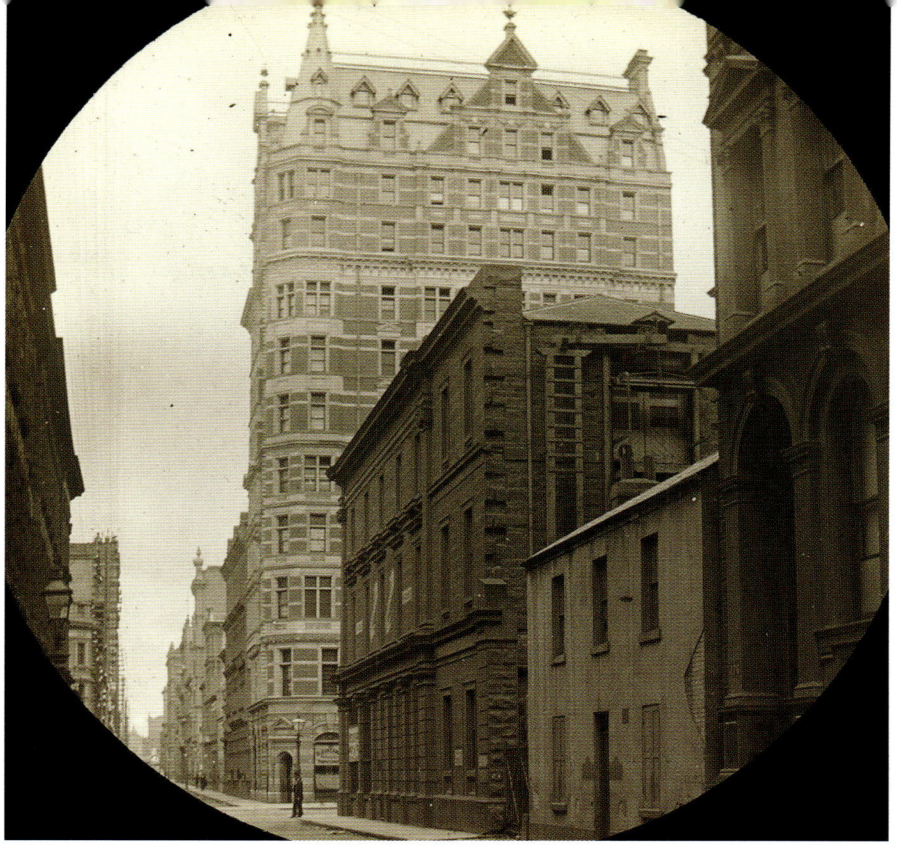

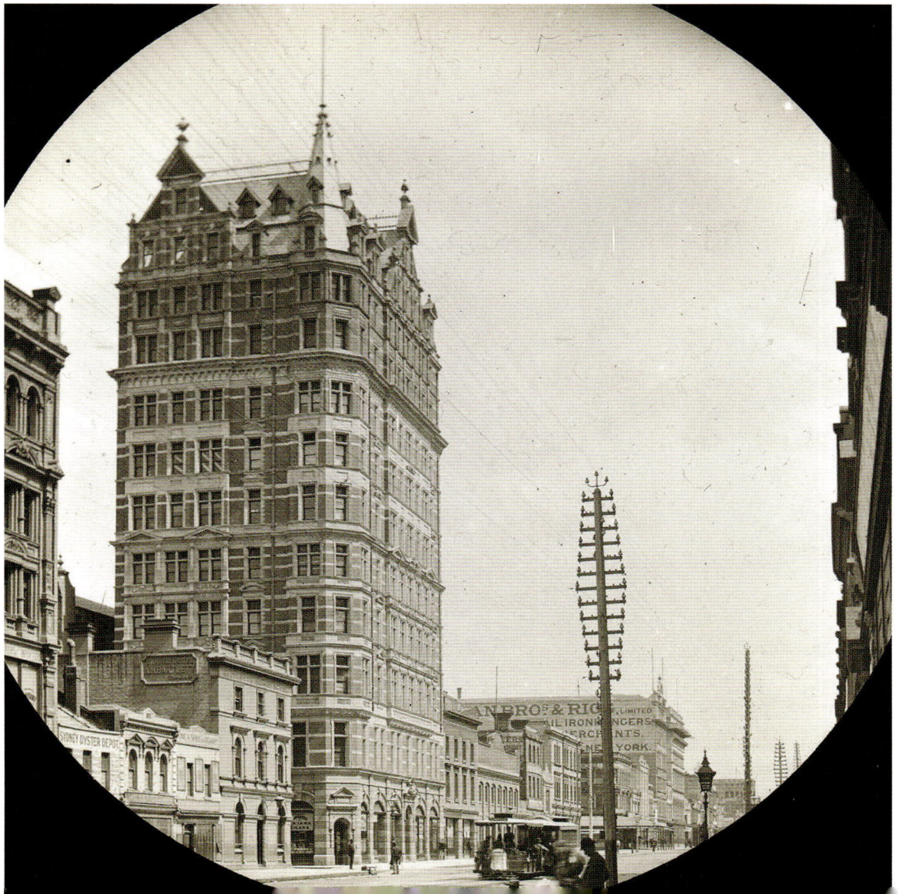

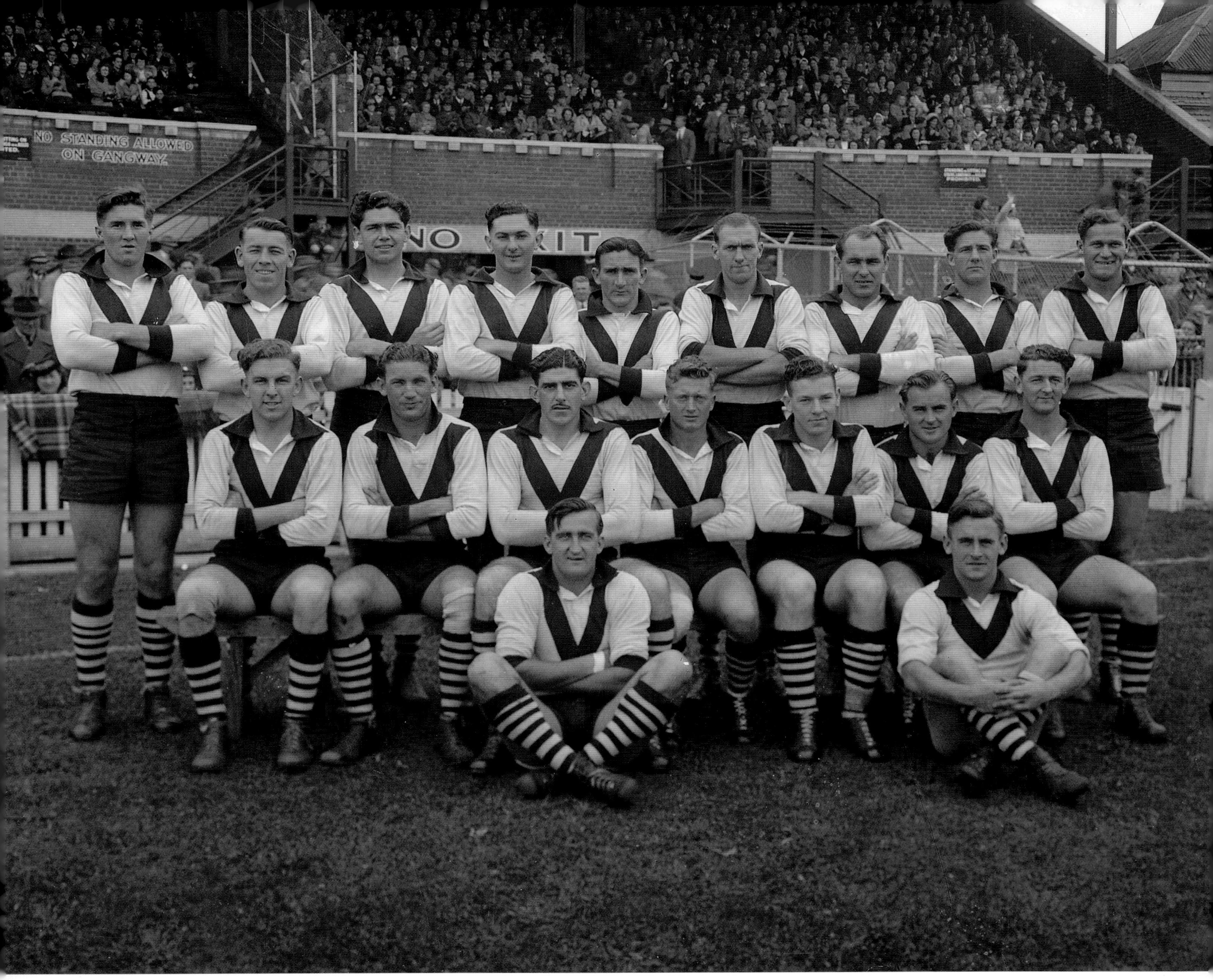
NO STANDING ALLOWED
ON GANGWAY.
NO EXIT

South Melbourne Football Club

BECAME THE SYDNEY SWANS 1983

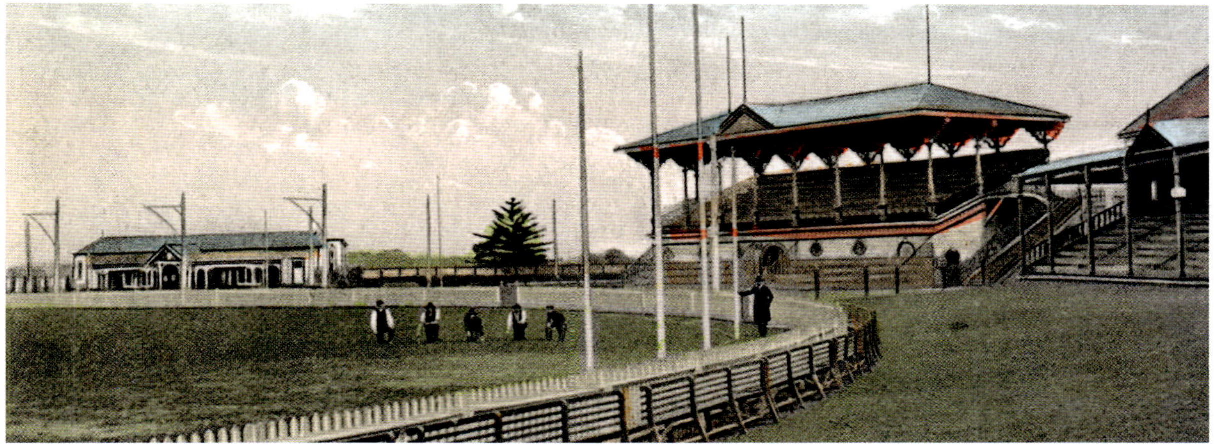

Clubs in South Melbourne and Albert Park played their own brand of Australian football in the 1860s, but it was in June 1874 that a group met to form a more cohesive football club. In July that year it took the name the South Melbourne Football Club. In 1880 they amalgamated with Albert Park and adopted the red and white colours of that team. South Melbourne were nicknamed "the Southerners" or "the Bloods" because of the bright red sash on their white jumpers. Their home was the Lake Oval.

South Melbourne at that time was probably the strongest football club in Victoria. Over its first decade it won five Victorian Football Association (VFA) championships. In 1897 though, it became one of the founding clubs of the new Victorian Football League (VFL) when they broke away from the VFA. The club had early successes, appearing in a number of finals and winning three Grand Finals. The 1930s were probably their most successful period and it was also the time when they earned the nickname "the Swans". This came about because so many of their players actually came from Western Australia, which has the swan as its state emblem.

Limited success followed the Swans in the 1940s, though they reached the Grand Final in 1945. Played against Carlton, the match became known as the "Bloodbath" because of a brawl that resulted in nine players being reported by the umpires. South Melbourne lost the match and over the next 35 years they played in finals only twice. They also won three wooden spoons (bottom) in this period.

During the 1950s to 1980s South Melbourne struggled. The traditional recruiting area was the inner-city, but people were moving to the outer suburbs so their pool of recruits diminished. Administrators worked desperately to keep the Swans afloat but it became apparent that they did not have the money to compete against other clubs in the drive for interstate and country players. Diminishing attendance and decreasing membership did not help. Country zoning was introduced to help the clubs but the area the Swans were to recruit from did not prove profitable. One of the Swans best known players during this era was Bobby Skilton who captained the side from 1961 to 1971. He was one of only four players to win the Brownlow Medal (the most prestigious award for individual players in the Australian Football League) three times.

The VFL (later the AFL) in the late 1970s wanted a club to be placed in Sydney in order to attract interstate interest. In 1982, instead of a 13th club being formed in Sydney it allowed South Melbourne to play 11 home matches in Sydney. South Melbourne was the first club in the competition to be based outside Victoria. In June that year they officially became known as the Swans and in 1983 the Sydney Swans. The initial success of this move was not to last. The Swans were bought by Dr Geoffrey Edelsten and, when that failed, by a group of investors. That too failed and it became necessary to restructure the club. AFL intervention meant that the Swans reverted to a traditional member-based system, rather than private ownership. It took some time, several coaches and a change of administration. All paid off when, in 2005, the Sydney Swans won the Grand Final against the West Coast by four points. They were to repeat this in 2012 against favourites Hawthorn, winning by 10 points. The Sydney Swans were once again a team to be reckoned with.

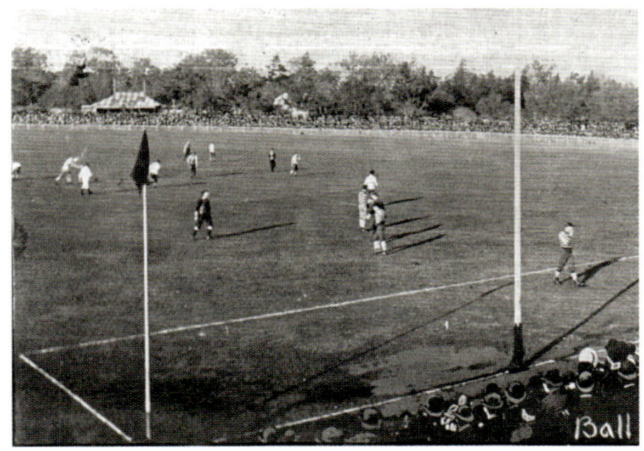

TOP *The Lakeside Oval with the grandstand, the home of the South Melbourne Football Club.*

ABOVE *The opening match of the football season in 1895, between South Melbourne and Melbourne.*

OPPOSITE *South Melbourne First Eighteen photographed at South Melbourne's Lake Oval in 1949 in front of a packed grandstand. Bert Lucas, the seated player with the moustache, was South's captain at the time of this photo.*

Allen's Sweets FACTORY DEMOLISHED 1987

The Allen's Sweets factory and its spectacular animated neon sign were landmarks in Melbourne for many years and the loss, particularly of the neon sign, is still mourned today.

Sweets or confectionery had been made in Melbourne from as early as the 1840s. Small cottage industries developed into family businesses and the history of the Allen's Sweets business reflects this development. Alfred Weaver (Alf) Allen started working in the confectionery trade for Sir Macpherson Robertson at the age of 17. He established his own business and in the 1890s was producing and selling confectionery in his shop in Fitzroy and supplying a stall in the Eastern Market. By 1909, Allen's was the third largest manufacturer of confectionery in Melbourne, after MacRobertson's and Hoadleys.

In the 19th and for much of the 20th century, the south bank of the Yarra was home to large industries, car parks, roads, remnants of railways and docks. The factories were initially attracted there because the land was flat, and cheaper, but it was also prone to flooding.

In 1922 A. W. Allen built a large factory on the southern bank of the Yarra, a factory designed by Joseph Plottel, a prominent architect. This large brick building with cement dressings of a neoclassical style was functional rather than decorative, but it became a major Melbourne landmark. Here sweets that became household names were manufactured. These included Kool Mints, Irish Moss Gum Jubes, Cure-'em-Quicks, Steam Rollers, Anticol lollies, and Butter-Menthol lozenges (the sweets where the "butter soothes the throat while the menthol clears the head"). Another jingle, "Moments like these you need Minties" was claimed to be the longest-running slogan in Australian advertising history. On the top of one of the buildings was erected an enormous neon sign, 30 metres wide and at least 12 metres high. The Allen's sign was the best known and certainly the most prominent of all the colourful neon illuminated signs to light the night sky in Melbourne.

A. W. Allen died in 1925 and after World War II chocolate production ceased, but Allen's continued to be one of Australia's largest and most successful manufacturers of confectionery. In 1985 Allen's, like some other iconic Australian brands, was taken over by a multinational, the UK-based Rothmans and later Nestle. By 2001 three foreign manufacturing giants, Nestle, Cadbury-Schweppes, and Mars controlled 75 per cent of the market. Victoria still produces 30 per cent of Australia's confectionery and 70 per cent of its exports. The Allen's brand continues, despite being owned by an overseas company, and their familiar sweets, like Butter Menthols, Minties, Freckles, Jaffas and Steam Rollers, are readily available.

In the 19th and early 20th century sweets could be bought in small quantities from corner shops and milk bars. Pocket money would buy a child a small white paper bag of lollies for very little money. Now most of the sweets are bagged and sold in convenience stores, self-service stores, service stations and supermarkets. The disappearance of some confectionery businesses could be attributed to high labour costs, healthier eating habits and the dominance of the large supermarkets, who can squeeze the producer and import the product more cheaply from overseas suppliers. By 1987 A. W. Allen had moved from South Melbourne and both the sign and the factory had been demolished. Everyone from politicians to the public wanted the sign to be saved but government and commercial interests could not agree on how this was to be done. Melbourne has lost an iconic part of its built history and, once gone, it can never be replaced.

BELOW *The Allen's Sweets factory and its huge neon sign viewed from one of the spires of St Paul's Cathedral.*

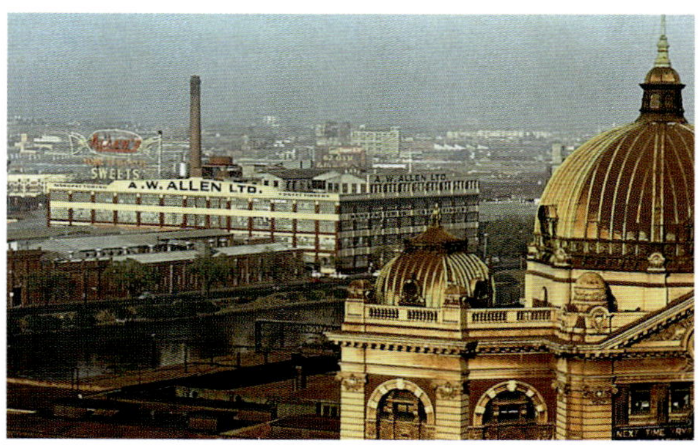

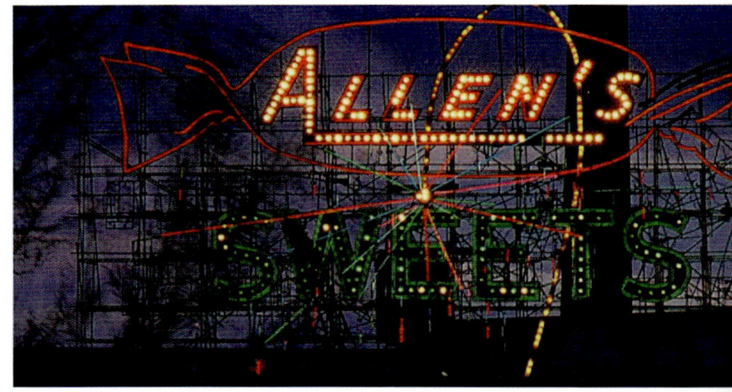

ABOVE *In 1955 the sign just announced "Allen's Sweets". In 1969 Claude Neon added several overlays that were a source of wonder and delight to Melburnians. Coloured neon lights showed "Cool, cool, Kool Mints", followed by "Anticol Cough Drops". The grand finale of this 35-second display showed a rocket that set off a display of sparks or fireworks and then cough drops falling from an Anticol packet.*

RIGHT *The Allen's factory and its iconic sign illuminated the night sky along the Yarra from the 1950s to 1987.*

BELOW *Magazine advertisements emphasised the goodness of Allen's Sweets in the 1950s and 1960s.*

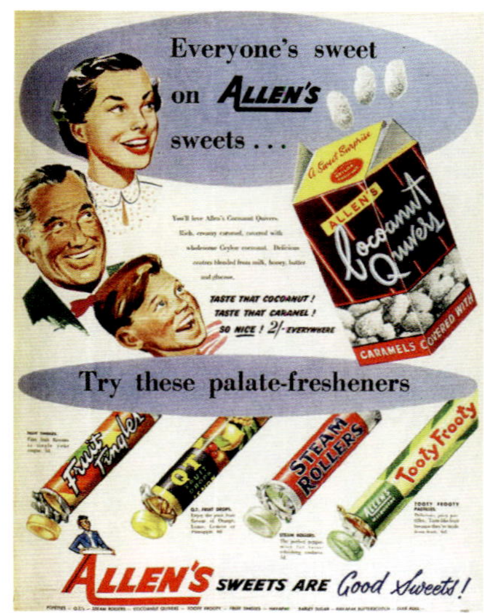

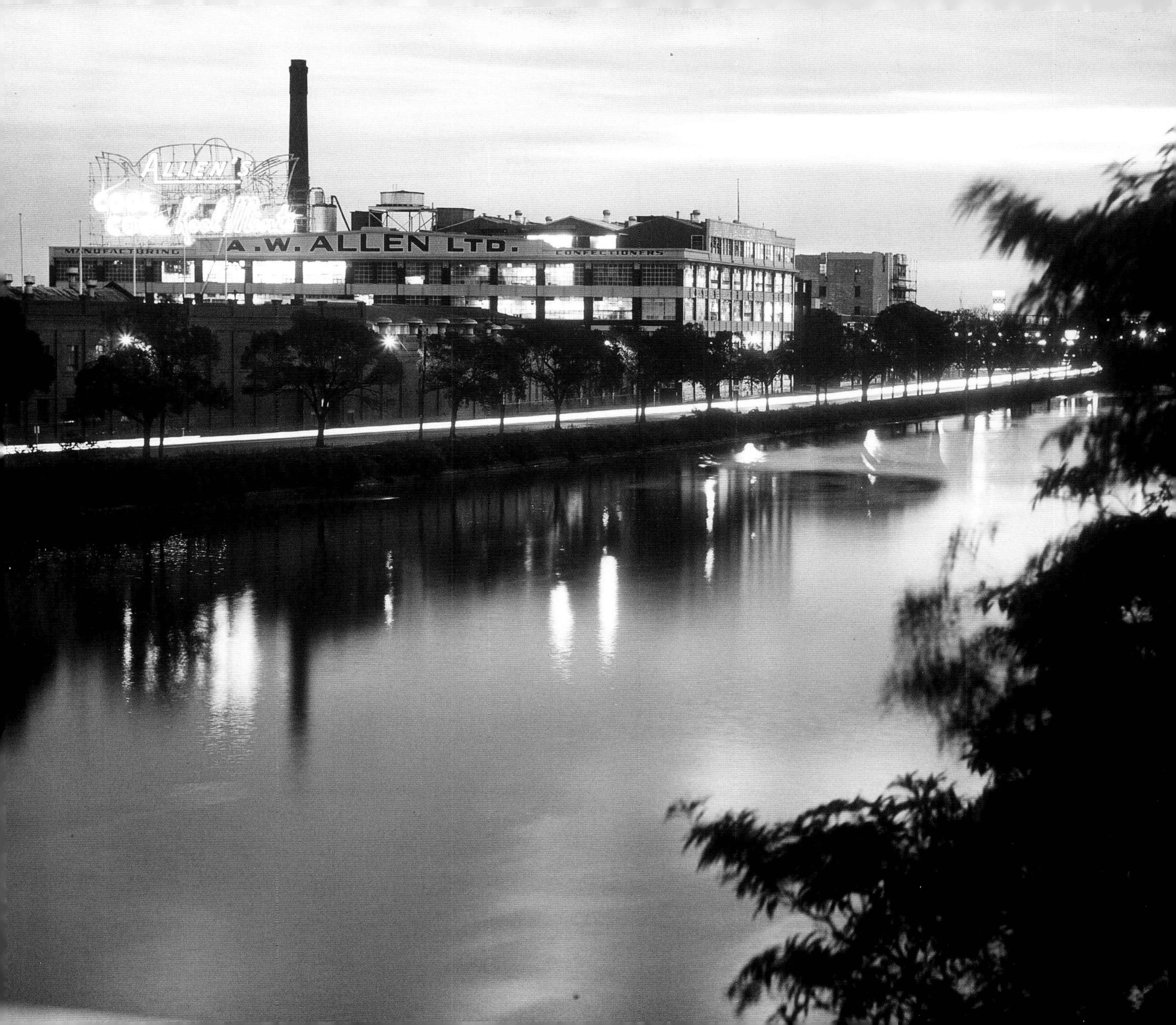
ALLEN'S
MANUFACTURING
A.W. ALLEN LTD.
CONFECTIONERS

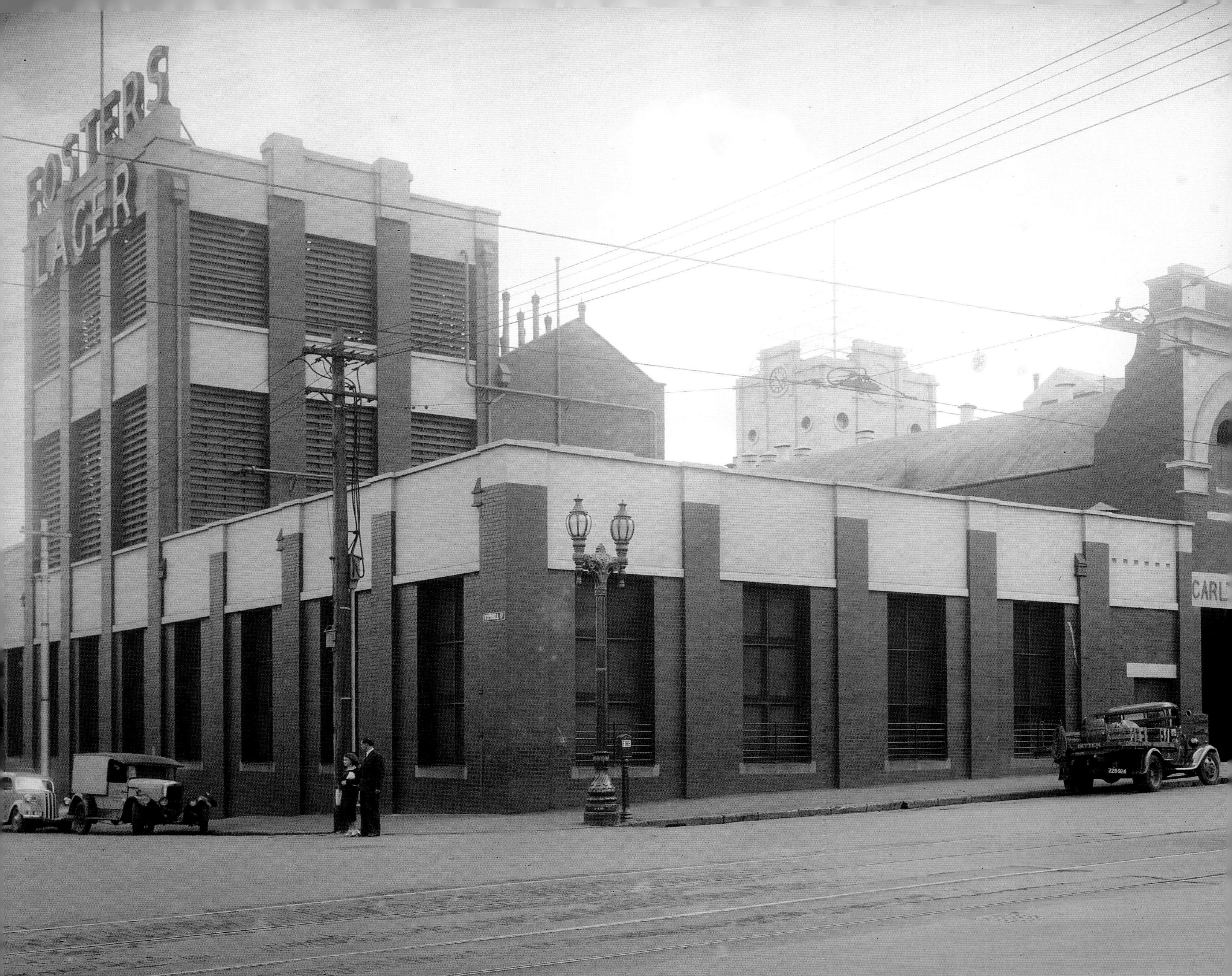
FOSTERS
LAGER
CARL

Carlton and United Brewery

SWANSTON STREET BREWERY CLOSED 1987

Beer drinking has always been a favourite pastime in Australia and in the 1870s more beer was consumed per person than it is today. The manufacture of beer was a very important industry and there were 126 breweries spread across early colonial Victoria. In Melbourne alone there were more than 100 hotels.

Beer manufacturing in the Carlton suburb of Melbourne began in 1858 when Rosenberg and Co. started brewing at Bouverie Street. This North Melbourne Brewery was an unsuccessful venture and in 1859 a Mr John Bellman bought the operation, renaming it the Carlton Brewery. This also failed. Edward Latham bought the brewery in 1865, and, over the next five years, successfully expanded its premises and its production, building bluestone offices, large stables for the essential draft horses and replacing the earlier plant with a tall tower of red and white bricks. A wine and spirit store and more bluestone warehouses were added in the early 1880s. Latham finally sold his interest in the brewery to the Melbourne Brewing and Malting Company. The Malt House was built in 1904 and hops, barley, and malted barley were stored here. In the basement were the fermenting tanks.

By the 1890s many hotels were tied to particular breweries. Those breweries not tied to hotels found that their outlets were dwindling. To combat this, the major Melbourne breweries formed the Society of Melbourne Brewers in 1903. By 1907 this group had become the Carlton and United Brewers (CUB), made up of the Carlton Brewery, and the McCracken, Victoria, Shamrock, Foster's, and Castlemaine breweries. In 1913 CUB was listed on the Stock Exchange. Between 1924 and 1982 CUB continued to expand, taking over many breweries across Australia, beginning with the Abbotsford Brewery in 1924. This was followed by Northern Australian Breweries in 1931, the Ballarat Brewing Company in 1958, the Queensland Brewery Limited in 1961, the Cascade Brewery in 1981, and Tooth's and Company in 1982. Through its long history of takeovers and mergers, CUB has become one of Australia's most successful companies.

As the breweries became larger they developed their own distinctive style of architecture. Many notable architects designed these breweries. Each brewery had a very tall brewing tower, generally five storeys or more. These towers were often topped with a mansard roof, decorative balustrade and a flagpole. The roof and the openings provided vital ventilation for the brewing process below. Many breweries were built of red brick, decorated with cream coloured cement rendering. This style was used for the arched windows and closed arches of the Swanston Street Malt House building. Until the 1950s most work was still done by manual labour. This backbreaking work was rewarded with good wages, job security, the support of a strong union and free beer.

The Swanston Street brewery closed its doors in 1987 when CUB moved its headquarters to Abbotsford. The buildings were largely demolished in the 1990s and today the huge neon Carlton sign has gone. All that remains of this Melbourne landmark is the Malt House and the bluestone building in Bouverie Street.

LEFT *The northern end of Swanston Street was dominated by the Carlton Brewery buildings from 1873 to the 1990s.*

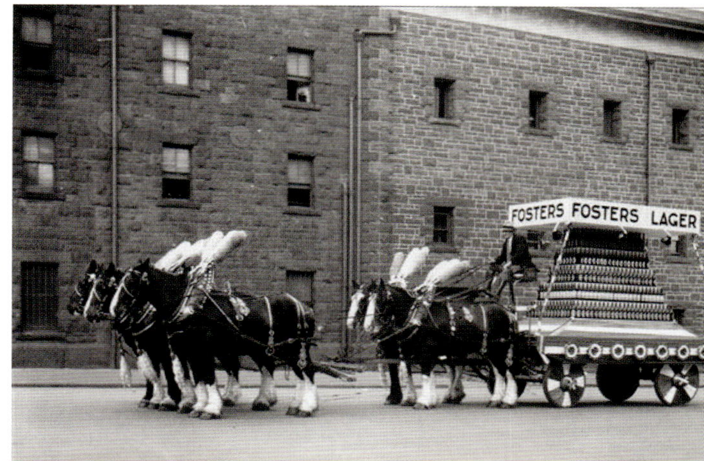

CARLTON AND UNITED CLYDESDALES

Clydesdale horses have played an important role in early Australian history. They were important in the clearing of the land, in all aspects of the farming industry, and they hauled timber and wool to ports. Teams of up to 30 horses were used in the construction of irrigation channels and dams across the country. As early as 1864 Clydesdales were pulling wagons with barrels of Carlton Ale and they did so until just after World War II. They were prized for their strength and their gentle natures. Their stamina was put to good use in the cities where they were used to pull the drays and wagons of the milkman, the baker and the brewers. Today Carlton maintains a stable of Clydesdales, used in ceremonial processions as a reminder of their past importance and a symbol of CUB.

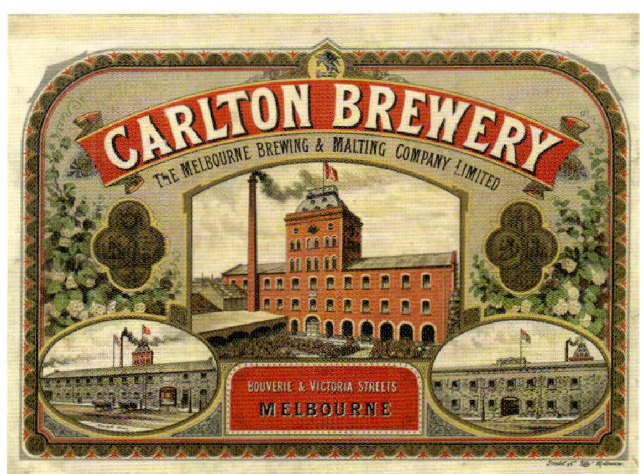

LEFT *This beer label shows the new brewery, erected in 1873, with its tall chimney and tower, as well as two images of the bluestone building at Bouverie and Victoria Streets.*

Cairns Memorial Church DESTROYED BY FIRE 1988

In the 1840s there were three branches of the Presbyterian Church set up in Melbourne by the migrants who had come to the colony from Scotland and Ireland. These Presbyterians became very influential in business, land and education, and the most influential of these were centred in the Scots' Church in Collins Street and the Chalmers Church in East Melbourne. Chalmers Church, under Dr Adam Cairns, was orthodox, while the Scots Church, under Rev Menzies, was more liberal and progressive.

Dr Cairns came from a family of Scottish ministers of religion. He was a very well-educated man and one of four clergymen sent to Melbourne in 1853 to establish more churches in the fledgling Colony of Victoria. Several sites had been granted to the Presbyterian Church and, when a site was found in Gipps Street, the Governor expedited the grant. This church became the Chalmers Church and the congregation quickly grew as people were drawn to Cairns' sermons. He was a dynamic speaker with a great knowledge of scripture, known for his diligence and hard work. Cairns always had about 12 sermons prepared and never repeated them. He travelled widely throughout his ministry and retained his strict orthodox beliefs. In time, Chalmers Church numbered many of Melbourne's wealthiest and most influential citizens among its congregation.

When Dr Cairns died in 1881 some of his congregation decided to establish a church in memory of this great leader. At the time some of the members of the Chalmers Church disapproved of statements by the new minister Dr Scott and they resolved to split and start another church. There were reports in *The Argus* showing that not all members of the Chalmers Church were happy to have another Presbyterian Church nearby in East Melbourne. Nevertheless, the Cairns Memorial Church was erected in Powlett Street, East Melbourne, in stages between 1883 and 1887. It was thought that the name of the church would attract a congregation and many donors.

Dr Cairns' widow laid the foundation stone in 1882, and in January 1883 plans for the church were displayed. The new church was built by Twentyman and Askew and was a very imposing construction of Barrabool Hills and Waurn Ponds stone with a nave and transepts featuring stained-glass windows, a tall arched entrance and a gable with a large cross and pinnacles. There was a square tower – a base for a spire that was never built. The interior was impressive, with an elevated gallery and raked floor that meant the congregation could easily see and hear the preacher. The organ made by Alfred Fuller in 1884 was an instrument of quality and beauty, its console polished walnut and the organ case and facade pipes elaborately decorated. During World War I the Cairns Memorial Church had a particularly colourful minister whose strong views alienated some of his parishioners, so much so that they left the church.

For many years the crypt was the home of the Melbourne Model Railway Society and it was here in August 1988 that a fire started. The solid outer walls were all that was left of this beautiful church. It was agreed that there was no money to restore the building and its congregation moved to other churches. Eventually the walls were saved and the Cairns Memorial Church was rebuilt as apartments.

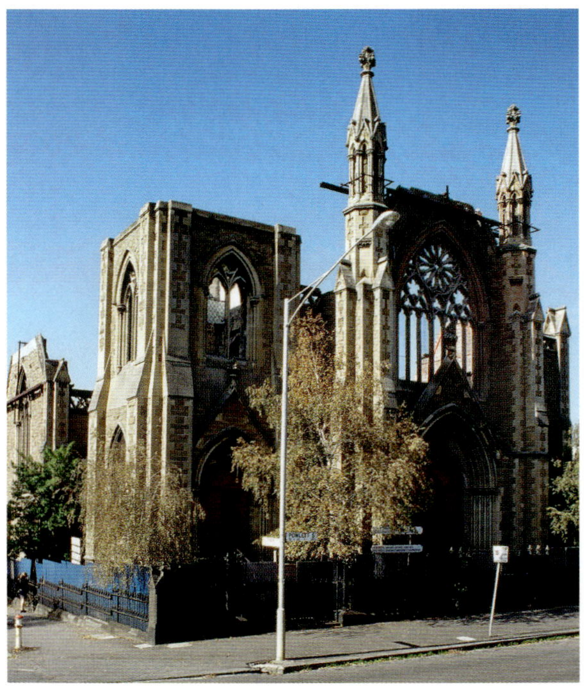

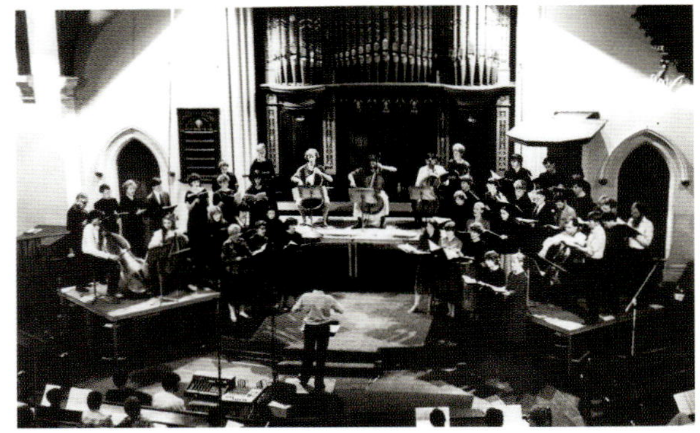

ABOVE *The Cairns Memorial Church sermons were frequently heard on national radio. The church had wonderful acoustics and many concerts were held there. Rudolf Oehr, secretary of the Melbourne Philharmonic Society, was the choirmaster for many years and the church's choral traditions were continued after the fire of 1988.*

RIGHT *The Cairns Memorial Church stood for more than 100 years, a testament to the respect and affection the Melburnian Presbyterians had for Dr Adam Cairns.*

LEFT *The burnt-out shell of the church in 1988. The walls became part of an apartment development.*

BELOW *The 1884 plans for the new Cairns Memorial Church showing the south elevation.*

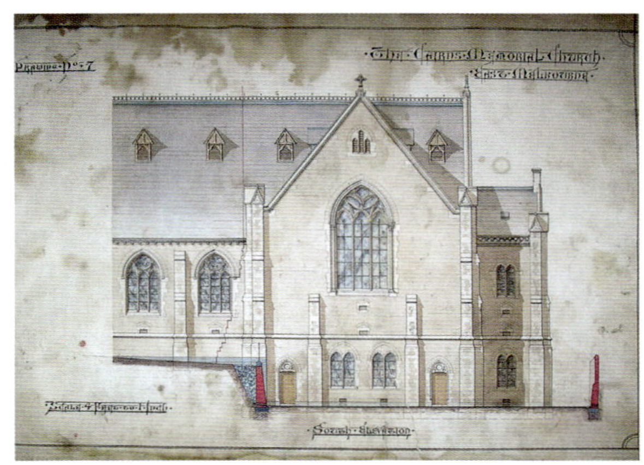

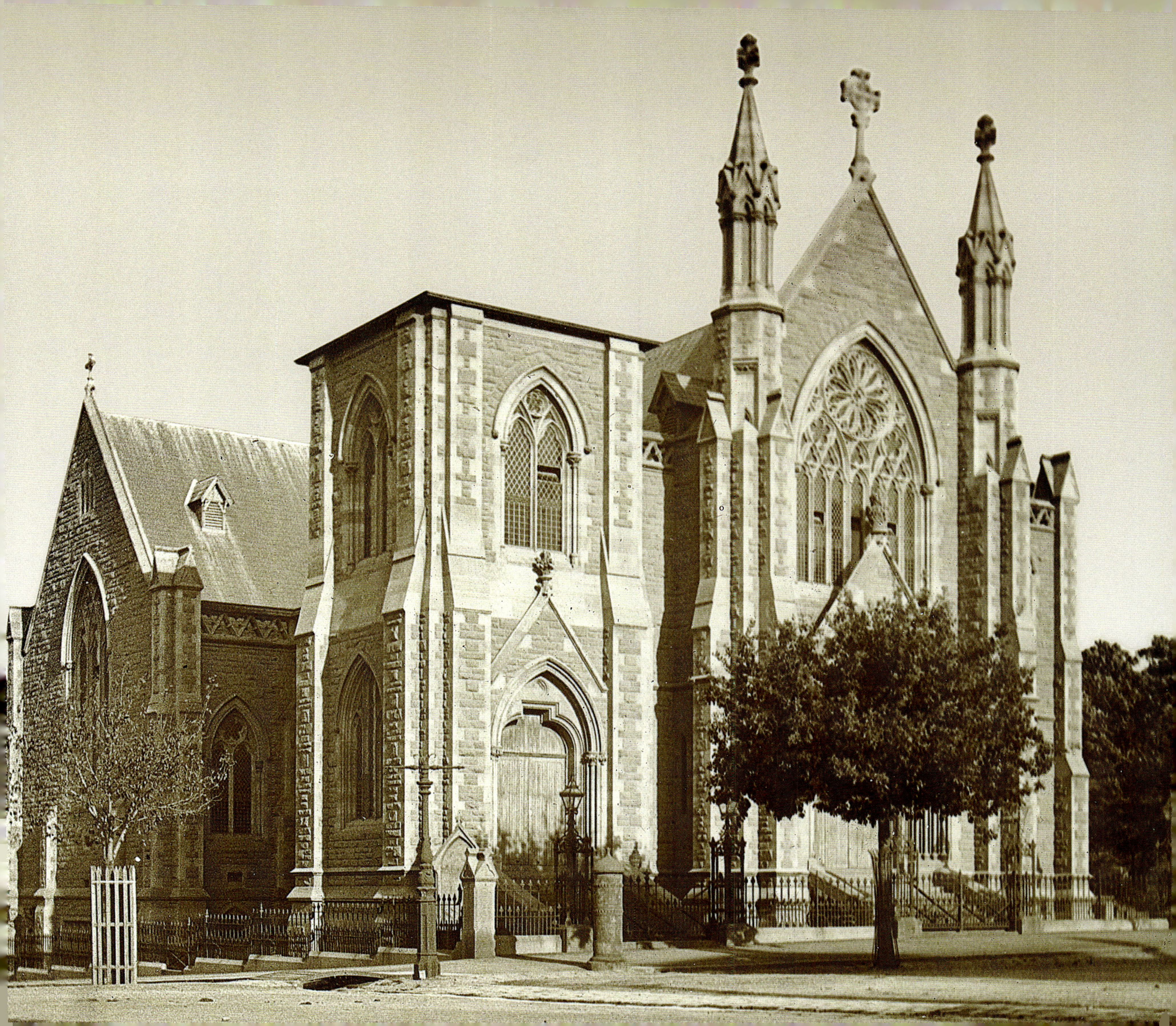

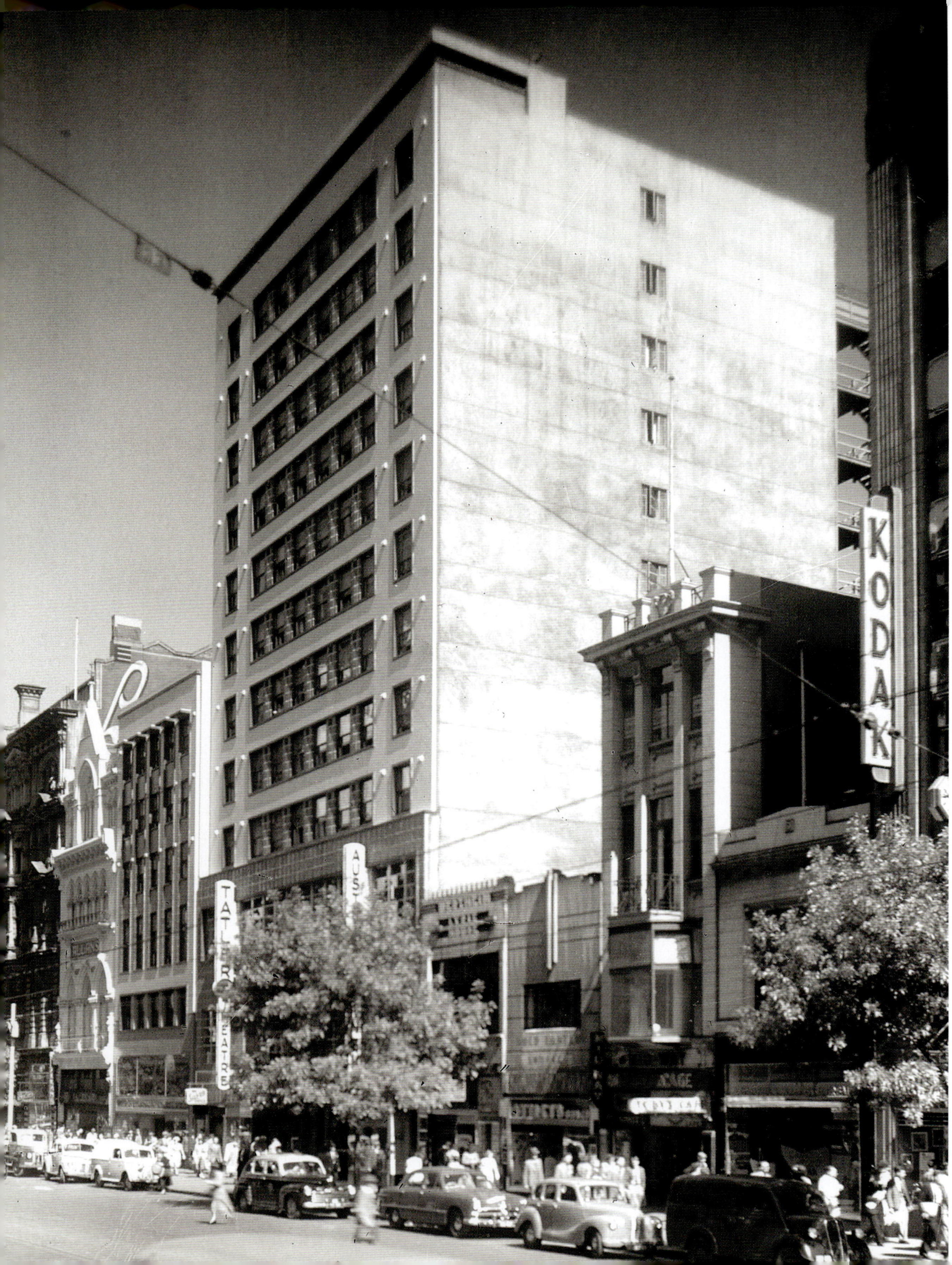

Hotel Australia

DEMOLISHED 1989

The Hotel Australia was built on the site of the Café Australia. Previously there had been two other cafés here: Café Gunsler (1879–90) and the Vienna Café (1890–1915). For many years this part of Collins Street had been the most fashionable part of Melbourne. The area was home to the Block Arcade, which is where Melbourne's high society liked to be seen. In the 1870s the shops in this area were Mullen's bookshop and circulating library, Fletcher's Art Gallery, Glen's Music Warehouse, as well as the Café Gunsler and the Vienna Café, which eventually took over five floors of the music shop.

In 1916 the well-known architect Walter Burley Griffin was engaged to remodel the interior of the Vienna Café and make it the "most beautiful café in Australia". It was also renamed Café Australia, as at that time, in the middle of World War I, the name "Vienna" lost its popularity. The new interior displayed fountains, many statues and art depicting Australian subjects. There were landscapes showing tea-trees, Port Jackson fig trees in the Fern Room and mountain ash trees in the dining room. In the 1920s Café Australia became the Hotel Australia. Fred Matear and Thomas Carlyle bought the building in 1938, but sadly many of the Griffin interiors were lost when the building was demolished to make way for a much grander hotel. However, some Griffin interior elements survived, and the Griffin ceiling was incorporated in the new ballroom of the hotel.

The new hotel, built in 1939, was to be called Hotel Australia and was built in the Functionalist/ Moderne style. It won much praise, particularly for its modern foyer. The hotel was 12 storeys high but it complied with the height limit in Melbourne of 132 feet (40 metres). Three of these storeys

LEFT *Hotel Australia in Collins Street in the 1950s was the place to be seen and a most desirable hotel to visit.*

were to be used for public space and nine for accommodation of about 94 bedrooms. There were two movie theatres in the basement and a large shopping area, Australia Arcade, accommodating 40 shops. It was claimed that this was the largest shopping arcade in Australia. Every day 26,000 workers and shoppers used this arcade, which was conveniently situated between Flinders Street Station and the Myer Department Store in Bourke Street. Some would also patronize the public bars or the coffee shop that was located in the elaborate foyer. There were private dining rooms such as the Cantala Room where the wood panelling had been brought from a demolished mansion, a new Vienna Café and the Georgian Banquet Room.

Just as the Block Arcade had been in the 19th century, in the middle of the 20th century Hotel Australia was considered to be the most desirable place to be seen in the inner city. Well-known theatre people and socialites were spotted here, as well as famous politicians like Sir Robert Menzies, Harold Holt, and the Packer newspaper owners, who kept a suite here for many years. It was also known for the celebrations and elaborate parties that were held at Melbourne Cup time and on New Year's Eve. During World War II, General Douglas MacArthur decided to take over two floors at the hotel as his headquarters for the South West Pacific Allied Forces. By September 1943 there were 119,000 American troops in Melbourne and the Hotel Australia became their main meeting place. In 1989 the hotel and some adjoining buildings were demolished to make way for a much larger hotel and shopping precinct to be known as Australia on Collins.

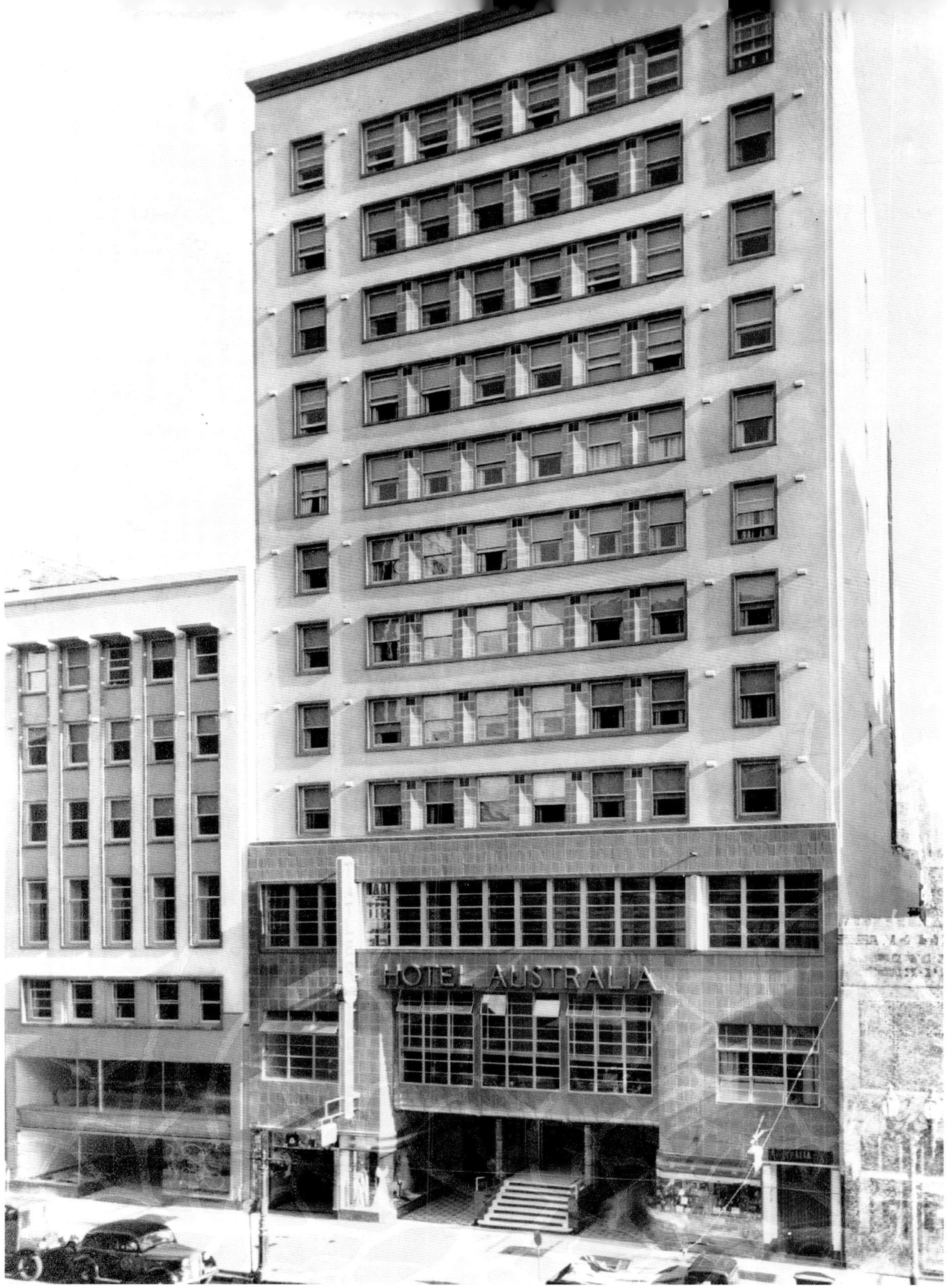

RIGHT *The Hotel Australia in the mid-1940s. The 12-storey landmark was demolished in 1989 to make way for the "Australia on Collins" shopping centre.*

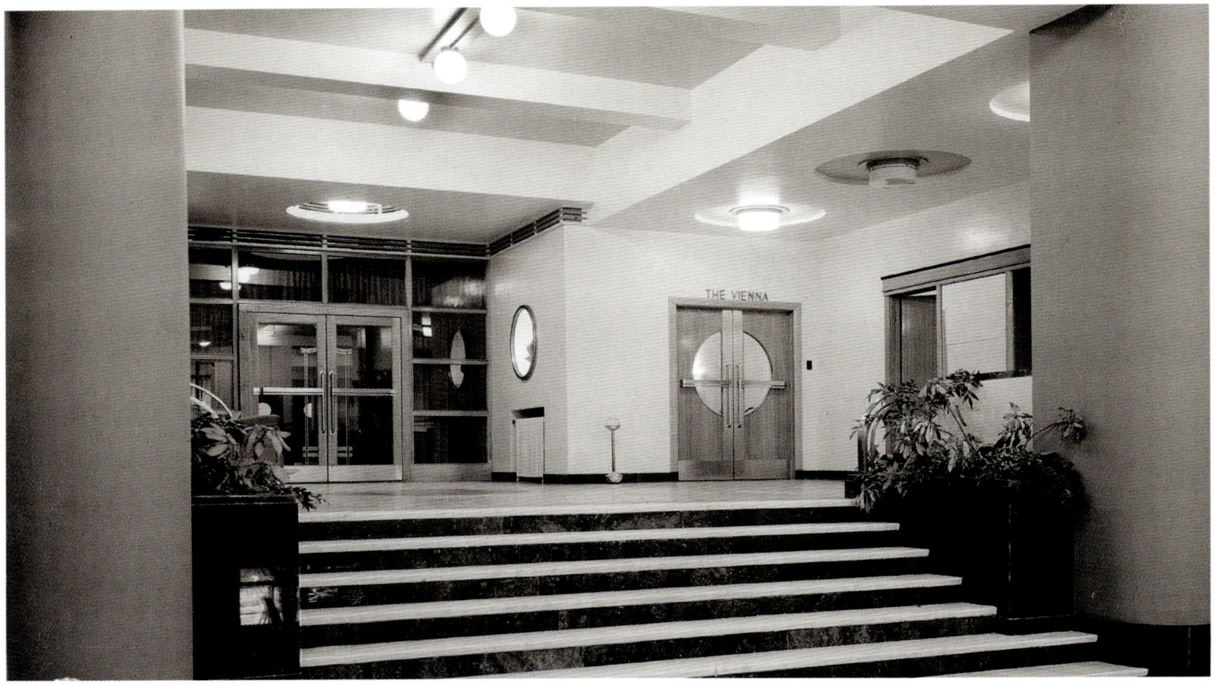

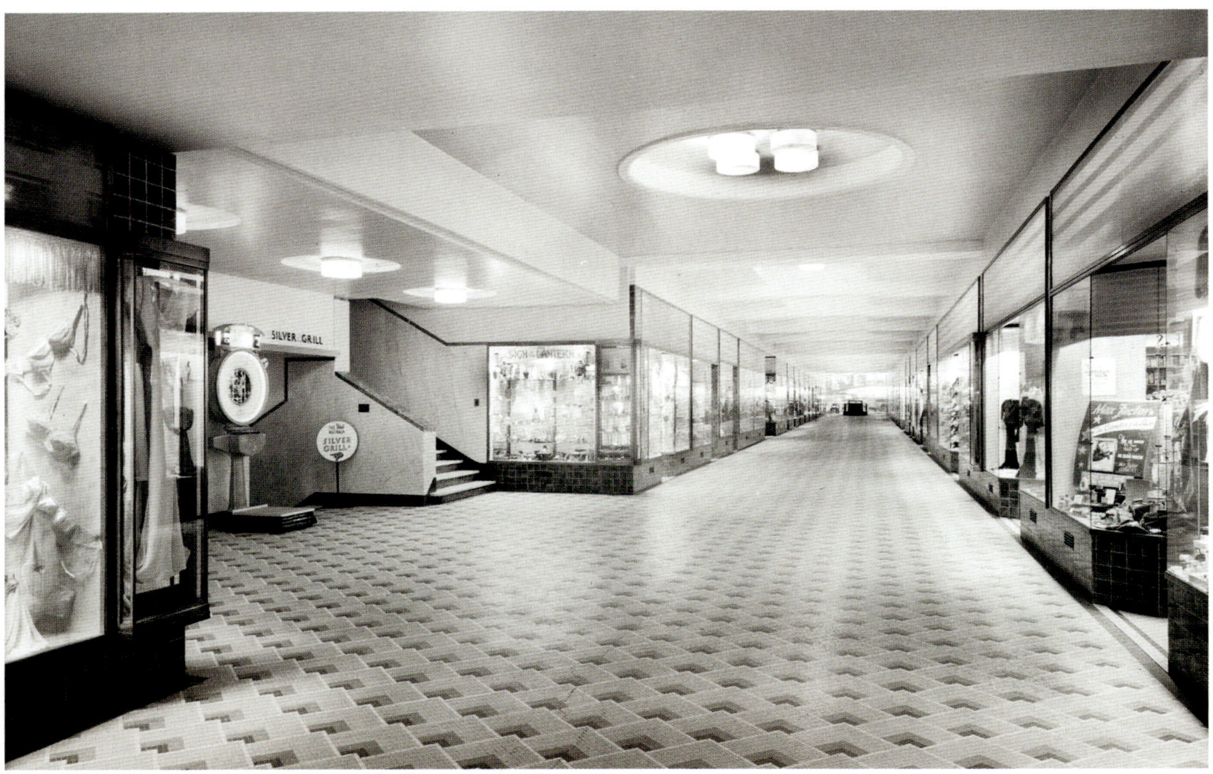

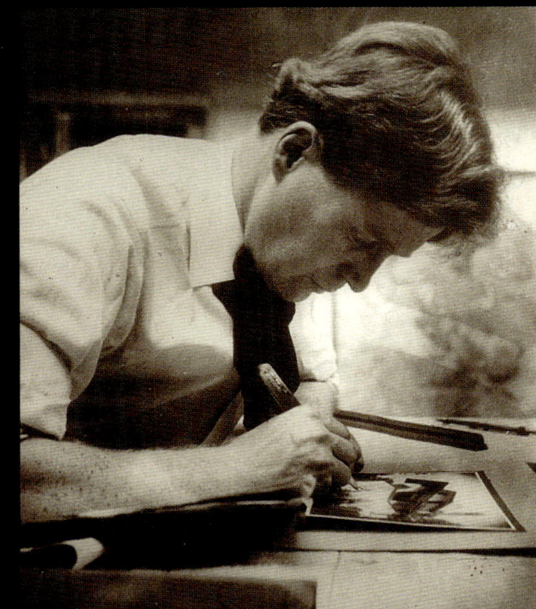

WALTER BURLEY GRIFFIN

Walter Burley Griffin is well known as the Chicago architect who designed the city plan for Canberra. He was responsible for designing many structures around Melbourne, including the Café Australia, which he was commissioned to redesign in 1916. His wife, architect Marion Mahony Griffin, was responsible for the furniture and decorative work in the café. Griffin has left a rich legacy in Melbourne and is best remembered for the Capitol Theatre, Newman College at Melbourne University and for the Palais de Danse in St. Kilda.

ABOVE LEFT *The hotel foyer and entrance to the new Vienna café in 1940.*

LEFT *The Australia Arcade, with its 40 shops, was thought to be the largest arcade in Australia at the time.*

RIGHT *The 1938 arched dining room ceiling of the Hotel Australia was preserved and included in the ballroom of the new building when the hotel was demolished.*

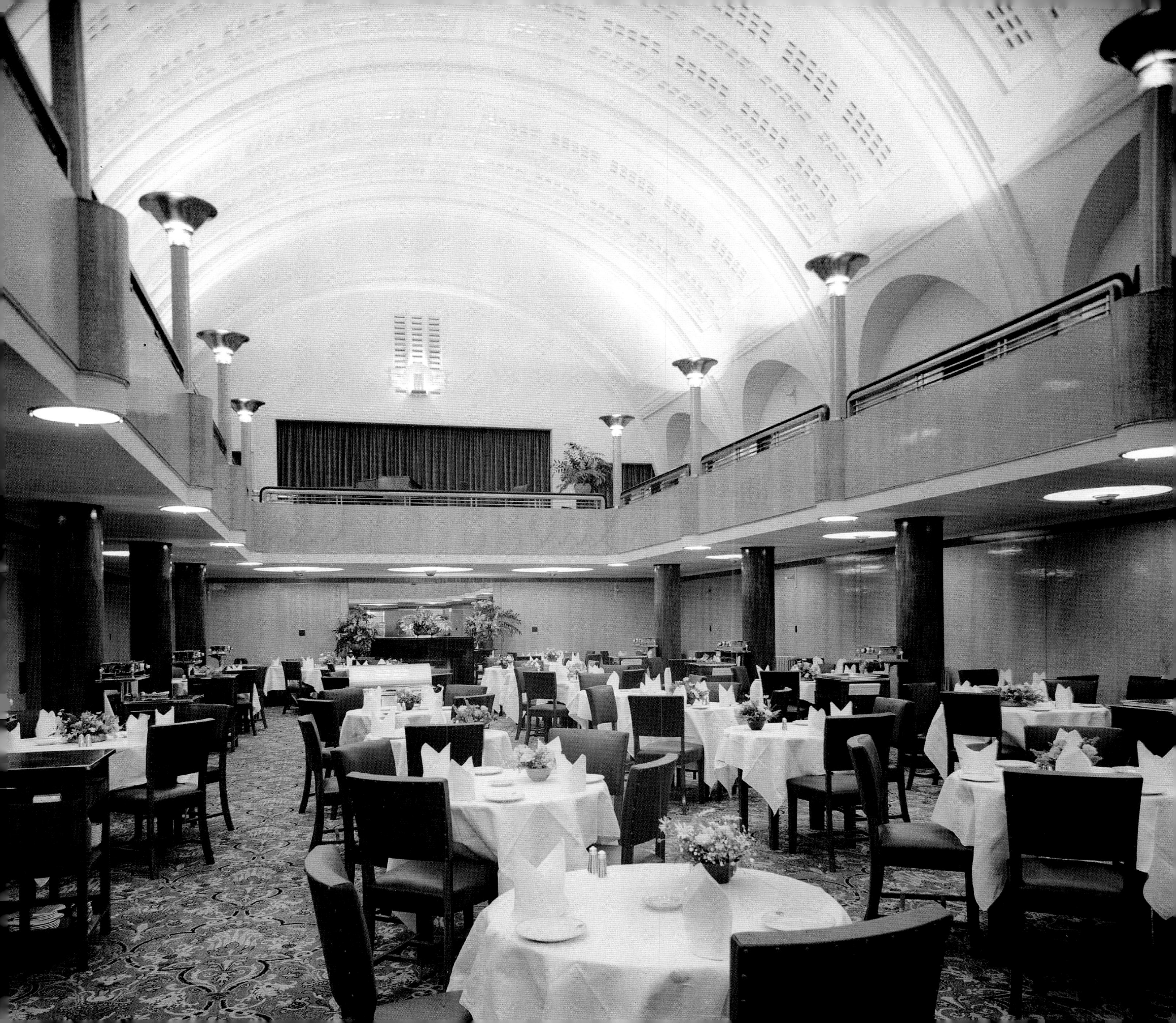

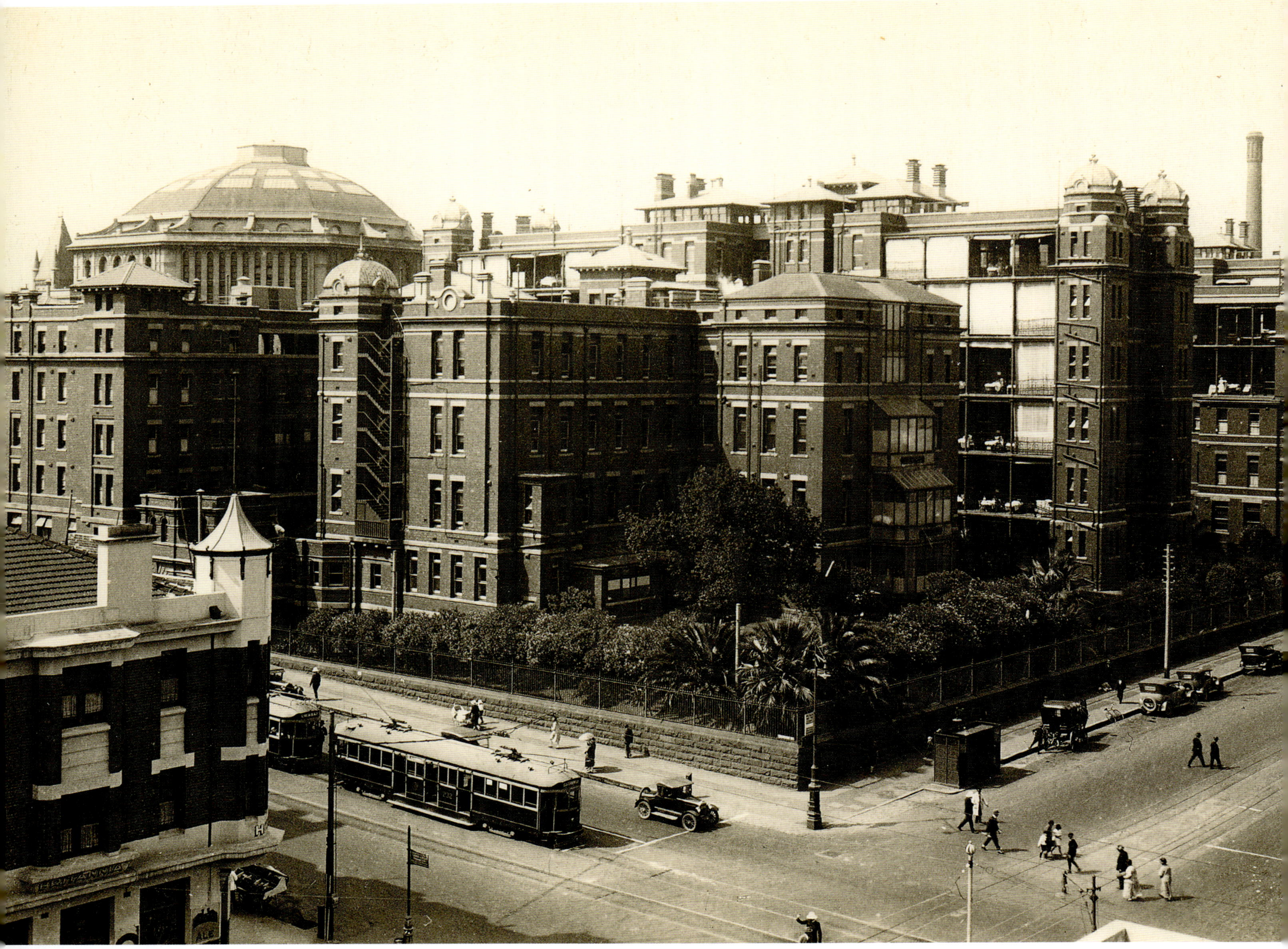
BRITANNIA
ALE

Melbourne Hospital / Queen Victoria Hospital MOSTLY DEMOLISHED EARLY 1990s

The foundation stone of the Tudor style building of the first public hospital in Melbourne was laid in a one-acre site at the corner of Swanston and Lonsdale Streets in 1848. It opened with 10 beds, which increased to 20 by the end of its first year of service. Of the 75 admissions only 53 survived.

Due to epidemics and a rapidly increasing and often sick population, the demand for access outpaced available capacity. Tents were often erected to provide shelter to hundreds of patients during outbreaks of fevers. To keep pace with patient demand and to facilitate developments in medical practices, between 1854 and 1867 seven extensions were built, bringing the hospital to a 300-bed capacity.

Unsanitary drainage and dilapidated structures resulted in the 1892 Royal Commission condemning the building and recommending that a new hospital be built at Parkville, closer to the University Medical School. Such suggestions were rejected and in 1908 it was decided to build on the existing site. J. A. B. Koch, architect of the condemned buildings, won the design competition but never built the new hospital. Amid controversy, Messrs J. J. Clark and Son, leading Australian architects, were awarded the build. Opening in 1913, it was of Edwardian Baroque style red brick with white "blood and bandage" highlights around the windows and walls. The skyline revealed cupolas and turrets aplenty with an overall style of pavilions networked by a central corridor. It was the most modern hospital building in Australia. In 1935 the hospital was renamed the Royal Melbourne and moved to a new building in Parkville after the American Military exited it in 1944.

In 1945 the old Melbourne Hospital site, which at this stage had 320 beds, four operating theatres, electrical lifts, X-ray equipment and areas for specialised departments, was sold to the Government for £549,000. In 1946 the Queen Victoria Memorial Hospital – set up by Dr Constance Stone, who was always looking for more room – moved from its Williams Street location to the Lonsdale Street site. Queen Victoria Hospital was one of only three in the world managed and staffed by women. The motto was "by women for women". In 1965 it became a family hospital, also treating and employing males, and was affiliated with Monash University as a teaching hospital for paediatrics and gynaecology. In 1977 it was renamed the Queen Victoria Medical Centre after amalgamating with McCulloch House and the Jessie McPherson Hospital. In 1989 the Lonsdale Street site was sold and the hospital relocated and integrated with the Clayton Campus, to be known as the Monash Medical Centre.

All that remains of the heritage-listed old Melbourne/Queen Victoria Hospital is the front portico and two-storey tower. The other two towers were demolished in 1994, despite a request for heritage protection. What remains is now the Queen Victoria Centre for Women. The heritage-listed bluestone and cast-iron palisade fence was carefully removed and relocated to Queen's College at Melbourne University.

The site is now split into four main structures, named QV1 through to QV4. Two structures are skyscrapers and dwarf the original hospital building. This one-acre site has been developed as an "urban village" with retail, living and commercial use. It is now known as the Queen Victoria Village.

OPPOSITE *An elevated view of the hospital buildings in 1933 with the dome of the State Library in the left background.*

BELOW *The old Melbourne Hospital in the 1880s.*

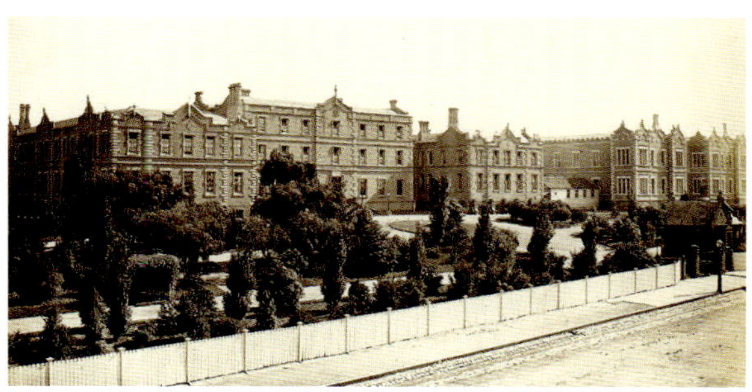

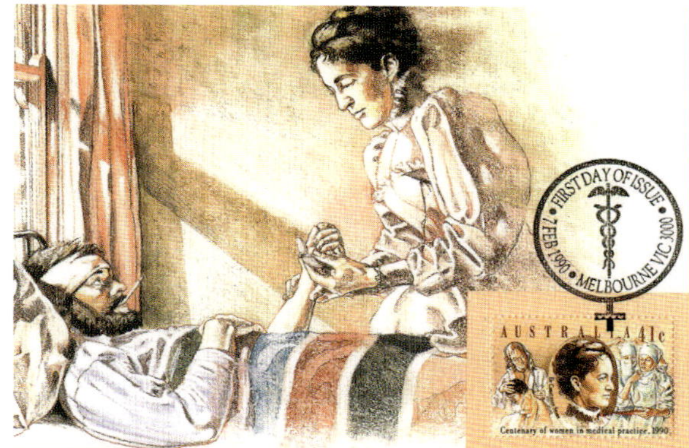

CONSTANCE STONE 1856–1902

In 1884 Constance Stone went to the USA to study medicine because women were not admitted to the Melbourne University medical course. Medically qualified, and following a period of visiting hospitals in the UK and Europe, Dr Stone returned to Melbourne and became the driving force behind the establishment of the Queen Victoria Hospital for Women and Children. She was the first woman to gain registration with the Victorian Medical Registration Board in 1890. Her overseas experiences and weekly work at the Free Dispensary in Collingwood inspired her desire to establish a hospital "by women for women" in Melbourne. This ambition was realised in 1896 when the Queen Victoria Hospital for Women and Children was opened in Williams Street, following a massive fund-raising effort through Dr Stone's "Shilling fund". In 1901, after the death of Queen Victoria, the hospital name was changed to the Queen Victoria Memorial Hospital. Within one year Doctor Constance Stone herself had died from Tuberculosis.

St. Moritz DESTROYED BY FIRE 1982; DEMOLISHED 1991

Ice skating began in Melbourne in 1906 when the Glaciarium opened in South Melbourne. In 1924, the building that would become the St. Moritz ice rink was constructed on the Esplanade in St. Kilda. From 1924 to 1939 it was to have a number of lives as the Paradise of Living Pictures, the Wattle Path Palais de Danse and Café, the Streets of Paris dance hall and a theatre and film studio for Frank Thring's Efftee productions. In 1939 it became an ice rink run by the Kleiners, who had formerly run the Streets of Paris dance hall. They knew nothing about ice skating but managed the front of house and brought in full-time refrigeration experts to run the equipment and a triple certificate nurse to administer first aid during opening times. The St. Kilda skating girl neon sign lit up the facade of the building.

St. Moritz had 20,000 square feet of ice surface and on the opening night, 11 March 1939, more than 2,000 people were catered for on the rink. During that evening, ornate decorations, colourful lights, seating arrangements for non-skaters (warmed by a steam heating plant) and a band all ensured that the evening was a success. Following its opening, St. Moritz held three sessions a day with an extra one for those wanting to learn to skate. As skaters moved around the rink, a spotlight was trained on a mirror-encrusted ball and this sparkled and covered the rink with moving lights. Three times a day, the surface was scraped and sprayed with water to give the ice its glistening appearance. In March 1940 *The Argus* reported that "there is no finer pleasure, no finer sport, no greater thrill for health and exercise, than ice skating."

Although many skaters had their own skates, in the early days St. Moritz provided 2,000 skates for adult visitors and another 2,000 pairs for children. A live band was introduced to accompany evening skating and Saturday afternoon sessions. Waltzes were played and on occasions there was a "fast skate", where faster-paced music was played for approximately 15 minutes. Skaters would put on their speed skates, which were longer than the normal, and the females, followed by the males, would race around the track. They were accompanied by music guaranteed to encourage active participation in the activities.

From 1939 to 1981 St. Moritz was one of Melbourne's social hubs and was popular as a dating destination and for weekend activities. Spectacular shows were held during World War II to aid the war effort. In 1946 it became a gathering place for Dutch migrants who joined together in the corners of the rink. Ice hockey was also played at the venue, particularly during the winter months, and the proprietors brought out shows from overseas. There was an annual ice show, carnivals and many schools throughout the city held excursions to St. Moritz.

For more than 40 years, St. Moritz was a St. Kilda landmark. But times were changing and rock and roll took precedence over waltzes. By the time the 1980s came, ice skating was not as popular and other activities were available to attract people. St. Moritz itself was showing the effects of age and poor ventilation. The ice rink closed in 1981 and the building was destroyed by fire in September 1982. It stood derelict until 1991 when it was demolished and a Novotel Hotel was built on its site. The Novotel Hotel and the Medibank Ice House both have a St. Moritz Bar named in honour of the famous rink.

RIGHT *The St. Moritz ice-skating rink, circa 1940.*

BELOW LEFT *The Gala Opening of St. Moritz in 1939 was attended by over 2,000 people.*

BELOW *The gleaming bar at St. Moritz, with an advert for Nestle's Malted Milk above the counter.*

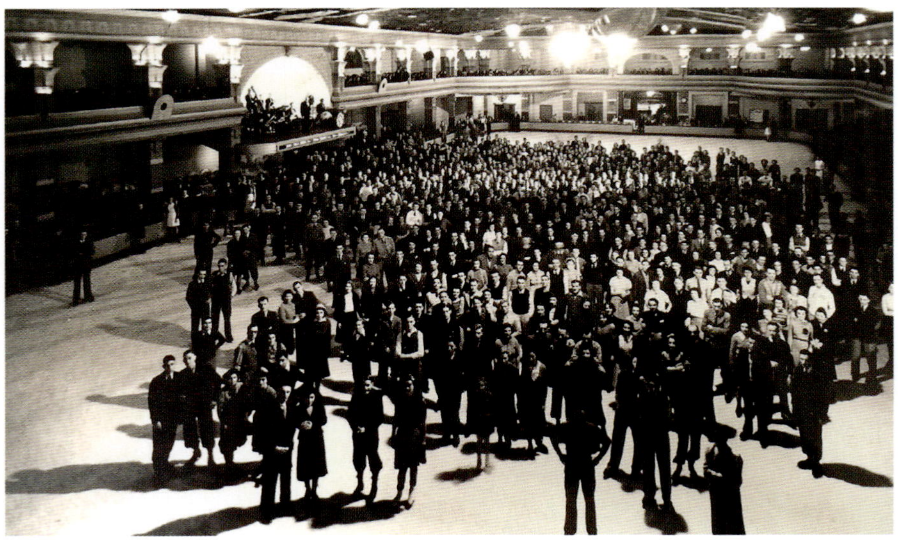

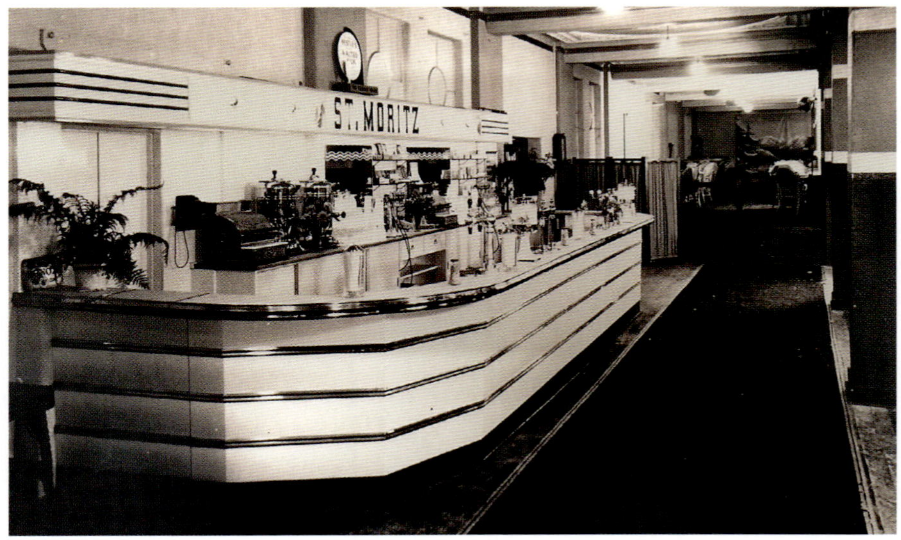

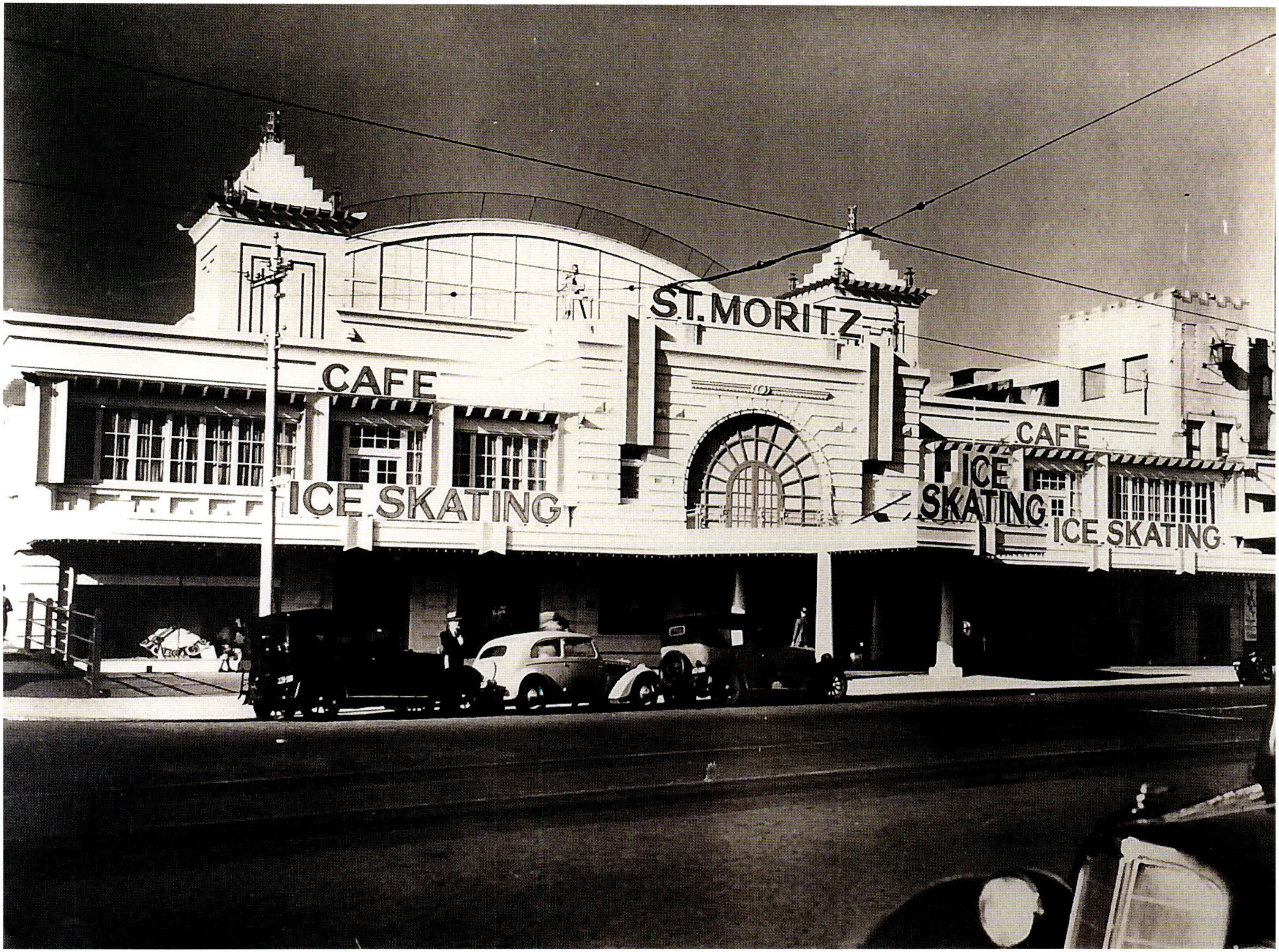
ST. MORITZ
CAFE
ICE SKATING
CAFE
ICE SKATING
ICE SKATING

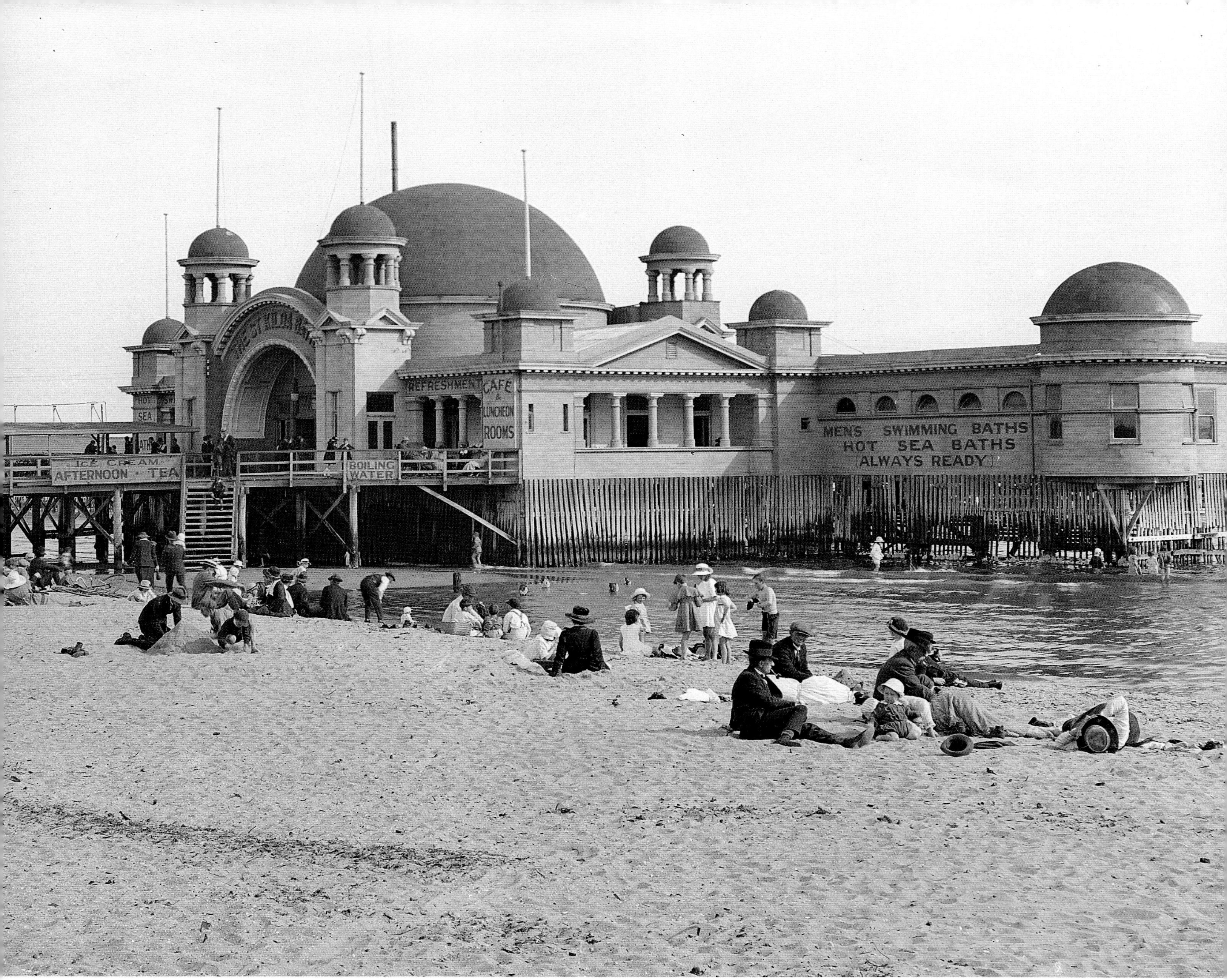
HOT
SEA
ICE CREAM
AFTERNOON · TEA
BOILING WATER
REFRESHMENT
CAFÉ & LUNCHEON ROOMS
MEN'S SWIMMING BATHS
HOT SEA BATHS
ALWAYS READY

St. Kilda Sea Baths CLOSED 1993

St. Kilda has always been Melbourne's favourite seaside place. The government auctioneer at the first land sales described St. Kilda as a "panoramic El Dorado that will replace the bloom on the pallid cheek and restore vigour to the weak."

In the 19th century swimming in the sea was prohibited during daytime and sea baths provided an alternative. However, men and women were never permitted to bathe together; such an occurrence was quite inconceivable and it would be considered an immoral act. In 1854 Captain Kenny scuttled a ship, the *Nancy*, just off the beach at St. Kilda and this bathing ship proved very popular and continued to operate until 1912. At this time Captain Kenny also ran a ladies' sea bath.

In 1856 a Government Select Committee recommended that a Sea Bathing Company be established to build two bathing houses at St. Kilda. A large swimming enclosure, refreshment room, gymnasium, a residence and offices were to be included in the plan. In 1860 the St. Kilda Sea Baths opened. They were simple structures made up of a fence in the sea and a building on the beach. They had separate sections for men and women; the women's section carefully screened because men often bathed in the nude. Women, on the other hand, had to cover up in voluminous costumes that were a dead weight when wet. The sea baths not only provided a bathing experience protected from sharks they also had lifeguards, swimming instructors, soap that lathered in seawater, and the freedom to enjoy bathing while preserving one's modesty. In the 1850s swimming carnivals were held but men did not like having to cover up in order to compete. The 1857 rail line from Melbourne to St. Kilda and the rail loop from Windsor brought many more people to the beachside and, by the mid-1860s, there were about 15 hotels catering for these day travellers and holiday-makers. The cable tram services of 1888 brought more people and between 1870 and 1890 St. Kilda's population had doubled to 19,000.

Bathing in the sea was thought to be therapeutic and it was a prescribed health treatment, a curative for all sorts of illnesses. This healthy activity was only a short distance away from Melbourne and available to most people. From the 1860s, the public had as many as five sea baths at St. Kilda from which to choose. By the mid-1920s bathers were deserting the St. Kilda Sea Baths in favour of swimming in the open sea. When several open-sea changing rooms were built on the beach they proved to be very popular, but the council imposed restrictions on beach behaviour. Bathers had to walk in a straight line from the changing rooms to the water, and cover themselves with a kimono or overcoat while on the sand.

New sea baths were constructed in 1929, sturdy structures designed by an engineer. The women's section had fretwork screens and Moorish domes, repeating those of the nearby Palais Theatre and Luna Park, and the men's section had Spanish Mission parapets. These baths opened in 1931 but public interest in sea baths had declined by then. Due to a lack of maintenance, the buildings deteriorated and the men's section was finally demolished in 1955. The women's section was refurbished.

Eventually, the St. Kilda Sea Baths structure was used by a series of nightclubs, some of which were notorious for the violence that occurred there. By the 1980s the sea baths were surrounded by a derelict building. Although the government discussed various plans to rejuvenate them, they were finally closed in 1993.

OPPOSITE *Fully clothed men and women enjoy the beach while children play in front of the baths, circa 1910.*

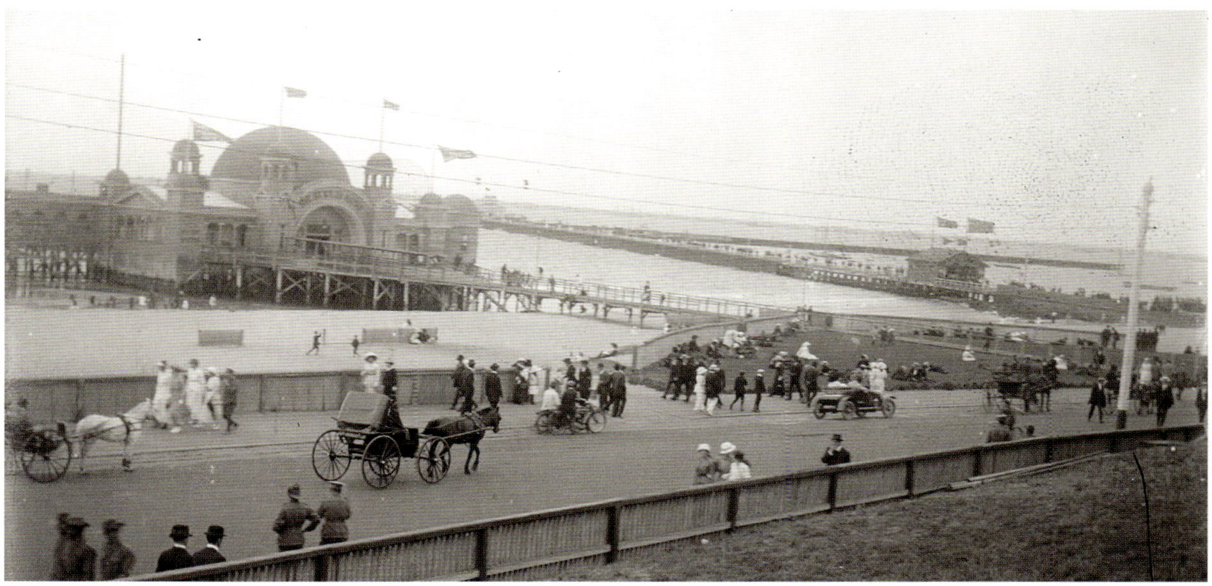

LEFT *The sea baths could be reached by an elevated walkway. St. Kilda Pier can be seen on the right of the baths.*

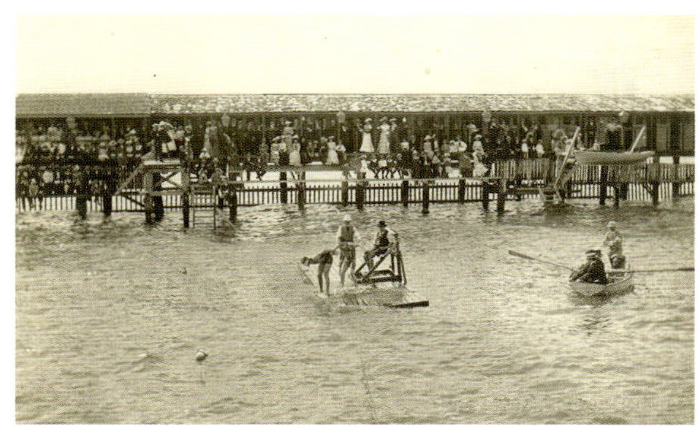

BELOW *The St. Kilda Sea Baths were described in 1913 as being the "largest and most up-to-date enclosed Swimming Area in the world. Hot sea baths, with every comfort."*

Prince Henry's Hospital DEMOLISHED 1994

Prince Henry's Hospital emerged in 1934 from the redefinition of roles and purposes of the Homeopathic Hospital situated on St. Kilda Road. It was named in honour of a visit from Prince Henry of Gloucester who became the 11th Governor-General of Australia in 1945.

It was intended for Prince Henry's to become a first-class hospital, incorporating plans for new operating theatres, treatment processes and the conduct of lectures and demonstrations in the wards. It was to become one of the most modern and best equipped institutions in Australia. As a postgraduate teaching hospital it was the first of its kind in the Southern hemisphere. Transformation into a modern hospital was seen to require a total rebuilding of the old Homeopathic Hospital. Construction commenced in 1936. A newspaper report at the time mentioned that "Plans for the rebuilding of Prince Henry's Hospital in St. Kilda Road (will) provide for the highest hospital building in Australia – a ten storey structure." The rebuilding was costed at £250,000.

It was proposed, ultimately, to have 400 beds and associated service facilities such as laboratory X-ray departments, medical and surgical departments and administration offices. The design, by nature of the narrowness of the site, and the need for essential services in the existing building to continue uninterrupted, presented difficulties for the architect Augustus Andrew Fritz. A plan for a T-shaped, multi-storey structure following the existing shape of the old Homeopathic Hospital, with a tall central block with extensions of north, south and west wings, was accepted.

The first new building, a pathology department, separate from the main block, was completed in 1936. The main central block was opened in 1946. This towering 11-storey, 48-metre high structure fronting St. Kilda Road, required alterations to the height restriction regulations. This block took advantage of new ideas, such as noise reduction treatments for ceilings and floors. Funds were available in 1940 for the construction of the new north and south wings. Struggling to overcome the impact of the Depression, building plans for the finances for the south wing and out-patient department were diverted to the war effort. They were completed in 1955 at an estimated cost of £1 million.

In 1952 Prince Henry's Hospital affiliated with the University of Melbourne as an undergraduate and postgraduate medical training institute. In 1962 this affiliation was transferred to Monash Medical Centre. Prince Henry's Medical Research Centre, specialising in endocrinology, was incorporated in 1990 and renamed Prince Henry's Institute of Medical Research. With changes in plans for hospital services and locations, Prince Henry's Hospital, along with Queen Victoria Medical Centre and Moorabbin Hospital, amalgamated to form the Monash Medical Centre. Prince Henry's Hospital closed in 1991 and was demolished in 1994. It was replaced by the most expensive luxury apartment project undertaken in Australia at that time.

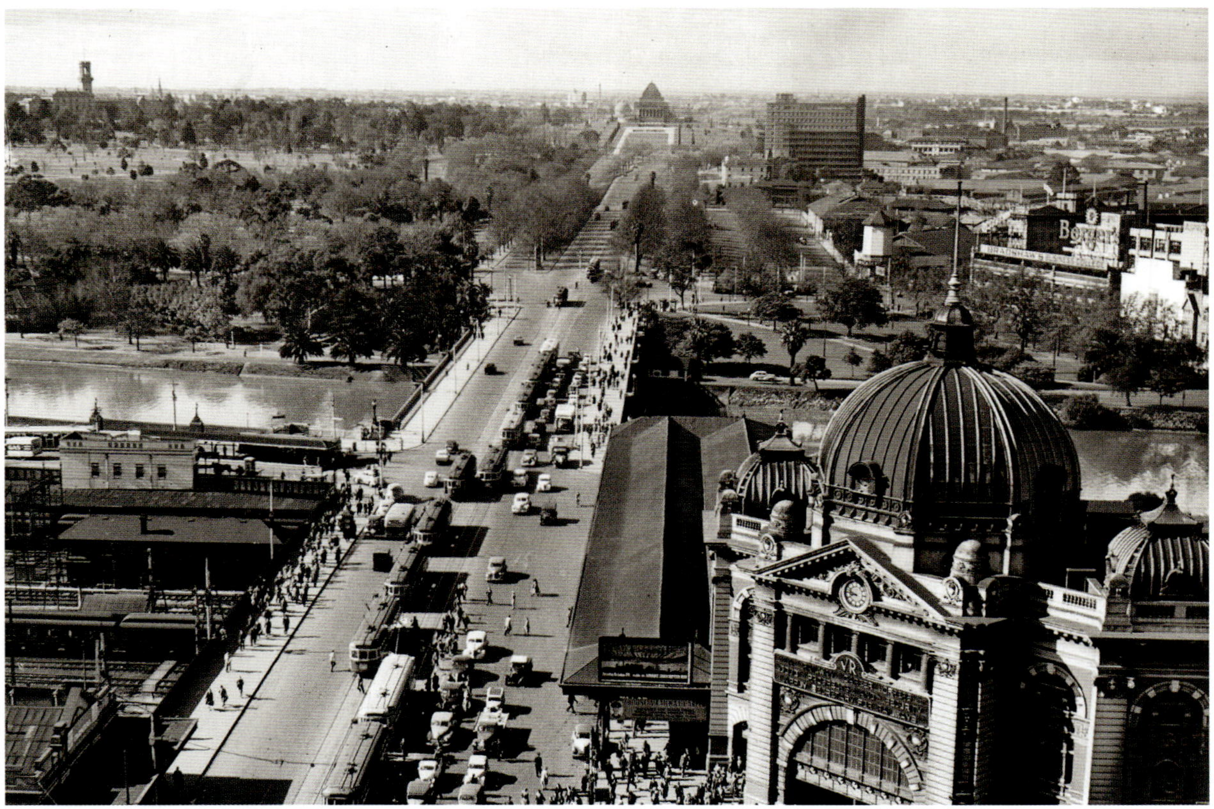

RIGHT *Prince Henry's Hospital, circa 1950. The old Homeopathic Hospital is on the right.*

LEFT *Looking along St. Kilda Road with Prince Henry's Hospital in the distance on the right.*

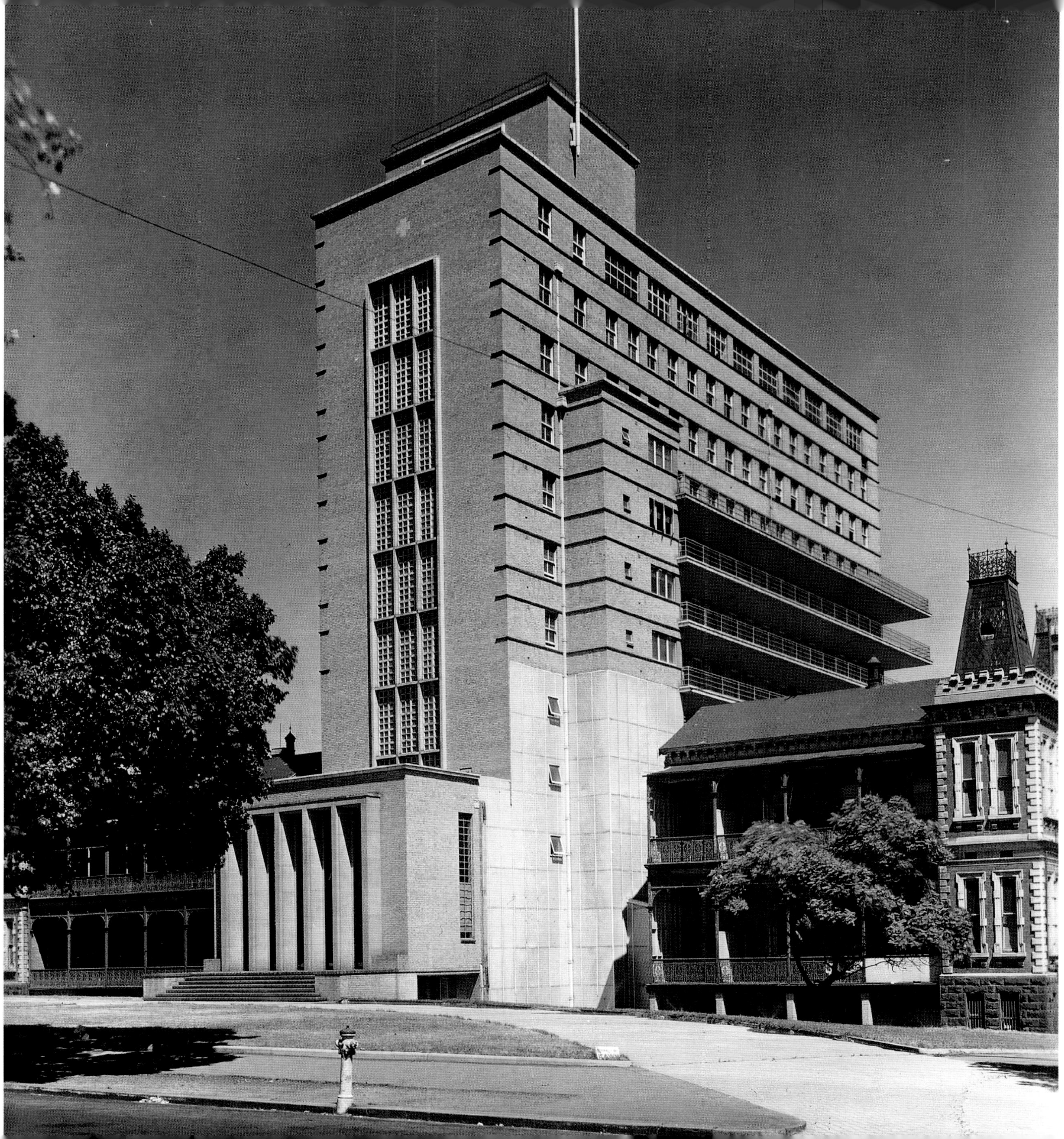

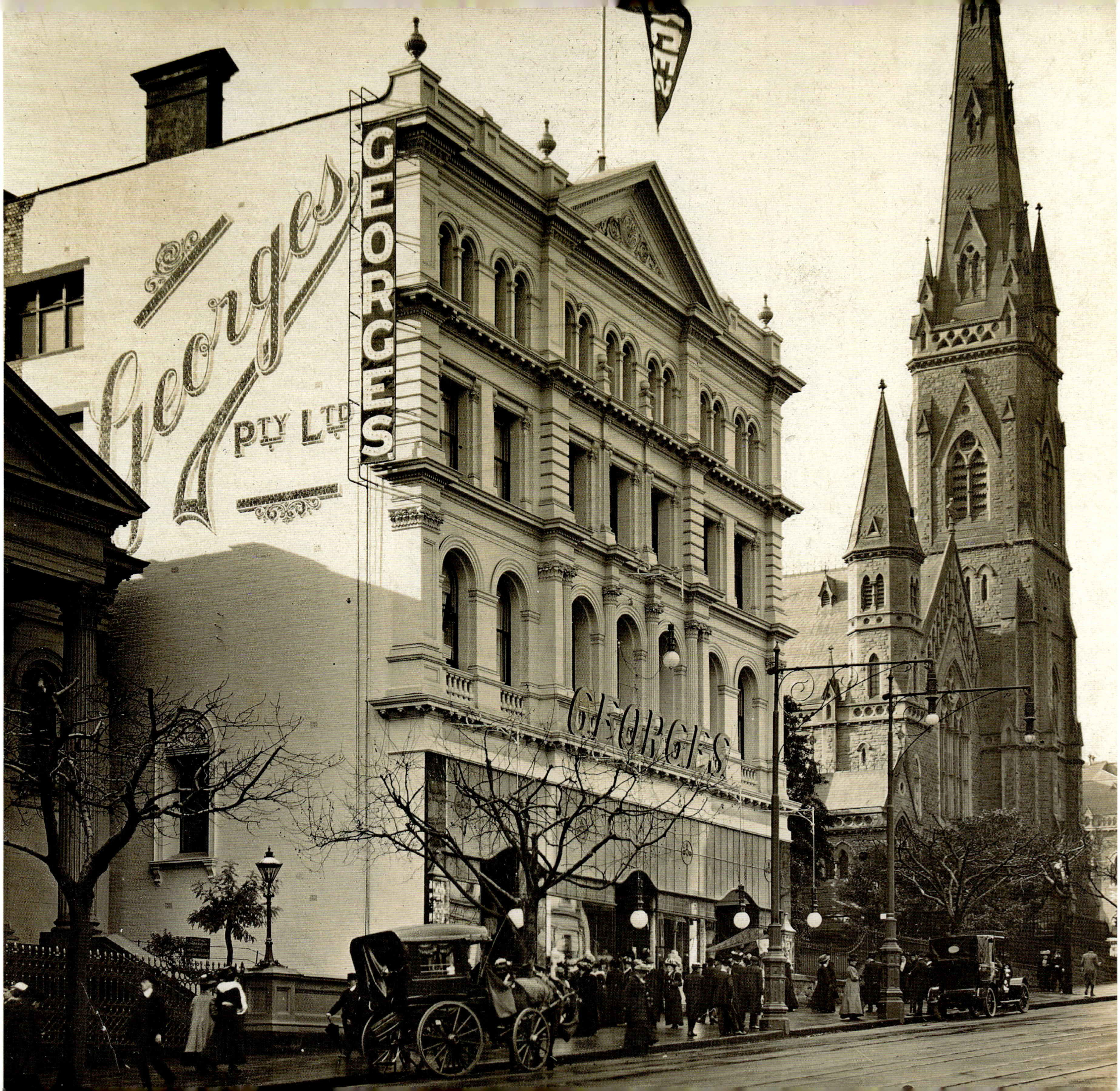
Georges
PTY LTD
GEORGES
GEORGES

Georges Department Store

CEASED TRADING 1995

When Georges Department Store closed its doors in 1995 Melbourne lost one of its most prestigious and much loved icons. William and Alfred George began their retail store in 1880, a time when Melbourne was at the height of the land boom and there was great wealth in the city. This was a time when a visiting English journalist dubbed the city "Marvellous Melbourne" and Collins Street was the centre of the city.

In 1883 the brothers moved to 11–17 Collins Street East, as it was named then, near where the Block Arcade is today. In 1888 they were forced to start looking for other premises as the owner, Benjamin Josman Fink, had plans to build the Block Arcade. In 1889, fortuitously for Fink, a fire broke out in the building and William and Alfred George moved, this time to 162–68 Collins Street, where the building still stands today. The store quickly became successful and gained a reputation that lived up to the Georges' advertising campaign. It was a store for the "smartest people in Melbourne", a store of elegance and refinement, with an atmosphere of peace and serenity. In the early years a wide variety of goods was sold, from drapery to napery, from carpets to coal. It was one of the first stores to introduce lifts, offer cash discounts, and have a bargain basement. In the late 1880s there were fashion shows and the Christmas Fun Fair included a Punch and Judy Show. A cyclotorium was introduced in the 1890s where ladies could learn to ride and then purchase a bicycle away from the public gaze. A Ladies' Lounge and the Regency Room Café were provided so that ladies could recover from their shopping adventures and sit, chat or perhaps listen to a German band amongst palms and ferns.

Although Georges was primarily a store for female shoppers, the Knight Club was a place where discerning gentlemen could purchase something for a lady, and then have it discreetly gift wrapped and placed in the distinctive Georges burgundy bag with its art deco logo.

The motto of Georges was "Quod facimus, valde facimus" translated to mean, "What we do, we do well". The staff were trained and strictly supervised to make sure the motto was adhered to. At all times they were to treat clients with respect, and make sure that the customer "should leave feeling a better person for the experience". Staff members were to address everyone as Mr, Mrs, or Miss, and there was to be no high-pressure selling of goods.

Georges' gallery was an innovation of the 1940s and notable artists such as John Olsen and Fred Williams won the Georges' Art Prize, set up in the 1960s.

Fashion had once been the preserve of the wealthy class but during the 1950s it became interesting to other classes as fashion was promoted widely in affordable women's magazines and on the new medium of television. Georges' fashion parades were popular with all. In 1995 this iconic Melbourne institution ceased trading after 115 years and closed its doors. Although there were attempts to revive it, none of the reincarnations could bring back Georges, a Melbourne institution. While the department store has gone, the building remains intact and is now occupied by a number of boutique stores and commercial tenants.

OPPOSITE *The department store in 1915, with Scots' Church behind. Georges' reputation for quality and service made it a Melbourne institution.*

RIGHT *Inside Georges there were three tiers with wrought iron balustrades. On the lower floor there were gloves and umbrellas, the middle level was for ladies' fashions, and on the third floor there was a café.*

BELOW *Georges' freestanding island windows were supposed to be the first in Melbourne. These display cabinets showed models wearing the very latest Parisian fashions of the Edwardian period.*

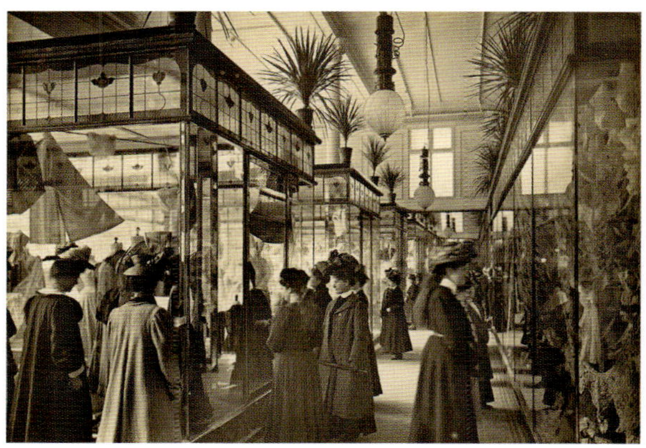

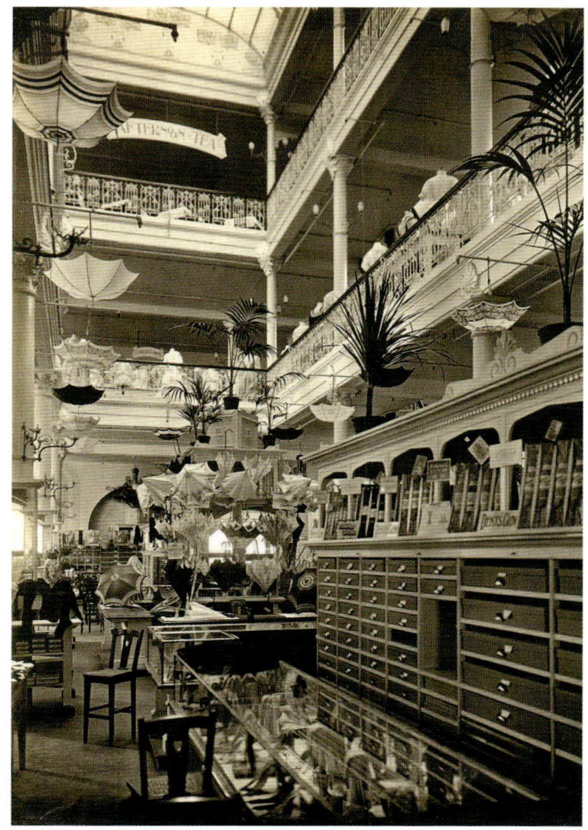

Gas and Fuel Buildings DEMOLISHED 1996–97

The 1960s was a time when there was a growing demand for real estate in Melbourne and the State Government decided to look at the corner of Flinders and Swanston Streets as a place for future development. Princes Bridge Railway Station had occupied the site since 1859, the terminus for all eastbound trains and an administration office for the Railways Department. The 1960s was also a period when tall buildings, higher than the previous height limit of 132 feet, or about 12 storeys, were beginning to be built. In 1957 the ICI building, just outside the Hoddle Grid, was the first to be allowed to exceed the height limit because it provided much open space at ground level. Instead of the previous height limit, new buildings were to be governed by a plot ratio formula and developers were anxious to take advantage of the change in regulation.

The mood of the public was sympathetic towards modernization and plans by the State Government for a grand redevelopment of the Jolimont railway yards was greeted with interest. When the plans were unveiled for the site in April 1963 they showed the outline of two tall buildings placed opposite Cathedral Lane and the two existing buildings that were to the east of the lane. It appeared as if the construction would not block the view of St. Paul's Cathedral when viewed from St. Kilda Road, but they would certainly block views to the south from the Ball & Welch department store.

The £5 million plans involved erecting twin towers of 15 storeys on the southern side of Flinders Street, covering part of the rail yards, and moving Princes Bridge Station underground. These buildings were to be used for commercial purposes, and a plaza and 14 shops were planned. The idea was to cover the entire rail yards, but in the end only part of the plan was completed. The architects were Perrot and Partners and the developers were Oddenino's Property and Investment Co. Ltd. of London and Lend Lease Corporation Ltd. of Australia. The twin brown brick towers were completed in 1967, the tallest buildings in Melbourne for a brief time. They were immediately controversial to some, but many liked the open plaza and the shops, with Central Station Records becoming a favourite of the music community.

The Princes Gate Towers or, as they were more commonly called, the Gas and Fuel Buildings, were often described in uncomplimentary terms. The author Barry Dickens called them "an antidote to beauty". Most of the criticism was because they intruded on what had previously been clear vistas to the south down St. Kilda Road. They were seen as a barrier, cutting the city off from the river and giving the city a defined edge that was not there previously. The Botanic Gardens could not be seen from parts of Flinders Street and St. Paul's Cathedral was partially obscured. The tall blocks seemed to loom over the Flinders Street buildings, their shape and colour so different from the sandstone 19th-century buildings opposite and many considered them ugly and featureless. The Kennett Government's decision to demolish them was generally greeted with approval, although there was some argument about what constituted "ugliness" and whether they should be preserved as an example of Modernist architecture. In the end, the towers were demolished in 1996–97 to make way for a new landmark construction, Federation Square.

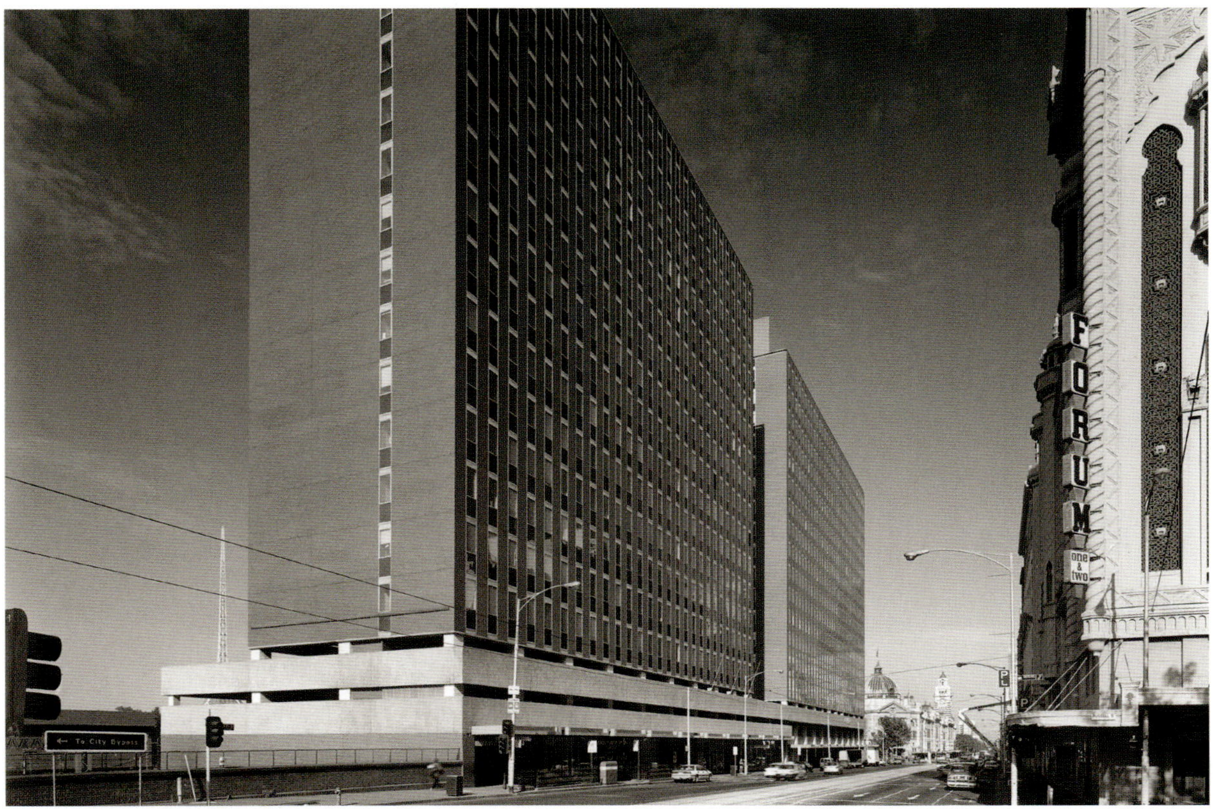

RIGHT *Advertisements for the Moomba Festival on the end of the Gas and Fuel Buildings prior to their demolition in 1996. Another sign said "These buildings are on the move".*

LEFT *The streamlined shape of these Modernist buildings is clearly seen; the small aluminium windows giving a vertical balance to the horizontal building. When constructed, they were not viewed as being particularly offensive, but over the years criticism increased and in the 1980s and 1990s they were viewed as intrusive and having little architectural merit.*

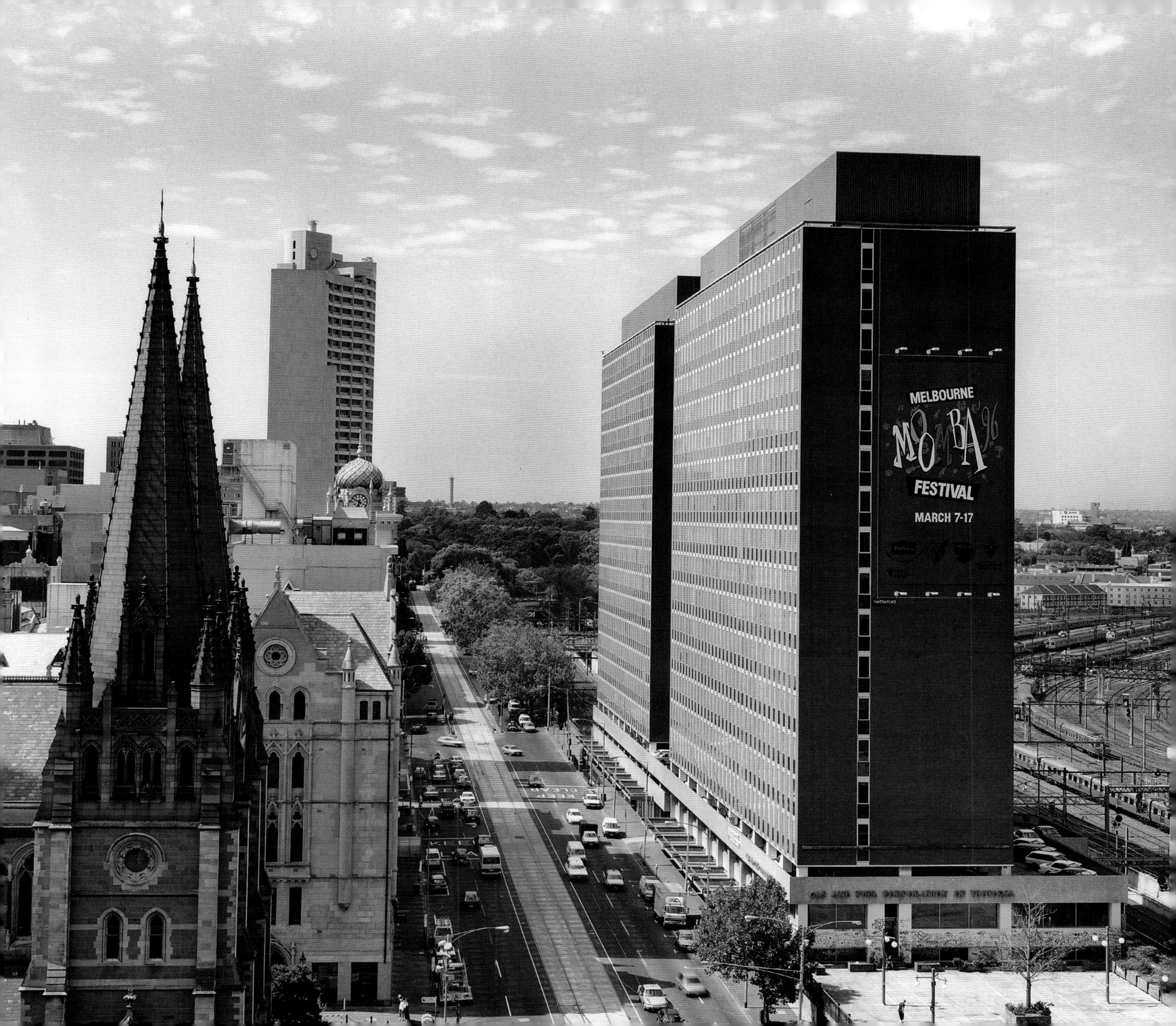
MELBOURNE
MOOMBA '96
FESTIVAL
MARCH 7-17
GAS AND FUEL CORPORATION OF VICTORIA

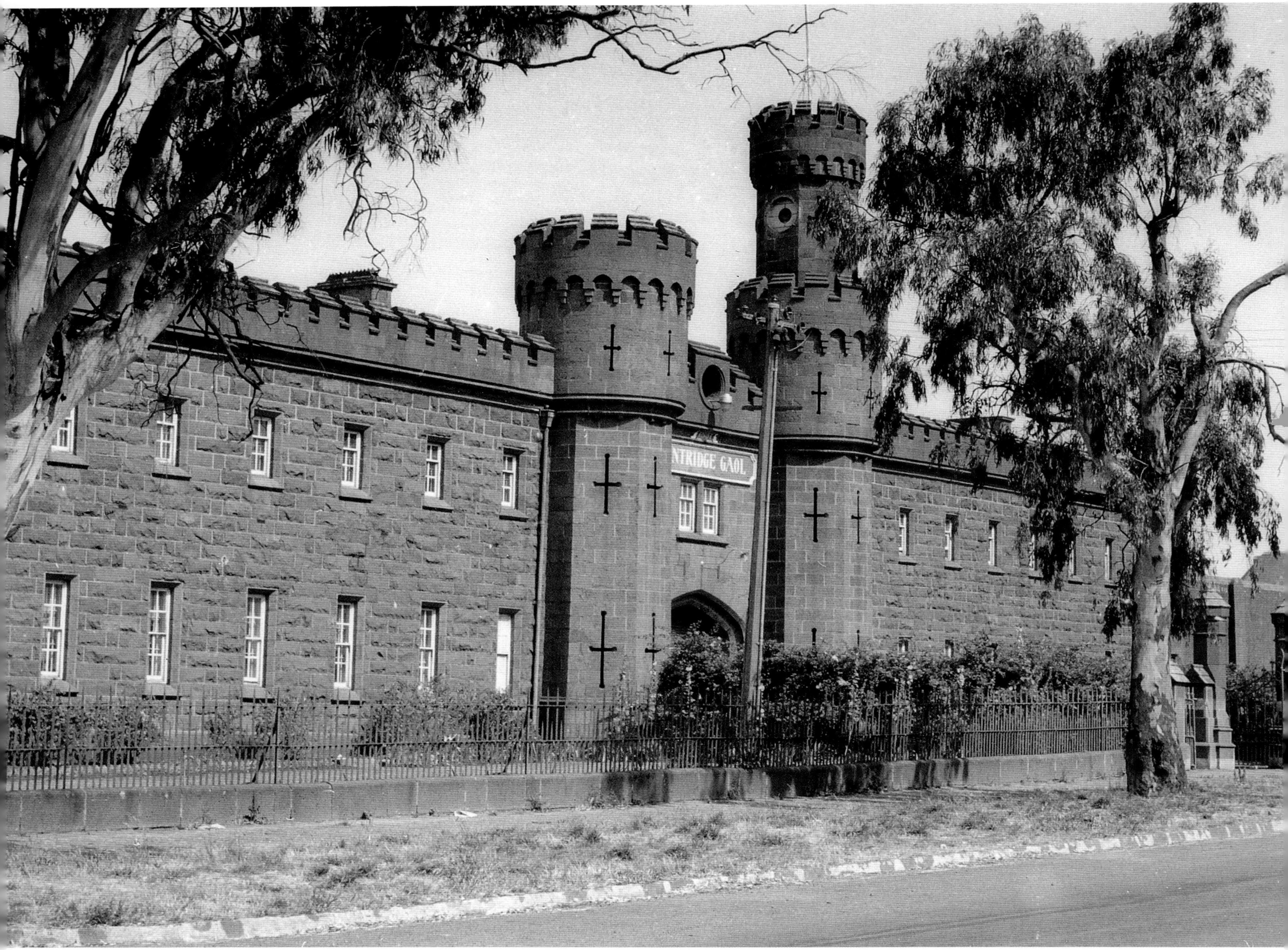
NTRIDGE GAOL

Pentridge CLOSED 1997

Sometimes known as the "bluestone college", Pentridge was set up in Victoria in 1850 because of the arrival of many "wild characters" from Van Diemen's Land and Norfolk Island at the time of Victoria's gold rush. Four stockades, or houses of correction, were formed in the Port Phillip area and one of the sites chosen was Pentridge, where unsold Crown land was still available. While near to Melbourne, it was not too close.

Not far from Pentridge, the road to link Melbourne with Sydney was being built. Around this area, bluestone was available and the prisoners could do hard labour to break up the stone and help build Sydney Road. The prisoners were divided into two gangs and were guarded by four or five constables with loaded rifles and fixed bayonets. The first stockade was an inadequate affair: log huts on wheels surrounded by a 1.2-metre fence. The prisoners were guarded by overseers while aboriginal police patrolled the perimeters. The second Inspector-General, John Giles Price, believed that punishment rather than reform would stop people from committing crimes. Accordingly, he devised the moveable stockade as a way to control the most troublesome prisoners. Conditions were appalling and the prisoners had to do everything in chains.

Between 1857 and 1864 a more permanent complex was constructed at Pentridge. It was to become the most concentrated gaol-building campaign in Australian history. Five parallel cell blocks, a 6-metre-high wall, workshops, hospital and a separate division for female prisoners were all built. Prisoners housed in A Division were isolated in their cells for 23 hours a day and allowed just one hour's exercise in a segregated yard. Talking was forbidden, and the prisoners' cell numbers were used instead of names. The hope was that solitude would bring moral reformation. C Division had the smallest, darkest, least ventilated cells, while executions were carried out in D Division. From the early 1860s until 1956 (when H.M. Prison Fairlea was opened), Pentridge was the main Victorian prison for female offenders.

Extensive building works occurred at Pentridge in the early to mid-1920s. The Melbourne Gaol closed in 1929 and all prisoners there were relocated to Pentridge. Pentridge now became Victoria's largest prison complex and was to house some of the state's worst criminals. It also became the site for all executions until 1967, when the last prisoner to receive the death penalty was hanged. Other divisions were also added, such as G Division for prisoners with psychiatric problems, J Division for young offenders and Jika Jika (maximum security), later renamed K Division.

In the 1970s, the rights of the individual came into more prominence and this was a period of unrest both at Pentridge and in the political and social arena outside. A need to reform prisons was recognised and by the 1990s the city of Coburg was campaigning to move the prison from what was becoming an increasingly urban area. In 1997 the government decided to privatise prisons and part of Pentridge was closed. It was completely closed in 1997 and sold to developers for residential, commercial and tourism activities. The outer walls, main entrance and D Division cells have been retained but a housing estate now sits inside the grounds.

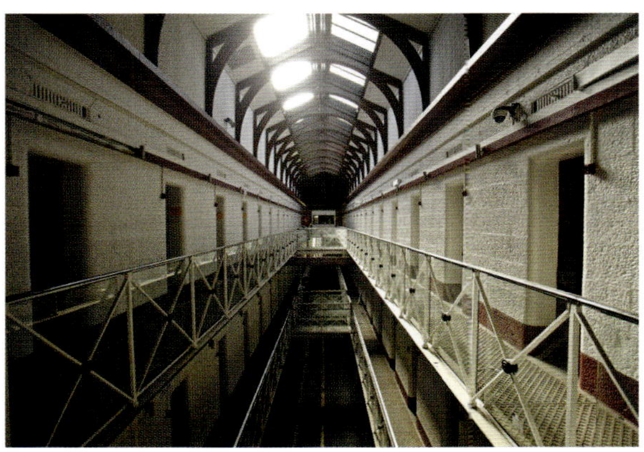

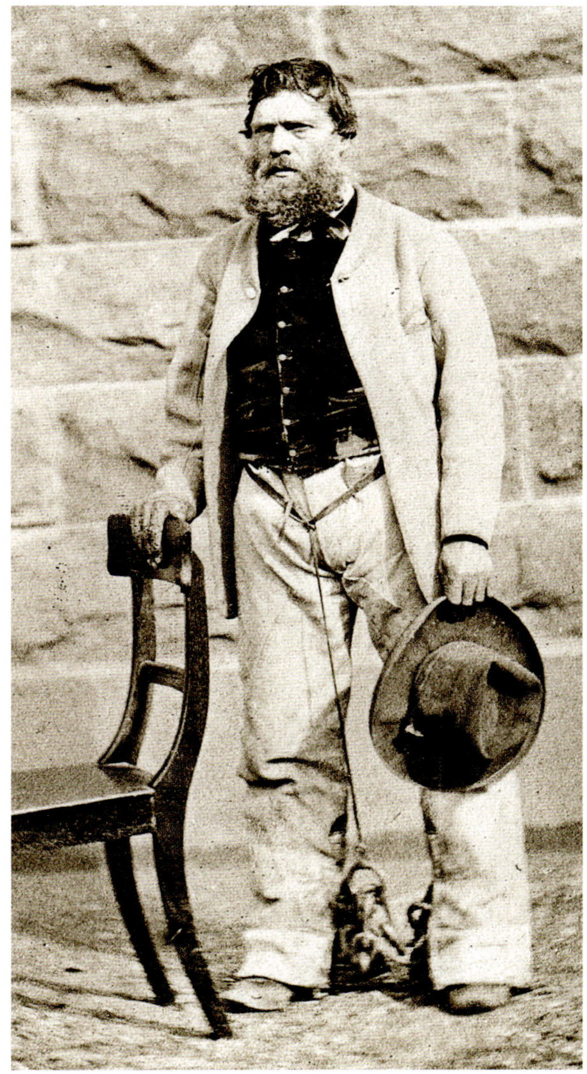

OPPOSITE *The walls surrounding the Pentridge Gaol at Coburg in the 1960s.*

LEFT *D Division, a former remand wing, is now hired out for parties, festivals and even weddings.*

RIGHT *Harry Power had been transported to Van Diemen's Land and had a long history as a criminal before he became a bushranger. He was sent to Pentridge but managed to escape by slipping inside a cart and lying beneath a pile of garbage. He was eventually re-arrested and returned to Pentridge to serve out his 15-year sentence for highway robbery.*

General Post Office CLOSED 2002

Every town, even one as embryonic as Melbourne in 1837, needs a place which is the centre of communication: a post office. In 1837 this was at a site in Collins Street, but when a postmaster was appointed in 1838 a post office was constructed on a more central site at the corner of Bourke and Elizabeth Streets. It was a wooden structure with a clock provided by the citizens. According to Garryowen, the colonial journalist Edmund Finn, this clock was capricious in its timekeeping and "was a great trial to its keeper", Joseph Greening. This made the post office hours unpredictable, as the workers delivered or dispatched mail according to the time shown on the clock. The post office was beset with problems from the beginning. Elizabeth Street was positioned on a natural watercourse named Williams Creek. It flooded periodically, washing away horses and drays in its notorious flash floods. The post office was prone to flooding, and had poor ventilation and vermin infestations. In a journal published in 1891, Hume Nisbet reported that "while waiting for my letters at the post office…I was startled by seeing a great tidal wave rolling along Elizabeth Street…with the water dashing around my waist."

In 1851 gold was discovered in Victoria and fossickers arrived in such numbers that the post office could no longer cope, despite countless additions to the building. In 1857 a royal commission recommended that a new grand building be constructed and a competition was announced. The architects Crouch and Wilson were awarded the right to build the post office but the chief architect for the Public Works Department, Arthur Johnson, who was placed second in the competition, effectively got the contract because he supervised the building and used many of his own ideas. The foundation stone was laid in 1859 and by 1867 the first stage of this building was completed, at a cost of £140,000. This comprised a two-storey building with a mansard roof and a short tower. The foundations for the building were bluestone, the basement red granite from Gabo Island, and the exterior was Grampians and Tasmanian sandstone. In 1879 the *Victorian Gazetteer* described the General Post Office as "by far the handsomest structure in Australia."

The next stage of building was in 1885 when another storey and a higher tower with a larger clock were added. This clock was made in Williamstown with imported parts from Glasgow. The original five bells, playing 28 tunes, were increased to 12 in 1890. In the early days it chimed every 15 minutes but today the clock only sounds every three hours during daylight hours. In 1907 the third stage added an arched colonnade along Elizabeth Street. In 1919 Walter Burley Griffin and the Commonwealth architect John Smith Murdoch made alterations to the interior of the building, converting the sorting hall into public space. By this time Melbourne had the grand Renaissance Revival Building that stands today. It is the place from which all distances in Victoria are measured, a meeting place for all generations and a city landmark. Many of the old photographs show men in hats sitting on the steps reading the daily papers. Today there are people doing much the same thing.

In 1992 Australia Post decided to stop using the GPO as a post office and in 1997 there were some plans to turn it into a five-star hotel. In 2001 there was a fire that destroyed most of the interior and in 2002 the Post Office closed. The building was turned into a retail store, with a small area of floor space put aside for postal purposes.

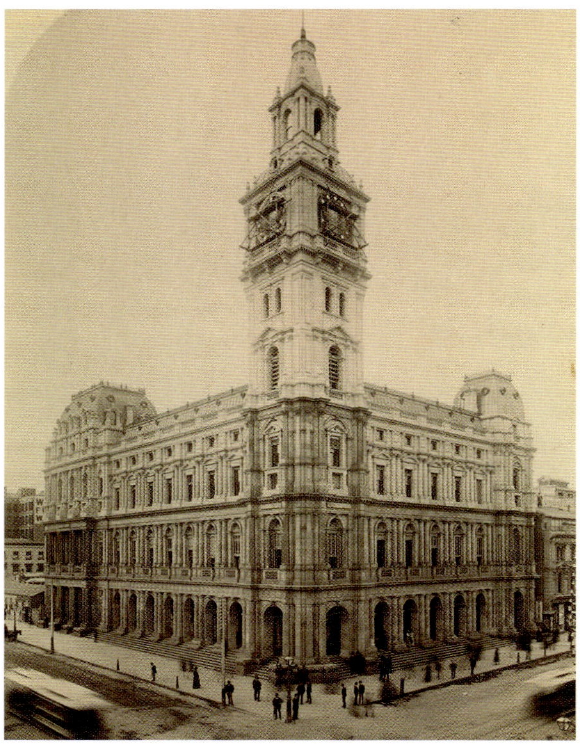

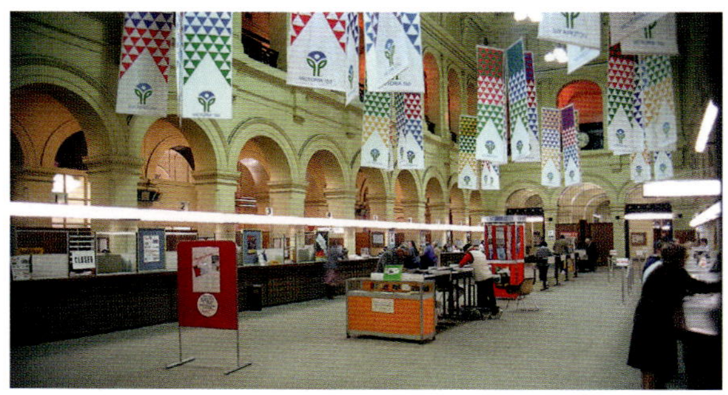

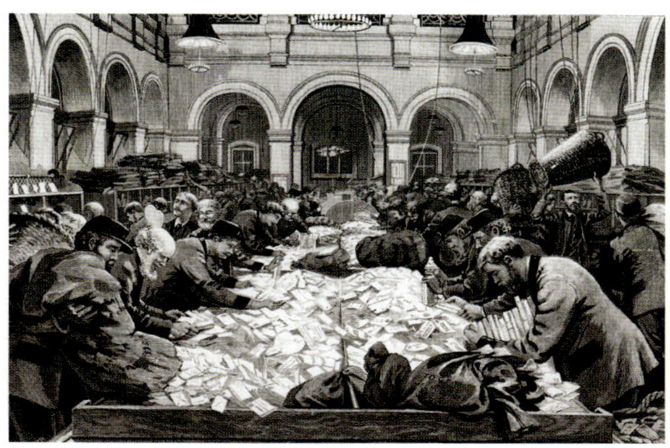

ABOVE LEFT *The Postal Hall in 1985, with hanging banners celebrating Victoria's 150th anniversary.*

LEFT *An engraving from the* Illustrated London News *of 1871 showing the Postal Hall on Valentine's Day. The hall was used as a mailroom before the building was extended.*

FAR LEFT *The GPO, complete with tower, between 1885 and 1892.*

RIGHT *The GPO prior to 1885, before the completion of the tower.*

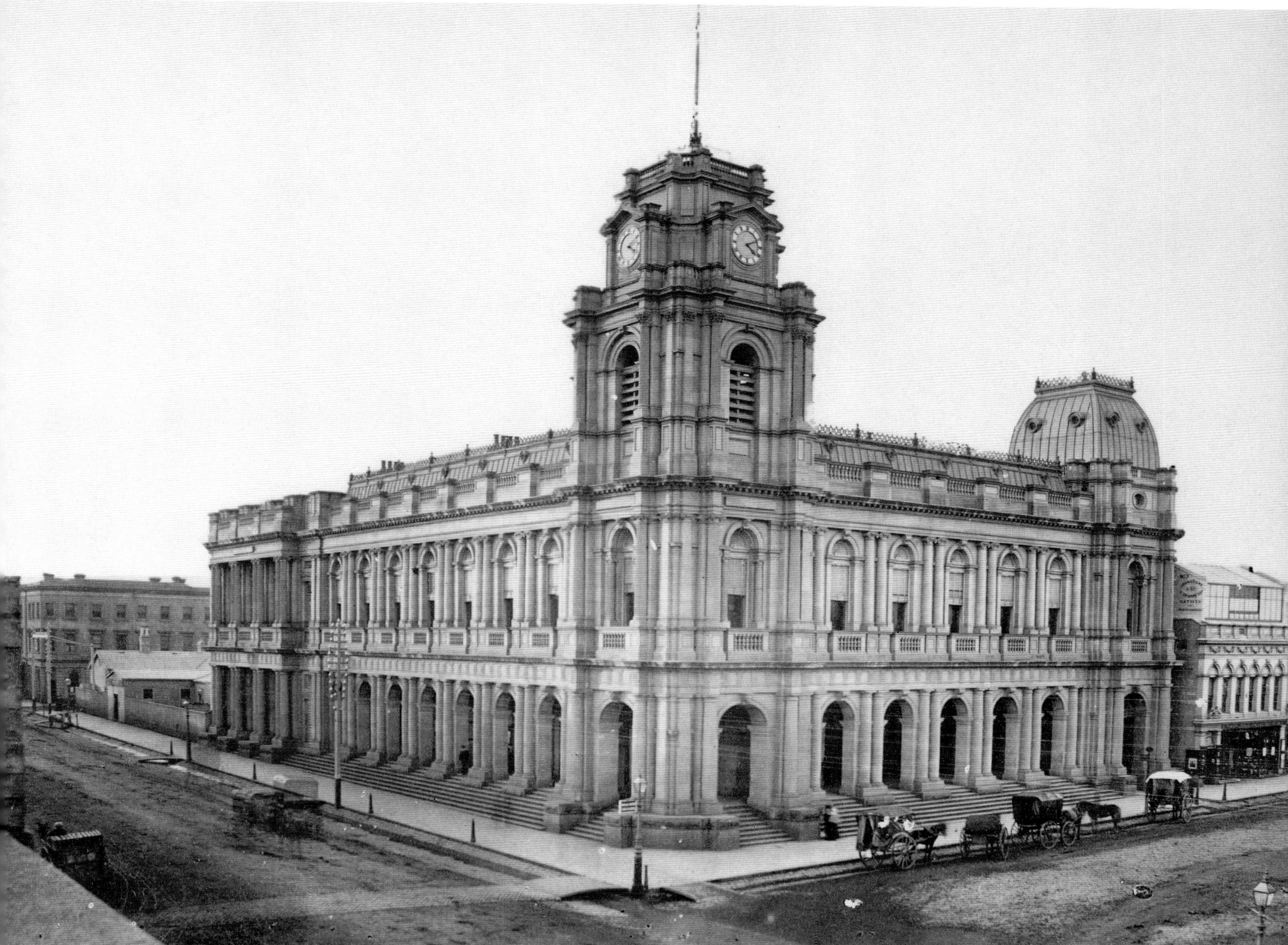

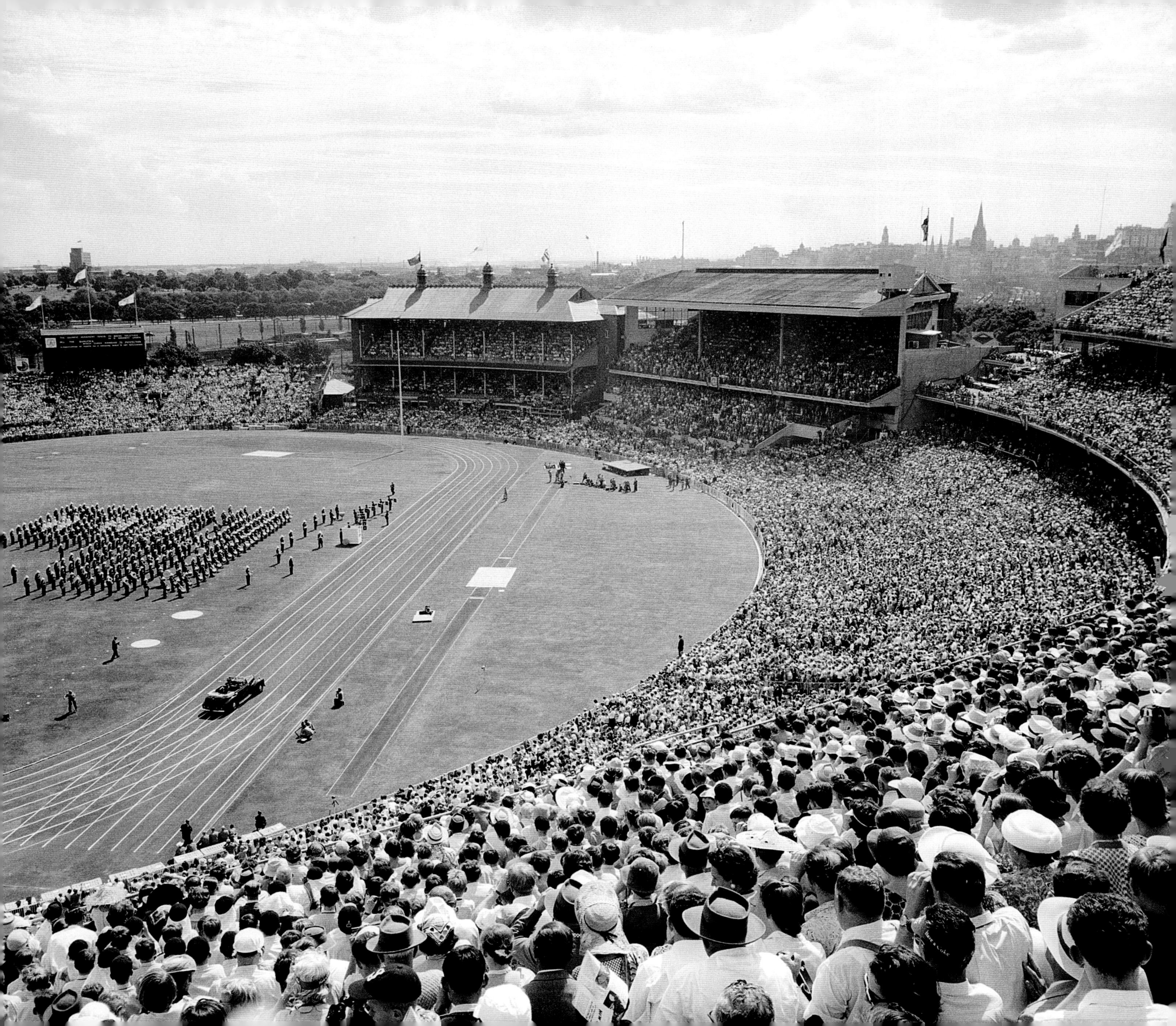

MCG Grandstands GONE BY 2005

There have been many grandstands at the Melbourne Cricket Ground (MCG). The first grandstand erected there was the Members' Pavilion. It was a wooden structure built in 1854. The Richmond Cricket Club bought this stand for £55 in 1881. Early photos indicate that perhaps 50 to 60 people could have been seated there, and it wasn't until 1881 that a brick grandstand of more substantial proportions was built. For a time, this grandstand was considered to be the world's finest cricket facility. Extended in 1886, at a cost of approximately £6,000, it was demolished in 1927 and replaced by the third Members' Pavilion – completed in 1928 at a cost of £60,000. This 1928 Members' Pavilion became the MCG's longest-serving grandstand, but in January 2004 it too was demolished as part of the Northern Stand redevelopment.

In 1876, a fire destroyed the first grandstand that was built on the Northern side of the MCG. It was replaced by a building that came to be known simply as "The Grandstand". Initially catering for 4,500 from the public and 450 from the members, the capacity was doubled in 1897 when another deck was added. In 1900 it was lit with electric light. Like the other stands, The Grandstand was itself to be demolished, though not until the 1950s.

The Grey Smith Stand was built on the Western side of the MCG in 1906. It was demolished in 1966 for the building of the Western (later the Ponsford) Stand. The 1936 construction of the Southern Stand saw the removal of the Harrison Stand (1908) and the Wardill Stand (1912). In the 1990s it too was replaced when it was found that the Southern Stand had concrete cancer.

On 5 April 1953, the Brisbane *Courier-Mail* reported that "Architects have finished plans to bring the Melbourne Cricket Ground up to Olympic standards. The plans envisage rebuilding and extension of some of the stands which will spread over two acres of park land being taken over." Melbourne had won the bid for the 1956 Olympic Games and part of the building venues for the Games meant that "The Grandstand" had to be demolished. This occurred in 1955, and it was replaced by the Northern (later the Olympic) Stand, which could accommodate more than 43,000. A series of modifications from 1984, however, reduced this seating and standing capacity to accommodate corporate boxes, dining rooms and a second scoreboard.

The replacement of the Southern Stand, the $150 million Great Southern Stand, was completed in 1992. As the Victorian Football League provided some of the funding, it was granted a 30-year deal to share the grounds with the Melbourne Cricket Club. Despite the difficulties in building this stand, it was completed on time and with very little interruption to the football and cricket seasons. The Great Southern Stand improved facilities and views for the public. The Ponsford, the 1928 Members' and the 1956 Olympic stands were all demolished between 2003 and 2005 to provide new facilities in time for the 2006 Commonwealth Games. Despite being one long unbroken stand, the names of Ponsford, Olympic and Members' were kept and today distinguish individual sections around the ground. The project cost more than $400 million and the grounds capacity is now 100,000.

OPPOSITE *Crowds fill the grandstands prior to the opening ceremony of the Olympics at Melbourne Cricket Ground on 26 November 1956.*

BELOW *Two circa-1915 views of the Members' Pavilion and "The Grandstand" at the MCG.*

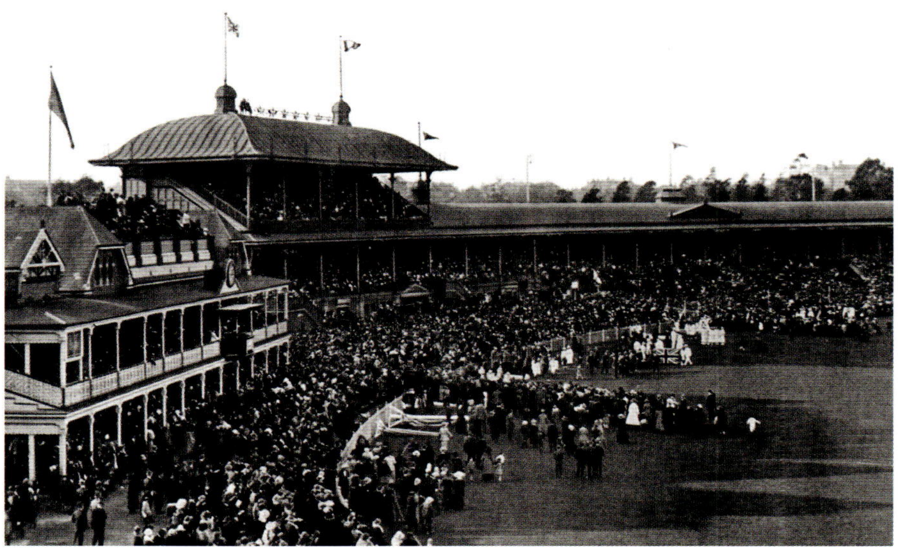

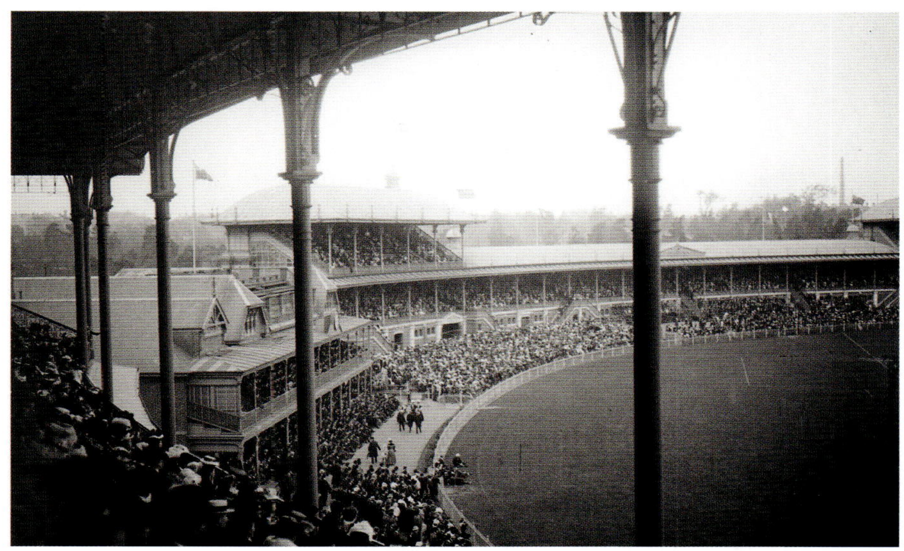

Royal Victorian Institute for the Blind

RENAMED 2004; SOLD 2007

Outbreaks of fevers and diseases such as measles were common during the overcrowding of the gold rush era, and many surviving children were rendered blind or deaf as a consequence. Public pressure during the 1860s to provide assistance to disadvantaged groups was successful, and land was granted for the erection of a building to specifically cater to the needs of the blind. The first institution of its type, the Victorian Asylum and School for the Blind opened its doors in 1868. Accommodating up to 120 children and adults, it pioneered education and welfare services for the blind.

A cobblestone apron, guarded by huge wrought-iron gates set back from the corner of St. Kilda Road and Moubray Street, Prahran, showed the way to the asylum. Located in spacious gardens with a curving tree-lined driveway, the imposing bluestone main building had white brick quoins and cement dressings. It comprised three storeys with mansard roofs, a central four-storey tower and white stone faced window treatments. It was unmatched by earlier institutions in Melbourne for size and style. The architects of its Neo-Gothic style were Crouch and Wilson, prominent architects of institutional buildings and churches in Melbourne in the 19th century. A feature inside the main entrance was a magnificent stained-glass staircase window, thought to be designed by Ferguson and Urie. Proceeding through the front entrance into a courtyard revealed a small bluestone chapel that housed an organ often played by blind students.

At the rear of the main building, workshops and a factory were soon built to teach blind people practical skills, which included making saleable mats, cane baskets and brushes. In 1872, a showroom for display of the workers' products known as the McPherson wing was added. In 1891, a hall funded and named after philanthropist Francis Ormond was built fronting Moubray Street. It was a major venue for entertainment and educational activities. Another heritage listed building was the Myer House, the only known remaining example of a prefabricated building constructed by the Commonwealth Aircraft Corporation and marketed by the Myer Emporium, post-World War II, to help overcome housing shortages.

Prior to the existence of the asylum, blind people were unable to earn a living and were restricted in travel freedoms; for example if they left Victoria they had to pay a £400 bond. The original purposes of the asylum were to provide both scholarly and musical education and training for employment in industry, enabling the inmates to become useful citizens. In 1891 the asylum was officially renamed the Royal Victorian Institute for the Blind (RVIB) so that these objectives could be more readily appreciated.

The Royal Victorian Institute for the Blind continued residential rehabilitation and training services for adult blind people until the late 1970s and the early 1980s. Residential services were discontinued under pressure from various rights groups. The buildings were heritage classified in 1990 and the grounds in 1993. In 2004 RVIB, with other blind service providers, merged to form a national organisation known as Vision Australia.

The buildings and the grounds of the St. Kilda Road complex were sold by Vision Australia in 2007 and the complex came under threat of severe subdivision for multi-storey development. In 2010 major restoration works, including that of the mansard roofs of the towers, were undertaken. The southern aspect of the grounds and Ormond Hall are now being used as a restaurant and hospitality venue. The northern grounds will soon become a 20-storey apartment building. The remaining buildings are heritage protected.

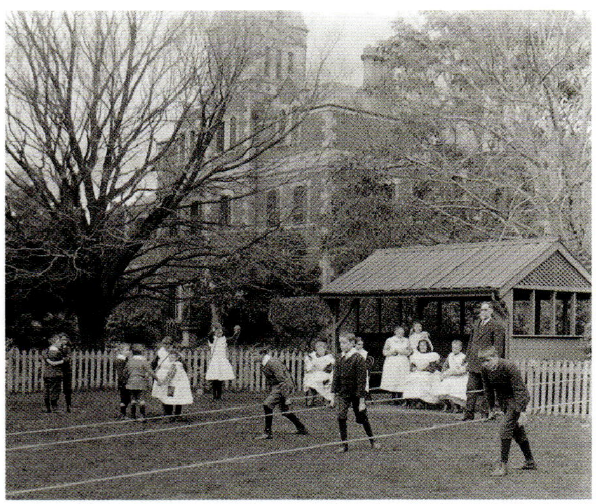

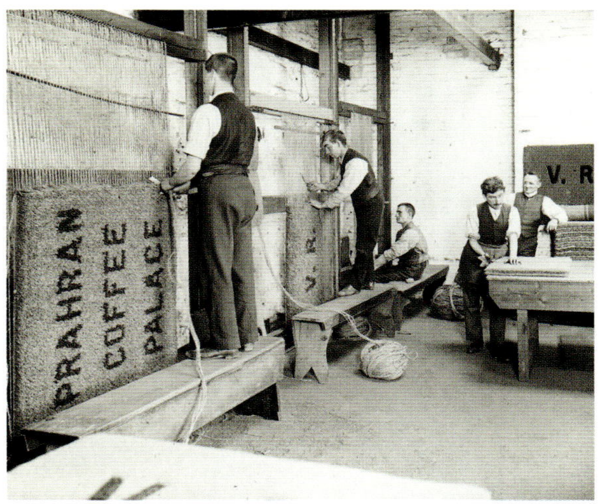

RIGHT *The impressive Royal Victorian Institute for the Blind in the 1890s, viewed from the front driveway.*

LEFT *Men weaving doormats, one for the Prahran Coffee Palace and the other for V. R. (Victorian Railways), circa 1890.*

FAR LEFT *Boys race one another using ropes as guides and children play "ring o' roses" at the RVIB in about 1912.*

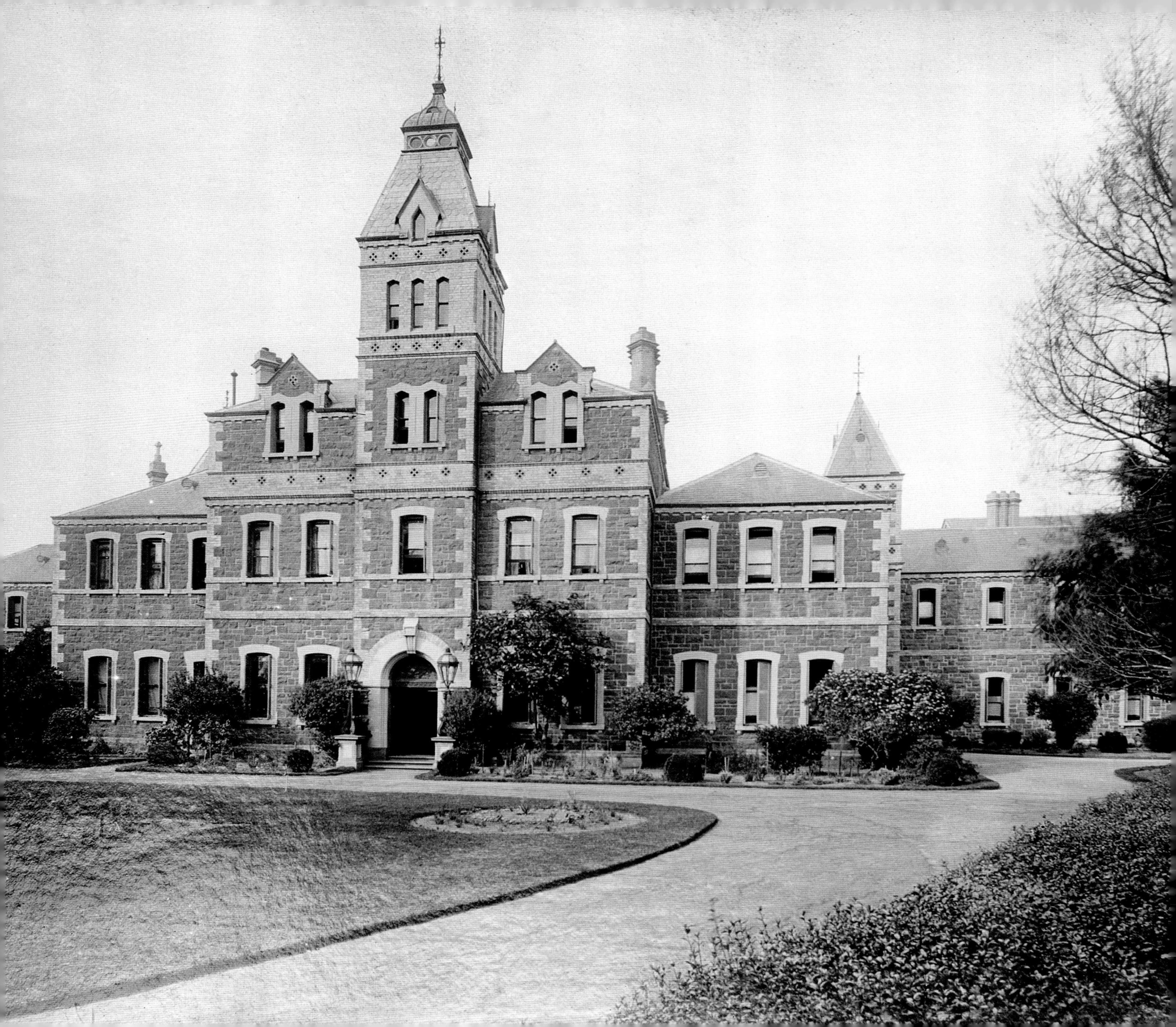

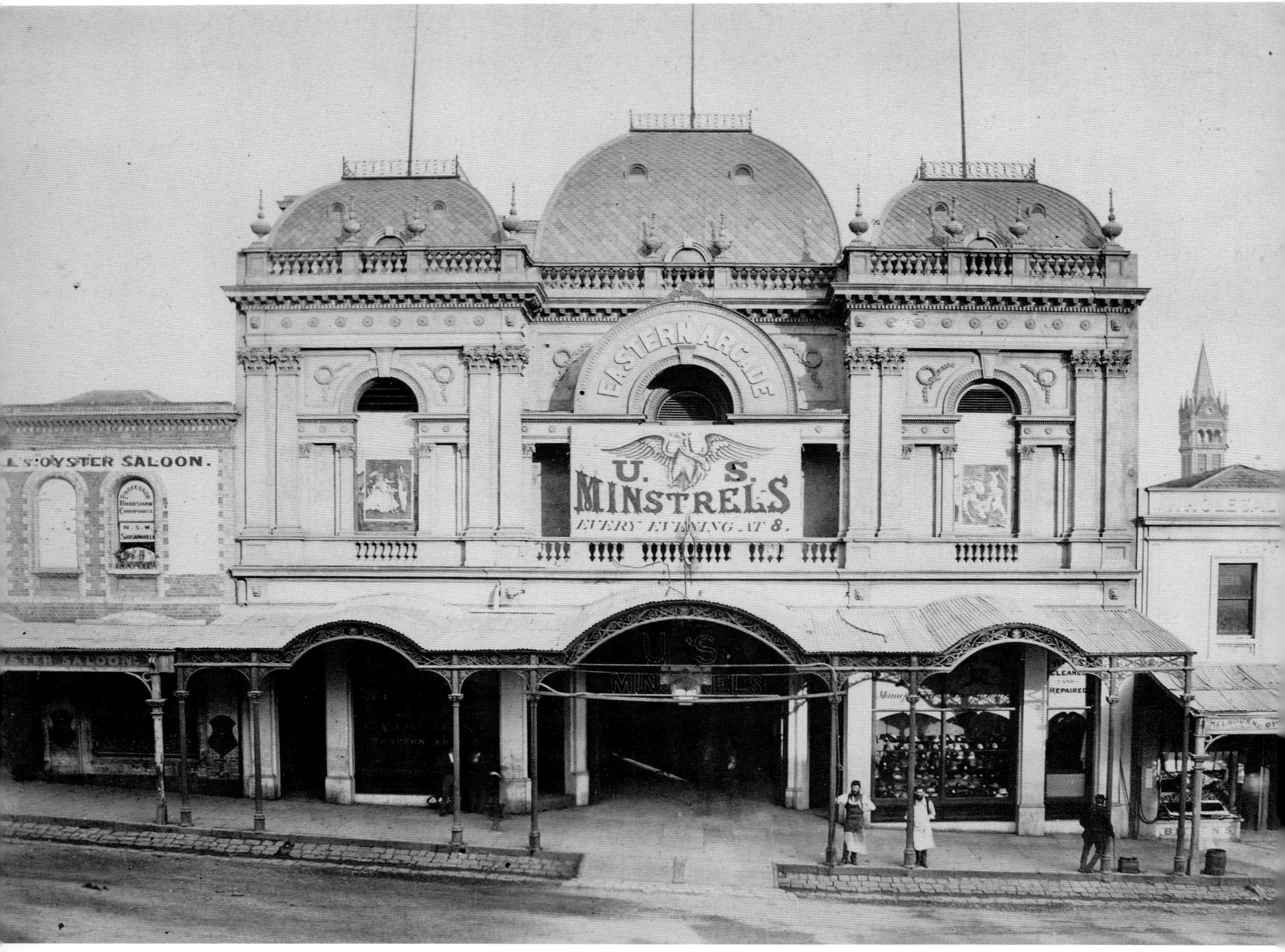
OYSTER SALOON.
EASTERN ARCADE
U. S.
MINSTRELS
EVERY EVENING AT 8.
N.S.W.
SARSAPARILLA
CLEANED
AND
REPAIRED

Eastern Arcade and Apollo Hall DEMOLISHED 2008

The Eastern Arcade was built in 1872, on the site of the former Haymarket Theatre next to the Eastern Market. It was the third arcade to be built in Melbourne and was larger than Queen's Arcade and Royal Arcade. The Eastern Arcade was designed by George Johnston and had 68 shops and an upper storey. There was a hotel, dining rooms and theatre spaces. In the late 1800s arcades were meant to be elegant places – social spaces where people could meet, chat, and dine.

In the Eastern Arcade in 1872 it was stated that there were to be no "offensive businesses such as butchers, fishmongers, greengrocers etc." In the early years this was generally true, with the exception of David Kinnear's shop, where chickens were bred and sold. Neighbouring tenants complained about the smell. The other shops sold gas stoves, sewing machines, rubber stamps, and pianos. There were gilders, painters, bespoke tailors, dressmakers, a Chinese merchant selling tea, firecrackers and ivory, and a phrenologist. There was a great turnover of tenants and by 1894 a new Moorish facade was built in an attempt to revive the fortunes of the arcade. After 1896 the type of tenant changed. There was far less emphasis on luxury goods and there were many more shops associated with the music industry. Theatrical agencies, rehearsal rooms and costume designers moved in. Bourke Street had for some years been the centre of nightlife in Melbourne and on Saturday night around the Eastern Market and Eastern Arcade there were pickpockets, drunks and ruffians amongst the partygoers.

The Apollo Hall at the Eastern Arcade provided many different types of entertainment, as had the old Apollo at the Haymarket Theatre. It was large enough to seat 1,000 people and provide them with boxing competitions, minstrel shows, and magic and mime artists, an "Ethiopian entertainer", "Impersonations Comique" and dramas such as *Cupboard Love*. In 1880, after the hanging of notorious convict Ned Kelly, his sister Kate and brother Jim sat on the stage and people filed past having paid 1 shilling to speak with them. *The Argus* thought that this was a "disgraceful affair" and polite society was outraged.

In 1921 the "Gun Alley Murder" filled the front pages of the newspapers. Alma Tirtschke, a 12-year-old girl, had been assaulted, murdered and left in a passageway off Gun Alley, where 80 Collins Street now stands. A wine merchant in the Eastern Arcade was convicted of the murder on the evidence of two unreliable witnesses and on scanty evidence. He was hanged. This was a terrible miscarriage of justice and it wasn't until 2008 that Colin Ross was granted a pardon, the first granted for a judicially executed person in Australia.

Many businesses had disappeared by 1921 and in 1926 the arcade shops were altered and it became one furniture store. Later in the 1950s it was occupied by other single tenants: Fletcher Jones clothing store, then Allan's Music store and finally Dimmeys discount store. The demise of the Eastern Arcade was probably due to a number of factors, but particularly its location away from the centre of the retail activity in Melbourne. The Melbourne City Council was involved in discussions aimed at preservation of the Moorish facade but the building was demolished with the planning minister's consent in 2008. The speed of the demolition created public outrage.

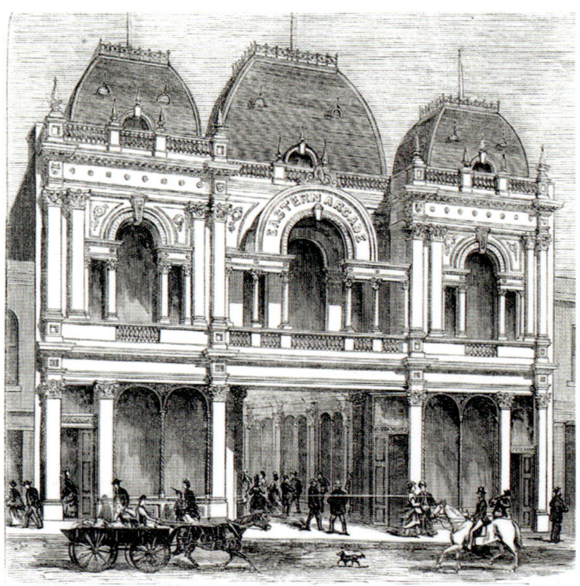

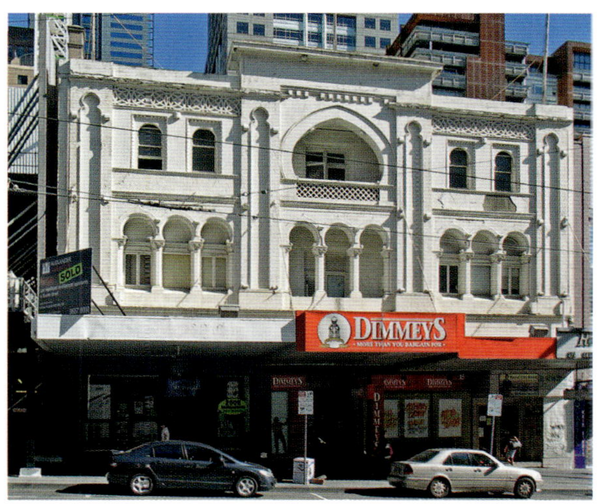

OPPOSITE *The Eastern Arcade had more than 60 shops, as well as the Apollo Hall, an entertainment hall, which at the time of this photo in 1877 was advertising a minstrel show.*

FAR LEFT *Arcades were usually reserved for genteel shoppers, as this illustration from 1872 shows.*

LEFT *The Moorish facade was added to the building in 1894. Dimmeys, a discount chain store, was the last business to occupy the building before it was demolished in 2008.*

Melbourne Power Station **DEMOLISHED 2008–9**

The Spencer Street Power Station provided Melbourne's first self-generated electric power and remained in operation from 1892 to 1982. The site was built by the City of Melbourne to supply electricity to the city. This was a departure from privately owned power generators of the time and the City of Melbourne was the first to do this. It was a Victorian-era, coal-fired power station and produced half of the electricity then needed for Melbourne. Each of the four generators in the first power plant was driven by a steam engine and the electricity was used for trams, lifts, city buildings and street lights.

The popularity of electricity within the city led to a rapid expansion of the facility. In 1901 the first underground mains were constructed in the city centre, supplying power at 230 and 460 volts. Further expansion occurred over the next few years, but it wasn't until 1908 that the first turbines were added. At the same time, the original station manager's office and residence were replaced by a large chimney and coal facility. This chimney was dismantled in the 1970s and reconstructed at the Williamstown Railway museum. Property owners paid for the public lighting in the city at a rate of 3d in the pound, reduced to 2d in 1913. In 1917, DC generators were replaced by motor generators and smoke was directed into two smoke stacks each 175 feet high.

From 1941 the Spencer Street Power Station came under the management of the State Electricity Commission of Victoria, though ownership remained with the council. In 1952, a chimney, 370 feet tall and designed by H. Tileman and Co., was added in Lonsdale Street. Then, in the mid 1950s a large part of this site was redeveloped as a modern gas-fired power station which operated until 1981. There were further upgrades to increase the capacity of the station as part of the state's electricity network into the 1960s. But newer power stations were opening in the La Trobe Valley and the Spencer Street station was increasingly being used only at peak times.

The Spencer Street Power Station buildings were architecturally significant, as examples of relatively elaborate industrial buildings, and were among the oldest buildings associated with electricity supply in Victoria. However, they were also located in a developing area with increasing prices for real estate. In 1982 the power station ceased operation, except for a substation on one section. Another building became a cleaning depot and a further one was leased as a theatre venue. The site was sold for $4 million in 2002. The company that bought the site went into liquidation and the site sat empty awaiting further development. In 2003 a man was arrested for painting a slogan on the chimney "No jobs on a dead planet" and in 2004 a girl died after falling down a 7-metre hole on the site. The site was considered an eyesore and in 2006 Russian developers bought it for $7.6 million. After asbestos was removed, demolition began. The historic tower was dismantled in 2007. In 2008–9 the turbine hall behind the office building (the one remaining structure from 1894), the 1950s section of the office buildings and other earlier buildings were demolished. What is left will be inundated by the more than one thousand apartments planned for the area.

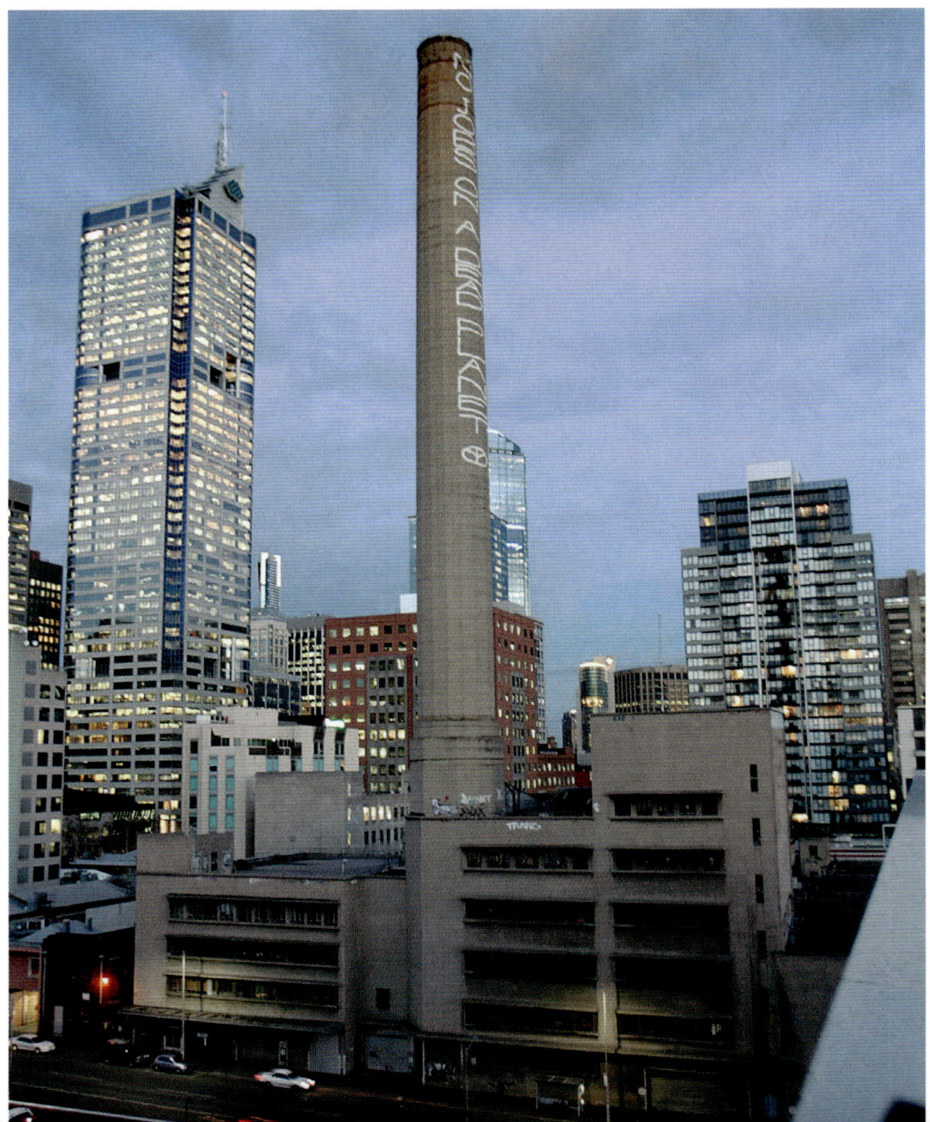

RIGHT *The graffiti on the chimney of the Melbourne Power Station added to its reputation as a city eyesore.*

LEFT *Designed by J. S. Lomdahl of British firm H. Tileman & Co., the power station's 370-feet chimney was the highest stack in the Southern Hemisphere when it was built in 1952.*

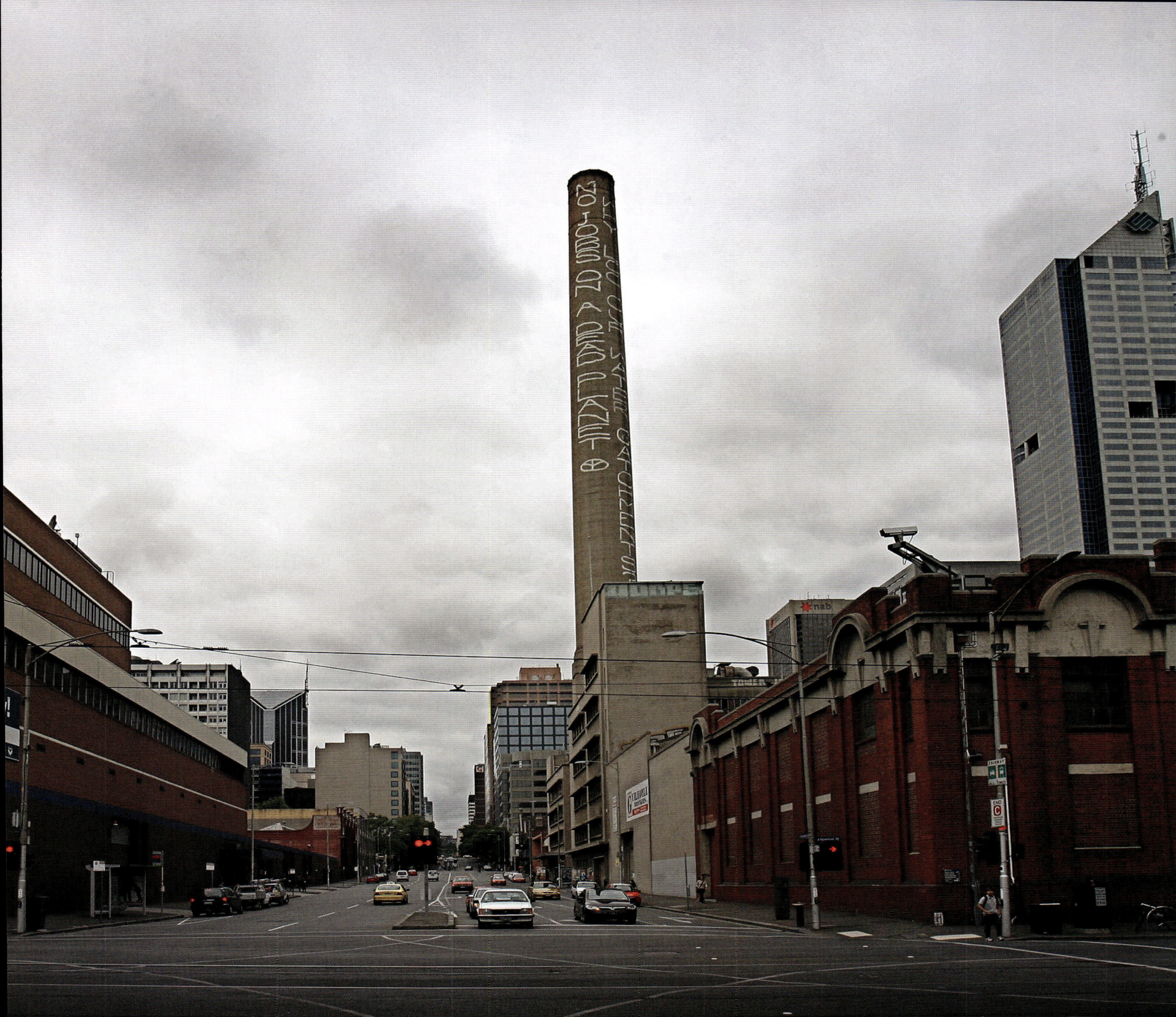
NO JOBS ON A DEAD PLANET
nab

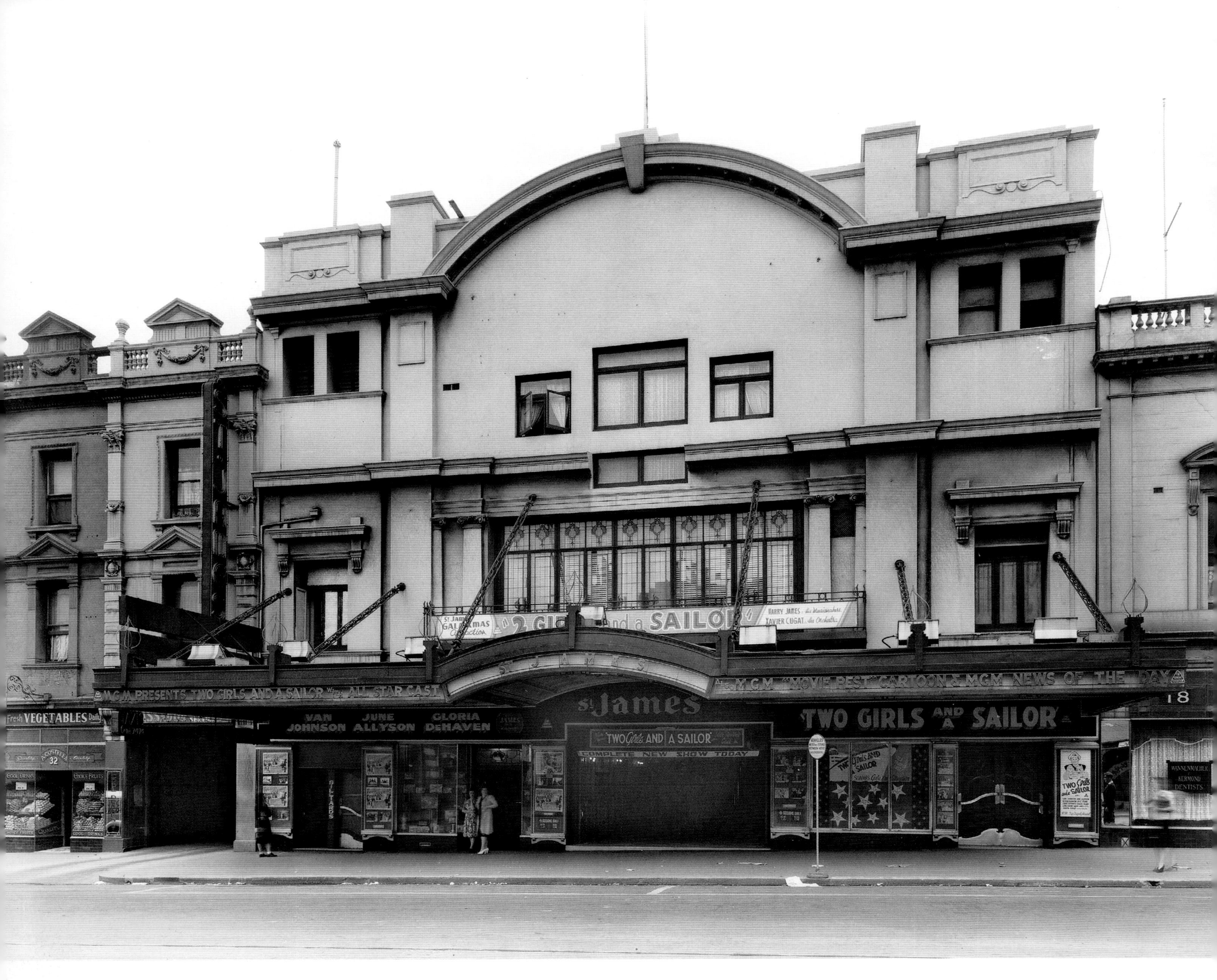
ST JAMES
MGM PRESENTS TWO GIRLS AND A SAILOR
ALL STAR CAST
M.G.M. "MOVIE PEST" CARTOON & MGM NEWS OF THE DAY
2 GIRLS and a SAILOR
HARRY JAMES
XAVIER CUGAT
St James
VAN JOHNSON
JUNE ALLYSON
GLORIA DeHAVEN
TWO GIRLS AND A SAILOR
TWO Girls AND A SAILOR
COMPLETE NEW SHOW TODAY
Fresh VEGETABLES
18
DENTISTS

Palace Theatre CLOSED 2012

The Palace Theatre at 20 Bourke Street has a long and colourful history, but today it is fighting for its life. Over 100 years ago, James Brennan asked Melbourne architect Nahum Barnet and Sydney architects Eaton and Bates to design a new theatre to be built on the site of the Douglas Theatre, which had been there since 1860. The new theatre opened in April 1912 and was called Brennan's Amphitheatre. Its total cost was £32,000. Later in 1912 Brennan sold the theatre to Fullers who kept it until 1940, renaming it the Nationa Amphitheatre.

During these years, the Palace was remodelled several times. In 1916 a complete renovation of the auditorium and lobby was undertaken by theatre architect Henry E. White, the architect of theatre interiors at the Palais, the Princess, and the Athenaeum in Melbourne. Ornate plaster decoration in a Louis XVI style was added and a three-tiered auditorium was built to seat 1,017 people. The theatre also became the centre of Fullers' dramatic companies. In 1923 the auditorium was again remodelled, the ornate features were retained and the auditorium was redesigned in the more elegant Adam style. The theatre was renamed the New Palace and it continued to be used for musicals, revues, and vaudeville. Fullers altered the theatre in 1934 and once more changed its name, this time to the Apollo Theatre. After being leased to a film company from 1936 to 1940, the Apollo was then sold to Metro Goldwyn Mayer, who renovated it yet again and renamed it the St. James cinema. Under the name of the Metro Bourke St. in 1951, the cinema projected only films made by MGM. The facade was rebuilt in the art deco style and a Cinemascope screen was installed.

In the 1970s, after a brief interlude as a live music venue, it reverted to being a cinema under an earlier name. Some cinema fans recall the films shown in the new "Sensurround" Palace Cinema, where a visitor would have a real-life experience in part due to the speakers installed under the seats. During a screening of *The Battle of Midway*, the aircraft bombing raid sounds were so realistic that patrons were said to have felt they were in the middle of the battle. The Melbourne Revival Centre was located here in 1980 and the theatre became a place for its Pentecostal congregation to worship and produce dramatic events. Its life as the Metro Nightclub dates from 1986, and even after another sale, this time in 2007, it remained a very important live music venue.

The last sale, in 2012, was to a property developer, Jinshan Investments, who planned to demolish the Palace and build a 30-storey hotel and apartment complex on the site at a cost of $180 million. There would be 205 hotel rooms and 145 apartments, which the developer felt would revitalize this end of Bourke Street, attract wealthy big spenders to Melbourne, generate 300 jobs while it was being constructed, and employ 620 people on completion.

The National Trust, the Melbourne City Council, people in the music industry and the general public were not happy. They felt that another breach of the existing height limits should be avoided. The streetscape is largely heritage and low rise now and the planned building would be unsympathetic to the existing Heritage Precinct. It was felt that the interiors were worth preserving, as was the facade, and that the existence of the Palace as an iconic live music venue should be retained. However, some of the interiors have already been destroyed and the ultimate fate of the Palace is unknown. Its future is still being determined and is uncertain.

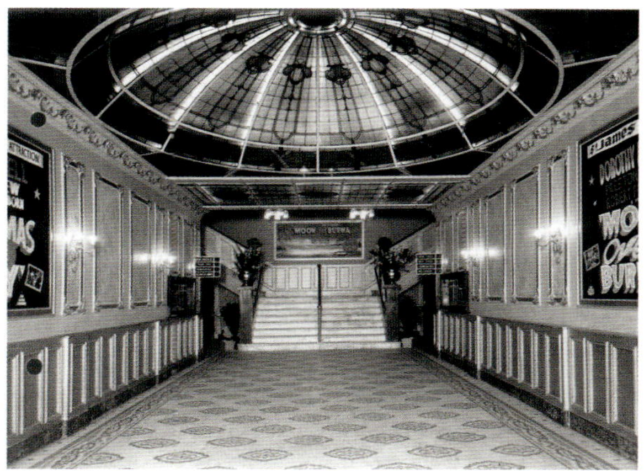

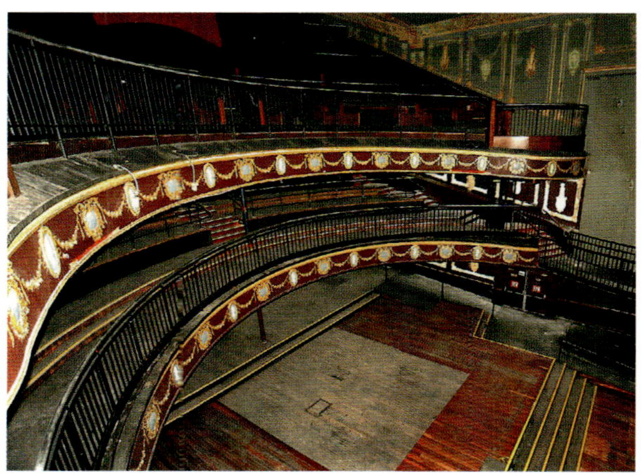

OPPOSITE *The Palace had many incarnations. In the 1940s it became an MGM cinema, the St. James.*

LEFT *The lovely leadlight ceiling in the foyer of the Palace Theatre, seen here in 1940.*

BELOW LEFT *The Palace Theatre auditorium in 2014.*

General Motors–Holden Limited at Port Melbourne PLAN TO CEASE PRODUCTION ANNOUNCED 2013

The story of General Motors–Holden at Port Melbourne begins in Adelaide where James Holden started a saddlery business in 1856. His J. A. Holden and Company became Holden and Frost Limited in 1885 when he took on a partner, Henry Frost. James's grandson Edward, who joined the firm in 1905, had a keen interest in automobiles and three years after his arrival the firm began to manufacture car upholstery. By 1913 they were producing motorbike sidecars and, when World War I interrupted many imports, Holden and Frost began making body shells for cars. J. A. Holden set up a new company, Holden's Motor Body Builders Limited (HMBB), in Adelaide and by 1923 they were producing 12,000 vehicles a year, as well as assembling bodies for Ford. By 1924 HMBB was supplying motor bodies for General Motors (GM) for their imported Chevrolet and Dodge cars and GM were setting up assembly plants in other states of Australia. In 1931 GM and HMBB merged and General Motors–Holden's Limited was born.

The Fishermans Bend (formerly Fishermen's Bend) factory at Port Melbourne was finished in 1936. World War I intervened and car production was delayed while energy went into the production of trucks, engines and guns. After the war the first Australian car was produced under the leadership of managing director Laurence Hartnett. Some of the names suggested for the new Australian car were the Boomerang, the Emu, the Melba, the Austral and the Canbra. In the end it was called the Holden, after Edward Holden. The birth of the Holden car introduced a new era in Australian car manufacturing. From the 1950s and 1960s new models were eagerly sought by the Australian public, and the phrase "football, meat pies and Holden cars" was born. A utility vehicle was an innovation that immediately caught the public's attention and the "ute", as it was known, quickly became much more than a farmer's workhorse. Young men all over Australia embraced the "ute", and then came the panel van. Equally successful GMH sedans and other models were being exported to New Zealand, Thailand, Malaysia and North Borneo. By the end of the 1950s Holden employed 19,000 people.

At the end of the 1960s the two millionth vehicle rolled off the assembly line. Holden was no longer making Chevrolets and Pontiacs, but it was manufacturing station wagons, cars with new automatic transmissions, front seat belts, V8 engines, the luxurious Premier, the Brougham, the Kingswood, Belmont and the Monaro. The 1970s success stories were the introduction of the Holden Commodore and the Torana, one of the few cars in the world engineered for 4, 6, or 8 cylinder engines. The Torana was very successful on the racing circuit of Mount Panorama in New South Wales. However, the 1980s was a trying time for Holden. It had large debts and there was much greater competition from Ford, Toyota and Nissan. The decision by the government that, after 1986, all new vehicles were to run on unleaded fuel, resulted in the closure of the South Australian Woodville plant. Holden reorganized and recapitalized. The Fishermans Bend factory in Port Melbourne was to specialize in engine production, while car body manufacturing was to be centred at Elizabeth, South Australia.

By the early 1990s Toyota had replaced both Holden and Ford on the sales tables and during the 2000s Holden's share continued to fall. By this time the workforce numbered 7,350 compared with 23,914 in 1964. In 2013 General Motors–Holden announced that it would cease making vehicles by the end of 2017 and, although it would still retain the world-class engineering and design section in Australia, the Fishermans Bend, Port Melbourne factory would close.

RIGHT *The end of the main assembly line in Plant I of General Motors–Holden at Fishermans Bend in 1951–52.*

BELOW LEFT *The vast GMH factory at Fishermans Bend, as seen from the air between 1940 and 1949*

BELOW *An advertisement for the "New Australian Car".*

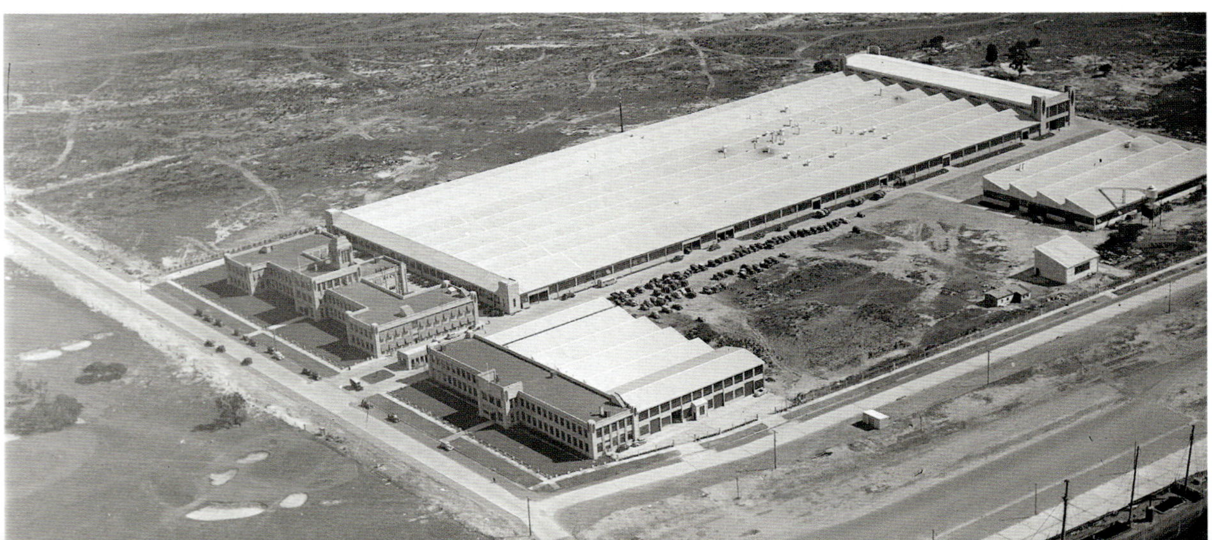

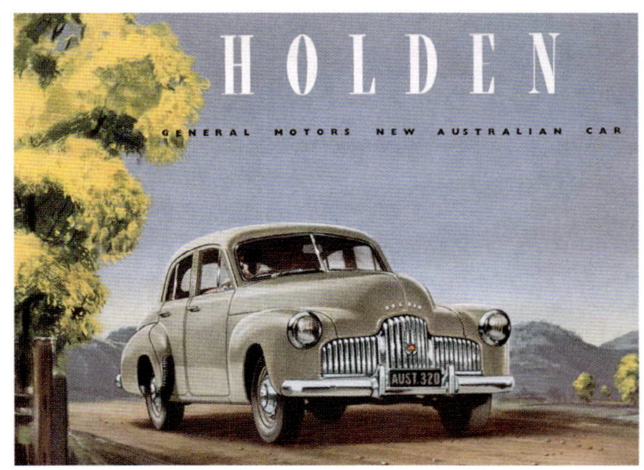

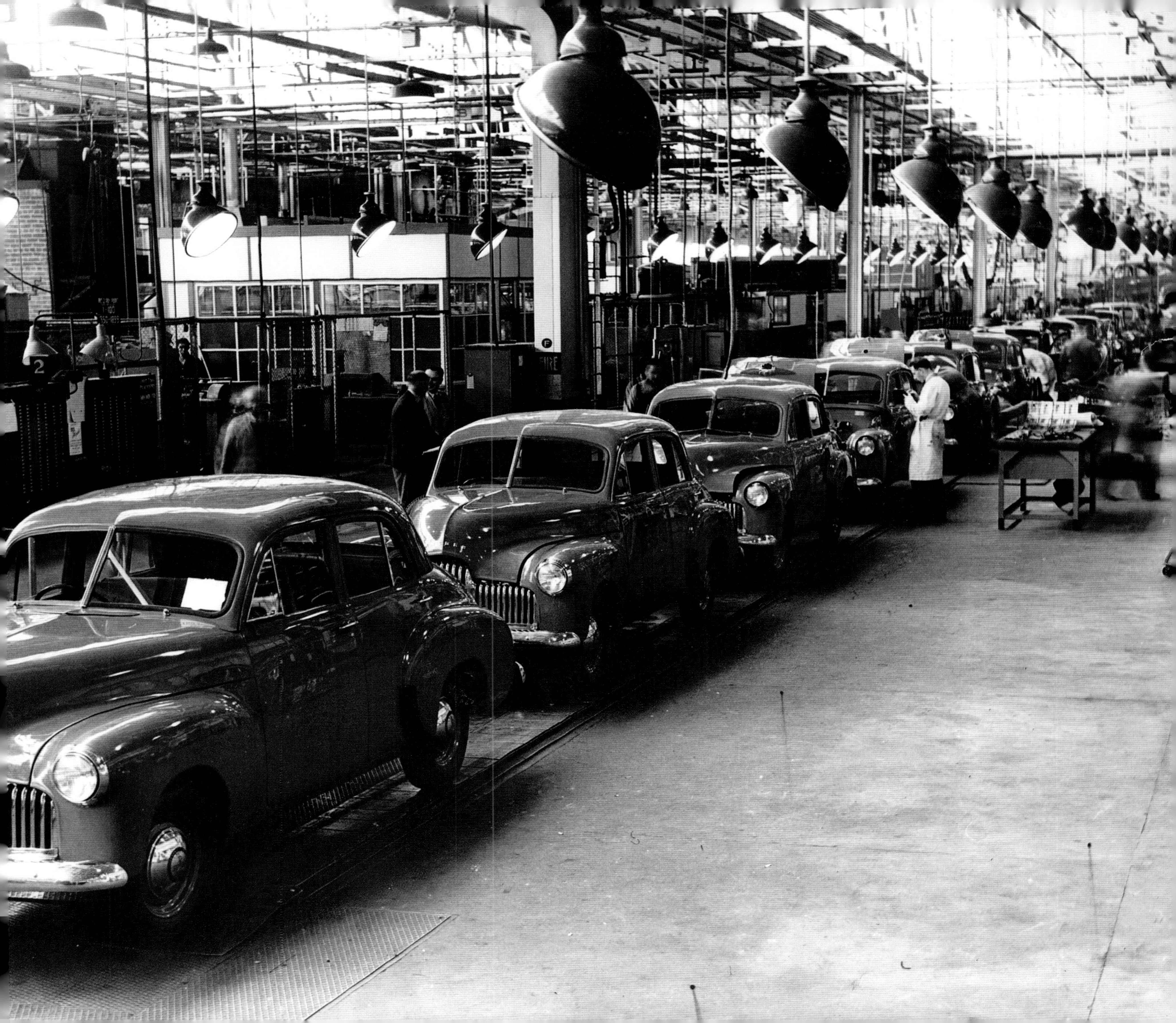
2
FIRE

Separation Tree CANOPY REMOVED 2015

The Port Phillip District was an historical administrative division of the Colony of New South Wales. During the late 1830s, a land boom took place in Port Phillip and the local inhabitants began to resent the fact that taxes were being sent to NSW rather than being used for the betterment of Port Phillip. As early as 1840, a few of Melbourne's gentry got together to discuss the issue of separation. A petition was sent to the British Parliament in England, but the advocate taking it died on the journey so the petition was dropped.

Port Phillipians had a number of grievances over the next few years. Comparisons were made with other imperial outposts and it seemed that Port Phillip was doing badly. To add to their distress, very little assistance came from Sydney, and on a revenue per capita basis they argued they received much less than Sydney. By 1842 most of the immigration into Australia went to Port Phillip. In 1845 the New South Wales Legislative Council voted against separation but a further petition was begun in 1846. Between 1846 and 1850, there were many disputes and arguments about separation and practical concerns were raised about the considerable distance from Port Phillip to the seat of government – it was nearly 600 miles away.

The Separation Bill was passed by the British Parliament on 1 August 1850, separating Port Phillip from New South Wales and calling the new colony Victoria. But it was 14 weeks before the news reached Melbourne, and even then it was only a small note in a South Australian paper. A reporter for the *Melbourne Herald* did see it and a special edition of the paper was printed. Much celebration occurred. Rockets were set off, giant hot-air balloons carried the word "Separation" and people rushed around cheering.

At 10.30 a.m. on 15 November 1850, Governor Charles La Trobe stood under the soon-to-be-famous River Red Gum tree and announced to a huge crowd the separation of the colony of Victoria from New South Wales. A great party was held that lasted for several days. The mood of the time can perhaps be seen in the number of "Separation" streets named at that time. When the actual day of separation arrived on 1 July 1851, the Proclamation was read outside the then courthouse. And, each year for the next half century, on the 1 July, Separation Day was celebrated as a public holiday.

The Separation Tree, believed to date from the 17th century, is in the Royal Botanical Gardens beside the ornamental lake. This majestic tree was one of the few left in the gardens that predated European settlement. The Separation Tree was placed on the Significant Tree Register of the National Trust of Victoria in 1982, so Melburnians were shocked in 2010 when the tree was ring barked by unknown vandals. Attempts were made to limit the damage but it was again ring barked in 2013, completely cutting off the tree's food system. The tree could not survive both assaults and it began to die. A difficult decision was made and in February 2015 the tree was reduced from 25 metres tall to a 10 metre high trunk. The trunk and scaffold limbs were left as a memorial both to the tree and the historical events that took place there. A plaque at the base commemorating Governor La Trobe's historic announcement will remain, as will a plaque commemorating the centenary of this event.

RIGHT *A postcard of the Separation Tree from 1907.*

FAR RIGHT *The plaque reads, "Under this tree on 15th November 1850, public rejoicings of citizens of Melbourne took place, in celebration of the authorized separation of the Colony of Victoria from New South Wales on 1st July 1851."*

OPPOSITE *The mature and healthy River Red Gum (*Eucalyptus camaldulensis*) in 1945.*

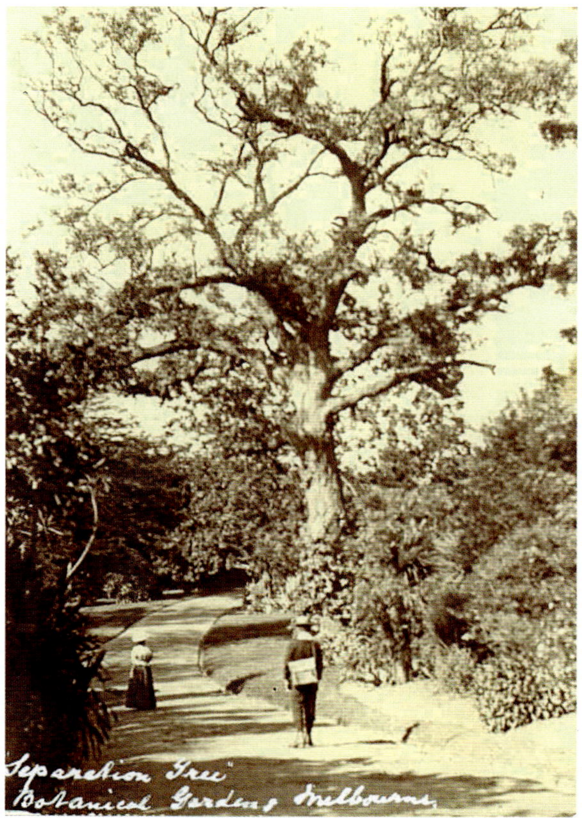

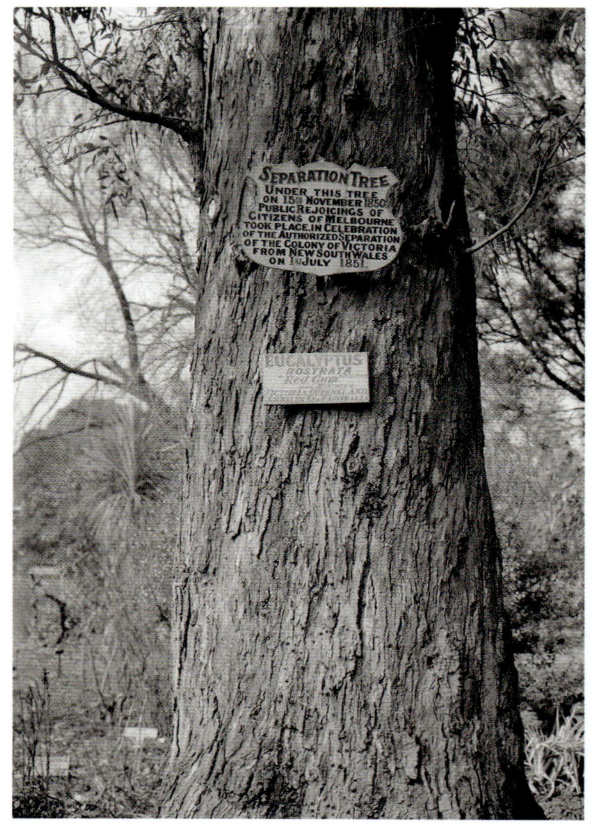

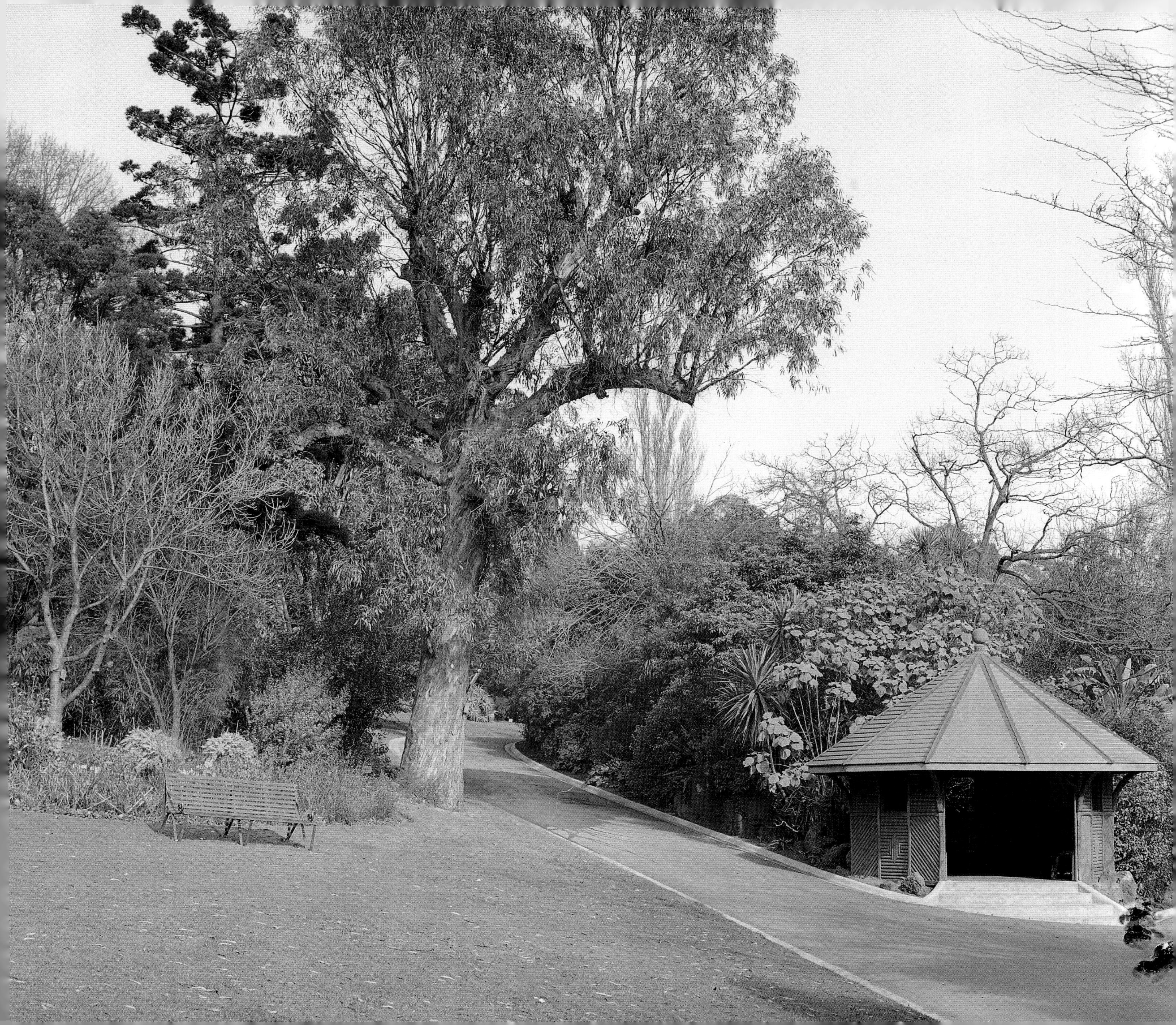

INDEX

Abbotsford 83
Albert Hospital 21
Albert Park 103
Alexandra Club 59
Alexandra Stage 32
Allen, Alfred Weaver 104
Allen's Sweets Factory 104–105
APA Tower 6, 94–95
Apollo Hall 134–135
Argus Building 38–39
Ariell, Thomas 60
Arts Centre 13, 32
Australian Building 6, 66, 95, 100–101
Baillieu Library 43
Barkly Street 92
Barnes, Frederick 44, 73
Barnet, Nahum 23, 139
Barry, John Michael 52, 87
Bateman, Edward La Trobe 31
Beach Street 60
Beale, Elizabeth 59
Beale, Octavius Charles 23, 59
Bedford Hotel 91
Bellhouse, E. T. 10
Bellman, John 107
Benevolent Asylum 14–15
Bent, Thomas 36, 67
BHP Plaza 73
Block Arcade 66, 67, 110, 111, 123
Blue Lake 87
Bourke Street 17, 23, 24, 35, 44, 48, 73, 74, 80, 128, 135, 139
Bouverie Street 107
Brack, John 63
Brennan, James 139
Bridge Road 24
Brighton 51
Brighton Beach State School 51
Brighton and St. Kilda Sea Baths 6
Brunswick 24, 96
Butler Street 51
Butterfield, William 44
cable trams 24–25
Café Australia 110
Café Gunsler 110
Cairns, Adam 10, 109
Cairns Memorial Church 109–110
Carlton 55, 103, 107
Carlton and United Brewery 106–107
Carlyle, Thomas 110
Carmichael, Sir Thomas 14
Cathedral Lane 124
Cavalier Tea Rooms 79
Central Common School 18
Chalmer's Church 108
Chapel Street, Prahran 23
Cheltenham 14
Clapp, Francis Boardman 24
Clarendon Street 64, 69
Clarke, Janet 69
Clarke, William 69
Cliveden 68–69
Cliveden Mansions 69
Coles, Edward William 6, 17, 44
Cole's Book Arcade 16–17
Coles Wharf 28
Collingwood 35, 69
Collins Place 91
Collins Street 17, 21, 39, 43, 44, 52, 56, 79, 86, 91, 95, 99, 108, 110, 111, 123, 128
Colonial Mutual Life Building 42–43
Commonwealth Bank Tower 80
Convention Centre 28
Coode, Sir John 28
Corroboree Tree 92
Craig, William 76
Craig, Williamson, and Thomas store 6, 66, 76–77
Crouch & Wilson 21
Customs House 28
Davitt, Arthur 18
Davitt, Ellen 18
Deakin, Alfred 23, 100
D'Ebro, Charles 23
Denton Hat Factory 82–83
Derham, F. T. 100
Duke of Rothesay Hotel 76
East Melbourne 18, 36, 64, 69, 84, 108
Eastern Arcade 134–135
Eastern Hill 84
Eastern Market 17, 44–45, 52, 104, 135
elephant rides 54–55
Elizabeth Street 18, 24, 39, 43, 48, 67, 76, 80, 95, 100, 128
Emerald Hill 9, 10, 51
Equitable Building 6, 42–43
Esplanade, St. Kilda 118
Exhibition Buildings 44
Exhibition Street 44
Fawkner, John Pascoe 47
Fawkner Cemetery 40
Fayrefield Hat Factory 83
Federal Coffee Palace 6, 86–87
Federation Square 124
Felton Building 95
Fink, Benjamin Josman 66–67, 123
Fink, Theodore 67
Fink's Building 66–67, 76
Finn, Edmund 128
Fisher, Arthur Henry 56
Fishermans Bend 140
FitzGerald, Sir Thomas Naghten 87
FitzGerald Brothers' Circus buildings 13, 32
Fitzroy, Governor 14
Fitzroy Terrace 64–65
Flemington House 27
Flemington Primary School 27
Flinders Lane 9, 47, 52, 95, 100
Flinders Street 7, 24, 40, 47, 67, 80, 91, 124
Flinders Street Railway Station 76
Foilacleugh mansion 56
Foy, Francis 35
Foy, Mark 35
Foy and Gibson's department store 34–35, 83
Fritz, Andrew 120
Frost, Henry 140
Gas and Fuel Buildings 6, 124–125
General Motors–Holden Limited 140–141
General Post Office Building 18, 128–129
George, Alfred 123
George, William 123
Georges Department Store 122–123
Giblins, J. T. 21
Gibson, William 35
Gipps Street 64, 108
Glaciarium 118
Glass, Hugh 27
Glen Waverley 51
Goold, Bishop 84
Gotha 22–23
Grainger, John Harry 80
Grand Hotel 91
Grand Junction 92
Green, Edward Bernard 46
Greening, Joseph 128
Greensborough 48
Grey Street 64
Grice, James 59
Griffin, Walter Burley 70, 110, 112, 128
Grosvenor Chambers 91
Gunst, J. W. 21
Haddon, Fred 39
Hadleigh Hall 22–23
Hallidie, Andrew 24
Hartnett, Laurence 140
Hawthorn Bridge 24
Haymarket Theatre 135
Hertz, Carl 74
High Street, St. Kilda 92
Hilton Hotel 69
Hoddle, Robert 6, 44, 47, 52
Hoddle Grid 40, 47, 124
Hodgson, John 47
Holden, Edward 140
Holden, James 140
Homeopathic Dispensary 21
Homeopathic Hospital 20–1, 120
Hotel Australia 110–111, 112–113
Howitt, A. W. 27
ICI Building 100, 124
iron houses 10–11
Jansen, Peter 86
Johnson, Arthur 128
Johnson, James 39
Johnston, A. E. 18
Johnston, George 135
Junction Hotel 92–93
Kellermann, Annette 13
Kensington Road 23
Kerr, Beatrice 13
Kerr, William 39
King Street 28, 40
King Street Bridge 92
Kings Domain 10
Kingston Centre for the Care of the Aged 14
Kooyong Road 59
La Trobe, Charles Joseph 10, 18, 39, 142
La Trobe Street 39, 73, 91
Laing, Charles 14
Lamb Inn 56
Latham, Edward 107
Lawson, Wilfred 55
Little Collins Street 17
Little Dock 28, 40
Lomdahl, J. S. 136
Lonsdale Street 80, 84, 87, 115
Luna Park 70, 119
Mac.Robertson Girls' High School 18
Madden, Henry 27
Maribyrnong River 28, 83
Market Street 52, 80
Masonic Hall 80
Matear, Fred 110
McIntosh, Hugh D. 74
McRae, Gordon 60
Meat Market 59
Medibank Ice House 116
Melbourne Cricket Ground Grandstands 130–131
Melbourne Continuation School 18
Melbourne Fish Market 28, 40–41
Melbourne High School 18
Melbourne Hospital 21, 87, 114–115
Melbourne Orphanage 50–51
Melbourne Town Hall 79
Melbourne Zoo 54–55
Menzies, Archibald 72
Menzies, Catherine 72
Menzies Hotel 6, 56, 72–73, 91
Mercy Hospital for Women 64
milk bars 96–97
Miller, Henry "Money" 52
Mirams, James 86
Mitchell, David 43, 73
Model School 18–19
Monash Medical Centre 120
Monash University 115
Montsalvat 31
Moondah 59
Moore, Henry Byron 99
Morton, William 56
Moss, Mark 6, 36
Moss, Rose 36
Moubray Street, Prahran 132
Mrs Dewar's milk bar 96
Munro, James 86, 100
Murdoch, John Smith 128
Museum of Victoria 17
Mutual Stores Building 76
Myer House 132
Nareeb 58–59
Nash, Lucinda 27
National Mutual Centre 52
New Dock 28
Nolan, Sidney 70
Norris, Harry A. 38
North Melbourne 11, 14
North Wharf 28
Northcote 24
Norwood 36–37
Novotel Hotel 116
Old Lamb Inn 47
Olderfleet Building 83
Olympia Auditorium 32
Oma 58–59
Opera House 74–75
Oriental Hotel 35, 90–91
Oriental Bank 8–9
Ormond, Francis 132
Paddy's Market 17, 44
Palace Theatre 138–139
Palais de Danse 70–71
Palais Pictures 70
Palais Theatre 70, 119
Parkville 115
Patterson, Robert 10
Pentridge 126–127
Phillips, Herman 70
Phillips, Leon 70
Pitt, William 74, 83, 86
Plottel, Joseph 104
Port Melbourne 60, 80, 140
Port Philip 14, 47, 127, 142
Port Phillip Bay 36
Port Phillip Club Hotel 46–47, 76
Port Philip Patriot, The 39
Powlett Street 108
Prahan 23
Prell, Friedrich Wilhelm 95
Prell's Buildings 6, 94–95
Price, John Giles 127
Prince Henry's Hospital 21, 120–121
Prince of Wales Opera House 74
Princes Bridge 6, 13, 32, 80
Princes Bridge Railway Station 124
Princes Court 6, 12–13
Princess Theatre 83
Queen Street 9, 28, 47, 95
Queen Victoria Hospital 114–115
Queen Victoria Village 115
Queenie 55
Queens Walk Arcade 78–79
Queen's Wharf 28
Raht, Edward 43
Ramsden, Samuel 64
Ranee 55
Reed, Joseph 31, 44, 73
Reynolds, Paddy 48
Rialto Building 83
Riches, E. A. 36
Richmond 23, 24, 69
Rickards, Harry 74
Robertson, Sir Macpherson 104
Rosebank 36
Rostella 86–87
Rouse Street 60
Royal Australasian College of Surgeons 18
Royal Botanical Gardens 6, 21, 59, 142
Royal Exhibition Building 43
Royal Insurance Building 56
Royal Mail Hotel 48–49
Royal Victorian Institute for the Blind 132–133
Russell Street 17
St. Kilda 70–71, 92, 116, 119
St. Kilda Junction 92–93
St. Kilda Pier 119
St. Kilda Road 6, 13, 21, 32, 120, 124, 132
St. Kilda Sea Baths 118–119
St. Michael's Church 44
St. Moritz 116–117
St. Patrick's College 84–85
St. Paul's Cathedral 6, 44, 76, 79, 84, 124
Saltwater River 28
Salway, William 59
Sandridge 60
Sandridge Pier 28
Sargood warehouse 76
Scanlan, Patrick 84
Scots' Church 44, 108
Scott, Edward 47, 56
Scott's Hotel 56–57, 91
Separation Tree 142–143
Shan, Emily 21
Shelmerdine, Thomas 83
Simmons, Alice 59
Simmons, Gertrude 59
Simmons, Walter 59
"six o'clock swill" 62–63
Skilton, Bobby 103
Snowden Gardens 13
South Melbourne 9, 10, 118
South Melbourne Football Club 102–103
South Wharf 28
South Yarra 18, 23
Sparrow, George 92
Spencer Dock 28
Spencer Street 24, 28, 40, 91
Spencer Street Bridge 28
Spencer Street Power Station 136–137
Spring Street 18, 91
State Bank of Victoria 6
State Savings Bank 80–81
Stephenson, Sir Arthur George 80
Stevenson, George 83
Stokes Street 60
Stone, Constance 115
Sugden, William 48
Sugden Place 48
Swallow, Thomas 60
Swallow & Ariell Factory 60–61
Swanston Street 35, 39, 48, 76, 79, 115, 124
Swanston Street Malt House 107
Sydney Road 96, 127
Sydney Swans 103
telephonists 98–99
Tewkesbury, Pearson 6, 91
Tilgner, Victor 43
"Tin Pan Alley" 10
Tivoli Court 74
Tivoli Theatre 64, 74–75
Toorak 24, 59
Travancore 26–27
Treasury Gardens 69
Treeby, Phillip 36
Trollope, Anthony 73
Turner, James Hobson 83
University of Melbourne 18, 31, 43, 84, 87, 120
Vernon, W. L. 69
Verona 64–65
Verona Lane 64
Victoria Brewery 83
Victoria Building 78–79
Victoria Docks 28
Victoria Market 44
Vienna Café 110
Wardell, William 69
Watson, James 27
Wellington Parade 69
Wertheim, Herbert 23
Wertheim, Hugo 23
Wertheim, Sophie 23
Wertheim Piano Factory 23
West Melbourne 28
Western Market 52–53
White, F. M. 31
White, Henry E. 70
William Street 52, 73, 87, 115
Williams Creek 128
Williamstown 28
Wilson, Edward 39
Wilson, Samuel 31
Wilson, William C. 56
Wilson Hall 30–31
Windsor Hotel 91
Wirth, May 32
Wirth's Circus 32–33
Women's Hospital 13
Wormal, David 79
Xavier College 84
Yarra House 47
Yarra River 6, 28–29, 32, 40, 83, 104
Young and Jackson's Hotel 76
Zoological Gardens 27